Stopping the Killing

Stopping the Killing

How Civil Wars End

Edited by
Roy Licklider

NEW YORK UNIVERSITY PRESS

NEW YORK AND LONDON

NEW YORK UNIVERSITY PRESS
New York and London

Library of Congress Cataloging-in-Publication Data

Stopping the killing : how civil wars end / edited by Roy Licklider.
p.   cm.
Includes bibliographical references and index.
ISBN 0-8147-5070-2
1. Civil wars. 2. War (International law)   I. Licklider, Roy.
JX4541.S84   1993
341.6′8—dc20   92-35075
                        CIP

New York University Press books are printed on acid-free paper, and
their binding materials are chosen for strength and durability.

Manufactured in the United States of America

c   10 9 8 7 6 5 4 3 2 1

For Our Children
with Hope
and in Memory of
Fern Eilers Newman
1919–1992
the Gentlest Soul I Ever Knew.

Contents

Acknowledgments   ix

PART I.   Introduction

1.   How Civil Wars End: Questions and Methods   3
Roy Licklider

2.   The Unfinished Agenda: Negotiating
Internal Conflicts   20
I. William Zartman

PART II.   Cases

3.   Civil Violence and Conflict Resolution:
The Case of Colombia   37
Jonathan Hartlyn

4.   The Peace Process in the Sudan, 1971–1972   63
Donald Rothchild and Caroline Hartzell

5.   The Civil War in Yemen, 1962–1970   95
Manfred W. Wenner

6.   The End of the Zimbabwean Civil War   125
Stephen John Stedman

7.   The End of the American Civil War   164
Stephen John Stedman

8. The Ending of the Nigerian Civil War:
    Victory, Defeat, and the Changing of Coalitions   189
    James O'Connell

9. The Doomed Revolution: Communist Insurgency
    in Postwar Greece   205
    John O. Iatrides

PART III.   Theoretical Issues and Problems

10. The Causes of Peace   235
    Robert Harrison Wagner

11. When War Doesn't Work: Understanding
    the Relationship between the Battlefield
    and the Negotiating Table   269
    Jane E. Holl

12. Political Order and the "Settlement" of Civil Wars   292
    Harvey Waterman

13. What Have We Learned and Where Do
    We Go from Here?   303
    Roy Licklider

    Bibliography   323

    Contributors   341

    Index   343

Acknowledgments

One of the pleasures of this project has been meeting and working with so many people who have found the topic worthwhile. My primary debt is clearly to the contributors, not only for their written chapters but for their willingness to participate in our ongoing discourse in various venues. We in turn drew liberally on the ideas of others at conferences of the International Studies Association and the International Political Science Association, but especially on other participants in the Conference on Civil War Termination at Rutgers University in March 1990, including Henry Bienen, Barbara Callaway, James T. Johnson, Jack Levy, Manus Midlarsky, Paul Pillar, Bikash Roy, Luigi Sensi, D. Michael Shafer, and John Vasquez. Paul Pillar also read and critiqued all of the theory chapters.

I have also personally benefitted immensely from responses to my papers at the City University of New York Political Science Conference, the Conflict Termination conference at Haverford College, the American Political Science Association, the Center for the Study of Social Change at the New School for Social Research, and the Rutgers International Relations Colloquium as well as helpful individual scholars like Robert Whealey. Charles Tilly's advice and support has been invaluable. My colleagues Jack Levy and Michael Shafer critiqued my chapters in this volume in detail. I acknowledge with gratitude the financial support of the United States Institute of Peace and Rutgers University. Most importantly, Patricia and Virginia Licklider helped keep me sane through the process.

Stopping the Killing

Introduction

How Civil Wars End: Questions and Methods

Roy Licklider

Civil violence may be rare or common, but it is always in some sense extraordinary, a challenge to one of the basic assumptions of civil normality.
—(Rule 1988, 2)

Our world is filled with violence of every sort, from the daily random killings of children by stray gunfire to mass murders and large-scale wars in places we can hardly locate on maps. But even in this environment of violence, civil war retains a particular horror.

Perhaps this is because of the peculiar *intensity* of many such conflicts. We say that family fights are the worst because the degree of feeling is so deep, that you really have to know someone to hate them. James Rosenau (1964, 73) argues that the intensity stems from the depth of prewar ties which have been destroyed. Certainly the degree of personal commitment, with its resulting heroism and savagery, in societies like Ulster, Lebanon, Cambodia, and Angola is hard for outsiders to comprehend.

At a deeper level, civil war reveals the fragility of our *own* social peace. Could our own society ever degenerate into the anarchy of Lebanon? The vision of people who would otherwise be living peacefully together deliberately killing one another retains its power to shock. The people in Ulster, for example, seem much like those of any Western industrial country; if they are unable to maintain social

3

peace, what does that say about us and our own future? Any stable society can be seen as a suspended civil war, and the troubles of others remind us of our own susceptibility to the condition. After all, the United States fought one of the bloodiest civil conflicts in history little more than a century ago. We know that it can happen here because it has.

We also worry about civil wars because, in this increasingly interdependent world, they are not private quarrels; they attract outside involvement and may escalate into international conflicts which will involve us directly. Some of the most intense Cold War confrontations, for example, resulted from interventions in civil wars in the Third World in places like Korea, the Middle East, Vietnam, and Afghanistan. Nor is this simply a modern phenomenon; after all, the French Revolution ignited a world war. Thus the end of the Cold War is unlikely to end this spiraling cycle of involvement and violence; indeed, if anything, the likely outbreak of new civil wars in the former Soviet bloc may increase it. Enlightened self-interest demands that we learn how such conflicts begin and how they may best be ended.

It is particularly hard to visualize how civil wars can end. Ending international war is hard enough, but at least there the opponents will presumably eventually retreat to their own territories (wars of conquest have been rare since 1945). But in civil wars the members of the two sides must live side by side and work together in a common government to make the country work. How can this be done?

Sustained wars produce hatred which does not end with the conflict. After half a century, American veterans were outraged at the idea of including some Japanese veterans in the fiftieth anniversary ceremony of the attack on Pearl Harbor. How do groups of people who have been killing one another with considerable enthusiasm and success come together to form a common government? How can you work together, politically and economically, with the people who killed your parents, your children, your friends or lovers? On the surface it seems impossible, even grotesque.

But in fact we know that it happens all the time. Fred Ikle's apt title *Every War Must End* applies to civil wars as well. The violence stemming from religious differences within Europe several centuries ago has ended. England is no longer criss-crossed by warring armies representing York and Lancaster or King and Parliament. The French no longer kill one another over the divine right of kings. Americans seem agreed to be independent of English rule and that the South should not secede. Argentines seem reconciled to living in a single state rather than several. The ideologies of the Spanish Civil War now seem irrelevant, and even the separatist issues there are not being resolved by mass violence. More recently, two separatist wars in South Asia have produced the independent states of Pakistan and Bangladesh. Conflict in the area remains likely, but no one seems interested in extinguishing the two successor states. Nigeria experienced one of the most brutal civil wars of our time, but the violence ended 20 years ago, and while the country is politically unstable, the divisions are not the same as in the civil war. Other cases can be found (including those in this volume). Somehow new societies were constructed after the war, involving most of the people who had fought on opposite sides.

But how did this happen? We know very little about the processes involved. How are armed societies disarmed? Do outside interventions (military assistance to one side or both, offers of mediation, humanitarian aid) help or hinder a settlement? Are lasting solutions more likely before or after total military victory by one side? Does it make a difference whether the underlying issues are ethnic divisions or political differences, whether the goal has been separation from the state or conquest of the state apparatus? Is peace more likely when both sides are strong or when they are divided? Can the central issues be compromised in the initial settlement, or does a draconian solution work best in the long run? Why do some "solutions" last and others collapse? Most importantly, what can we learn from these experiences about the circumstances under which civil societies may be constructed from civil violence? That is the central focus of this book.

How Important Is Civil War?

Jimmy Carter recently said that of the 116 wars since World War II, all but the Iraqi invasion of Kuwait were civil wars. (Jack Levy notes that Saddam Hussein would disagree, viewing Kuwait as part of Iraq.) Statements like these depend on the definitions being used, but the systematic studies of recent wars demonstrate the importance of civil war, no matter how it is defined. In 1973 Robert Randle asserted that "since the first use of the atomic bomb against Japan, there have been at least 18 wars between states and 55 civil wars" (Randle 1973, x). The seminal Correlates of War project identified, between 1945 and 1980, 43 civil wars, 12 international wars, and 18 extrasystemic (colonial and imperial) wars (Small and Singer 1982, 56–57, 80, and 222). Paul Pillar (1983, 21) lists 16 civil, 14 international, and 9 extrasystemic wars after 1945. Gantzel and Meyer-Stamer (1986; cited in Wallensteen 1991, 215) developed a list of 31 wars going on in 1984; 26 of them were classified as internal. Hugh Miall (1992, 115–116 and 124) constructed a set of about 350 conflicts between 1945 and 1985. From this he worked with a subset of 81 and found 6 international conflicts with major violence as compared to 28 civil or civil/international ones. Ruth Sivard (1988) counted 24 wars being fought in 1987, 22 of which were civil wars or wars of secession. The common ground of these studies is that civil violence is a major phenomenon in the current world.

It therefore seems unreasonable to omit such struggles from theories of conflict and violence. Nonetheless they have received much less attention than interstate conflicts, for reasons that are not altogether clear. Practitioners tend to focus on individual civil struggles rather than looking for patterns; few people, after all, are likely to have had direct experience in resolving more than one. Academics might be expected to take a wider view, but they are sometimes restrained by the sociology of their disciplines. Among political scientists, for example, interstate war is part of the field of international politics, while the study of internal wars is often included in another field, comparative politics. Perhaps as a result, the very substantial amount of research on interstate war has had little impact on the study of civil wars. Historians tend to focus on individual conflicts rather than generalizations about many such wars, and neither discipline has much contact with sociology, which alone among the disciplines has produced a substantial literature on the topic.

Indeed, the termination of civil violence is relevant to a wide variety of intellectual fields of study.

The 'problem of order' . . . is often alleged to be the most fundamental on the agenda of social science. . . . Most of the major currents in social and political thought since Hobbes's time have contributed something to the debate on the origins of civil violence. Most of the key methodologies current among social scientists today have served as vehicles for arguments on the subject. As much as any other relatively delimited issue, it offers a microcosm of social science thinking. (Rule 1988, xi and 3)

Conflict resolution has focused primarily on less violent disputes within states and interstate wars, omitting civil wars; the recent interest in what are often called protracted or intractable conflicts (Kriesberg, Northrup, and Thorson 1989) has begun to compensate for this and offers one way to bring these two different areas together. The immense literature on revolution has focused primarily on the *origins* of such conflicts, with very little concern given the process by which they *end* and produce major social impacts. The recent concern with ethnic groups often encourages us to look at conflicts among them, some of which escalate into violence; it is perhaps more important to determine how they can coexist in the same state relatively peacefully, especially after they have been killing one another. The failure to end such conflict may sometimes produce genocide and policide, the study of which has developed into a specialty area of its own (Kuper 1981; Walliman and Dobkowski 1987). We cannot seriously study political and economic development without looking at how civil wars are ended. The list goes on.

Analysis of civil violence has focused on explaining its *origins* (a prominent exception is Gurr 1988.) It is particularly infuriating that two of the best books on internal war (Eckstein 1964 and Rule 1988) both explicitly note the importance of studying how such conflicts end and then proceed to ignore the topic. Of course this is also true of interstate wars, whose *causes* have been extensively studied while the equally interesting question of how and why they *end* has been, for the most part, curiously neglected.

Little has changed in the quarter century since Harry Eckstein lamented:

No questions about internal war have been more thoroughly neglected by social scientists, in any generation, than these long-run ones. . . . This neglect is most serious in what may well be the most crucial practical question that can be asked about internal war . . . : How is it possible to re-establish truly legitimate authority after a society has been rent by a revolutionary convulsion? How does one go from a "politics of aspiration" to a settled civic order? It is extremely common for internal war to grow into an institutional pattern of political competition by force, less common for a truly "civil" society to emerge from a major internal war, except in the very long run. What then are the circumstances under which the self-renewing aspects of internal war become, or may become, muted? (Eckstein 1964, 28–29; cf. Modelski 1964b, 126)

But does it make any sense to look at civil wars separately from large-scale conflict in general? After all, if even the experts can't agree on the distinctions between civil and interstate wars, why should we expect them to end differently? We don't really know, but there is good theoretical reason to expect that civil wars may be resolved differently than wars among states.

In conflicts that are predominantly civil wars . . . outcomes intermediate between victory and defeat are difficult to construct. If partition is not a feasible outcome because the belligerents are not geographically separable, one side has to get all, or nearly so, since there cannot be two governments ruling over one country, and since the passions aroused and the political cleavages opened render a sharing of power unworkable. (Ikle 1971, 95)

The civil war that ensues will be a violent military struggle between two societies so committed that victory for one means extinction for the other. Thus a society organized as either envisions would be incompatible with the continued existence of the other; the alternative becomes Victory or Death, God or the Devil, Freedom or Slavery. Once the battle has been joined, the war is total and the outcome is seen only as total victory or total defeat. Neither side at any stage can seriously contemplate any alternative to victory except death—if not of the body then of the soul. (Bell 1972, 218; cf. Modelski 1964b, 125–126; Pillar 1983, 24–25)

This general argument is developed eloquently in the next chapter in I. William Zartman's powerful analysis of the difficulties of ending civil wars based on a large number of current examples.

If this is true, we would expect civil wars to be both more *intense* and more *difficult to resolve* than interstate wars. There is some support for both hypotheses. Hugh Miall's conflict data shows that 15% of international conflicts involved major violence, while a full 68% of civil and civil/international conflicts did (Miall 1992, 124). Paul Pillar's data (1983, 25) show about two-thirds of interstate wars ending by negotiation as compared to about one-third of civil wars. Using a somewhat modified data set, Stedman (1991, 9) found that, when colonial wars and other "special" cases were eliminated, the civil war figures declined to about 15%.

These data have somewhat ambiguous implications. On the one hand, casualties do seem to be higher and settlements more difficult in civil conflict, suggesting that there may be interesting theoretical differences between the different sorts of violence. On the other hand, while suppression, genocide, or partition are certainly possible, negotiated settlement in civil violence does in fact occur, as seen in the cases of Colombia, Sudan, and Yemen in this volume.

What Is a Civil War and When Does It End?

This line of reasoning also suggests that the conventional definition of a civil war, large-scale violence between two or more groups holding sovereignty within a recognized state, is inadequate. The problem is the notion of recognized state, which is essentially a legal criterion. Using this definition, it's not clear that, for example, the Palestinian uprising in the territories occupied by Israel is a civil war, since one can view Israel as an occupying force rather than a recognized state in the occupied territories. Similarly, as Robert Mortimer has pointed out, the war in Zimbabwe can be viewed as a colonial struggle, since there was no legitimate government in place before the end of the conflict.

However, Ikle's argument suggests that the particular intensity of a civil war stems from the *nature of the stakes*, from the expectation that after the violence, regardless of the results, the participants will have to live together in the state which is being shaped by the conflict. Thus we use the term civil war to mean *large-scale violence among geographically contiguous people concerned about possibly having to live with one another in the same political unit after the conflict*. In particular it incorporates two different kinds of criteria.

(1) There must be *multiple sovereignty*, defined by Charles Tilly as the population of an area obeying more than one institution.

They pay taxes, provide men to its armies, feed its functionaries, honor its symbols, give time to its service, or yield other resources despite the prohibitions of a still-existing government they formerly obeyed. (Tilly 1978, 192)

This criterion differentiates civil wars from other types of domestic violence, such as street crime and riots.

(2) In addition, a civil war, by our definition, involves physical violence to people. We have used the operational definitions of the Correlates of War project: (a) 1,000 battle deaths or more per year and (b) effective resistance (either at least two sides must have been organized for violent conflict before the war started or the weaker side must have imposed at least 5% of its own casualties on its opponent), to distinguish between civil wars and political massacres (Small and Singer 1982, 214–215).

As defined, the term civil war thus logically includes wars of *conquest*, where one group tries to incorporate another into the same state, but very few of them can be found after 1945. (Even the Iraqi invasion of Kuwait remains somewhat debatable, as noted above.) The Palestinian uprising would be included in this definition since Arabs and Jews are likely to cohabit some states, regardless of the outcome. Similarly Zimbabwe becomes a relevant case because the issue of the conflict was the nature of the government which would control the state in which most of the combatants expected to reside.

But what does it mean to say that a civil war *ends*? It is commonplace, for example, to say that the American civil war has not yet ended, that the struggle between differing cultures in the north and south continues to this day in various ways. Here we distinguish between *war* and *conflict*. The distinguishing qualities of *war* are multiple sovereignties and violence, as set forth above. The *underlying conflict* which triggered the violence may well continue, but *if (1) the violence or (2) the multiple sovereignty ends, the war ends* as far as we are concerned.

Research Strategy

When this project began in 1987, these questions represented something of a chicken and egg problem. There were neither applicable *theories* to test nor *case studies* which might be used to generate such theory. Moreover, the problem was clearly larger than any single person could handle. The obvious approach was a collaborative and iterative strategy, combining the intimate knowledge of specialists in particular examples with the broader interests of theorists, moving back and forth between cases and theory.

To get started, I sketched out some very tentative ideas about why civil wars might end, including questions and variables which might be relevant (Licklider 1988). This framework (it was far from a theory, since there was no serious discussion of how these variables were related to one another) is summarized in the following diagram:

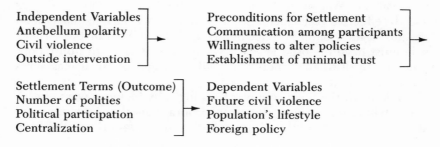

Independent Variables ⎤
Antebellum polarity ⎥ ⟶
Civil violence ⎥
Outside intervention ⎦

Preconditions for Settlement ⎤
Communication among participants ⎥ ⟶
Willingness to alter policies ⎥
Establishment of minimal trust ⎦

Settlement Terms (Outcome) ⎤
Number of polities ⎥ ⟶
Political participation ⎥
Centralization ⎦

Dependent Variables
Future civil violence
Population's lifestyle
Foreign policy

There were lots of problems with this initial framework, and it was largely abandoned later. However, it did have the advantage of specifying that the reason civil wars end the way they do was interesting, that we were concerned with the consequences of such conflicts on people, states, and the international system, and that the connections between these factors should not be ignored in our research.

In the second phase of the project, this framework served as the basis for a group of comparative case studies prepared by area experts with particular knowledge of the individual conflicts. These cases were to be used to develop and refine the original set of variables inductively, hopefully allowing us to move toward something closer to testable theory about the conditions under which civil wars end.

Clearly case selection was critical. We can all recite litanies of civil wars which seem endless—Ulster, Lebanon, Cambodia, etc. But we seem to know less about those which have ended. Therefore, the cases were deliberately chosen as examples of large-scale civil violence which had *ended*, at least for a considerable time. They were designed to encourage *theory development*. Clearly they could *not* be used to *test* theory, since they were all "successful" in reducing conflict. Theory testing would require comparable cases in which the violence had *not* ended (although even within this sample of "successes," longitudinal comparisons were still possible by asking why a settlement had not been reached earlier).

The cases were chosen from large-scale civil conflicts which had ended, at least for some considerable time and were identified by the Small and Singer (1982) data. We classified a civil war as ended when the level of violence had dropped below the Small-Singer threshold of 1,000 battle deaths per year for at least five years. This criterion produced at least two apparent anomalies among the seven cases. Colombia 1957 was included because violence diminished for several years and, when it was renewed, involved different contestants and issues. The 1972 settlement in Sudan was included because violence declined for over five years, even though the agreement eventually broke down and resulted in renewed conflict with essentially the same participants and issues.

In order to narrow the focus of the study, pre-1940 cases were excluded. This is a conventional strategy, especially in the study of international relations because of major changes in the power distribution of the international system from World War II. However, several people pointed out that there was no obvious change in the fundamental problems of reconciliation and state formation which this study addresses. Moreover, these processes seem likely to take a very long time (generations is a term that gets used a lot), and post-World War II settlements by definition haven't lasted very long yet. Lastly, there is an enormous literature on some of the earlier conflicts. In the end, I decided to add a chapter on the American Civil War to see if it would be useful in the theory-building exercise, and it was quite helpful.

Small and Singer (1982, 222) list 44 civil wars which began after 1940 and classify all but three as having ended (so much for endless civil wars). Cases were selected within this group on the basis of their diversity and my ability to persuade a first-rate specialist in the conflict to work within the general lines of the project, since bad cases were not going to be of much use. This is obviously *not* a random sample of the Small-Singer post-1940 data set, which itself is subject to legitimate question. However, since the cases were to be used for *theory development* rather than theory testing, it seemed an appropriate strategy. The seven cases were the American Civil War, Greece, Colombia (1957), Yemen, Nigeria, Sudan (1972), and Zimbabwe. The initial versions of the cases were written and presented at meetings of the International Political Science Association in 1988 and the International Studies Association in 1989.

The cases are remarkably varied in a number of aspects, which makes them particularly useful for theory construction. They include three negotiated settlements (Yemen, Sudan, and Colombia), two total victories (Greece and Nigeria), and two mixed examples of military dominance combined with negotiation (more negotiation in Zimbabwe, less in the United States). Some of the conflicts were separatist (Nigeria, the United States, and Sudan, although the latter is not entirely clear); others were revolutions (Greece, Yemen, Colombia, and Zimbabwe). There was extensive outside intervention in Yemen and Greece, somewhat less in Nigeria, Sudan, and Zimbabwe, and much less still in Colombia and the United States. Their only apparent shared characteristic is that large-scale civil violence ended for a considerable time after the settlement.

The third phase of the project was to refine the case materials by making them more theoretical and more comparative and to move back again to the theory-building process. The centerpiece of this activity was a three-day conference in March, 1990, supported by the United States Institute of Peace and Rutgers University. The case authors were brought together for the first time to discuss the cases systematically, along with several theorists on war termination and selected members of the Rutgers faculty, both to enrich the cases and to encourage some theorists to address the general question of how civil wars end.

Coincidentally, a conference on Internal Security Negotiations was held two weeks later at the Paul Nitze School of Advanced International Studies of Johns Hopkins University in Washington, supported by the MacArthur Foundation. It focused on a group of cases in which large-scale civil violence was *currently being negotiated*. This added a number of fascinating cases and some intriguing theoretical ideas which are summarized by I. William Zartman in the next chapter.

After some discussion, participants at the Rutgers conference agreed on the central focus of the research. The major issue was agreed to be *why some civil wars end so that large-scale civil violence is not resumed*. This can be divided into two separate questions: (1) *Why does the fighting end when it does?* In particular, why do some civil wars end in negotiated settlements while some are fought until one side or the other attains a total victory? (2) *Why doesn't the civil violence start again later*, especially since the underlying issues often remain when the killing stops?

This stress on *empirical relationships* allows the apparatus of modern social science to be applied, hopefully in testing hypotheses in ways that can be replicated. The advantage of this approach is that people with very different political beliefs can work together and hopefully reach agreement on how these empirical relationships actually work, which would otherwise be very difficult. However, the approach avoids a set of normative issues by implicitly assuming that violence is bad and should be avoided. But this ignores the reasons why people choose to fight and die in the first place. Presumably the insurgents saw the pre-war situation as intolerable, perhaps involving "structural violence" where the status quo systematically injures people (Galtung 1969). For example, would Americans have appreciated a foreign mediator who negotiated a compromise settlement of our Civil War in 1862, saving hundreds of thousands of lives while leaving slavery intact, or was that sacrifice of much of a generation justified by the goals of the struggle? Are we studying this topic because we are interested in peace or because we are interested in justice (accepting that there will be no agreement on what that term means)? And how useful is our research when the two values conflict?

We may try to square this particular circle by assuming that only a "just" settlement will really assure a lasting peace, but the empirical evidence for this proposition is unclear. Alternatively, one may argue that our work is purely theoretical and that it does not necessarily imply that policymakers *should* be more concerned with ending violence than establishing justice, although in fact most of us find the topic interesting precisely because it seems to have policy relevance. My own position is that violence is clearly not a good thing and that the purpose of this project is to suggest ways by which it can be avoided or ended. The study does not address either the empirical question of how "justice" may be established or the normative issue of when a resort to violence is appropriate.

Framework for Research

Most of the case authors at the Rutgers conference agreed that the initial framework had been too complex and not particularly useful in their work, and we spent a good deal of time discussing it. As a result of these discussions, I drastically simplified the framework, focusing on five factors or variable clusters which seemed relevant in explaining why violence ended: issues which caused the conflict, internal politics of each side, military balance, activities of third parties, and terms of the settlement. It was agreed that the cases would be revised around these factors. This process reflected a set of guesses about explanations which can be formulated as tentative (and sometimes conflicting) hypotheses. These will be refined here in light of the case studies and formulated and tested more systematically in the future.

(1) *The nature of the issues which underlie the conflict* is important, although its impact is unclear. The *scope* of the conflict can be defined in terms of the *purposes* for which the war is waged. (a) We can distinguish between wars of *secession* and wars of *revolution*. In the latter category, the insurgents may seek to change personnel (who hold certain offices), authority (changes in government but not society), or structure (changes in society as a whole); presumably the conflict will be more intense and foreign intervention more likely as we move up this scale (Rosenau 1964, 60–69).

(b) We also have arguments that *identity issues* (ethnicity, race, nationalism, etc.) are more difficult to resolve than *economic* or *political issues*, since they provoke deeper levels of commitment and are harder to compromise (Gurr 1990, 96; Wedge 1986, 56–57; Smith 1986; Rothchild 1991, 201–203). An alternative position is that identity issues are *easier* to resolve, either because they are primarily symbolic (flying two flags together rather than one doesn't cost much more) or because security for one side in a conflict will increase the security of the other side (Burton 1987, 42).

Leaving aside the degree of difficulty, different strategies may be more useful in dealing with each type of issue. Richard Bensel has suggested, for example, that secessionist conflicts are best resolved by devolution of power, while a revolution is best handled by centralizing power and defeating the rebels.

(2) The *internal politics of each side* will also be significant. Each side in a civil war is likely to be a *coalition*, and successful political analysis will require that this be taken into account. (a) Ending a civil war involves a *policy change* by at least one side, perhaps both. Such a change is more likely to take place after a *leadership change* than with continuity. (b) Moreover, each side in a civil war is usually a coalition of different factions. Internal rivalries may reduce the ability of the leadership to enforce unpopular agreements with the opposition; thus a *strong leadership* may be necessary for a negotiated settlement. Without such united leadership, the war may have to go on to its bitter end because no one is strong enough to change the policies which maintain it. Obviously, however, while united leaderships may be a necessary condition for ending the violence, they are certainly not sufficient; one or more united leaderships dedicated to continuing the war can make any agreement impossible. But without such unity, negotiation may be fruitless (Zartman 1989, 274–275).

(3) The *military balance in the field* is likely to be reflected at the bargaining table, although future *expectations* of military success or failure may be more important than the current situation (Modelski 1964b, 143–144; see also Jane E. Holl's chapter in this volume). (a) Measuring the military balance is very difficult, particularly if the conflict is being waged using guerilla rather than conventional military tactics. Moreover, the notion of balance implies knowledge of the *opponent's position* as well, and that will be even less clear. There is thus likely to be considerable debate among the coalition

members about what the balance actually is at any given time. As a result, *prominent military outcomes* will have a disproportionate impact on the perceptions of the elites, often creating agreement among them on issues which have been long argued.

(b) Zartman (1989, 266–273) has developed the concept of the "hurting stalemate," where each side is willing to change policies only if it believes that it cannot achieve its desired ends by violence at a tolerable cost and that its relative position will decline in the future. The hypothesis would be that a stable agreement is possible only if *both* sides believe this at the same time.

(4) *Third parties* may encourage or inhibit the violence by actions ranging from military assistance to mediation in all its forms. George Modelski (1964a, 28, and 1964b, 126–129) argues that "every internal war creates a demand for foreign intervention." The range of such activities is enormous. However, we know relatively little about their *impact*. Broadly framed, what can third parties do to make a settlement more likely? (a) A negotiated solution may be more likely if weapons are given to the weaker side, since that will create a balance which may lead toward a hurting stalemate. Alternatively, weapons given to the stronger side may bring about a victory which will end the war quickly and with fewer casualties. A third possibility is that withholding weapons from both sides may encourage both to negotiate. (b) What kind of outside actors have more or less influence under what circumstances? Private parties may be able to establish contacts with both parties in ways that government cannot, and their lack of power makes them less threatening and perhaps better able to facilitate negotiations. An alternative model is called "mediation with muscle," the idea that settlements will require pressure on one or both sides as well as good will and that governments are best able to apply such pressure. There is a considerable literature on both mediation and military assistance, but much of it is anecdotal, and it has not yet been linked to how civil wars end.

(5) Assuming some sort of settlement is reached, how long is it likely to survive? *The nature of the polity which emerges from the settlement* seems likely to affect its duration and what will follow it. (a) We may label the "liberal" or accommodation hypothesis the argument that, if rivals have been successfully included in the governing process, a settlement is more likely to survive. This position is supported by a massive literature on conflict resolution, but there seem to be no empirical tests of the hypothesis in post-civil war

societies. This in turn is related to the question of centralization, and it is interesting that one of our cases (Nigeria) was a federation both before and after the conflict.

On the other hand, there is clearly a major risk in bringing former armed opponents into the national government; the techniques used in the United States to cope with this danger over several decades after the American Civil War are particularly interesting (Bensel 1990, 405–413). Thus the "repressive" hypothesis is that stability is more likely when governments are strong and unified and therefore able to deter future attempts at collective violence.

(b) Aside from the structure of the state, its *performance* on a number of *issues* may be important. How are the sides to be disarmed, for example? How can a common political system be created over different territories? Moreover, even after settlement the original issues underlying the conflict usually remain. Many people have been willing to kill and die for them; how can they be handled so as to avoid renewed civil violence on a large scale?

The third phase of the project concluded with the case authors' rewriting their initial papers, using the revised framework as a guideline and benefitting from the discussions and interactions at the Rutgers conference. In a parallel process, four other conference members wrote theoretical studies, building upon the cases and discussions of the conference but informed by their own quite different backgrounds and interests. No attempt was made to impose a common focus on these four chapters; their value consists precisely in their variety, in their demonstration of both the utility of different literatures and approaches to the understanding of how civil wars end and the illumination thrown on theoretical issues in various fields by analyzing this topic.

Where Are We Now?

What did all this produce? Having used seven non-random cases to generate and refine but not test hypotheses, any patterns must be labeled tentative in the extreme. Perhaps the clearest lesson is that *stable settlements can emerge under a remarkable variety of conditions*. In a sense we knew this already; the cases were picked as examples of stable settlements, by our definition, and they were very varied. Perhaps more striking, we have examples of *negotiated settlements* to civil wars, which we know to be relatively rare, in separatist and revolutionary conflicts, where the issues are identity and otherwise, with and without increased unity of command, when the military balance varies, with very different kinds of third-party involvement (including non-involvement), and with postwar regimes which stress both accommodation and repression.

The second general point is that the five factors which we isolated do indeed play important roles in explaining how civil wars end. To be more precise, the issues which caused the conflict, while difficult to isolate, do indeed seem related to the eventual resolution. The internal politics of each side are clearly relevant to decisions about termination, as are the military balance and the widely varied actions of third parties. Lastly, the nature of the political settlement clearly is useful in explaining why civil violence does or does not renew itself. These effects can be seen in our cases and can also be explained in theoretical ways that are consistent with other bodies of ideas. They can thus serve as the basis for hypotheses to be tested in further work.

Interestingly, however, these variables have different sorts of impacts under different circumstances. Thus, rather than a single pattern whereby civil violence is ended, it seems more useful to conceive of the termination of civil violence as a set of *processes* in which there are certain *critical choice points*.

Selections at these points form *alternative strategies* of conflict termination. The identification of these strategies is clearly a major goal for future research; already we can distinguish, for example, between strategies of *accommodation* and *repression*, both of which seem to work under the right circumstances.

Over time, the question under discussion has shifted. At the beginning of the study, the focus was very much on *how the violence stopped*. However, increasingly the question of *why it did not start again* became more intriguing. It is easy to imagine a number of contingent events (deaths of prominent leaders, temporary military setbacks, policy of outsider actors, lack of supplies, divisions within the coalition) which might persuade one side to end civil violence temporarily. But if the basic problems have not changed, we would expect the participants to renew the violence when these circumstances changed, and as I. William Zartman reminds us in the next chapter, such renewals of civil violence are indeed quite common. The *nature of the settlement* became more intriguing, and it soon became clear that we were really talking about *state formation* in a new guise. After all, one definition of a state is precisely a group of people who can work together without killing one another in an organized way. Moreover, the postwar problems of disarmament, demobilization of at least two armies, and the likely collapse of the winning coalition in an environment where resources will be scarce and demands will be high mean that effectively the state will have to be recreated, even if the government has won the conflict. This reformulation of the central question brings in an entirely new set of perspectives and literatures with whose implications we are only now beginning to wrestle.

At this point in the project, it seemed imperative to move the discussion to a broader intellectual community. This book is the result. It is composed of three parts. The first lays out the problem in two introductory chapters. Mine sets forth the background and intellectual assumptions of the project; I. William Zartman then discusses the difficulties of resolving civil conflicts based on both theory and the cases analyzed at the Nitze School conference.

The second part of the book consists of the seven revised cases of the ending of large-scale civil conflict. The authors do not address each of the many questions raised above. Nonetheless, each case is framed in terms of these five types of questions. The result was a unique series of comparable case studies of the ways in which civil war has actually ended. The chapters are arranged in rough order of the method of settlement, starting with the examples of negotiation (Colombia, Sudan, and Yemen), followed by the two mixed cases (Zimbabwe and the United States), and concluding with the two military victories (Nigeria and Greece).

The last part of the book builds upon these materials. Rather than a single conclusion, there are four different chapters, each written by a participant at the Rutgers conference looking at some particular aspect of the settlement process in a theoretical, comparative way. Robert Harrison Wagner uses a rational-choice approach to develop a unique analysis of interstate war termination and looks at how similar processes work in civil wars. Jane E. Holl compares the relationship between military and political success in international and civil war termination. Harvey Waterman explores in more depth the complexities and ambiguities of the concept of a settlement in a civil war. I then try to bring the cases together to respond to the issues raised in this chapter, to suggest what we have learned, to evaluate the project as it now stands, and to suggest a number of different ways in which we can move forward in this important and challenging field.

The Unfinished Agenda: Negotiating Internal Conflicts

I. William Zartman

Not all internal conflicts have been successfully negotiated. Many are still under discussion, negotiations having been tried but settlement not having been reached. The striking characteristic of all of them is the protracted nature of the conflict. "Protracted conflict" is a term formerly taken to refer to the Cold War (Strausz-Hupé et al., 1959); it is now understood that internal, frequently ethnic conflicts are even more durable (Mitchell, 1992). More than interstate conflict, internal conflicts seem to have the ability to continue for decades and arrive neither at victorious resolution for one side nor at satisfactory reconciliation for both. Why do internal conflicts last so long? Why is negotiation so difficult? How can a mutually satisfactory solution be found through negotiation?

As the prevalent bipolar conflict that has dominated our century fades away, the salient events of the end of the millennium are not the parallel resolution of lesser conflicts but their persistence. Alongside the cases analyzed in this volume for their successful negotiation are a number of others, no less important, that rise and fall in intensity, start and drag in negotiation, sometimes reach a temporary and artificial "settlement," only to burst out all over again later on.

This chapter is part of a larger project of Negotiating Internal Conflict (NICon) funded by the MacArthur Foundation, whose support is gratefully acknowledged.

The Eritrean conflict (Ottoway, 1993; Lyons, 1991) with Ethiopia delayed the disposition of the British-occupied, formerly Italian colony until 1952, when the more developed Eritrea was federated with imperial Ethiopia; the Emperor's dissolution of the federation a decade later brought on a war of national liberation, led eventually by the Eritrean Peoples Liberation Front (EPLF) and other factious groups, that lasted over thirty years through a major revolution in Ethiopia, punctuated by shifting fortunes in the field and a number of ultimately abortive attempts at mediated negotiations. The final collapse of the Ethiopian government in 1991 brought promises of a referendum in Eritrea by 1994, but the chicken had not yet been hatched.

Next door, British colonial indecision about the status of the racially and culturally distinct southern part of Sudan (see chapter 4 in this volume; Deng, 1993; Deng and Zartman, 1991; Deng and Gifford, 1987; Assefa, 1987) created the context for military mutiny in 1955, opening a war that accompanied the declaration of independence for the country at the end of the year. Moving toward secession in despair of ever attaining their desired goal of federation in a single country, the rebels in the Anyanya movement reached a mediated agreement in 1972 bringing a federation into existence. A decade later, after the same Sudanese government that signed the agreement abrogated it, the Sudanese Peoples Liberation Movement/ Army (SPLM/A) reopened the conflict, calling for a revolution throughout the country and coming several times near a negotiated agreement, only to have the government of the moment collapse and the process start all over again.

In southern Africa, two major factions of the Angolan nationalist movement continued their conflict even after one, the Peoples Movement for the Liberation of Angola (MPLA), won control of the state with foreign support at independence in 1975 (Rothchild, 1993; Marcum, 1978; Zartman, 1989, chapters 4 and 5; McCormick, 1991; Kitchen, 1987; Wolfers and Bergerol, 1983). The other, the National Union for the Total Independence of Angola (UNITA), gained competing foreign support and, after the mediated agreement on neighboring Namibia in 1989, engaged a number of mediators to end hostilities and turn the war into an electoral contest. The agreement that was finally signed in Estoril in May 1991 ended the civil war, but a judgment on civil peace hangs on the conduct of the elections in the fall of 1992 and the evolution of politics thereafter. Similarly, the Front for the Liberation of Mozambique (FreLiMo) has been contested since independence in 1974 by the National Resistance Movement (ReNaMo), and a number of countries since 1985 have attempted to mediate an agreement to bring about a multiparty system (Isaacman and Isaacman, 1983; Isaacman, 1985; Kitchen, 1987).

In Sri Lanka (Wriggins, 1993; Montville, 1990, part III), the Tamils, an enterprising minority with ties to compatriots in neighboring India, accentuated their demands for greater recognition in the early 1970s and developed a generational split over tactics, with the young Tamil Tigers contesting the Tamil United Liberation Front (TULF) and waging a full-scale guerrilla war since 1983. Direct negotiations brought the parties to a search for a compromise, and mediated negotiations brought Indian army occupation of troubled areas, but neither has brought a solution. In Spain (Clark, 1990), a similar ethnic minority, although without the support of a major population of compatriots and a state across the border, long sought self-determination as a national Basque movement, despite periodic reconciliation policies and bilateral negotiations from Madrid. In Cyprus (McDonald and Bendahmane, 1985), a formula for power-sharing at independence in 1960 was destroyed by the Greek majority government, leading to conflict and a negotiated settlement in 1964; another attempt to revise the regime in the Greeks' favor led to a similar round in 1967; and a third led to a Turkish invasion and secession of the Turkish part of the island in 1974. Conflict and negotiations have continued since then, with no solution.

In the Philippines (Druckman and Green, 1993), as in other Asian countries, a communist-oriented nationalist movement arose to fight the Japanese occupation and then continued to press the demands of a poor peasant population primarily in Luzon after independence in 1947 as the Hukbalahap movement. The Huks were won over by a populist government in the 1960s but leftover followers and new grievances among the poor and the Muslim populations in outlying islands led to a second round of insurgencies by the National Peoples Army (NPA), the Moro National Liberation Front (MNLF) and a number of other groups. Some of them found a more acceptable government in the change of regimes in 1986 and in subsequent negotiations but the rebellion has not ended.

Historic communal—then interstate—conflict between Muslims and Bantus in central Africa was controlled by French colonization but revived in Chad in 1965 five years after independence when southern administrators replaced the French in the north (Buijtenhuijs, 1978; Thompson and Adloff, 1981; Zartman, 1986). The northern rebels, organized into factions of the National Liberation Front of Chad (FroLiNaT), finally overthrew the government in 1978 but then fell to fighting among themselves, as one leader (1978), then another (1982), and then a third (1990) evicted his predecessor and met further rebellion, despite repeated mediations and negotiations.

A power-sharing agreement negotiated in 1943 as the basis for Lebanese independence fell prey thirty years later to changes of the demographic balance on which it was based, and to the trigger of a disruptive foreign presence, the Palestinians (Day, 1986; Deeb and Deeb, 1993). The Lebanese civil war broke out among multiple political factions of multiple religious communities, despite repeated truces and negotiations, until the Syrian occupier finally imposed peace in 1990. Yet even the extant amount of peace depends on Syrian dominance, while civil strife stands waiting in the wings. With as many similarities as differences, the arrival to power of the Afrikaner lower class of the white minority in South Africa in 1948 and their dispossession of the black majority on whom they increasingly depended for both the labor and consumer factors of economic growth led to a series of majority outbursts of increasing militancy in 1960, 1976, 1984, and 1990, along with a slowly rising terrorist campaign (Zartman, 1993b; Cloete, 1991; Stedman, et al., 1992). Negotiations in the late 1980s and in 1990 have been only preparatory to more substantive rounds of revolutionary proportions in the future. Also similar in many ways was the situation created in 1958 in Colombia when the nearly twenty-year war termed *la violencia* was ended by a power-sharing agreement between the two elite factions, closing out new social forces (see chapter 3; Garcia, 1993). After 1970, these forces, organized into the M–19 Movement, the Revolutionary Armed Forces of Colombia (FARC), and lesser but equally violent groups waged war on the System and the Establishment until several rounds of negotiations throughout the 1980s gradually integrated most of the groups and prepared for the opening of a new political system.

Finally, in Afghanistan (Bokhari, 1993; Dupree, 1986), a Soviet invasion in 1979 imposed a government that met immediate resistance from the predominantly Islamic Mujahidin. A decade later, the US and the USSR negotiated the withdrawal of Soviet troops, but the guerrilla war continued, despite attempts to mediate between the government remaining in place and the Mujahidin supported from neighboring Pakistan.

There are other cases of protracted internal conflicts; El Salvador, Cambodia, Rwanda, Somalia, Peru, and Northern Ireland, to name a few (Zartman, 1989, chapter 3; Laitin, 1983; McClintock, 1989; Montville, 1990) could also be added to this list of thirteen headline-grabbing cases. The selection here was random; the inclusion of other cases would strengthen but not fundamentally alter the conclusions and generalizations drawn as answers to the initial questions.

Three different if interrelated questions are being asked about the protracted nature of internal conflicts. First, why are settlements so difficult? Internal conflicts last a long time because negotiations are as hard to produce as victories. Mutually satisfactory, second-best settlements are unattractive to parties playing for ultimate stakes. "Protracted" means "extended," impervious to any kind of settlement. Second, why don't settlements stick? The cases show that most conflicts are many times settled, only to burst forth again, a fire that will not be put out. "Protracted" here means "recurrent," even though apparently successful negotiations occur. Third, what strategies can be devised to overcome these problems? "Protracted" means "intractable." Therein lies the answer to the first two questions. It is more difficult to answer the third. Some things one understands better in order to know how to overcome them; others one understands better only to see how hard they are to change.

Internal Conflict and Ripe Moments

One of the basic findings about the negotiation process in general is that it functions best under conditions of equality, and indeed only takes place when the parties have some form of veto over each other's outcomes (Rubin and Brown, 1975, 199, 214–21; Zartman and Berman, 1982, 57ff.). Generally, there must be a basic power equivalence of the parties themselves even if their sources of power differ. This condition can favor conflict resolution when it takes the form of a mutually hurting stalemate, where the countervailing power of each side, though insufficient to make the other side lose, prevents it from winning (Zartman, 1989, chapter 6). Also, the parties to a negotiation have an existence—and therefore other interests—independent of the conflict, and therefore the cost/benefit calculations that contribute to the dynamics of their relationship—conflictual or conciliatory—concern the proportion of their power and interests to devote to the particular conflict, among others (Zartman, 1991). These conditions of negotiation are basically very different from the asymmetries which characterize negotiations in internal conflict (Zartman, 1993a; Mitchell, 1991).

In internal conflict, the government enjoys an asymmetry of power, but the rebels compensate with an asymmetry of commitment. In the beginning they seek a redress of grievances within the rules established by the government. But when they get no satisfaction, their rebellion enters into a new phase, protesting both the government's inattention to their grievances and its right to decide the rules by which protest shall be conducted. They contest the legitimacy of government itself and take on a total and exclusive commitment to rebellion. Conflict becomes their raison d'être; rebellion becomes their sole concern. On the other hand, the government's capabilities are diluted and distracted by its many other concerns. Existence is not its only issue, and probably not its issue at all until the very end (when it may be too late). The desperation of the power asymmetry reinforces the rebels' commitment, makes them economize their resources, and counterbalances capabilities. Theirs is not just a romantic attachment to life in the maquis, to the lifestyle of an outlaw. It is the starting point for their cost/benefit calculations (Pillar, 1983, 24, 162, 245). Anything less than their goal is an unacceptable cost, whereas total and ongoing struggle is not a cost but simply the normal condition of life. Their capabilities are magnified by their commitment.

This situation gives the rebellion tremendous staying power, evening up the otherwise asymmetrical relation with the government. "The guerrilla wins if he does not lose," noted Henry Kissinger (1969, 214); "the conventional army loses if it does not win." Since the rebellion's only issue is existence, just not losing makes it win by preserving its existence, even if it has not yet achieved conclusive victory. Since the government has other things to do, including maintaining security, not performing them properly makes it lose, even if it has not undergone conclusive defeat.

This situation leaves no room for many of the basic ingredients of negotiation. On the rebel side, there is little possibility of trade-offs and compromise. Recognition is both their top and bottom line, with nothing in between to contribute to the give and take of negotiation and bargaining. There is nothing to give up but the rebellion and their commitment to their cause, so that once the agreement is made to negotiate, remaining trade offs only concern details. For both sides, the question of valid spokesmen, usually a precondition for negotiations, is a zero-sum issue. Each side contests the other's legitimacy, since to recognize the claim of the rebels to speak for their population or of the government to speak for the entire country is to accede to their principal demand. Since there is no agreement on the legitimacy of spokesmen, there is no condition of equality between the parties, another formal condition necessary for fruitful negotiations.

Furthermore, conditions which should lead to negotiation become comfortable outcomes in themselves, rather than unstable preconditions to search for a lasting outcome. In internal conflict, stalemate is stable and supportable, an acceptable alternative to losing for both sides, a compromise already favorable to the rebellion rather than a costly deadlock driving the parties to negotiate. Stalemate generally means unrecognized partition of the country, formalizing in the extreme both the rebellion's grievance of regional neglect and its demand for regional autonomy. To the government it provides on-the-job experience for training its army and a national cause for mobilizing its people. In a reverse of the usual situation, stalemate is compromise, negotiation is one-sided victory. Even in a dynamic sense, with the ups and downs that typify insurgencies, stable mutually hurting stalemates are hard to find. The government sees a small improvement in fortunes as the beginning of its reestablishment of legitimate authority over its country; the insurgency sees an upswing as the beginning of justified self-determination. But if the insurgency weakens, it merely draws back to its hills, bush or maquis and to its referent population, who are its invisible redout; if government weakens, it withdraws to its capital and practices its recognized sovereignty over a slightly smaller part of the country. The mutually hurting stalemate that is almost a prerequisite for negotiation or even for mediation is characteristically absent, yet neither side has the power—with rare exceptions—to dislodge the other fully. Fluctuating stalemate becomes a way of life.

Finally, when stalemate settles in, without being mutually hurting, it produces polarization, not pacification. Sunk costs on the government side, and true belief on the insurgents' side, reinforce each party's source of power and their desire to dig in and hold out. Rather than seeing a stalemate as an indication of the maximum each side can achieve and then negotiate from there, as often happens in interstate war (as the history of boundaries indicates), internal conflict parties retrench on their element of strength and harden their positions. The symbolic epitome of this situation has been the status of the Western Saharan conflict throughout the stalemate of the 1980s, where each side clung to its element of strength—the Polisario Front to diplomatic recognition (commitment) and Morocco to military occupation (capabilities)—and neither was willing to negotiate because each hoped to pull the other onto its terrain of strength and defeat it (Zartman, 1989, chapter 2). Polarization is not merely a matter of positions but of leadership styles, so that stalemate leads to less conciliatory leaders, as Cyprus, Eritrea, Sri Lanka, Lebanon, Sudan, and Chad have shown. Stalemate does not produce what is sometimes termed a reconciling or composing mentality, the necessary shift in perception that is needed for negotiation, but instead reinforces the winning mentality that makes negotiation impossible. The basic conditions of the insurgency lie at the root of this paradox: It is possible to take refuge in a winning mentality because the unlikeliness of losing hides the impossibility of winning.

In sum, the nature of internal conflict works against the component conditions for a ripe moment for negotiation. Instead of moving toward either a decisive escalation or a decisive stalemate, internal conflicts are characteristically indecisive, yet their indecisiveness produces extremist leadership. If ever the parties do become involved in negotiation, usually through the insistent efforts of a third party, they continually look for ways of seizing an opportunity to escalate their way out of the stalemate, convincing the other party of their basic bad faith. The long histories of painful negotiations in Lebanon, Eritrea, Cyprus, Sudan, Sri Lanka, and Chad are colorful testimonials to the difficulties.

Protracted Conflicts and Normal Politics

To understand the ongoing nature of internal conflicts, one has to go back to the basic notions of politics. In an ideal condition of internal governance that may be referred to as "normal politics," issues are brought before government as petitions and are disposed of through appropriate policy responses. Absolute (or time comparative) grievances would be handled through measures to increase production or other causes of resource availability; comparative grievances would be handled through just divisions, allocations, and compensations. Production and distribution, or growth and development, in whatever magnitude, are the normal concerns of government. This is true whether the exercise is a rather underdeveloped one of limited government, such as a king dispensing justice under a tree, or whether it is part of the highly complex process of democratic governance in which the people send up not only groups of petitioners according to the issue but also delegates and representatives to receive them and dispense policy responses. The point, basically obvious, is that normal politics is a matter of satisfactorily meeting groups' concerns and grievances, of sending the petitioners back home satisfied, and not a matter of eliminating demands or even of conflicts of interest between demanding groups. Development theorists have emphasized interest articulation and aggregation, as well as output functions, as the business of normal politics.

Internal conflict occurs when this process breaks down. It begins with disadvantaged, deprived or discriminated groups, since internal conflict involves part of society against the rest, represented by the government. In some cases, the conflict is a majoritarian protest, in the name of the excluded population as a whole, and seeks to install a new and better system of dealing with anyone's grievances; in other cases of minoritarian protest, the conflict comes from a particular group's sense of exclusion. In either case, a basic element in the initial stages of the conflict is the building of solidarity among the followers of the protest and of legitimacy and representativeness among the leaders, two sides of the same coin. This is done in only two available terms—ideologically for the majority and ethnically for minority protests (or a combination of the two).

These terms of solidarity are always partial inventions and always only partially inventions. Minority protests arise when people feel ascriptive blockages, that is, discrimination by the majority because of who they are, in predefined terms. Majority protests appear when people feel achievemental blockages, that is, discrimination by the privileged minority because of where they are in the social pyramid. These senses of solidarity and discrimination have both an objective and a subjective component; protest leaders need to turn the former into the latter and arouse the subjective source of solidarity. It is because of this objective and subjective relationship, incidentally, that the ethnic component in minority protests is always asserted by the protestors, contested by the government and debated by the analysts.

Thus Tamils, Basques, Lebanese, Moros, and Eritreans reinforce an undeniable ethnic aspect to the protest with ideological appeals and divisions. In Mozambique, banditry with ideological origins developed an ethnic base. Majoritarian protests in South Africa also combine ethnic and ideological appeals, while a minority, regionalist, ethnic protest in Sudan appeals for majority support by turning its protest ideological. In Afghanistan, Mozambique, the Philippines, and Colombia, non-ethnic protests seek ideological solidarity but suffer from ethnic divisions.

Unlike states at war with each other, these groups so self-defined never surrender and never disappear. Their insurgent organization may suffer defeat and its leaders may be killed, but the group remains and its sources of grievance still remain potentially alive. The struggle is not over the existence of the group, but over the particular deprivations it suffers and the effectiveness of the mechanisms for handling them. The groups continue to exist, in a more or less heightened self-awareness because of the conflict and its outcome, and their existence continues to serve as the basis of politics. In sum, since normal politics involves group demands, internal politics never really goes away; it only becomes political, quiescent, normal.

It therefore makes as much sense to regard internal settlements as truces as it does to consider internal conflicts as violent aberrations. Internal settlements at best provide regimes and mechanisms for handling group grievances, or in other words for reinstituting normal politics. They are only provisional settlements, in that the group will continue to monitor them while practicing them to make sure that the new dispositions are effective in handling their problems. If not, new incidents, new generations not exhausted by the past struggle, even new groups created by the past settlement will revive internal conflict.

Thus Eritreans, southern Sudanese, Cypriots, Tamils, and northern Chadians all achieved a settlement to a previous round of conflict, but the settlement in some way proved inadequate to their perceived blockages and grievances. The Eritreans' and southern Sudanese' federations were abolished by central government after a decade of more-or-less implementation, in what amounted to a declaration of internal war. The Cypriot government did the same thing at more frequent intervals, supported by hardliners from irredentist Greece.

Young Tamils, known as Tigers, were disillusioned by the pace of recognition achieved by their elders precisely through normal politics, and they took up arms. Northern Chadians finally took over the central government after fifteen years of war, and then set about to continue the war among themselves, claiming that the representative of their cause who won at any given time monopolized the benefits of power for himself, his ethnic group, or simply his friends, excluding other leaders, tribes, or factions.

In Angola, Mozambique, Lebanon, Colombia, and an earlier Sudan, a new regime was established—often by negotiation—that satisfied old combatants but created new losers, who then rose to challenge the presumed settlement. In some cases, the settlement marked a victory over colonial rule, but the victors neglected to provide for all the factions and groups among them. In others, notably Lebanon, Colombia, and Mozambique, changes brought in by new social forces, uneven demographic growth, and simply bad government brought a new conflict out of the old settlement.

The lesson is that, precisely because internal conflict settlements are agreements to return to normal politics that necessarily leave at least the informal groups intact to play the normal game, against a background of conflict, exhaustion, and suspicion created by the rebellion, each such settlement is necessarily a trial-and-error affair, with the parties participating to see how it works. In symbolic terms, the arms of the rebellion are buried, out of reach under the trial regime, but ready to be exhumed when necessary again. Meanwhile, normal politics keeps alive the very groups that the settlement disarmed.

Internal Conflicts and Negotiated Outcomes

Since the situationally determined behavior of the parties is the cause of protracted internal conflict, it is useless to provide prescriptions that amount to simply saying, "Stop it!" While external rationality would suggest doing something else, such as negotiation, the internal logic of each party dictates extended, recurrent conflict. It is often seen as a Prisoners' Dilemma Game, so the beginning of a way out is for one or both parties to view the situation as a Chicken Dilemma Game, where continued conflict is viewed as even worse than giving in. But again, the fact that each party understands this, and tries to convince the other that protracted conflict is worse than conceding, merely reinforces its own need to see making concessions as worse than conflict (Brams, 1985, chapter 2; Snyder and Diesing, 1977, 108 ff.).

There are only a few ways out of the dilemmas, and all depend on a skilful use of persuasion and a reordering of perceptions. One returns to timing. Whereas "ripeness" has generally been discussed as a symmetrical property preparatory to resolution, the characteristic asymmetry of internal conflict suggests that it be examined in terms of one side alone (Zartman and Berman, 1982; Zartman, 1990). Rather than looking for a ripe moment in the attributes of the conflict, a search for a ripe moment in the position of one side alone can give some clue as to how that party can act to bring the other to conciliation. If either side follows up a successful escalation with conciliatory terms, the conditions can be created for a Chicken Dilemma perception and a move to conciliation on the other side. Similarly, if one party seeks to escalate its way out of the conflict and the other meets it with an "escalation to call" rather than an "escalation to raise," checking but not overcoming, the functional equivalent of a stalemate is created that can favor a conciliatory outcome (Zartman and Aurik, 1991; Pillar, 1983, 247).

But why would it be in the momentarily stronger side's interest, contrary to the preceding logic, to show itself conciliatory? The answer is not always obvious to the conflict party but it is found in the understanding that victory is at best a long shot, for either side. As seen, unless it resorts to genocide, government cannot eliminate the side that the rebels represent, and the rebels are not likely to eliminate government. That is a broad judgment and one that is not likely to be the perception of either party much of the time, but it is the only one that provides the basis for an outcome reconciling minimal goals of both sides.

There are historic examples, none of them conclusive since the cases referred to here are all incomplete. In 1984, after a successful military campaign, the Sri Lanka government opened a round table with the Tamil insurgents to examine appropriate outcomes. After the installation of the new monarchial democracy, the Spanish government opened talks with the Basque insurgents and met many of their grievances. In Colombia, the gradual process of negotiation conducted under presidents Turbay, Barco, and Gavaria took place under increasing polarization and retrenchment by both sides in which both were strong and both increasingly persuaded of the impossibility of victory; there was no galvanizing sign of ripeness nor clinching catastrophe but simply the growing feeling on both sides that the conflict was tearing the country apart, the consequent willingness of the government to offer a wide opening of the political system, and the willingness of the insurgents to trust the offer, with no guarantees on either side as to the stability of the outcome.

Another way to find an answer in timing is to deal differently with different historical phases of the conflict. In the beginning, the conflict is easier to resolve because solutions can be found within the framework of the governmental system; restive minorities grumble either because they are neglected or because they are oppressed, and solutions to these two forms of grievance are conceptually easy. The implications are clear. Ethnic conflicts are best handled early, before they get out of hand, and they are best handled through an increased role in their own or general affairs and an elimination of blockages and discrimination. Above all, regional arrangements, such as those in Sudan and Ethiopia, should be implemented and respected, since their retraction not only restores the conflict but also exhausts a potential solution.

In the later stage under consideration here, however, when the conflict has gone to the point of challenging the legitimacy of the system itself, it is difficult to go back to first-stage solutions. Not only are specific responses exhausted but the problem which they addressed has changed in nature in the course of the protracted conflict. More radical solutions are needed. This is a crucial point, and one that the "needs" school has reached toward but failed to grasp in its unquestioning support of all ethnic causes. What is required is not simply self-determination for any ethnic cause at any stage, nor victory for internal rebellions over governments, but a new synthesis of the two sides' demands when the conflict escalates beyond more local grievances to the legitimacy of the whole governance system. At this stage, there is no going back to local solutions, and no hope of an escalation to one-sided victory. A totally new formula, involving the reform of both sides, is required.

The best examples, still incomplete, come from Colombia and Angola; South Africa, Sudan, and Ethiopia provide a partial illustration as well. In Colombia, a new constitution and an opening up of the system established forty years earlier to end *la violencia* was required as a basis of reconciliation between the various rebels and the government. Simply allowing the rebels legal existence as parties within the old system of two-party dominance was not satisfactory. In Angola, the 1991 accord withheld victory from either side and transferred the conflict from the military to the political arena, with elections, coalitions, and accountable government as means to handle grievances.

In South Africa, the outcome is obvious; only the way to get there is mined and unmapped. The optimal solution, again, is not a victory of one side over the other but a redesigned political system in which the rights of the majority are operative without the rights of the minority or minorities being trampled. The dual threats of one-sided victories mark the outset of the path to that solution; unfortunately, toward the end of that path, one of the threats will be removed and only wisdom will keep negotiations on track and keep the majority from eliminating the minority (or minorities). In Sudan, the SPLA demands a reform—it uses the term "revolution"—of the northern government, including secularization and the sharing of power and resources. Simply returning to regional autonomy is no longer sufficient.

In Ethiopia, there was an apparent victory of the Eritrean forces in mid-1991, and the commitment of the government to a referendum and independence for Eritrea within two years. While this may appear as simply a victory of the Eritreans and a defeat for the Ethiopian government, in fact the outcome as discussed also includes economic association, interdependence between portland and hinterland, and other elements of cooperation. The case is an extreme, and like the Sudanese revolution, it has not yet come into full shape or reality. But it too illustrates the need for overarching solutions and new formulas as the only way out of protracted conflict.

Two other cases illustrate the uncertainty of presumably stable new outcomes, one already in force and the other generally accepted as the only stable outcome toward which to work. In Lebanon, an apparent solution has come about only because it was imposed by a powerful neighbor, Syria. It is unclear whether the new government represents a restoration of order tenable only as long as the neighbor remains or whether the neighbor's imposition itself is the mark of a newly restructured system, the only one that could substitute stability for conflict. In Cyprus, mid-1991 was seen as an opportunity for creative diplomacy, with the United States helping exhausted patrons troubled by other concerns—Greece and Turkey—move the two Cypriot parties toward an equal two-party federation. Again, the stability of the outcome that purports to transfer conflict from military violence to constitutional politics will have to be tested.

The other half of the cases still elude even a clear notion of a resolving formula, let alone an implemented outcome. What but a lasting defeat of the insurgency would resolve the conflict in Sri Lanka, Mozambique, Spain, Chad, Afghanistan, or the Philippines? But how could such a defeat be engineered? Desultory negotiations under various mediators have gone on since 1986 in Mozambique; much of the Basque insurgency has reached an agreement with the government in Spain; peace has come many times with the defeat of the incumbent government in Chad, only to be broken by a new form of the insurgency. Meeting the Tamil and Basque problems will require some measure of regional autonomy and much more; even the type of formula required for the other conflicts is less clear.

The other requirement will be some change in the military fortunes of the parties and a corresponding change in their leadership (in one or both parties). Both are necessary to bring about a revision in the perceptions of stalemate and the relative cost/benefit calculations over toughing it out vs. coming to terms. Yet they do not guarantee a reconciliation, as potential lost opportunities in Sudan and the Philippines indicate, nor do they assure that an agreement will be stable, as overturned victories and agreements in Chad and Spain testify. These ingredients are only the preconditions to creative thinking about new, overarching formulas bringing a reformed government and a revised opposition together to transform violent conflict into political competition. And even then, when the necessary conditions for a responsive, reconciling outcome have been identified, it must be remembered that they may not be sufficient conditions, and produce no guarantees, since the parties are only human, prone to missing opportunities, behaving offensively, and acting stubborn enough to botch a sure thing.

Cases

3.1 Colombia. From Jonathan Hartlyn. *The Politics of Coalition Rule in Colombia.* Copyright © 1988 by Cambridge University Press. Reprinted with permisison of the Publisher.

36

Civil Violence and Conflict Resolution: The Case of Colombia

Jonathan Hartlyn

In Colombia, from the late 1940s to the early 1960s, some 200,000 Colombians died during an extensive bloodletting known simply as *la violencia* (the violence). In the 1980s, violence once again picked up force, and by the late 1980s, there were some 2,000 to 3,000 political homicides per year in a country that had an overall murder rate five times higher than that of the United States. This kind of violence is not new to the country. Following the major post-independence conflicts of 1827–32 and 1839–42, the country suffered seven major civil confrontations in the second half of the century as well as numerous other smaller-scale regional conflicts. The "War of the Thousand Days" at the turn of the century (1899–1902) resulted in approximately 100,000 casualties. And, in this century, prior to the violence of the 1940s, there was smaller scale civil conflict particularly in the early 1930s.

Yet, in addition to—and partially as a consequence of—its history of violence, Colombia also has a rich history of accommodation and conflict resolution. An examination of how civil conflicts end could fruitfully examine all of these civil conflicts in Colombia. However, the goal of this paper is the far more modest one of exploring the country's two most recent periods of violence, *la violencia* of the 1950s and the violence of the past decade.[1] In particular, after considering the definitional issue of whether these two periods of violence can properly be considered "civil wars," three basic questions will be examined:

1. How did *la violencia* end, and what factors are most important in explaining it?
2. What relationship, if any, is there between the current violence and that of the 1940s and 1950s?
3. What are the short-term prospects for a negotiated end to the current violence in Colombia?

To anticipate, my principal conclusion is that the Colombian case suggests several factors that need to be incorporated into any model that examines conflict resolution, particularly with regard to the nature of the polity that emerges and the longer-term consequences of the process by which civil conflicts end. Issues related to the counterproductive consequences of an initially positive conflict-reducing arrangement and to the autonomy and coherence of the state turn out to be of critical importance in the Colombian case. They are likely to be of particular relevance in national contexts with historical legacies and cultural memories of intense violence, where one side is not decisively defeated by another.

Colombia and Civil Wars

The definition of a civil war provided by Small and Singer is an armed conflict with military action (a minimum of 1,000 battle deaths per year) internal to the country, the active participation of the national government and effective resistance by both sides (with the weaker inflicting at least 5% of the fatalities it sustains). For purposes of this paper, the definition will be accepted.[2] *La violencia* would appear to satisfy all three criteria, although more ambiguously toward the end. In the absence of clearer statistics, it would appear that the current violence could minimally fit the description.

A little background is in order. In Colombia, the period of *la violencia* began in 1946 as a consequence of an unexpected, pivotal victory by the minority Conservative party in presidential elections to which the majority Liberal party, badly divided, presented two candidates. Violence was most immediately a consequence both of Conservative efforts to replace Liberal public employees and Liberal resistance. Then, violence was further fueled by Liberal fears that the Conservatives, as a minority party, would attempt to consolidate a permanent grip on power by force and Conservative concerns, mindful of earlier Liberal exclusivism from power, that if they were to lose the presidency they would be able to regain it only with great difficulty if at all. Although this violence resembled incidents surrounding the 1930 elections (when the divided Conservatives lost the presidency to the Liberals), there were now substantially more economically integrated and politically mobilized groups in society as a consequence of economic growth and diversification.

In the 1940s, political sectarianism and social mobilization interacted in a more dynamic and explosive fashion than in the country's past. This process is difficult to comprehend without understanding the role of the country's two political parties. The parties, identifiable by the mid-19th century, divided the country politically while serving to integrate the nation. The series of civil wars in that century were channelled though bands that identified with the parties; party affiliation therefore became an ascriptive trait inherited by families of all social groups. Subsequent industrialization and incorporation of the working class also proceeded in a bipartisan fashion, though the Liberals gained more adherents in the country's growing urban areas. As one Colombian analyst noted, the parties are better characterized as "deeply rooted *subcultures* than [as] distinct programs for the conduct of the state or of economic development" (Sánchez, 1985, 796).

The violence increased dramatically in intensity following the assassination of Jorge Eliécer Gaitán, a Liberal populist leader, in April 1948—an individual who almost certainly would have been the sole candidate of his party in the 1950 presidential elections and thus the likely winner. The regime finally broke down in November 1949 when Conservative President Mariano Ospina declared a state of siege, closed Congress and imposed other measures. Another Conservative, Laureano Gómez, ran unopposed and won the elections that had been moved up to late 1949.

The inability of some and the unwillingness of other elements of the top leadership in both parties to negotiate in good faith with each other ultimately led regional conflicts to spiral into the breakdown of the regime, a "partial collapse of the state"[3] and one of the "greatest armed mobilization[s] of peasants . . . in the recent history of the western hemisphere."[4] However, the violence had different characteristics across regions, and it gradually evolved into other modalities. The worst casualties (well over the 1,000 threshold required by the operational definition) were suffered in the earlier years, when the partisan motivation, strictly speaking, was strongest (see Figure 3.1). However, it would appear that many of the deaths were brought about by small bands without central coordination. Mostly, they sought to defend their political position at the local level or enhance their economic well-being or security; over time, some developed a more explicit and radical political project, whereas the actions of others bred fears among party leaders that such was their intention. At the same time, although I am not aware of precise casualty figures for police and military, it is implausible that guerrilla groups did not inflict at least 5% of the fatalities that they received. In the most virulent period of *la violencia* in the early 1950s, army and police troops joined by irregular Conservative forces (and paid assassins) fought Liberal and Communist guerrillas and more apolitical "bandits," all of whom also fought each other on occasion. In some areas, vendettas between adjoining villages of different parties re-emerged; and in others, the situation of violence permitted struggles over land and crops to expand.

Levels of violence declined dramatically following the military coup of General Gustavo Rojas in June 1953, as he declared a general amnesty that was accepted by some 6,500 guerrillas (see Figure 3.1). However, in late 1954 and in 1955, army troops clashed with Liberal and Communist-organized peasants and violence escalated in 1956 as some bands began moving into banditry and others began to articulate more clearly revolutionary objectives. Even after the transition to the consociational (power-sharing) National Front between

Figure 3.1 *La Violencia* Fatalities: 1948–1957

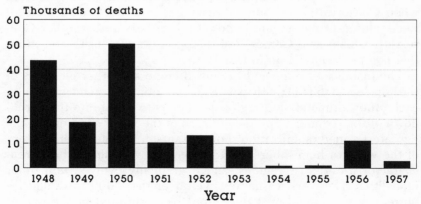

Oquist, 1980, 6–9.

the two parties that facilitated the removal from power of General Rojas and the return to civilian rule, fairly high levels of violence continued (see Figure 3.2). Gradually, though, as the central government reestablished its authority, effectively integrated local political leaders and permitted the army to operate, rebel and bandit leaders became isolated and most were eventually defeated by the armed forces.[5] Communist guerrilla leaders, though, survived army efforts to destroy them in the early 1960s and eventually joined together in 1966 to form the Revolutionary Armed Forces of Colombia (FARC).

Definitionally, then, *la violencia* can be considered a "civil war," although it must be recognized that the partisan disputes that unleashed the violence gradually became superseded or even replaced by other conflicts in the country. As will be argued below, these two facts—that it was a civil war whose precipitating cause and principal channel was partisan conflict and that this conflict generated others that top party leaders felt had escaped from their control even as over-all levels of violence declined—help to explain the way in which the conflict was resolved.

The violence in Colombia in the past decade would appear to meet the definition of "civil war" minimally. The number of fatalities, high as they are, do not appear to have approximated the highest levels of fatalities of the period of *la violencia*, and the country's population is roughly double what it was in the 1950s. However,

Figure 3.2 *La Violencia* Fatalities: 1958–1966

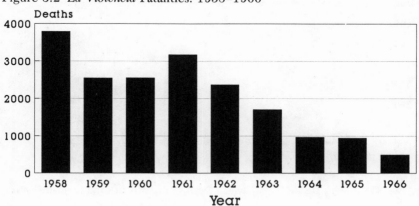

Oquist, 1980, 7–9.

the current violence has resulted in the deaths of many prominent
political leaders, government officials, judges and journalists and has
been reported more comprehensively by the country's mass media
and internationally than was the case in a far more rural and less-
educated country 30–40 years earlier. Government statistics illustrate how political violence has escalated from the mid-1970s to the
mid-1980s (Figure 3.3). These numbers lie below the definitional
threshold (1,000), but there are reasons to believe they underesti-
mate the true extent of casualties. An independent researcher has
estimated violent deaths in Colombia in the mid-1980s at around
16,000 per year (excluding traffic accidents), of which some 2,000
to 3,000 are attributable to political violence (struggles between
guerrillas and the military, deaths by paramilitary squads of leaders
of organizations such as unions or peasant leagues, assassinations of
local-level party officials or elected officials, etc.). Colombian human
rights organizations assert there were 3,457 political homicides between 1981 and 1986, between 1,000 and 2,000 in 1987, and about
3,000 in 1988.[6]

Thus, as in the 1950s, other kinds of violence than those traditionally considered under the guise of civil war have been contributing to the incredibly high number of fatalities in Colombia over
the past decade. These include deaths caused by drug trafficking,
private paramilitary groups' killing leftist leaders, perceived common

Figure 3.3 Military & Civilian Casualties: 1974–1985

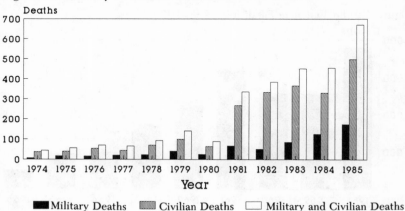

Colombia, Ministerio de Gobierno. 1985. *Paz: Política de la paz del Presidente Be-
tuncur.* Boqotá.

criminals, or other "undesirables" (with apparent police or military cooperation in at least some cases), violent conflicts over land (including large landowners' ousting peasants and Indian groups' seeking to defend their communal lands from encroachment), and criminality, with regional variations depending upon the local circumstances. The most important "public" and "political" violence is associated with the military, guerrilla groups, right wing paramilitary organizations, and drug-trafficking groups (particularly the so-called "Medellín cartel"). The complex relationships among these groups and the destructive impact on state capacity of their violent interactions are important factors in helping to explain the difficulties encountered in trying to bring the country's current wave of violence and civil conflict to an end. Although numerically this does not represent the largest number of fatalities in the country, its prominence and its impact on state institutions, particularly the judiciary, has facilitated the emergence or intensification of common criminal and other kinds of violence.

Conflict Resolution: *La Violencia* in Colombia

The establishment of the consociational National Front between the two traditional parties in 1957 can be viewed as a negotiated end to a civil war. That is largely because *la violencia* was unleashed through traditional party channels. As Gómez, the Conservative president in the early 1950s, did little to stop the escalating violence and sought to perpetuate his grip on power by means of a constitutional reform, Ospina and other elements of his own party actively encouraged a military coup against him in June 1953 (with the eager acquiescence of the Liberals, though most of their top party leaders were in exile). The new government, led by General Rojas, remained closely identified with the Conservative party (with the obvious exception of the Gómez faction) which retained many important posts in his administration. However, as Rojas gradually sought to continue in power by promoting a new political movement outside of the two political parties, leaders of the two parties began seeking each other out and Ospina and his followers began backing away from the military government.

Inter-party violence was not new in Colombia, but the threat of loss of power to a populist military officer and an emerging challenge of revolutionary violence by certain guerrilla groups were. Although the majority party in the country, Liberal leaders saw the most likely route away from military government was to seek an agreement with Conservatives in which they pledged to support a Conservative candidate for the 1958–62 term. Liberals recognized that Rojas, given his Conservative leanings, would be unlikely to hand power over to a Liberal, even as Conservatives, because of their strong position in Rojas' administration, were unlikely to sign an agreement that would require them to relinquish substantial power. In 1956, the Liberals chose Alberto Lleras to direct their party in order to seek an agreement with the Conservatives. Lleras had played no direct role in the failed negotiations between the parties in the 1948–49 period (he had been Secretary-General of the Organization of American States at the time) and thus, Liberals reasoned, he could have easier personal access to Conservative leaders.[7] The Liberals approached Ospina first, but he was reluctant to negotiate with them; he felt his standing within the Conservative party had been weakened by his association with Rojas and feared that if he reached agreement with the Liberals that the wrath of Gómez would descend on him, further hurting his reputation within his own party.

Thus, Alberto Lleras sought out Gómez, who was in exile in Spain. In July 1956, the two leaders signed the Declaration of Benidorm (Spain) that called for a return to republican rule by means of one or more coalition governments. Gradually, a "Civic Front" of opposition began to grow within the country, as Liberals continued to promise they would support a Conservative for the presidency. An extensive document (the "Pact of March [1957]") was signed by leaders of the two parties (except for Gómez supporters) calling for civilian two-party rule with guarantees for parity and alternation in power, and in April the parties officially launched the candidacy of Conservative Guillermo León Valencia for the next presidential term. An unsuccessful attempt by General Rojas on May 1, 1957, to place Valencia under arrest precipitated demonstrations that finally led to Rojas' resignation ten days later. He was replaced by a five-man military junta that formed a bipartisan cabinet and promised to hold elections to replace itself in August 1958 (which would have been the end of Rojas' presidential term).

The parties now faced two critical issues. One was to determine the specific mechanisms by which they would provide each other with mutual guarantees and the other was to resolve the question of the presidential candidacy of Valencia, supported by Ospina Conservatives and Liberals but to which Gómez and his followers remained unequivocally opposed. Lleras returned to Spain, where he signed the "Pact of Sitges" with Gómez. This document called for a bi-partisan "National Front," in which there would be parity in Congress and in the cabinet for twelve years and formal incorporation of these promises into the constitution by means of a national plebiscite.

Complex negotiations continued. The conflict over the Valencia candidacy was finally resolved by having a Liberal, none other than Alberto Lleras, serve as the first president, instituting presidential alternation and extending the Sitges agreement from 12 to 16 years so that the last presidential term would be held by a Conservative. Thus, as it finally emerged, the parties' National Front agreement— most of whose conditions were overwhelmingly approved by a national plebiscite in December 1957—sharply limited the operation of mechanisms of majoritarian representative democracy in the country, while permitting the civilian transition to succeed. The agreement stipulated that from 1958 to 1974 the presidency would alternate between members of the two parties, and that all cabinet offices, legislative and judicial posts and other government jobs not covered by civil service were to be divided equally between the two parties. Most measures would require a two-thirds vote in Congress for approval.[8]

In explaining successful conflict resolution, this project has identified four major clusters of factors as potentially significant: the nature of the underlying issues, the internal politics of each side in conflict, the military balance in the field, and the role of third parties. All of these are relevant to explaining the resolution of conflict in the late 1950s in Colombia, though the last one only minimally and indirectly.

What was at stake in the conflict in Colombia? Here, it is critical to identify not only the degree or intensity of polarization, but also the nature of the issue(s) and whether and how they evolved over time. In the 1940s and 1950s, the central issue between the political parties revolved around control of the state to aid one's own adherents. Once that issue was resolved by the National Front agreement to share power equally (and exclusively), less divided the top leadership of the two parties than united them. They shared a mutual interest in displacing a military leader who appeared increasingly interested in extending his rule, blocking a potential if still weak revolutionary threat in certain rural areas and insuring that inter-party violence with its horrendous casualties and unpredictable consequences would not accelerate anew. Furthermore, party leaders received strong support from economically dominant interests upset with General Rojas' statist and populist policies. Party leaders did not have significant differences regarding the country's socio-economic order or central political procedures or constitutionalism. This suggests that settlement of conflicts by consociational or other "power-sharing" arrangements, such as occurred in Colombia in the 1950s, are probably easier when the conflict is over how to "live and let live" (group autonomy) or over how to share divisible goods (patronage).

Two background conditions were also of vital importance; the fact they were also present in the 1940s when *la violencia* began, though, indicates they were not sufficient in themselves. One was the historic population-wide identification with the two parties. As the tumultuous negotiations inched along, it was evident that party leaders were in control of collectivities with entrenched loyalties and the principal stumbling blocks lay less in their ability to bring along their party followers than in generating inter-party trust at the leadership level in the face of a split in the leadership of one of the parties. The other background condition was that, if there were strong historical antecedents for violence in the country's past, there were also many prior examples of bipartisan collaboration to which leaders could turn. None of these, though, including failed efforts at power-sharing in the 1940s, had provided for equality between the parties, nor been so elaborate and constitutionally enshrined.

As the process also involved the withdrawal of the military from power, it was also necessary for the political parties to address their fears and concerns. Party leaders successfully pursued a strategy of *de-linking* the government of General Rojas from the armed forces as an institution. They argued that in their view the attempts to create an independent political movement, his government's economic policies and most of the financial "irregularities" (corruption) were committed by members of the "presidential family" and a few civilians closely tied to Rojas, not by the military. This strategy was facilitated by the fact that Rojas' dictatorship was relatively benign, even in comparison to other Latin American military governments of the 1950s. Pro-Rojas military conspiracies still emerged, including a major coup attempt in May 1958. However, senior military officers perceived that the National Front did not threaten them either individually or the armed forces as an institution; it promised, instead, to strengthen the coherence and improve the image of the military even as it provided them with considerable autonomy to manage their own internal affairs.

As described above, the internal politics within each party were significant and were in part related to the changing circumstances of the violence in the countryside, to the military balance in the field. *La violencia* was unleashed because national intra-party leadership was fragmented, particularly in the Conservative party, though Liberals were also divided between regional "war" groups and a national "peace" faction. The national Liberal leaders did not condemn their own party members' acts of violence nor did they feel they could ignore the attacks and counter-attacks by the Conservative-dominated police and (less often) army. Ultimately, national party leaders probably aided their regional associates; however, unlike previous civil wars in Colombia, in the period of *la violencia* no national political figures took to the field.

Why did many of the same party leaders who had helped usher in *la violencia* in the late 1940s, successfully come together some ten years later? In this case, the horror of the unexpected intensity of *la violencia* they helped to unleash, somewhat unexpectedly, played a key role, as it did, as well, for the Roman Catholic Church which initially had backed the Conservatives but then became a firm supporter of the National Front.[9] It certainly was important that Gómez, the arch-Conservative figure overthrown in the 1953 coup, was willing to negotiate a power-sharing arrangement with the Liberals, even if he did so at least partially with the hope that it would strengthen his own somewhat weakened position within his own party. Thus, contrary to what appears to have been true in other cases, in Colombia leadership change was not necessary for eventual agreement. On the contrary, the absence of such change meant that concessions—based on a "political learning" of the violence their earlier intransigence had sparked and fear of possible displacement from power—could be made by prestigious national party figures, with a positive impact on public opinion.

By the late 1950s, violence was less clearly between demarcated bands of one party or another. Thus, there was not a clear "hurting stalemate" between the two parties. However, leaders of both parties recognized that efforts to establish one-party governments would almost certainly re-kindle partisan conflict. Liberals deliberately underplayed their potential power and majority electoral status, agreeing to complete parity in government and eventually to presidential alternation, both because it was unlikely they could succeed in achieving hegemonic control given the fact the military government was predominantly Conservative in orientation and because they feared the consequences of seeking such control.[10] Conservatives, although well represented in the Rojas government, distrusted Rojas' intentions and knew that seeking their own one-party rule was not a viable option.

Outside intervention played a role, but only a relatively minor one. The United States had no particular reason to favor one side in the civil war over another, one political party over another. Historically, the Liberal party had retained extremely close relations with the United States, and this had been especially evident during World War II when Liberal governments collaborated extensively with the United States. The Conservatives, particularly Gómez, had openly supported Francoist and Falangist notions. Thus, Conservative efforts to link Liberals and Communists together did not convince United States government officials, and prosecution of Protestants during the Gómez years did not please them either. Although "Communist subversion" was accused for the violence associated with the *bogotazo* in 1948, which overlapped with the presence of numerous foreign diplomats for the Ninth International Conference of American States, Liberals were largely not tarred by the charge (which in any case was supported by little evidence). And, once Gómez came to power, he was extremely solicitous of the United States, and Colombia was one of the few Latin American governments which actually sent a contingent of soldiers to fight in Korea at the request of the United States.

There is no evidence that the United States played any role in the 1953 military coup, although it probably welcomed General Rojas' initial efforts to pacify the country. Although the U.S. was preoccupied by the violence in Colombia in the 1940s and 1950s, it occurred mostly in remote rural areas and largely did not threaten either strategic or private economic interests of the United States. Eventually, however, the Rojas government met with strong hostility from the United States government and from international financial agencies such as the World Bank, because of Rojas' flirting with Peronism, his populist economic policies and the growing opposition from the two traditional parties which appeared to be more secure allies and to promise more stable economic policies. The U.S. government and the World Bank withheld credits from Rojas' government and rapidly re-established them for the interim military junta that replaced him and for the subsequent civilian government. However, the dominant economic fact during this period remained fairly constant through these three administrations: serious balance of payments problems due to low world prices for coffee, the country's major export.

The United States supported party conciliation efforts in Colombia, but in a passive rather than an active sense. Support for the civilian National Front governments did increase as strategic fears were heightened following the Cuban Revolution (Castro assumed power in January 1959). In the early 1960s, Colombia became one of the "showcase" Alliance for Progress countries, and the United States provided extensive military aid to buttress Colombian counter-insurgency efforts against remaining guerrilla groups, particularly those that espoused openly revolutionary or Communist ideologies (see Maullin, 1973).

In sum, one could argue that in Colombia the structural space and opportunity for negotiations to succeed by the late 1950s were high. Nation-wide identification with the two traditional parties made the establishment of a third political movement, such as Rojas sought to bring about, extremely difficult. Levels of violence had already begun to decline, but the population recognized its partisan origins and feared its continuation or intensification. Major economic actors, the Church, and in the background, international actors, all encouraged inter-party accord. National-level party leaders had not expected the ferocity of violence they had helped unleash and began to fear its consequences as well as displacement by the very military government they had helped bring to power; thus, they were more willing to compromise.

La Violencia of the 1950s and the Violence of the 1980s

The National Front arrangement was a conservative one. Though it was born out of crisis, its purpose was neither to confront directly the socio-economic aspects of the breakdown and of the violence nor to seek to deepen political incorporation. Rather, the party leaders and their socio-economic allies saw the National Front at least in part as a restoration of their rule in a more secure, "civilizing" fashion, a rule that had been challenged due to their previous sectarian partisan intransigence by *la violencia* and then by Rojas' rule.

At the same time, a return to civilian rule in the late 1950s was essentially inconceivable without extensive mutual guarantees between the two parties, such as those embodied in the National Front agreement. The major alternatives to some version of shared two-party rule were extended and increasingly unstable military rule or an attempt to promote one-party (Conservative) rule with the likelihood of kindling renewed partisan violence. In both these cases, violence by Communist guerrilla groups or radicalized Liberal groups, combined with banditry, could have intensified.

Yet, one can ask if such a lengthy, formal, and rigid constitutional agreement was necessary. The National Front accord reflected the fact that national politicians "learned" to distrust local-level leaders and fear mass mobilization since they had gotten out of their control. Gradually, the violence came to an end, though some guerrilla groups spawned by it continued to exist. Various ones of them joined together in 1966 to form the Revolutionary Armed Forces of Colombia (FARC), the country's oldest and most significant guerrilla organization, with ties to the (Soviet-oriented) Colombian Communist party. And, new guerrilla groups formed. In the 1960s, these included the Castroite-influenced National Liberation Army (ELN) and the Maoist-oriented Popular Liberation Army (EPL). In the 1970s, the most significant guerrilla group to form was the Movement of the 19th of April (M–19) which took its name from the date of the 1970 elections it felt fraudulently kept the presidency from General Rojas, at that time campaigning ambiguously as a Conservative and as head of his own populist movement.[11] Those groups that had a rural orientation began their operations in areas of past guerrilla activity in the country, and a number of their leaders or adherents had suffered as a consequence of *la violencia* (murders of close family members, forced migration, etc.). Some built upon regional traditions of resistance to central authority and promotion of self-defense, local democracy or self-defense. However, these "background conditions" helped spawn renewed guerrilla activity and intensified civic protest due to the evolution of the country under the National Front.

The National Front period was one of dynamic social and economic change in the country, as the population doubled and became substantially more urban and educated, and as the economy diversified and became more complex. However, these significant factors were not accompanied by more dramatic redistributive changes in a country that began the National Front with a highly unequal distribution of wealth and income. In particular, land reform was only weakly implemented.

At the same time, the country's socio-economic changes, combined with the National Front regime structure, which twice required voters to elect a presidential candidate from the opposing party, led to a dramatic decline in party segmentation. For the first time in the country's history, an independent electorate emerged largely in urban areas, potentially mobilizable by any party or movement. Additionally, coalition rule encouraged party factionalism as partisan conflict shifted from inter-party relations to intra-party negotiations. The parties became dominated by regional politicians in control of small captive electorates who lacked substantial links to mass organizations. Politicians, particularly of the minority Conservative party, were reluctant to change the model of coalition rule with its guaranteed access to government resources. Ironically, the return to competitive elections in the 1970s made it more difficult for opposition movements to gain electoral representation even as the traditional parties were increasingly incapable of channelling dissent. Non-electoral opposition emerged or was strengthened: popular sector organizations, civic strikes, and guerrilla organizations.

The regime confronted a growing legitimacy crisis as political actors sought to justify and retain a political model (coalition rule) that no longer responded to the country's social structure, in part due to changes induced by the model itself. The problems of the 1970s and 1980s reflected the predicament of an unchanged regime in a changed society. Thus, the country would almost certainly have suffered considerable political turmoil in the 1970s and 1980s in any case. However, the situation deteriorated because of the additional violence, corruption and partial deflation of state capacity brought about by drug trafficking and by the complex alliances and forms of violence engendered by drug-trafficking groups.

The problems of political violence of the 1980s were at most only partially attributable to a "birth defect" of the National Front regime. The focus should be more directly on the inability (and for some, unwillingness) of political leaders to transform the regime structure. Some form of coalition rule was almost certainly necessary to bring *la violencia* to an end, but the rigid and excessively lengthy form it took under the National Front had conservative implications regarding the possibilities for social reform and made both the peaceful channelling of dissent and the transformation of coalition rule to permit such dissent exceedingly difficult. The structure of incentives (access to power, economic benefits, levels of insecurity and mistrust) for regional politicians and economic elites led them to oppose changes that would have opened up the regime. Thus, the reasons for the growth in political violence stemmed in part from the nature of the polity that emerged from the settlement but probably more from the inability of that polity to meet new challenges as the country's society and economy changed and as the two-party sectarian identifications largely disappeared. Eventually, drug trafficking was to represent an additional critical factor helping to explain further escalation of violence.

The final outcome of the current wave of violence in Colombia is still unclear. Much of the attention on violence in the late 1970s and early 1980s focused on that produced by the guerrilla groups. President Julio César Turbay (1978–82) attempted to address it primarily by means of a repressive response, which militarily weakened in particular the M–19 guerrilla group. Upon assuming office, Conservative President Belisario Betancur (1982–86) actively sought "peace," including negotiation with the guerrillas (amnesty and political incorporation) and political reforms (democratization). He was able to achieve a truce with most guerrilla groups in 1984. And, Betancur also ushered through a constitutional reform establishing the popular election of mayors (previously they were appointed), which, combined with a degree of fiscal decentralization, was intended to help open up the country's political process. Other reforms intended to assure opposition forces greater representation in Congress, access to the media, and so on either were not approved by Congress or were significantly watered down.

However, Betancur's efforts largely failed to bring peace to the country. Political violence actually increased in his last years in office and continued to escalate under the subsequent administration of President Virgilio Barco (1986–90) as well. This failure is best explained by the nature of the issues and the internal politics of each side. Divisions within the state as well as lack of unity among the guerrilla groups over whether to give up the goal of seeking state power militated against the success of the negotiations over the

1980s. The Colombian armed forces' opposition to negotiated settlements with the guerrillas was dramatically strengthened by drug
trafficking groups during this period. The actions of these groups
and of state efforts to control them added multiple kinds of additional
violence and had a tremendous impact on state coherence.

The military balance in the field has also been relevant. The state
found itself unable to defeat the guerrillas militarily or to stop terrorist violence on the part of drug traffickers. At the same time, the
likelihood of a takeover of state power by guerrilla groups was always
very low and probably diminished over the past decade. Under the
Barco administration, this "military stalemate," in the words of one
Colombian analyst, combined with the problems of political legitimacy related to the exhaustion of the country's political model, facilitated negotiations in 1989 and 1990 with some of the guerrilla
groups, principally the M–19. This led to their legal reincorporation,
participation in the 1990s congressional and presidential elections,
representation in the cabinet of the Gaviria administration inaugurated in August 1990, surprising plurality victory in the special elections for representation to a constitutional convention, and active
role in the convention in early 1991 (Pizarro, 1990). Other guerrilla
groups (principally the FARC and the ELN) continued their attacks
against the state, even as relations with drug traffickers moved in
cycles from violence—principally kidnappings and terrorist bombings—to truce and back again.

Under the Betancur administration, the problems of divisions
within the state and within guerrilla groups were further complicated
by an ambiguous negotiating strategy on the part of the administration and negative short-term economic circumstances. The "peace
process" began auspiciously with the approval, in November 1982,
of the broadest amnesty law ever passed in the country's history.
However, the next stage was not clear. The government finally opted
to negotiate truces directly with the various guerrilla groups, a process that came to fruition in 1984. Eventually, the FARC created a
political party, the Patriotic Unity (UP), to compete in elections. But,
the agreements made no mention of handing over arms, though guerrilla groups promised to halt all attacks and kidnappings. The government, in turn, pledged to implement or seek passage of a variety
of political reforms and social programs. Yet, soon after the truces
were signed, the administration announced it would have no money
for social reforms. The need for economic austerity at this critical

moment (symbolized by agreeing to an "enhanced surveillance" agreement with the International Monetary Fund) was especially unfortunate.

Other factors, however, also militated against the success of the negotiations. There were significant divisions within the state, with the armed forces skeptical and increasingly obstructionist. The consensus regarding the need for political reform among national political leaders was difficult to translate into concrete action because of occasionally tense relations between a Conservative president and a Liberal-dominated Congress, and between regional politicians fearful of losing their local power base to new political movements and national leaders not fully able to control them.

Guerrilla groups also played an ambiguous game. The M–19, which had most benefited from the amnesty program in 1982, then sought to increase its military capabilities while pressing for political concessions from the government. Coordination among guerrilla groups was poor, and even within some of them there was no agreement over the objectives they should be seeking in negotiations with the government. As a result of these factors, by late 1984 opposition to the peace process expanded beyond the military and initially skeptical political and economic groups to growing sectors of public opinion.

A final complicating factor was the increased violence and corruption engendered by drug trafficking. Narcotics traffic was initially accepted in Colombia because of the foreign exchange it generated and the jobs it provided. It was also viewed as essentially a consequence of the U.S. demand for drugs. However, it gradually became a worrisome problem for the Colombian government, because of its corrosive impact on state institutions (especially the judiciary), U.S. pressure, increased domestic consumption, and the brutal tactics of assassination and intimidation by drug traffickers seeking to continue to do business, as well as to gain acceptance within Colombian society. With regard to negotiations with guerrilla groups, the negative effects of violence by drug traffickers were both indirect, by contributing to an atmosphere of violence and helping to provoke the collapse of the judiciary or the capacity of the state to investigate crimes successfully, and direct, by their apparent targeting of left-wing political figures and social activists, sometimes alone and sometimes in collaboration with others, such as regional landowners or elements of the armed forces.

A central example has been the violence and intimidation of leaders and activists of the leftist opposition party, Patriotic Unity (UP). The UP was formed by the country's oldest and largest guerrilla group, the FARC, in March 1985 following the truce established with the Betancur government in 1984. It was intended to symbolize the willingness of the guerrilla organization to rejoin the political process through electoral means. Unlike what occurred with other guerrilla organizations, the truce between the Betancur government and the FARC was never formally broken. However, as tensions built anew the FARC began to claim it was organizationally distinct from the UP. The UP participated in the 1986 elections, winning a plurality or a majority of the votes in over a dozen municipalities and 12 congressional seats (including seats in coalition with Liberal party factions). From January 1986 to April 1988, 334 members of the UP and of popular organizations were assassinated, including their presidential candidate for the 1986 elections, 4 congressmen, 2 mayors, and 11 mayoral candidates.[12]

A self-reinforcing cycle of polarization was established in which UP leaders, lacking trust with regard to their personal safety and the democratic process, remained ambiguous with regard to the guerrilla option and the use of force; this in turn, helped right-wing groups (whether drug traffickers, landowners, or members of the armed forces) to justify the use of the violence against them. Shadowy death squads, of which some 140 were identified by the Barco administration, have taken responsibility for many of the assassinations of UP activists and leaders. In Barco's last years in office, these groups were involved in many larger-scale massacres. Given the serious threat to democratic institutions and democratic values represented by the violent alliances and actions of the country's major drug traffickers, primary supporters of many of these death squads, the Barco administration sought to stop their actions and bring them to justice. But, with a weak and penetrated state, its few successes were at best partial and incomplete. Its greatest success was the discovery and death of a major figure of the Medellín cartel in December 1989. Yet, among the many victims of violence over 1989–90, there were three presidential candidates, including the Liberal Luis Carlos Galán, widely considered the likely winner in the 1990 elections if he had lived, and candidates of both the UP and the M–19. Nevertheless, by demonstrating its tenacity, the Colombian state prevented a process of further state collapse.

The incredible violence generated directly by drug trafficking, and the increase in criminality it helped foster by its contributions to the collapse of Colombia's judicial system, made the "political violence" of guerrilla groups appear to be just one more kind of violence, rather than separate and distinct. The country became "multi-polarized" rather than, as the guerrillas had hoped, "polarized" (see Leal Buitrago, 1988). At the same time, state efforts seeking their political reincorporation might have progressed further in the absence of drug trafficking, as those opposed to agreements with the guerrillas within the state or from traditional sectors would have been missing a critical, even if at times only indirect, support. Guerrilla groups would also have confronted a more coherent state, perhaps better able to enforce agreements and assure the physical integrity of political leaders, forcing them to define their own objectives more clearly, even as the financial importance of certain remote areas under their control would have been much less. In addition, cynicism, corruption, resentment, the loss of trust in public institutions, and the breakdown of social solidarity would also not have reached current heights. (For a more extensive discussion of drug trafficking and Colombia, see Hartlyn, forthcoming.)

A number of international factors bear on the current violence. One has to do with drug trafficking. The United States has been much more interested in the "war on drugs" than it has in efforts to end the political violence and seek the peaceful reincorporation of guerrillas into the country's democratic process. U.S. policy regarding drug trafficking has shifted slightly over time toward an increased recognition that a strategy focused primarily on the supplying countries will not work; it has also become somewhat more sensitive to the constraints under which governments such as that of Colombia must operate. However, its policy efforts have still been more unilateral than cooperative and more focused on boosting the military than on strengthening institutions or recognizing the underlying economic imperatives.

As the so-called Medellín cartel group of drug traffickers targeted government officials, journalists, political leaders, and others for assassination, the Colombian government increasingly came to view them as a national security threat. The precipitating event, especially in terms of Colombian public opinion, was the assassination of the popular Liberal presidential hopeful Galán in 1989. Particularly under the Gaviria administration, the Colombian government has sought to distinguish "narco-terrorism" from drug trafficking, and has set the alleviation of the former as its immediate goal while insisting that the latter can only be dealt with over the long-term, on a cooperative, multilateral basis. On this basis, the government began moving away from the use of extradition of drug traffickers to the United States as a tool, even before it was banned by the constitutional convention, promising leniency and trials in Colombia to traffickers that voluntarily turned themselves in. Several major figures of the Medellín cartel turned themselves in over 1990 and 1991, and drug-related terrorist incidents declined.

The U.S. government has been unhappy with the ban on extradition and has continued to pressure the government on drug-trafficking issues. Aid has focused more on boosting the armed forces and directly involving them in the drug issue, than on strengthening the police or the Colombian judiciary. Similarly, although it is widely recognized that the foreign exchange and employment generated by the drug traffic would not be nearly as important if more significant debt-relief measures, more aid and more open trade practices were forthcoming, legislation in the U.S. Congress to facilitate these measures has been slow to gain approval. The logic of the Colombia government is clear: over the medium-term, declines in drug-related terrorist violence and recomposition of the Colombian judiciary should facilitate a decrease in other political and criminal violence as well.

In contrast to many other on-going civil conflicts, there has never been a significant role for international mediators in Colombia. At certain moments, Colombian governments did seek cooperation from the Cuban government because of its ties to guerrilla groups, but these links were never viewed as a determining factor in explaining either the rise or the strategy of these groups. In specific instances, governments such as those of Felipe González in Spain or Carlos Andrés Pérez in Venezuela, offered their countries as sites for meetings. But Colombian governments have resisted involving international mediators in specific negotiations.

Thus, the behavior of the guerilla groups is best explained, not by their international connections but by how their own analyses of changes in the international system, particularly in the Soviet bloc and in Central America, have affected their goals and calculations of likely success. These changes include the inability of the Soviet Union to provide aid, disillusionment with the Cuban model, the defeat of the Sandinistas in Nicaragua, the inability of guerrillas in El Salvador or in Guatemala to realize their goals, and the predominance of U.S. military might in the region as evidenced in the intervention in Panama. Based on discussion with M–19 leaders, Pizarro (1990, 21–23) considers that their international analysis and their weak military situation were crucial in their decision to put down their arms.

Writing in mid-1991, the picture in Colombia appears marginally more hopeful. Efforts toward political reincorporation of willing guerrilla groups and toward political reform continue. The M–19 demonstrated unexpectedly strong electoral successes in the 1990 elections and gained a cabinet seat in the Gaviria administration. It subsequently received a plurality of votes for representation in the constitutional convention that successfully re-wrote the Colombian Constitution, instituting a more democratic and participatory framework. A new strategy of promising major drug traffickers trials in Colombia, reduced sentences and a guarantee of no extradition to the United States appeared to be reducing levels of drug-related terrorism. The most dramatic success was the surrender of Pablo Escobar in June 1991, a major figure of the Medellín cartel. Yet, whether the multiple "stalemates" could lead in the short-term or even in the medium-term to a more long-ranging peaceful outcome was far from obvious. Several major guerrilla groups continued their violent actions, several drug trafficking groups retained considerable power and capacity for violence, and the judiciary and other state institutions were still extremely weak.

Concluding Reflections

In a country with a history of violence, such as Colombia, it is difficult to sort out the ways in which different periods of violence are related to each other. Both violence and accommodation have strong historical antecedents in the country, and thus both have significant "cultural carriers" and are available as "options" at critical moments. There probably are young guerrillas in contemporary Colombia whose parents fought in the days of la violencia and whose great-grandparents, in turn, were active in the turn-of-the-century War of the Thousand Days. In addition, areas with a history of guerrilla struggle against state authority have been among the most receptive to new guerrilla groups as they have begun.

Yet, ultimately, I would argue that this "culture" and "geography" of violence is neither necessary nor sufficient to explain the current outbreak of violence, though it should be considered an important contributory factor. If I had the data, I believe it would indicate that a significant percentage of those committing violent acts today do not have a direct link to *la violencia*, while many with such connections are not committing violent acts. Similarly, violence in the 1980s has extended far beyond areas affected by *la violencia* in the 1950s, to rural regions of recent colonization and to cities such as Cali and Medellín.

Two other factors would appear central. First, the political framework of two-party coalition rule was superseded by a dynamic society that changed in part due to the political structure of the National Front itself. The National Front, in some guise, was probably necessary to end *la violencia*. But, the attraction of continued coalition rule remained high, for different reasons, for regional party leaders, major economic groups and international actors, long after there was any need for it. The Colombian case suggests that solutions to periods of violence may be imposed in too rigid a fashion and may generate excessively powerful incentives for their continuation past the time when they should be changed. Coalition rule helped transform a society and reduce traditional party segmentation. Yet, it was also such a cozy arrangement that it resisted changing in the face of new societal demands and pressures.

The other factor has to do with state autonomy and state capacity.[13] Part of bringing *la violencia* to an end involved re-articulating state authority over disparate regions of the country, coupling regional party figures to central authority and separating them from guerrilla and bandit leaders who could then gradually be defeated. In contrast, the ability of the Colombian state in the 1980s and 1990s to negotiate effectively with the guerrilla opposition and to proceed with democratizing reforms has unquestionably been hurt by the actions of drug traffickers. The state has been unable to insure the physical safety of amnestied guerrillas or left-wing activists, or even of its own top officials. Its judicial system, already inept and overloaded, largely collapsed under the intimidation and corruption of drug trafficking, even as the corrupting presence of drug money was felt, to differing degrees, throughout Colombian society. Successful conflict resolution requires functioning state institutions, and any model of conflict resolution should incorporate directly issues related to state autonomy and state capacity.

Notes

1. This paper borrows liberally from the discussion and analysis of these conflicts in Hartlyn, 1988. For a table summarizing the major protagonists and the nature and outcome of the 19th-century conflicts, see Hartlyn, 1988, 21–24; on the period of *la violencia*, see Hartlyn, 1988, 42–48 and 54–74; and on the most recent period of violence, see Hartlyn, 1988, 191–99 and 216–35.

2. See Small and Singer, 1982. In my view, what is absent from this definition is any discussion of the goals or objectives of the non-state actors. This should logically comprise some political project, such as state power, or a related—if less ambitious—goal, such as power sharing, partition, or regional autonomy. I am not sure that it is helpful analytically to consider conflict between groups such as drug-traffickers and the state as a "civil war" unless the traffickers develop a clear political project, and I would expect the way in which such conflicts are resolved to differ from the way in which "civil wars" come to an end.

3. This is the basic thesis of Oquist, 1980, still one of the best treatments of *la violencia*, though his notion somewhat exaggerates the extension and coherence of the Colombian state in the 1940s.

4. Hobsbawm, 1963, 16, cited (as Oquist above) in Hartlyn, 1988, 43–44.

5. One of the best works on the "late violence" is Sánchez and Meertens, 1983.

6. Guzmán, 1988. The initial data of this Colombian sociologist was employed in preparing Sánchez et al., 1987. Figures from human rights organizations for 1981 to 1987 are from Fellner, 1988, 6; as she notes, these numbers refer to political assassinations targeted almost exclusively toward leftists or critics of the status quo. For 1988, the figures are from Americas Watch Committee, 1989, 1. The multifaceted nature of Colombian violence is apparent in the fact that one splinter guerrilla group from the FARC took credit for a massacre of over 200 of its own members in late 1985, ostensibly on the grounds that they were all "infiltrators."

7. Details regarding these negotiations are based on taped interviews with many of the central actors in 1979 with Luis Pinilla to which I was given access, interviews by this author with them in 1982, and other sources (Hartlyn, 1988, 54–74).

8. A 1968 constitutional reform provided a partial dismantling of the agreement. It reinstituted simple majority vote for most measures in Congress, opened elections to all parties, and eliminated parity in the legislative branch at the municipal and departmental level in 1970 and at the national level in 1974. Parity in the executive branch was extended until 1978, after which the majority party was required *to offer* "adequate and equitable" representation in the executive branch to the party receiving the second

highest number of votes in the elections. This representation was accepted until 1986, when Conservatives refused participation in the government of Liberal President Virgilio Barco (1986–90). Under Barco, efforts to reform the Constitution which would have removed this requirement ultimately failed. However, in 1990, newly inaugurated Liberal President César Gaviria offered cabinet representation to the (re-named) Social Conservatives as well as to the M–19, a guerrilla group turned political party, which both initially accepted.

Political reform efforts finally succeeded over 1990 and 1991. Special elections in December 1990 determined the membership of a Constituent Assembly which on July 4, 1991 promulgated a new, more expansive and participatory Constitution, putting an end to all vestiges of the National Front agreement.

9. This shift in the attitude of the Church was facilitated by compromise moves on the part of the Liberals. For example, they permitted a special preamble, affirming the centrality of the Church to the country, which they had removed in the 1930s to be reinserted in the Constitution.

10. The fact that the Liberals thus had more to gain from an agreement and that they allowed themselves to be "exploited" by the smaller Conservative collectivity is consonant with arguments regarding collective action (Olson, 1971, 29–43).

11. Under the National Front rule of presidential alternation, in 1970 only a Conservative could be elected president. As General Rojas had always identified with the Conservative party he was a legal candidate. Much of his support came from poor urban Liberal sympathizers who had no Liberal candidate for whom they could vote.

12. During this time period, 149 Liberals and 83 Conservatives were killed, including 5 congressmen, 11 mayors, and 11 mayoral candidates (de la Espriella, 1988, 25, citing a document from the Presidency of the Republic). The government reported that 383 members of the armed forces or the police were killed in 1986, 408 in 1987, and 199 in three to four months of 1988 combatting guerrillas or drug-traffickers (Colombia, Office of the President, n.d., 29).

13. Helpful in understanding these terms are the conceptualizations of Skocpol, 1985. State autonomy refers to the ability of the state to formulate and pursue objectives independent of societal demands or interests; state capacity refers to the ability of the state to implement its goals or objectives and depends on such essential factors as the integrity of its sovereignty and military control of its territory, as well as its internal coherence and administrative and financial capabilities.

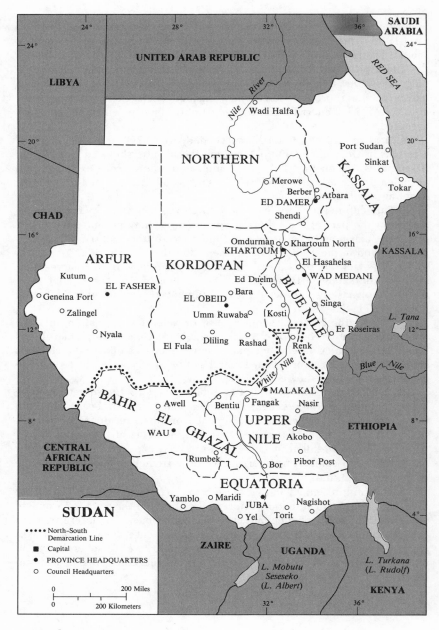

4.1 Sudan

The Peace Process in the Sudan, 1971–1972

Donald Rothchild and Caroline Hartzell

Africa's civil wars, and especially those which hold out the prospect of the break-up of the state, are not normally amenable to political compromise and negotiation. However, this grim scenario does have its notable exceptions. In the Sudan, a rather unique process was set in motion that led, in 1972, to a negotiated settlement of a protracted civil war. The resulting Addis Ababa Agreement was implemented, and the country settled down to a near decade of seemingly peaceful relations.

Does a mere decade of peace justify the conclusion that the Addis Ababa Agreement constitutes a case of successful negotiations? We are inclined to agree with Nelson Kasfir's (1977: 165) conclusion, put forward in the more peaceful times of 1977, that however deep the differences between Northern and Southern politicians or among themselves, "the agreement has amounted to far more than a mere interlude in war." Support for this view can be found in the theoretical literature on negotiation and mediation, such as Saadia Touval and I. William Zartman's (1985: 14) remark that successful negotiations and mediation cannot be limited to "the final resolution of all conflict and the reconciliation of the parties"; rather, successful ne-

We wish to express our appreciation to Lako Tongun, I. William Zartman, Aggrey A. Majok and Robert O. Collins for helpful comments on the first draft of the paper.

gotiations should be viewed in narrower terms, as "the conclusion of an agreement promising the reduction of conflict."

To gain an insight into the process of peacemaking in the Sudan, we briefly discuss the conflict-making environment, emphasizing how hostile perceptions and stereotypes, varying religious and educational practices and values, and uneven regional development and cultural differences affected the conflict process. We then turn to the processes of negotiation, analyzing both the favorable preconditions unique to the Sudanese situation at the time and the factors explaining the specific negotiating success at Addis Ababa in 1971–72. But the negotiations on the agreement cannot be isolated from the implementation process; therefore, we will look briefly in the subsequent section at the processes of implementing the Addis Ababa settlement. And, finally, we will relate the unique to the generalizable and will consider the implications of the Sudan's peacemaking process in the 1970s for the management of civil wars.

The Conflict-Making Environment

Although serious cultural and social divisions among peoples and subregions did create intense conflicts in the Sudan (Wai, 1981:37), these conflicts were not so all-encompassing as to prevent meaningful negotiations. Certainly, distinct ethnic identities and histories reinforced by regional separation and uneven economic development are likely to produce conflict in the best of circumstances; this combination of factors did in fact lead to grave tensions as independence came and old stratifications between a dominant and more developed North and a vulnerable and less developed South remained. The ensuing struggle for ethnoregional equality has remained bitter and at times violent, but we stress that it did not preclude negotiations as such. In John Howell's (1978: 427) words: ". . . racial antagonism, while often strong, did not in itself create an insurmountable barrier to a settlement once favourable conditions had been created" (also Legum, 1988a: 2–3).

For Southern Sudanese, the struggle was "against internal colonialism" and most specifically against what they perceived as the "cultural orientation of the Arab, Northern-dominated government's policies toward the South," something that they described as constituting "a form of oppression" (Wai, 1983: 306). For Sudanese government officials, with their power base in the North, it was erroneous to view the struggle as a racial one; not only was the description of Northerners as a homogeneous "Arab" collectivity inaccurate, but the country's political system included representatives from all sections of the population in positions of power (Eprile, 72: 3). Ethnic stereotypes clearly existed on both sides and created distance between groups; in the end, however, various key leaders did manage to rise above sectional loyalties, displaying sufficient political will to find an accommodation. This pragmatism, facilitated by the encounters between rival elites during the negotiating process, showed ethnoregional leaders to be considerably less totalist in their perceptions of one another than many observers assumed (Rothchild, 1986: 87–93; Amy, 1983: 354).

Until the 1940s, the Sudan was an example of low-level national integration, what Ali A. Mazrui (1969: 334) describes as a "bare coexistence" of ethnoregional identity groups. This minimal level of integration was a consequence both of the interplay of local forces and of colonial design. The opening up of the South to Northern traders, administrators, and religious proselytizers sharpened an awareness of Southern isolation and vulnerability. Much more frightening was the intermittent contact with Northern slave dealers, an experience that created negative remembrances and images among Southerners which remain poignant to this very day (Republic of the Sudan, 1956: 4; Wai, 1981: 29). After the initial encounters, remarks a South Sudan Resistance Movement statement,

There followed numerous ivory traders and adventurers, who turned to slaving when the supply of ivory diminished. The disruption and loss of life caused to peoples of the South by the slave-traders was extremely heavy, particularly among the Shilluk, the Bari, and the smaller tribes of the Bahr-el-Ghazal. The slave-traders and their private soldiers were mainly 'Khartoumers' (Northern Sudanese). (South Sudan Resistance Movement, n.d.: 2)

The divisions introduced by British administrators compounded the awareness of collective differences in group power, advantage, and opportunities. British colonial officials, determined to insulate the South from Northern commercial, religious, linguistic, and educational practices and competition, put special administrative policies into effect (the so-called "Southern Policy") that provided for the use of English as an official language, denied trading licenses to Northerners, suppressed Muslim religious activities, discouraged the use of Arab names and dress, and transferred Northern administrators to the North.[1] The Southern Policy was abandoned in 1946, but not before creating "fear and mistrust in the mind of a Southern Sudanese against his fellow countryman in the North. . . ." (South Sudan Resistance Movement, n.d.: 17). Mental and emotional boundaries between Southerners and Northerners were erected and fortified, producing tensions that would live on in the period after independence.

The paternalistic colonial policy on separate ethnoregional identities and developmental paths produced conflict largely because it left the South with negative remembrances of contacts with the North and unprepared for a shared fate in a common Sudanese state. The protective policy of allowing the South "to develop along its own lines" had a variety of harmful political, economic, and social consequences (Grey, 1971: 113). Not only did the development of a Southern-based political consciousness and participation lag behind that occurring in the Northern parts of the country, but relatively few Southerners had been recruited into the country's civil service (as a consequence of educational disparities and inexperience, Southerners secured only six of the 800 senior government posts vacated by British officials just prior to independence) (Eprile, 1972: 6; Collins, 1985: 8). Separation inhibited the growth of a web of political exchanges and reciprocities that would have facilitated elite cooperation once independence came (Beshir, 1975: 45–49). Given the level of Southern suspicions and animosities it is not clear whether increased patterns of political exchanges would have been sufficient to unite the country after the colonial-erected scaffolding had been removed, but it seems likely that at the least it would have promoted learned experiences with joint problem solving.

The South's relative unpreparedness for Sudanese independence was even more apparent in terms of the subregion's economic neglect. The Southern Region was clearly one of the most disadvantaged in the Sudan, having a per capita income estimated at half that of the country as a whole and only one-fourth that of the relatively advantaged provinces of Kassala and Khartoum (International Labour Office, 1976: 199). As of the 1970/71 Industrial Survey, 73 percent of the industrial establishments producing 66 percent of the value of production were located in Khartoum province; in the South, virtually no industrial activities were reported (International Labour Office, 1976: 289). Cotton, the country's major cash crop, was produced in the Gezira scheme, just south of Khartoum, and the country's infrastructure, in terms of railroads and communications links, was heavily concentrated in the more developed areas. Well might a leading Southern scholar, Dunstan Wai (1981: 37), criticize the Southern Policy as a cause of uneven economic modernization, concluding that such deprivation left the South "dangerously vulnerable to the pursuits of the North."

The consequences of a "protective" colonial policy were also painfully evident in social and cultural relations. Determined to thwart the spread of Islam to the South, the British assisted Christian missionaries while restricting Muslims entering the South and discouraging the use of Arabic by administrative personnel (O'Ballance, 1977: 28). Christian missions exercised a decisive control over education, using this influence to promote a political culture distinct from the rest of the country. Robert Collins (1985: 5) notes the intended impact of this emphasis on the process of political recruitment:

. . . all administrative staff, including clerical and technical personnel, speaking Arabic were to be replaced from indigenous sources. Local boys were to be procured from the mission schools and 'every encouragement should be given to those in charge of mission schools to cooperate in that policy by sending boys into Government service.'

This policy not only inhibited nation building, but it did little to overcome the country's uneven development. Decades after independence the subregional imbalances in educational opportunity still persisted: aggregate statistics on educational opportunities in the early 1970s showed the Southern schools enrolling only one-sixth as many students as the rest of the country (International Labour Office, 1976: 128). And General Joseph Lagu, noting that the Southerners were hopelessly unprepared to administer their country after independence, blamed the British for offering the peoples of the subregion an inadequate educational training (O'Ballance, 1977: 151).

In sum, *class, culture, ethnicity, and region in the Sudan all tended to coincide and to reinforce one another.* In objective terms, the differential rates of subregional modernization, caused in part by colonial contacts and policies, resulted in sharp cleavages between the relatively advantaged peoples of the North and the relatively disadvantaged peoples of the South. In subjective terms, unmistakable evidences of uneven development became the foundation for group antagonisms grounded in negative remembrances and current perceptions. Although often built upon false myths and stereotypes, these perceptions (or misperceptions) gained a cumulative accept-ance over time, with disastrous consequences in terms of intense conflicts in North-South relations in the postindependence period.

Most importantly, the commonly used dichotomy between an "Arab" North and an "African" and "Negroid" South was an ov-ersimplification that greatly distorted reality. In fact, an intermin-gling of peoples and cultures had been pronounced, resulting in considerable heterogeneity on both sides of the North-South divide. In the North (where some 70 percent of the country's population lives), the four million Arabs made up nearly three-fifths of the re-gion's population. The Southern ethnic peoples are often re-divided into clans or sub-ethnic peoples, increasing the complexity of the demographic picture in the area. In addition, while the South was homogeneously "African," it was divided further along religious lines, including a small number of Muslims and Christians as well as a substantial number of peoples adhering to traditional religions.

The overarching identity as a Southerner or Northerner, then, reflected subjective and symbolic factors at least as much as objective reality. Historical experiences with conquest, assimilation, and ex-ploitation, including slavery, combined with current perceptions of difference to create a separate consciousness. The objective aspects of uneven development coincided with the subjective factors of his-torical enmities, memories, and perceptions to produce a powerful conflict-making situation in the Sudan. But it is important to em-phasize that this combined thrust toward conflict, strong and im-pelling as it was, did not in and of itself preclude negotiation and compromise between North and South. How were Northern and Southern leaders able to rise above 17 years of civil war to reach a peaceful settlement in the 1971–72 period? To answer this, we turn to the processes of negotiation at Addis Ababa.

The Favorable Preconditions

The convergence of region, ethnicity, class, and religion contributed to a deep and protracted conflict between the Northern-led Sudanese state and the Southern-based guerrillas. Nevertheless, by the late 1960s a number of general factors facilitated a constructive nego-tiating process. Taken together, these favorable factors were criti-cally important to the successful outcome of 1972 because they es-tablished a context in which strategically placed mediators could overcome a stalemate of power. As Douglas Amy (1983: 358) observes, "the context of power in which negotiations take place" is critical to the success of mediatory initiatives. In the Sudan, these facilitating factors were uniquely in place, helping to explain that country's rather atypical success with negotiating an intense conflict between acutely divided societal groupings. Hence it is important that we turn at this point to a discussion of the main favorable preconditions that set the context for successful negotiations in the Sudan in 1971–72.

1. The Emergence of Identifiable Bargaining Parties

As in many conflicts between state and ethnoregional interests, the conflicting parties were in fact coalitions of factions, not homogeneous parties. In the state coalition, President Gaafar el-Nimeiry had to balance diverse elements in the army and bureaucracy. The resignations of the Defense Minister and the Chief of Staff prior to the February 1972 negotiations, reportedly because of their aversion to meetings with the guerrilla leaders, indicate the existence of opposition elements within the Northern coalition at this critical time (O'Ballance, 1977: 142; Beshir, 1975: 105). The Southern coalition was, if anything, more divided than its state counterpart. The Southerners disagreed strongly among themselves as to means and ends, and there were pronounced splits between the elements who remained within the Sudan and those who went abroad to Uganda, London, and Ethiopia as well as between the various elites in Khartoum and in the South. As one of the mediators noted regarding negotiations with Southern leaders: "There were many groups, and the question came up many times—who is the one to approach. You have to approach many leaders, and not only those who think themselves leaders; leadership changed quite often" (Conflict Research Society, 1973: 2).

As the civil war dragged on, a number of developments clarified the nature of the bargaining parties and their key leaders. With the crushing of a military coup attempt in 1970, Nimeiry moved swiftly to eliminate opposition elements in the army, the Muslim Brotherhood, and the left (most particularly, the Communist Party). Among those eliminated was a Southerner, Joseph Garang, the Cabinet member responsible for Southern affairs who supported regional autonomy but expressed strong reservations about the separatist-minded Anya-Nya insurgent movement. Garang's execution, along with the fall of other active opponents of compromise within the army and the Muslim fundamentalists, left Nimeiry with considerable freedom to pursue a political solution to the Southern problem. Much of the responsibility for handling Southern affairs was immediately transferred to another Southerner, Abel Alier, who played a key role in the subsequent negotiations with Southern leaders.

Although the coalition of Southerners never reached quite the level of cohesiveness manifested by the elite around Nimeiry, the Southern Sudan Liberation Movement (SSLM), led by Colonel Joseph Lagu, did come to represent a reasonably united party for negotiating purposes. Lagu's role in bringing together diverse Southern interests is most impressive. Consolidating his base of power in eastern Equatoria, Lagu then went on to unite the various Anya-Nya forces under his command. By August 1971, Lagu had been so successful in gaining support among Southern military commanders and politicians that he was in a position to announce the formation of the SSLM and to declare himself its leader (O'Ballance, 1977: 132–135). Lagu had been greatly strengthened by the leverage gained from controlling military supplies funnelled into the Sudan from abroad (allegedly by the Israelis) (Conflict Research Society, 1973: 2–3). The result was to establish the acceptability of the SSLM among its constituents in the South and to clarify the decision structure within the SSLM. This was important to the negotiating process, for the Nimeiry state was able to recognize that Southern leaders could deliver on the bargains that they ultimately struck (Licklider, 1988: 6).

2. Leaders Determined upon a Political Solution

It requires political will on the part of the leaders of the main rival parties to the conflict to extricate themselves and their supporters from a mutually hurting stalemate. Their sense that time is running out and that both the conflict and their situation will worsen through inaction may impel the key leaders to begin the difficult search for a political solution. In the Sudan, the competing elites did alter their preferences around the same time, reflecting their joint realization that the continuance of the civil war was likely to prove self-destructive. In other conflict situations, intransigence has seemed preferable to at least one of the parties; as a result, their military struggle has continued, even escalated. Hence the parallel movement toward joint problem solving can be viewed as somewhat unusual, and it represented an important facilitating factor in the achievement of the 1972 settlement.

Political preferences favoring a peaceful solution emerged on both sides around the same time, but for very different reasons. Nimeiry, recognizing that the Sudanese state was "soft" and therefore incapable of imposing its peace terms upon the South, was committed to overcoming the deadlock in North-South relations with a series of conciliatory initiatives (*Africa Confidential*, 1971:1). During the 1969–72 period, he proposed a solution offering the South a degree of regional autonomy within a unitary Sudanese state; replaced (the executed) Joseph Garang as Minister of Southern Affairs with a moderate Southerner (Abel Alier); asked Alier to begin discussions with the guerrilla spokesmen, leading to negotiations; appointed Alier to head the Sudanese delegation at the Addis Ababa negotiations; unilaterally ratified the Addis Ababa Agreement; and promulgated the subsequent Southern Provinces Regional Self-Government Act (Assefa, 1987: 72; Kasfir, 1987: 152). Clearly, he was prepared to take calculated risks in dealing with his coalition opponents on the issue of a negotiated solution of the Southern problem. In achieving this objective, Nimeiry was ably assisted by Abel Alier, who played a key role in the successful negotiations at Addis Ababa in 1972. Not only was Alier's appointment as head of the government delegation taken as a positive signal of the government's seriousness of purpose regarding the negotiations, but he was to go on and contribute importantly to the 1972 settlement, putting forth constitutional proposals on regional autonomy that became the basis for the final accord (Epps, 1971).

Within the Southern coalition, SSLM leader and Anya-Nya Commander-in-Chief Major-General Lagu played a critically important role in the process culminating in a settlement. Once Lagu consolidated his position of political and military leadership within Southern ranks, he was able to overcome the reluctance of some of his commanders to begin negotiations and to respond positively to government overtures (*Africa Confidential*, 1971). Seeing political negotiations as inevitable, Lagu declared himself ready in October 1970 to enter into serious negotiations with government representatives. "We have been all impressed," Lagu wrote,

that the *enemy now feel our pressure and would want to have talks with us. . . . We welcome the idea to prepare for talks* because we are not just trouble makers, we are a people struggling for a cause, and if that can be achieved by talking we see no reason why we do not accept to talk. (Lagu, 1978, emphasis in text).

Although agreeing in principle to talks, Lagu nevertheless set a number of preconditions before serious discussions could begin: that the Sudanese army stop all hostilities and stay in the positions they held at that time, that Southern Sudanese political prisoners be freed, and that the Anya-Nya be recognized publicly as "the only element to negotiate with in the Southern Sudan" (Lagu, 1978). Subsequently, Lagu indicated a willingness to agree to Nimeiry's preconditions for talks. He indicated that if the Khartoum authorities showed themselves to be "sincere and serious," his delegation would be willing to enter into negotiations to reach a settlement of the conflict *within the framework of one Sudan* (Ankrah, 1971; 1972: 63). Not only was Lagu prepared to be cooperative, but he was willing to accept Nimeiry's non-negotiable principle on Sudanese unity as well. From that point forward Lagu played a central role in promoting the peace process—maintaining the unity of his delegation, responding to initiatives, and delivering on agreements.

In brief, the leadership skills and commitment of Nimeiry, Alier, and Lagu to the peace process during the 1969–72 period created a uniquely positive environment that facilitated joint problem solving. As Nelson Kasfir (1977: 145) concluded, ". . . the decisions of Nimeiri and Lagu to fully commit themselves to peace and the patient efforts of Alier for two and a half years to establish conditions permitting those commitments were crucial."

3. A Mutually Hurting Stalemate

By 1971, a number of the actors involved in the conflict in the Sudan appear to have become aware that a mutually hurting stalemate had developed between the Nimeiry state and the Southern coalition of forces. This stalemate was principally of a military nature but involved financial and political elements as well. It was primarily with respect to the military aspect of the stalemate, though, that leaders of the state and Southern coalitions came to recognize that an impasse in the conflict had been reached. Neither the Sudanese state nor the SSLM possessed, nor seemed likely to be able to acquire, such resources as to lead to an overwhelming power disparity. As a result, both coalitions came to the realization that total victory for one or the other was not possible. Thus, an awareness of the fact of a mutually hurting stalemate can be seen as constituting a significant factor leading to the search for a non-military settlement to the Sudan conflict.

While a mutually hurting stalemate between the two sides to the conflict may have been reached a year or two earlier, only in 1971 was there a willingness to recognize the implications of the stalemate. In the previous years of the conflict neither Northern governments nor the Anya-Nya had succeeded in gaining the upper hand militarily, yet each side had pressed on, seeking to gain an advantage on the battlefield. During his tenure as President of the Sudan, from 1958 until 1964, Ibrahim Abboud pursued a primarily military solution with respect to the South, seeking to quell the newly emergent guerrilla army there. His failure to solve the Southern problem was one of the reasons for his downfall. While the succeeding governments of Premiers el-Khatim el-Khalifah, Mohammed Ahmed Maghoub, and Sadiq al-Mahdi initially put forward political proposals to resolve the conflict, they too reverted to the use of the military.

Once in power, Nimeiry appears to have realized the inability of the Sudanese state to press on to a military victory in its conflict with the SSLM. On August 1, 1969, for example, Nimeiry stated: "There is no military solution to the rebellion in the south." The period he spent from November 1966 to December 1967 as the officer in charge of restoring order in Torit, Equatoria province may have been important in leading him to this conclusion (O'Ballance, 1977: 116). Other members of the political elite in Khartoum at this time also doubted that a military solution to the Southern problem was possible and recognized the existence of the mutually hurting stalemate (*Africa Confidential*, 1971: 1).

A mutually hurting stalemate such as that reached in the Sudan in 1971 is by no means an inevitable outcome in civil war situations. This stalemate must be understood in light of the fact that the Sudan was in many respects a "soft" state, with resource scarcity, limited regulatory and coercive capacity within its boundaries, and weak social relations among societal elements (Rothchild and Foley, 1988: 234). Such state softness made it difficult, if not impossible, for the Sudanese government to win a military victory over the South, and it continually raised the costs of attempting to do so.

Although the Southern forces had fought their way to this stalemate, apparently they lagged behind Nimeiry in recognizing that such a state of events had been reached between North and South. After all, the Anya-Nya had become stronger over the course of the conflict, growing from a small, nearly unarmed force of some few hundred to a movement, unified under General Joseph Lagu, consisting of 10,000 to 12,000 men. Even though the Anya-Nya's actual control over much of the South remained limited, its armed strength and degree of popular support made it a force to be reckoned with (Howell, 1978: 426). Nonetheless, events in 1971 may have contributed to the Anya-Nya's realization that it could not score a final victory over government forces. Foremost among these was a reduction in its war materiel arising from the blocking of the Israeli channels. An agreement reached in November 1971 between President Nimeiry and Emperor Haile Selassie had closed the Ethiopian line of access. Another route was cut off when President Amin expelled the Israelis from Uganda.

Certainly the lag between stalemate and remedial action proved hurtful to both antagonists. As one observer (Assefa, 1987: 153) noted: "The Anya-Nya had made the South virtually ungovernable, but an internationally recognized secession was as far away as ever." It had taken years for the conflict in the Sudan to reach a recognizable deadlock and yet more time was to prove necessary before the parties could come to grips with this state of affairs. The costs to both sides of battling to an impasse proved extremely high. Yet had such a stalemate of power not been reached and had either side continued to believe in the possibility of a military triumph, it seems unlikely that either actor would have been willing to consider a non-military solution to the conflict.

4. External Pressures to Reach Agreement

As noted above, initiating a peace process requires cooperative political decisions by the rival leaders. Pressures by external actors to end a conflict are not likely, by themselves, to move antagonists to the bargaining table. Nonetheless, the actions of regional and international actors may serve to facilitate the negotiation process. In the Sudan, a number of external political factors were at play throughout the 17-year civil war. Several of these external pressures appear to have been significant in influencing the two contending coalitions to seek a non-military settlement of the conflict.

Ethiopia and Uganda were two regional actors with a long-term interest and significant involvement in the Sudanese conflict. Like the Sudan, Ethiopia faced secessionist challenges, most particularly in Eritrea and the Ogaden. The Eritrean Liberation Front (ELF) and, after 1970, the Eritrean People's Liberation Front (EPLF) used the Sudan for arms running and refuge; in turn, Emperor Haile Selassie allowed military supplies to be funnelled to the Anya-Nya through Ethiopia and gave safe haven and training to rebel troops. Such actions were indispensable to Anya-Nya forces and constituted a source of pressure on the Khartoum government; however, when the leaders of Ethiopia and the Sudan agreed in March 1971 to cease aiding and abetting each other's secessionist movements, it had the effect of facilitating an internal settlement between the Nimeiry state and the SSLM. Nimeiry and the Emperor moved to this agreement in part because both the Anya-Nya and the Eritrean liberation movements had grown strong enough to expand, and possibly to internationalize, what still remained essentially internal wars (Howell, 1978: 432).

Moreover, with the overthrow of President Milton Obote in January 1971, Ugandan pressures on the conflict in the Sudan became critical. Langi and Acholi troops opposed to the Amin coup fled to the southern Sudan for safety where, supported by the Sudanese army, they were able to regroup. During this period, plans were afoot to invade Uganda from eastern Equatoria to restore Obote. These actions were countered by Idi Amin who gave support to the Anya-Nya; among other things, the Anya-Nya was allowed access to a supply route through Uganda. These events came to an end when, in late 1971, Nimeiry and Amin signed an accord; Nimeiry agreed to terminate support for Obote's forces in exchange for an expressed willingness on Amin's part to curtail external access to the Anya-Nya through Uganda.

The Ethiopian and Ugandan agreements severed the two major supply routes to the rebels. In addition, Amin expelled the Israeli military mission from Uganda. This cut off Israeli support for the Anya-Nya, an important factor because the Israelis had apparently become arms suppliers sometime in 1969 (Howell, 1978: 430–433). Thus, the termination of Ethiopian and Ugandan support for Southern forces influenced the Southern politicians to consider seriously an agreement with the Nimeiry state.

Although none of these external factors in and of themselves proved sufficient to impel the contending parties toward an agreement, they may have heightened a joint awareness of the urgency to end the stalemate. In addition, implicit in many of the aforementioned influences was the possibility of isolation that each of the antagonists could ill-afford—diplomatic isolation for the government of the Sudan and strategic isolation for the Southern forces. The coincidence of a number of these external pressures in 1971 made both antagonists aware of the dimensions and consequences of the stalemate.

5. Mediator Actively on the Scene

The third-party mediator in the Sudan was not removed from the scene of the conflict, but rather had interacted with parties involved in the conflict for a number of years before its resolution; this appears to have facilitated the process leading to the Addis Ababa Agreement. The presence of the World Council of Churches (WCC) and the All Africa Conference of Churches (AACC) in Africa and their ongoing contacts with various Sudanese political leaders allowed them, as mediators, to take advantage of any windows of opportunity that presented themselves. The mediators understood the shifting negotiation context, the rise of new actors, and changes in political will; they were therefore able, at the appropriate moments, to lend their services and to help move the parties beyond stalemates in the negotiation process.

The WCC and the AACC had been involved in the conflict in the Sudan, in one way or another, for a number of years. A primary form of this involvement was engagement in refugee relief efforts. In addition, in 1966 a goodwill mission from the AACC visited the Sudan, seeking to evaluate the situation there and to offer its services for peace negotiations. In 1970, after some years of exposure to the conflict, the WCC undertook a re-evaluation of "what leadership the World Council of Churches should offer to its member-bodies on the Sudan situation." According to Kodwo E. Ankrah (1972: 61), the African Secretary of the Division of Inter Churches Aid, Refugees and World Service of the WCC:

We became convinced that anyone who had been aware of the situation in the Sudan would *not* attribute the problem to one specific cause; it had a complexity of reasons—which might include religion, race, political, social and economic factors—all of which had combined to create a political problem. . . . We furthermore became convinced after exchanging a series of internal staff memoranda that we should advocate strongly that the Church leaders in Africa should approach the Sudan problem from a political angle.

Thus, their presence at the scene of the conflict allowed the third-party mediators to change their approach to the conflict when circumstances called for such a shift.

Because they were actively on the scene, the WCC and the AACC were able to assess the implications of changes in leadership, the emergence of identifiable bargaining parties, and other events as they took place and make the most of opportune moments in order to advance the negotiation process. Among other things, WCC representatives urged the SSLM, through its London spokesman, Mading de Garang, to create a consensus position within the Anya-Nya by resolving some of the internal problems that existed among the many Southern groups.[2]

Mediators who can recognize windows of opportunity and use them to move the negotiation process forward must be seen as familiar with the conflict and the parties involved. One WCC official put this well, declaring that

reconciliation efforts had to be based on a long period of preparation beforehand—perhaps five or six years. You had to nourish good relations with both sides, even if there was no hope of a settlement on the horizon. A relationship of trust was not unimportant, and it took time to establish our reliability and impartiality before people would 'enter into confidentiality' with you. (Conflict Research Society, 1973: 23)

In the case of the Sudan, the WCC's and AACC's familiarity with the conflict, their contacts with SSLM supporters such as the Makerere Group and the Kampala Committee, and visits to the Khartoum government gained them the confidence of the parties to the conflict.

The presence of a third-party mediator actively on the scene was certainly not sufficient to move the conflicting parties to reach agreement. If there had been no political will on the part of the coalitions to reach a settlement, no amount of effort by the mediators would have sufficed to resolve the conflict. However, the fact that a mediator had been on the scene for a number of years meant that it could act when the moment was advantageous, facilitating agreement between the actors and helping them to move beyond deadlock.

The Process of Negotiation

In the Sudanese negotiations of 1971–72, the five favorable preconditions discussed above set a uniquely propitious context in which state-ethnoregional bargaining could take place. Let us turn now to the peacemaking process itself. Following the overthrow of the oppressive regime of General Ibrahim Abboud in 1964, the new Prime

Minister, Sir el-Khatim el-Khalifah, pursued a more conciliatory approach to the South. In particular, Khalifah appointed two Southerners to the Cabinet, relaxed the state of emergency in the South, and invited Southerners inside and outside the country to a Round Table Conference in Khartoum. After some initial discussions on the normalization of the situation in the South and the recognitions of certain human rights, the Conference, unable to reach a unanimous agreement on the system of government to be adopted for the South, appointed a twelve-man committee to make recommendations on a constitutional arrangement which would "protect the special interest of the South as well as the general interest of the Sudan" (Wai, 1973: 208). The 1965 twelve-man committee, which met for more than a year, ruled out separation and centralized unitary government, and proposed instead a scheme of regional autonomy within a united Sudan. Northern and Southern representatives disagreed strongly on whether the South should be considered as a unit (as preferred by the Southern delegates) or divided along provincial lines (as preferred by the Northern delegates); however, there was broad agreement on the division of central and regional powers (Wai, 1973: 211–217). These proposals, while not put into effect at the time, set appropriate guidelines for the Addis Ababa settlement.

With the accession of Sayed Saddiq al-Madhi to the premiership in 1966, the tone of North-South relations changed. The new regime, intent upon encouraging an Islamic revival, urged the adoption of an Islamic constitution. By departing from the general guidelines on regional autonomy and group rights set out by the twelve-man committee, the al-Mahdi and Mohammed Mahgoub regimes represented a temporary break in the progress toward a North-South settlement in the late 1960s. With the war continuing and these regimes unable to offer a way out of the impasse, it is not surprising that the military, led by Nimeiry, decided to intervene.

It quickly became apparent that Nimeiry favored a new effort at political reconciliation with the South. In June 1969, he announced plans to broaden the amnesty for southern opposition elements; to initiate an intensive social, economic and cultural program for the South; to appoint a Minister of Southern Affairs; and to train Southerners to take up positions of responsibility. He thus offered the goal of regional autonomy within the framework of a united Sudan, the same objective that had been put forward previously by the Round Table (Legum, 1971: B55).

In the years that followed, Nimeiry remained firmly committed to the objective of a political settlement that would give Southerners responsibility for local affairs in their region. He authorized work on the implementation of the regional autonomy plan, a task that was undertaken separately by Southern intellectuals and by Dr. Gaafar Mohamed Ali Bakheit, the Minister of Local Government, and Sayed Abdel Rahman Abdullah, the former chairman of the twelve-man committee and later Deputy Minister of Local Government. Both implementation plans were similar in proposing to maintain the unity of the South, to have a head of the region with the status of a minister, to have a regional assembly and executive, and to give the region the power to raise money through taxes (Nimeiri, 1971). In brief, there was considerable continuity in the process—both in terms of personnel and program specifics. The recommendations of the Round Table and the twelve-man committee reached forward to the negotiations at Addis Ababa in 1971–72, creating linkages over time that narrowed differences and facilitated agreement on the final terms.

An important variable was the willingness of both parties to engage in an ongoing process of reciprocal concessions. This willingness went beyond environmental factors and favorable preconditions and evidenced a political will on both sides to move toward a settlement. One of the most important examples of such reciprocal concessions involved the agreements by the Nimeiry state and the SSLM on the conditions each had set for entering into negotiations. The government of the Sudan asked that Southern representatives be individuals who had influence over those actually involved in the fighting and that negotiations be conducted within the framework of regional autonomy of the South within one Sudan.[3] In turn, the SSLM required that negotiations take place in an independent, non-Arab, African state and that they make use of an African leader as mediator. The SSLM also asked that the Sudanese government recognize the Anya-Nya as "the only element to negotiate with in the Southern Sudan" (Lagu, 1978). What is significant, then, is that the two parties agreed to the conditions that the other set prior to negotiations, thereby demonstrating that each was serious about embarking upon the process of political exchange.

In addition to these concessions, which were critical for initiating the negotiations, at least three other major sets of concessions surfaced during the negotiations. First, Northern representatives contended that Arabic should be the country's sole official language, arguing that the development of local languages was a part of the national culture and heritage and that the existence of two or more official languages could prove divisive. Southerners sought to make English the official language of the Southern region, fearing that non-Arabic speaking Southerners might later be disadvantaged when seeking government positions. The issue was resolved by both sides agreeing that Arabic would be "the official language for the Sudan and English the principal language for the Southern Region" ("Addis Ababa Agreement," 1972, Chapter III, Article 6).

Second, the government wanted a single national army controlled by the central government. The SSLM argued that there should be three armies: one for the Northern region, one for the Southern region, to be composed of Anya-Nya troops, and a third army to guard Khartoum, to be controlled by the central government and made up equally of Northerners and Southerners.[4] This proved to be a very contentious issue; nevertheless, a formula was finally devised which each side found minimally satisfactory and which affected only the composition of the Southern Defense Corps. The armed forces in the Southern region were to consist of a unified force made up of 6,000 troops from the Anya-Nya and 6,000 troops from the North. Such a formula met the desires of the Sudanese state for one national force and the Southern coalition's concern for the incorporation of Anya-Nya troops into the army.

Third, while some Southern politicians had favored secession of the South from the North, others had sought a federal structure between the two regions. The North, on the other hand, had entered into the negotiations urging limited regional autonomy for the South. Mutual concessions led to an agreement whereby the South's three provinces of Bahr el Ghazal, Equatoria, and Upper Nile constituted a self-governing unit within the Republic. As Mohamed Omer Beshir (1975: 110) observed: "This was not a compromise but a realistic and practical formula which removed the two extreme positions, separation and the *status quo*. The national aspirations of both parties were satisfied."

These reciprocal concessions appear to have built up a certain minimal level of trust on the part of both groups. They demonstrated to each that the sacrifices entailed in an agreement would not be unilateral. After 17 years of prolonged warfare, one could not expect any single action to create trust on the part of an adversary party,

nor to legitimate the entire negotiation process. However, the reciprocal concessions that were made did serve to create a history of
positive responses between the two groups and to build a network
of relationships between them. Through reciprocal concessions, each
side was able to test the negotiation process at various stages, and
to receive concrete evidences of its rival's political will to reach and
implement a settlement. As part of the negotiation process, reciprocal concessions also encouraged participants to alter their perceptions of one another. Growing interaction between the parties during
the negotiations, combined with the give and take of concessions,
prompted the evolution of perceptions from totalist ones toward
something more pragmatic in nature and more conducive to bargaining outcomes. An early example was the North's agreement to
negotiate with the SSLM outside the Sudan, in Addis Ababa. Such
a concession accorded a certain degree of legitimacy to the Southern
movement, both because it met one of the Southern politicians' demands and because it placed the parties on somewhat more diplo-
matically equal terms than would have been the case had they met
in the Sudan. An even clearer example of evolving perceptions was
the government's willingness to treat the SSLM as a legitimate bargaining party in the secret negotiations preceding Addis Ababa (Niilus, 1973: 12).

Although perceptions were altered during the negotiation process, they remained within a certain range. For example, negotiations
between the contending groups could not have occurred had the
Southern coalition insisted on secession. Once the Southern politicians agreed to the Northern government's "one Sudan" condition,
the parties then diverged on interests rather than principles. Interests proved to be negotiable and were something on which both
sides were willing to make concessions. By acknowledging tacit limits
and recognizing that some principles were non-negotiable, the two
sides were able to move forward, circumventing issues that might
have led to deadlock and the breakdown of negotiations.

As third-party mediators the WCC and AACC were involved in
moving the Sudan negotiations forward. As we mentioned before,
their familiarity with the conflict and their presence on the scene
were factors enabling these organizations to act in the productive
manner they did. What remains to be explored is the nature of the
role played by these mediators and its importance to the negotiation
process. We argue here that if the five favorable preconditions we

set out are in place, a mediator can play a facilitating role, but no more than that. To borrow the language used by Douglas Amy (1983: 356–360), it is possible to speak of both the importance and the unimportance of a mediator within the negotiating context.

Some of the important roles played by the WCC and AACC, such as promoting contacts between groups, have been examined previously. In addition, the two mediators helped to facilitate concessions between the contending parties at Addis Ababa, offering formulas for the two groups to debate and discuss, reminding each side of the dilemmas faced by its opponents, recalling what was at stake when the negotiations grew heated, and slowing down the pace of the negotiations when that became necessary (Welton, Pruitt, and McGillicuddy, 1988: 182, 185–186). The mediators, and the tone they set for the negotiations, may also have helped alter perceptions. For example, when agreement was reached at the conference on the question of the army, Canon Burgess Carr stood to pray aloud, crying as he did so. According to others present, one of the generals in the Northern delegation was crying as well, out of admitted remorse for the slaughter between brothers that had taken place over the years (Assefa, 1987: 142).

Why were the WCC and AACC able to succeed where other intermediaries (such as the London-based Movement for Colonial Freedom) had failed? At least part of the answer to this question may be found in the fact that the two groups were able to gain the trust of both of the contending parties. The North's trust had been at least partially won by the fact that the AACC's 1966 report, "Mission to the Sudan," was somewhat sympathetic to the North. This became important later because the government had to participate if there were to be any negotiations.

Even though a number of Southerners had been put off by the 1966 report, their trust was gradually gained by, among other factors, the willingness of the third-party mediators to meet with them in places like Uganda under the auspices of the Kampala Committee and the Makerere Group. In addition, the fact that the AACC was an African organization, and that some of the key mediators, among them Burgess Carr and Kodwo Ankrah, were Africans, may have helped to make the third-party mediators more legitimate in Southern eyes. Finally, the willingness of the mediators to provide the SSLM with money for travel and lawyer's fees, thereby empowering the Southern coalition and enabling it to participate more effectively in the negotiations, probably reassured the South that the WCC and AACC were not inherently biased in favor of the North's position.

In addition, the WCC and AACC appear to have been able to play the role they did because of the nature of their organizations. As private, activist organizations with relatively limited resources, the WCC and AACC were unable to either coerce or threaten the actors involved in the Sudan conflict. This may have been yet another reason the two sides trusted them so much and decided to allow them the needed leeway to facilitate the mediation process. The mediators were certainly aware of what being a non-state actor and a private, non-partisan organization meant for the negotiation process. As Leopoldo J. Niilus (1973: 10) put it:

There is no government which could call in bodies like the UNO or the OAU to 'intermediate' between it and its 'rebels'. For to do so would be to give to the rebels formal status, parallel to that of the government. However, bodies like the WCC and the AACC, which can give no diplomatic *status* to anybody can be made use of, *provided*, of course, that they are understood to be objective and *informed* enough and not suspected of having their own stake to interfere in a Nation's internal affairs.

The fact that the WCC and AACC were private organizations was very important to the Sudan government. Their non-diplomatic and unofficial status meant they were able to perform an important face-saving function. Once there was sufficient political will on the government's part to embark on the negotiation process, Northern officials were able to turn to the WCC and AACC, which were already on the scene, to facilitate the process. Doing so meant the negotiation process would not be publicly subjected to the pressures of state and other international actors and that the government did not have to accord the Southern coalition any more legitimacy than it was initially prepared to give. The unofficial status of the mediators, combined with the private manner in which they handled the negotiation process, allowed the two parties to move gradually away from their pre-negotiation stances without losing face and legitimacy as coalitions. This face-saving mechanism, which stems from the non-threatening nature of private organizations, lends them a capacity to facilitate mediation processes. This is a capacity that states tend to lack.

The third-party mediators did have a role to play in facilitating the Sudan negotiations; however, it would be a mistake to overstate their contribution. The WCC and AACC faced certain limitations that prevented them from overcoming a stalemate reached in the negotiations at Addis Ababa. The WCC and AACC had only limited power to make credible threats or to coerce the parties involved; once deadlock was reached in the negotiations, the resources they possessed as private organizations proved insufficient to persuade the parties to compromise and move on. Such a point of deadlock in the negotiations arose over military/security issues, specifically the future of an army for the Sudan. Negotiations nearly broke down at this point for neither side could be persuaded to make any concessions on this matter. None of the negotiating techniques that had been employed in the discussions on other issues worked on this one. The WCC and AACC, unable to do more, turned to an arbitrator, Emperor Haile Selassie of Ethiopia.

The Emperor played a unique role during the negotiations, but one which should be seen as coming into play only when other efforts to keep the negotiations on track had failed. Although Haile Selassie was willing to have the contending parties meet under his auspices, he insisted that his role not be regarded as that of a mediator. This was made clear to the WCC and AACC, who were told they could refer only to "His Imperial Majesty's *good offices, under his auspices*" (Niilus, 1972). This position may have stemmed from the Emperor's fear that secessionists in his own country would attempt to pressure him to submit those conflicts to mediation. When deadlock was reached on the military/security question, Canon Burgess Carr was able to persuade the Emperor to use his good offices to attempt to settle the matter. The Emperor met separately with the Northern and Southern delegations, putting a 50–50 proposal to them by which half of the armed forces in the South would be Anya-Nya troops (i.e., 6,000) and half Northern troops. Concessions were made by each coalition, leading to agreement on this proposal.

The Emperor's formula on splitting the differences was one the third-party mediators might well have suggested themselves. A proposal from the Emperor apparently moved the negotiations out of deadlock when all the efforts of the WCC and AACC had failed, an action largely explained by the fact that the Emperor represented a state with a substantial amount of implied coercive capacity. As such, he could threaten the parties involved by raising the costs of stalemate should they fail to reach an agreement on the issue at hand. The Emperor could threaten the Nimeiry government with the possibility of once again aiding the SSLM should the Northern coalition prove recalcitrant or of no longer allowing Sudanese refugees to remain in Ethiopia, thereby flooding the Sudan with refugees it was ill-equipped to handle. In turn, the agreement the Emperor had signed with Nimeiry pressured the Southerners to reach a settlement with the Sudan government; dwindling military supplies would not only affect the fire-power of the Anya-Nya, but in the longer term, it might also weaken the unity of the Southern coalition itself. Moreover, he gave his personal guarantee against any reprisals or repression of Anya-Nya returnees, should the South reach an agreement on the military issue (Assefa, 1987: 141). Hence, the Emperor, backed by the power of a state active in the region, was in a very favorable position to influence the two parties to the conflict— thereby helping to overcome a deadlock at a critical point in the negotiations. State and private third parties cooperated in an effective manner, with the Emperor backstopping the private, unofficial mediators at critical points, and this yielded impressive results in this instance.

Post-Agreement Relations

The successful negotiations between the Nimeiry state and the SSLM at Addis Ababa in 1972 brought an end to the first Sudanese civil war. Although suspicions remained very much alive on both sides (both Nimeiry and Lagu had antagonized their colleagues and coalition partners by their unilateral actions in ratifying the agreement), the agreement did provide for some basic rules of relationship for the period that followed (Kasfir, 1977: 143–144). Thus the Sudan's conflict process had gone full circle, returning to a hegemonic exchange relationship under the aegis of President Nimeiry and his ruling coalition.

Under the provisions of the Addis Ababa Agreement and the follow-up Southern Provinces Regional Self-Government Act of 1972, the Southern Region (including the provinces of Bahr el Ghazal, Equatoria, and Upper Nile) was constituted a "self-governing region" within a united, socialist Sudan. A High Executive Council and Peoples Regional Assembly were created for the Southern Region, with authority to deal with a specified list of regional subjects—in particular the preservation of public order, internal security, efficient administration, and the promotion of economic, social and cultural development. The regional authorities were empowered to establish a separate budget and to levy regional duties and taxes.

The leading position of the central government in center-regional relations was never in doubt. Not only was the central government given exclusive authority to deal with an extended number of national matters (defense, external affairs, currency, communications, customs and foreign trade, nationality and immigration, economic and social development, educational planning, and public audit), but the president of the Republic was given broad authority to organize relations between the central ministries and the regional organs. The Peoples Regional Assembly could, by a two-thirds majority, request that the president postpone the coming into force of any law which adversely affected the welfare and interests of the citizens of the Southern Region; however, it was left up to the president to determine whether he would accede to such a request. Under the 1973 constitution, central-regional relations remained ambiguous. Douglas Johnson (1988: 5) notes that Nimeiry took advantage of this lack of clarity to intervene in regional elections and to make economic decisions without reference to Southern authorities.

Shortly after the Regional Self-Government Act was put into effect, Nimeiry appointed a Provisional High Executive Council, headed by Abel Alier, to act as the regional government for a transitional 18-month period (Betts, 1974: 2). A series of other steps intended to reassure the South followed quickly. Lagu was commissioned a Major-General in the Sudanese Army and three Southerners were appointed to the central government. The Nimeiry regime cooperated with neighboring governments and the United Nations High Commissioner for Refugees to repatriate, resettle, and rehabilitate a half million or more refugees in the bush or living abroad (Betts, 1974: 3) and integrated 10,000 SSLM troops into the People's Armed Forces, the police, and prison forces (Alier, 1976: 4). A financially-strapped, soft state such as the Sudan which had just experienced a brutal civil war would have had difficulties healing the wounds of the past; yet for all the anger and resentment within and between both coalitions, the transition to peace proved as smooth as could be expected. Conditions were created under which ties of reciprocity and norms and rules of interaction could emerge among politicians, from both North and South, in the future. That this failed to materialize is less a commentary on the peacemaking process of 1971–72 than on the short-sightedness of President Nimeiry and his entourage, as they sought to strike a balance between the Northern-dominated state coalition and Southern demands in the period that followed.

The Addis Ababa Agreement represented a positive beginning, but it was up to the political leaders, and most especially those in the Sudan's ruling coalition in Khartoum, to make this beginning a substantive reality. The integration of Anya-Nya troops into the People's Armed Forces and the holding of elections for the Regional Assembly in the South in November 1973 were important signs among others that the Nimeiry regime remained serious about implementing the spirit of the Addis Ababa Agreement. However, by the mid-1970s, Southerners had reason to be concerned over signs that Nimeiry had begun to shift his priorities.

Signs of a reconsideration of Southern autonomy began to emerge soon after the initial transition period. Although the 1973 elections to the Regional Assembly in the South augured well in terms of the introduction of the democratic process to this area, there were concerns over Nimeiry's intervention into the process to assure Alier's nomination as the official candidate of the Sudan Socialist Union for the presidency of the High Executive Council. Although some have concluded that Alier, a key Southern politician who had played an important role in the Addis Ababa negotiations and the implementation process that followed, would likely have been elected anyway, Nimeiry's intercession as president of the party was an embarrassment which weakened Alier's position in the years ahead.[5] At least as serious was the harm done to the spirit of Addis Ababa; Nimeiry's action "caused some misgivings" about the procedures on the election and, more generally, about what seemed a shaky power relationship between the central government and regional authorities (*Africa Confidential*, 1974: 7).

By the mid-1970s, evidence appeared indicating that the Nimeiry regime had not committed itself fully to a stance of reconciliation toward the South. For example, Southerners expressed general disappointment over the level of central expenditures allocated to rebuild the war-devastated infrastructure in their region. Subsequently, Nimeiry took a series of actions which pointed even more clearly to a shift in regime priorities away from compromise and accommodation. The result was most destructive of the Addis Ababa Agreement. Nimeiry, the advocate of a political solution in 1969 and immediately after, backtracked decisively from his earlier position and thereby undercut the very agreement he had once championed.

In the eyes of militant Sudanese leaders (and most notably Dr. John Garang de Mabior, the current leader of the Sudan People's Liberation Movement (SPLM) and Sudan People's Liberation Army (SPLA)), a number of state initiatives caused a new flare up of guerrilla warfare in the Sudan (Garang de Mabior, 1984: 5; 1987: 19–25). The most significant of these "provocations," as Garang describes them, include the following.

First, because half of the water passing through the Sudd evaporates, the Nimeiry government, in alliance with Egypt, decided to build a 175-mile canal between Jonglei and Malakal, thereby saving water to be used in Northern Sudan and Egypt. Some Southerners were highly critical of this proposed Jonglei Canal, fearing that the drying effect in the swampy Sudd area would drain pastures, dry up wells, change the climate, and generally undermine the Dinka's pastoral life style. Despite demonstrations against the scheme in Juba in October 1974 and criticism from both Southern leaders and Western environmentalists, the Nimeiry government proceeded to plan and begin implementation of the project. SPLA military forces attacked the Jonglei Canal construction site in 1984, kidnapping and killing some foreign employees in the process, and work on the project came to a halt (Tinker, 1978; Kasfir, 1976: 13).

Second, on various occasions Nimeiry intervened in Southern executive and legislative affairs; he altered electoral processes and dissolved legally constituted bodies in ways that Southern politicians felt contravened the constitution (Garang de Mabior, 1984: 5).

Third, Southern members of the National Assembly protested against legislation that would have changed the border between North and South, removing certain mineral-rich and prime agricultural lands in the Northern Upper Nile, Bentiu, and other areas from Southern control (SUDANOW, 1981: 13; Garang de Mabior, 1987: 21).

Fourth, with Chevron's discovery of a substantial oil find in Bentiu district in the Southern Sudan, Southerners were hopeful that a refinery would be built in their region close to the oil find (Africa Confidential, 1981: 1; SUDANOW, 1981: 14). Such a project would not only create economic opportunities in the Bentiu area, but might contribute to the development of the region as a whole. These hopes were dashed, however, as Nimeiry decided in the summer of 1981 to locate the refinery at Kosti in the North. Nimeiry's decision led to widespread resentment in the South, touching off riots and open expressions of student militancy. The following year, Nimeiry scrapped plans for an oil refinery, choosing instead to allow Chevron to lay a pipe line to the ocean at Port Sudan. The South felt betrayed by this decision and, not surprisingly, Garang's SPLA mounted efforts to prevent it from being put into effect.

Fifth, in 1983, in a major bid to gain support from some key Northerners, Nimeiry imposed Islamic *Sharia* law upon the country as a whole, including the South (Heraclides, 1987: 227). *Sharia* law, which applies traditional punishments (including whippings, stonings and amputations) in certain specified cases as a means of "retribution, deterrence and rehabilitation" (*SUDANOW*, 1983: 8–12), is strongly opposed by Southerners who view it as a harsh legal system that violates the human rights and cultural autonomy of the largely non-Muslim people of the South (*Africa News*, 1985: 7; *New African*, 1984: 6–7). All three of the Southern regional assemblies passed resolutions in the 1983–84 period rejecting a proposed amendment to the Sudan constitution that would impose *Sharia* law and urged that in any event it not be applied to non-Muslim peoples (*Guardian*, 1984: 7). By late 1984, Nimeiry, under pressure from Western governments as well as leaders in the Southern Sudan and in Eastern Africa, backtracked a bit, declaring that he was suspending the further use of *Sharia* law (*Weekly Review*, 1984: 1; *Manchester Guardian Weekly*, 1984: 15). But the announced suspension was not a decision to end the application of Islamic law to non-Muslims, leaving Southerners apprehensive about their future in a politically centralized Sudanese state.

And sixth, Nimeiry's determination to redivide the South into three regions was viewed by Garang de Mabior (1984: 6) and many (but not all) Southerners as an effort to weaken the South as well as an "abrogation" of the Addis Ababa provision on maintaining the region as a single entity. The redivision of the South followed an earlier decision of the Sudanese government to decentralize and devolve limited powers under the Regional Government Act of 1980 to five new regional governments in the North. With this in place, Nimeiry was eager to extend the decentralization policy to the South, thereby increasing his influence over rival elements in the region (*SUDANOW*, 1983: 1).

Toward this end, he received important encouragement from Vice-President Lagu, the champion of the smaller ethnic (non-Dinka) peoples in Equatoria province. Arguing that administrative decentralization was necessary to promote cultural distinction as well as stability and progress in the South, Lagu struck out forcefully against what he described as Dinka domination in the area. He wrote (Lagu, 1981: 3, 7):

The truth . . . is that many of the leaders of the Dinka tribe have chosen to mark time of [sic] the issue of decentralization so as to effect the spread of members of their tribe in all areas of the South, and thereby guaranteeing themselves the control of any government formed at any level. The annual intake to the police and administrative institutions are very clear revelations of this ambition.

Other Southern politicians (among them, some important Dinka leaders) were quick to challenge Lagu's call for redivision; one booklet (The Solidarity Committee of the Southern Members 4th People's National Assembly, n.d.: 6 *passim*) described the proposals as "nakedly tribal[istic]" and a threat to the unity and integrity of the Southern Region. Nimeiry, preferring to conform to the guidelines agreed upon at Addis Ababa, initially prepared for a referendum on the issue. However, as conflicts between the pro- and anti-divisionists became intense, he abandoned these plans and, in June 1983, decreed the South split into three regions. "By that act," writes Bona Malwal (1985: 34), "he took the 'final' step which in effect totally abrogated the 1972 Self-Government Act for the South which had embodied the Addis Ababa Agreement." Nimeiry and his redivisionist supporters had won, but at great future cost to the peace of the country. Ominous signs soon became evident, for the decree on redivision coincided with an increase in guerrilla activities in the South (Gueyras, 1983).

Step by step, then, Nimeiry subverted the very agreement he had helped to create at Addis Ababa. His motives in this were less than clear, although his desire to strengthen his coalition base in the North appears to have been a significant factor. As Nimeiry's base of support shrank, he tended to be increasingly responsive to the demands made by more traditional religious elements in the North for *Sharia* laws and the redivision of the South, policies which subverted the 1971–72 peace accord (Gueyras, 1983). The Anya-Nya II guerrilla forces emerged as a serious challenge in 1983, soon to be overtaken by Garang's SPLA. Isolated and broadly unpopular, Nimeiry was overthrown by General Abdel Rahman Siwar el-Dahab, his defense minister, in April 1985.

The takeover of power by el-Dahab, and that of his legally elected successor, Sadiq al-Mahdi, the following year did little to restore the spirit of the Addis Ababa Agreement. As peace disintegrated, leaders on both sides turned again to the military option, with the cruelest of consequences for the civilian population in the South. The fighting intensified, as Garang's forces grew and gained control over much of the rural areas, and as the Sudanese army, supported by well-armed tribal militias, fought to extend its hold over the area (Gurdon, 1988: 11). Al-Mahdi seemed unprepared to accommodate basic Southern demands. To be sure, he compromised on the issue of re-division, urging that Equatoria be accorded a special status within a reunited South, and took steps to soften (but not to abrogate) the system of *Sharia* law (Johnson, 1988: 8; Legum, 1988b: 4). Garang, rejecting such compromise measures as insufficient, ruled out meaningful negotiations with Khartoum until the al-Mahdi regime agreed to end the application of *Sharia* laws, adopt a secular constitution, and restructure the country's political system (Garang de Mabior, 1987: 22). At heart, then, the two sides remained locked into diametrically opposed positions regarding the government's commitment to the application of Islamic principles. Nor did this situation change following Brigadier Omar Hassan el Beshir's intervention and suspension of the constitution in 1989. El Beshir's failure to remove Nimeiry's *Sharia* laws from the statute books, as well as his appointment of a new government with substantial connections with the Muslim Brothers, further complicated the process of reaching another political solution in the Sudan.

Conclusion

What are the implications of Sudan's peacemaking process in the 1971–72 period for the management of civil wars? As we show in the body of the paper, the emergence simultaneously of the five favorable preconditions in the Sudan was somewhat unique and contributed substantially to the achievement of an agreement at Addis Ababa. Certainly one would anticipate the existence of the first three favorable preconditions (the emergence of identifiable bargaining parties, evidence of a mutually hurting stalemate, and the existence of leaders determined upon a political solution) in any successful negotiation of conflict in a deeply divided society; however, when these preconditions are combined with pressures by external political actors conducive to positive conflict management outcomes and a mediator actively on the scene, then a uniquely propitious situation can be said to be in place.

Certainly the unofficial mediatory agencies built effectively upon these favorable preconditions to facilitate the peacemaking process. Although the WCC and the AACC did show great commitment and skill in gaining the confidence of the rival parties, in narrowing their differences through communication and caucusing activities, and in coordinating their efforts with official authorities in Addis Ababa, we contend that it is important not to overstate either the room for maneuver of the third-party intervenors or their capacity to influence the disputants in a conflict of this type and intensity. The Sudanese leaderships converged in their preference for overcoming the deadlock through a political solution; under these circumstances the unofficial mediators, backed at critical moments by official external actors, were in a fortuitous position to promote a mutually acceptable settlement.

With the Addis Ababa Agreement in place and with initial measures put into effect to give substance to the accord, the two sides to the conflict cautiously began to edge toward peaceful relations. Suspicions remained in evidence on both sides; nevertheless, the Addis Ababa settlement was viewed as something of a beginning that might lead to positive outcomes. Yet even as the Sudanese elite began to work out norms of relationship and reciprocity among themselves, evidences of mixed signals began to emerge at the top. President Nimeiry, a key champion of a political solution prior to the Addis Ababa Agreement, took steps soon after the implementation process that undercut the spirit of the accord. Then, as he became isolated and in need of new coalition partners in his Northern base, he initiated a number of policies in the early 1980s that contravened the terms of the 1972 Addis Ababa Agreement. The South felt betrayed and guerrilla actions mounted rapidly. Nimeiry's sabotage of the very agreement he had championed undermined the fragile norms of relations slowly developing within the elite. Moreover, the unwillingness of Nimeiry and his successors to respond generously to Southern demands on such issues as the *Sharia* system of law and the adoption of a secular constitution deeply polarized the society.

Clearly, the fact that the conflict cycle has gone full circle has grave ramifications for the Sudan. To build the necessary coalitions and make the required adjustments to bring about peace, only to see it slip away as a consequence of insensitive state policies, is disheartening in the extreme. In the period that followed, cynicism and distrust came to prevail, creating a kind of negotiating fatigue that inhibited the next serious effort to negotiate the conflict. With the costs of civil war mounting, the new leaders of the Sudan may find it extremely difficult to build support within their diverse constituencies for conciliatory moves. If simple reciprocal acts are no longer sufficient to move the negotiating process along, then something more—such as either a series of conciliatory moves by one of the antagonists (preferably the state, as the stronger actor) or a third party intervenor—may be necessary to break out of the current stalemate. Such initiatives may be very difficult to orchestrate where both coalitions are heterogenous and the state is weak; even so, the costs of inaction may in time compel a change in policy preferences.

Notes

1. As late as 1953, the British government still justified the "Southern Policy" as a necessary "protective barrier . . . against those who, whether northern Sudanese or Europeans, might try to exploit [the Southern peoples]" (British Information Services, 1953: 26).

2. Undated document in WCC Archives, Geneva. The three-page document appears to be the minutes of a meeting between WCC members Leopoldo Niilus, Dwain Epps, Theresa Scherf, Jan Orner, and Kodwo Ankrah and the Sudanese-in-exile Mading de Garang and Arthur Aiken. Ankrah's statement to de Garang and Aiken is "you make it easier if . . . you can solve internal problems in your camp, if you can bring them together to see the situation."

3. All Africa Conference of Churches, 1971: 1. These are notes on the 25 May 1971 meeting between the AACC and "the involved parties," in Kampala, Uganda.

4. Minutes on the third day of negotiations at Addis Ababa, Feb. 18, 1972, WCC Archives, Geneva.

5. According to southern Sudanese informants, Alier did not welcome this move on Nimeiry's part and requested that his nomination be withdrawn. However, as pressures were brought to bear he changed his mind and accepted the nomination, not wishing to undermine the agreement (Majok, 1989).

Republic of Yemen

5.1 Yemen. Copyright © 1991 by Manfred Wenner

The Civil War in Yemen, 1962–1970
Manfred W. Wenner

Introduction

The contemporary state known as the Republic of Yemen officially came into being on 22 May 1990 as a result of the unification of the two previously existing Yemeni states: the Yemen Arab Republic (often known as North Yemen) and the Peoples Democratic Republic of Yemen (usually known as South Yemen). The previous experiences of the YAR and the PDRY were markedly different, in both political and economic terms. For North Yemen, the most important political event of the post-war era is unquestionably the civil war which wracked that country from 1962 to 1970, and eventually resulted in the political system which signed the unification agreement of May 1990.

Background

North Yemen achieved *de facto* independence upon the withdrawal of the Ottoman Turkish authorities from Yemen at the end of World War I. Responsibility for governance was turned over to the spiritual and temporal leader of the Zaydi sect of Islam, known as an *imam*; at the time the Zaydis clearly dominated the political and social, and quite probably the economic, systems. The specific individual, Imam Yahya ibn Muhammad, had led the major domestic political movement against the Ottoman administration and presence.

During his reign, which lasted until 1948, Imam Yahya strove to accomplish a number of goals: (1) to make Yemen as autarkic as possible, so that its patrimony, territory, and resources would not fall into the hands of others (non-Zaydis); (2) to assert his control over the entire territory of the state as then constituted (and perhaps additional lands which had been part of Yemen some 150 years earlier); and (3) to create the ideal of a Shi'a state, i.e., a "church-state" governed by a member of the Prophet's House, headed by an imam, and committed to promoting the Shari'a as the "law of the land." Within this system, the non-Zaydi Muslims in the population (Sunni Shafi'is as well as other Shi'as, the Isma'ilis) generally had second-class status, and the Jews constituted a traditional *dhimmi* ("protected people") population.

In general, Imam Yahya accomplished his goals; on the other hand, by 1948 his autocratic and often repressive policies produced an organized effort—a revolution—to bring about significant social change. Imam Yahya's son, Ahmad, was able to put together a counter-revolutionary coalition and succeeded in re-establishing the *ancien régime*. In barely altered outlines and operations, it continued to 1962, despite some assassinations and abortive revolutionary efforts in the 1950s. When Imam Ahmad died in September 1962, his son Muhammad al-Badr became Imam. Although it was widely anticipated that he would institute major reforms, he never had the opportunity to do so: on 26 September a coalition of army officers and their civilian supporters shelled his residence, assumed they had killed him, and declared the creation of the Yemen Arab Republic.

The imam, however, survived the shelling and escaped into the rugged mountains of the northern area of Yemen. The traditional support of the Zaydi imams has always come from these mountains: the fiercely independent tribes of this area have been strongly committed to the cause of the imamate ever since its founding in the ninth century A.D. However, the northern tribes have not always been united in their political goals and interests. The tribes of North Yemen are more like small nations, each with its own network of allies, its own lands, its own set of interests, its own towns and villages, etc. Essentially they act as a small international system. In the past, many imams desperately sought to curb their influence and power. Imam Yahya had tried to create a truly central authority, in both political as well as legal terms, during his tenure. Despite these tensions, the tribes, in general, accepted the minimum role of the imamate in political terms, and strongly supported his religious role (as imam of Zaydi Muslims). Therefore, it was possible for Imam Muhammad al-Badr to put together a coalition of *some* of these tribes for the purpose of defending the imamate, and destroying the re-public. The country was soon in the throes of a civil war to decide the nature of the political system.

For roughly the next eight years, this civil war affected every part of the country; no region or settlement was spared. It was not until the spring of 1970 that a unified political system was once again in place, at least in theory responsible for governing all of (North) Yemen.

The following essay seeks, in five headings, to analyze various aspects of this conflict in order to contribute to a more synthetic and theoretical analysis of the ending of civil conflicts. These five head-ings are derived from preliminary work and discussions undertaken under the leadership of Professor Roy Licklider, of Rutgers Univer-sity.

1. The Nature of the Underlying Issues

Tracing the origins of any civil conflict is an extremely difficult and complex task; it may be argued, at least in the case of Yemen, that the revolution would never have taken place had not the domestic policies of Imams Yahya and Ahmad been so severe, restrictive, pu-nitive and autocratic in nature. Without them, the intellectual, eco-nomic, and military opposition which eventually culminated in the revolution might not have developed. And, of course, without the revolution, there probably would not have been a civil war. The difficulty is in the line of causality: at what point do we decide that the chain should begin (or end)?

One thing is clear: to begin with the revolution itself would be completely inaccurate and inappropriate. One needs a discussion and analysis of the society as a whole, and the frictions, divisions, and conflicts which eventually proved to be irreconcilable within the traditional framework, and therefore eventually led to war.

In one sense, pre-World War II Yemen was a relatively well in-tegrated, relatively homogeneous society, if only because the various elements had developed organically and rather isolated from many of the political, economic, and social currents prevailing elsewhere. The elite—in the politico-religious sphere, in the economic arena, as well as in social affairs—was relatively homogeneous, in the sense that everyone knew which elements of the social structure were included and which were excluded. Perhaps of some importance was the fact that the differences in overt wealth between the highest and the lowest were not egregious.

There were, of course, some elements which were more closely tied to the politico-religious leadership of the country. Foremost among these were the *sayyids* and the *qadis*. The first is the group of people who can trace their lineage back to the Prophet Muhammad, and who therefore enjoyed special status and privileges (since the imamate could only be in the hands of one of their numbers). The second group is a class of educated persons who, precisely because of their education, enjoyed rank and position within the system (as administrators, civil servants, etc.).

Eventually the "national unity" which had been created as a result of the policies of the Ottoman Turks (in the late 19th and early 20th centuries) began to erode. Alternative ideas of political responsibility and public participation in decision making began to surface and spread; alternative views of the social structure began to be heard; alternative ideas of social and economic justice found greater receptivity, and last but not least, discontent over the low standard of living began to spread.

As has happened elsewhere, political change did not stem solely from progressive opposition to the continuation of the *ancien régime*. Indeed, in Yemen, a strain of progressive opposition eventually joined forces with a strain of conservative opposition to bring about the first attempt at political reform in 1948.

One particular element of the opposition warrants special treatment, however: the commercial interests of the Shafi'i portion of the population. The foreign trade of Yemen, limited though it was as a result of the imams' policy of strictly limiting all foreign connections and the desire for autarky, was almost wholly in the hands of the Shafi'is of the south and southwestern regions of the country—the logical location for such trade links, via Aden and the Red Sea ports. And, despite efforts to limit Shafi'i economic power, such trade continued, leading to the development of an economic grievance against the imams which overlapped the politico-religious one, i.e., the fact that the imams might possibly be accepted as "king" of Yemen, but certainly not as religious leader, imam, of the Sunni Shafi'is.

In sum, then, though there were significant cleavages within the population, it was not until the 1940s that they became a significant

factor in the political system's viability. The decision by the revolutionaries to establish a republic, however, heightened and exacerbated some of the earlier frictions and divisions. In one sense, then,
the terms which the Western media used to describe the adversaries
in the civil war were appropriate: "republicans" vs. "royalists." The
republicans were the progressive political elements, the economic
liberals, as well as the social reformers and modernists; the royalists
were the conservative political elements who wished to retain the
traditional forms (and sometimes the content) of the Zaydi imamic
system which had developed since the departure of the Ottomans.
Such sweeping generalizations always have their exceptions, of
course: there were elements among the republicans who did not wish
to see all Yemeni tradition and cultural patterns swept away, and
there were elements among the royalists who devoutly wished to
see major reforms of the previous imamic system adapted to the
social, economic, and political realities of the end of the 20th century.

The republicans sought, from the outset, to avoid having religious
frictions and divisions affect the new political order: Shafi'is as well
as Isma'ilis were made a regular feature of the cabinets which constituted an important part of the direction of policy in the republic.
Nevertheless, it is somewhat ironic that the percentage of Shafi'is in
republican cabinets never approached equality with the Zaydis despite the fact that most observers believed that (a) the population of
Yemen was approximately equally divided between Zaydis and
Shafi'is, and (b) few Shafi'is supported the royalist cause, whereas
some significant elements of the Zaydi tribal elements (e.g. Shaykh
Abdullah al-Ahmar of the 'Usaymat) supported the republic.

Can it be said, then, that the republic recognized the political
equality of the Shafi'is, and that this recognition was an important
part of the success of the republic? While this would make the story
a coherent and logical one, things are never that simple. First, the
Zaydis have, as indicated, continued to dominate the political elite
of the republic (though this situation may change with the unification
agreement), even though certain elements continued to resist the
republic into the 1980s; second, the level of economic development
and change which characterized the country since the early 1970s
seems to have disproportionately benefitted the Shafi'i areas, thus
presumably "taking the edge off" the political discrepancies which
exist.

How much of the success of the republic may one attribute to its ability to minimize identity issues (Zaydi vs. Shafi'i), as opposed to its ability to deal effectively with such tangible issues as economic development, an increased standard of living, or promoting a more "open" social structure? No easy answer is possible or available, though one would have to argue these are an important part of the republic's viability, especially after 1970.

One thing, however, is clear: during the civil war years, when Yemen suffered one of its periodic droughts, the republican government was able to draw upon resources from outside Yemen and provide food and services in the areas under its control which were not available to the royalist side. In other words, the republic's control over tangible resources at a critical juncture in the conflict contributed (though to what degree can never be reliably ascertained) to the perception that the republic's powers and influence were greater than those of the royalists.

2. The Internal Politics of Each Side

The outcome of the Yemeni conflict can be analyzed in a variety of terms; one of the most useful for our purposes is in terms of the coalitions which were created on both sides. However, for the sake of accuracy, it is essential to distinguish between the international coalitions which were tied to the domestic forces, as well as the actual domestic coalitions themselves.

A. International

In view of the variety of international tensions and disputes which characterized the 1960s—an important decade in what has become known to the historians as the "Cold War"—any local conflict almost inevitably become internationalized, and so it was with Yemen.

The foreign participants' motives were quite diverse and involved "principles" and concerns often quite distant from the issues as perceived by the Yemenis. For example, those who supported the imam and the *ancien régime* were concerned with such issues as the model for the export of revolution which it seemed to represent (Jordan), the consequences of revolutionary Arab nationalism as a threat to an Arab minority and the country's influence in a subregion of the Middle East (Iran, and the Persian Gulf), or closer to home, as a threat to the continued existence of a traditional Arab monarchy

(Saudi Arabia). Other more traditional political systems saw an increased risk to their stability and influence as a result of the existence and stated objectives of the Yemeni republic: Morocco, in the Middle East, and Great Britain, among Western powers.

On the other hand, the republic's supporters also had multiple motives. The Soviet Union and other states in its Bloc, which provided most of the arms and equipment as well as the credits needed to finance their purchase, seem to have had at least two distinct motives: first, an expansion of Soviet influence into what was perceived as a highly strategic area of the globe (i.e., the Red Sea Basin, Bab al-Mandab, and the Horn of Africa, extending even into the Indian Ocean), and second, promoting the image and influence of the Soviet Union as an ally of the Arab states in their "battle" against Western imperialism and colonialism in the Middle Eastern region. These motives presumably also explain Soviet policy toward South Yemen, given the role of the British there, and the (assumed, on the part of Western analysts) Soviet desire to obtain a naval base in the Arabian Sea.

In some respects, the most important power was the United States. President John F. Kennedy wished to distance himself from the alignments and policies of the previous Eisenhower administration, namely, support for conservative and monarchical regimes. Consequently, the Kennedy administration chose to recognize the republican government (in December 1962). The decision to recognize the revolutionaries had additional motives. The U.S. assumed that its bestowal of diplomatic recognition would be followed by others, that this would provide the opportunity and justification for Egypt to withdraw, and that this would, in turn, deter Saudi Arabia and Jordan from providing additional assistance to the royalist faction, especially since both of these countries were dependent upon American military assistance.

In the event, the United Nations also recognized the republican government and turned over the UN seat to them, and some 50 additional states followed the American lead in granting recognition. However, Great Britain was not among them, Egypt did not withdraw, and the Saudis did not terminate their support.

In fact, the American role was less than illustrious—both in terms of its analysis of the issues involved, and its implementation of mechanisms designed to ameliorate the conflict. The additional motives and policies will be discussed in greater detail below (see section 4, "The Role of Third Parties").

B. Domestic

Multiple motives were at work among the domestic participants, including old grievances and jealousies involving land, water, prestige, influence, resources, and the like; occasionally real principles were involved, for example, concerning the rights and privileges of groups, sects, and the like; last but not least, there were individuals (with followings) who had their own agendas, some of which were quite principled, others of which were only of immediate benefit to the individuals involved. The political life of Yemen has, in any event, revolved around multiple motives for thousands of years; in recent years, the political and social influence of the tribal groups seem to have been the most prominent.

In the case of Yemen, the civil war brought to the surface disputes over land, tax policy, commercial and trade policy, religion, water, various and assorted civil and criminal grievances and conflicts between families, clans, tribes, and tribal confederations, the role of the government in conflict resolution, etc. In many instances, these issues were raised only when domestic participants (villages, tribes, etc.) were asked or coerced into taking sides.

The war, in addition, produced a number of other, less admirable motives for participation: the size of the payment offered by other parties to the conflict (domestic and/or foreign), the nature of the weaponry being offered as an inducement, the choice of affiliation by a traditional opponent or rival in the domestic arena, specific individual grievances against the personnel or policies of the old government, etc. In addition, there were offenses committed against traditional morality and principle such as violations of the principle of *hijra* (sanctuary/refuge) by the Egyptians and/or the republicans; the indiscriminate use of violence against other participants (allies), including poison gas, torture, massacre of innocent civilians in order to intimidate opponents, as well as real or imagined slights to tribal prestige, honor, etc.

It is possible to argue (Dresch, 1989) that the sheer scale of foreign support dwarfed the old complex of motives—social, economic and political; on the other hand, any full account of the war has to take into account these additional motivations which remained relatively "pure," localized, and often rooted in tribal rights and laws. The result was that some tribal confederations found themselves split, with some clans/elements siding with the royalists, and some with the republicans. There are too many instances to tally, moreover, of tribes switching their allegiances, often during the course of the conflict—sometimes for base reasons, sometimes on matters of principle.

Among the non-tribal portion of the population, the division of support was relatively clear cut and obvious. The Shafi'i portion of the population, which owed no religious allegiance to the imams and which had, in fact, been disadvantaged by many of the imams' policies, overwhelmingly supported the republic. Since the two main sects are to a large degree geographically distinct, this meant that the south and southwestern areas of the country, where the Shafi'is are clearly in the majority, were firmly pro-republican. More importantly—for the outcome—was the fact that the Zaydi population was divided in its loyalties to the republic and the imamate; some very important Zaydi tribal leaders elected to support the republic (for various motives). (This makes it possible to entertain the argument that had the Zaydis been united, they would have succeeded in retaining the imamate, in at least some form.) In many instances, Zaydi tribes and tribal leaders invoked no more elevated principle in their decision concerning political affiliation than who paid more, or who provided the better weaponry to the troops. In other instances, however, there *were* more elevated principles at work: traditional loyalty to the imamate, defense of what was perceived as Yemeni, as opposed to the "foreign" system and policies associated with the Egyptians, etc.

The important point which needs to be made, in sum, is that the domestic coalitions and alignments were, in whole or in part, influenced as much by external participants and motives—at least at the outset of the conflict—as they were by internal ones: who could and would provide money, weapons, and other supplies (including food, clothing, etc.). It was only later, as the Yemenis became increasingly alienated from their foreign advisors, supporters, and suppliers, that more clearly Yemeni motives and goals began to influence the process which eventually led to a settlement.

The most important process of coalition building during the conflict was on the side of the republicans. This is not to suggest that there were no differences of opinion among the royalists, either with respect to goals, or the desirability of negotiations. However, it took longer for the republicans to admit to themselves that they could not completely defeat the royalists, and that the cost of continuing was too great in terms of Yemeni lives, resources, and culture. The royalists, though also originally convinced that they would be completely victorious, realized earlier than the republicans (no doubt due to the nature of the forces arrayed against them—domestic and foreign) that the only realistic conclusion to the conflict was negotiations.

The "troubles" of the republican side begin with the development of their dependence upon their Egyptian allies and supporters, without whom, of course, the republic would have been defeated rather early in the conflict. When it became obvious, at least to some Yemenis, that a resolution of the conflict was not possible unless various (Yemeni) "hardliners" and Egyptian advisors were eliminated from positions where they could thwart or at least seriously inhibit negotiations between royalists and republicans, real progress began to be made.

C. The Process of Negotiations

The financial, diplomatic, military, and domestic political costs associated with the conflict led the two major external participants, Egypt and Saudi Arabia, to begin the process of extricating themselves relatively early, i.e., only months after their first intervention. However, they both wanted extrication *and* the political victory of the party they were supporting. It took about two years before extrication became the top priority, instead of something to be accomplished as a side-effect of seeing one's Yemeni ally emerge victorious.

On the other hand, both of the Yemeni groupings similarly believed that a complete victory was inevitable, if, of course, the appropriate aid were provided. It took the Yemeni participants a few years to reach the conclusion that continuation of the conflict was a greater evil than compromising on the characteristics of a new political order.

The first maneuvres actually took place in 1963 but resulted in nothing more than mutual recriminations and similar accusations. The first efforts by outsiders, the United States and the United Nations, to act as "neutral" mediators were also complete failures. It was not until the Second Arab League Summit Conference, in September 1964, some two years after the start of hostilities, that direct negotiations between Egypt and Saudi Arabia took place; these led to a meeting on neutral ground (Erkwit, Sudan) in November 1964, at which time a national congress in Yemen, to be attended by representatives from all sides, was proposed. This congress never took place due to significant disagreement in the ranks of the republicans over the role of the Egyptians—the first clear signal that there were doubts concerning the policies of the republic's major supporter.

There was, however, an important development within republican ranks as a result: the rise of what became known as the "Third Force," a group of well-respected republican figures who reached the conclusion that negotiations with the royalists were not only desirable but necessary, since only a compromise solution was possible. A number of secret talks between elements of the republican and royalist sides took place in 1964 and 1965; that they were not universally approved was evident in the reactions of the Egyptians and those republicans who remained intransigent (for example, Abdullah al-Sallal, one of the original conspirators and organizers). This disapproval, however, went even further on occasion: one of Yemen's most respected statesmen, poets, and long-time opponents of the imamate, Muhammad Mahmud al-Zubayri, who was also an organizer of the Third Force, was found assassinated (presumably by Egyptian elements) shortly after the existence of the secret talks was discovered.

One could argue that his death was not in vain: his long-time associate, Ahmad Muhammad Nu'man, organized a National Peace Conference shortly thereafter, at which he tried to organize all republic supporters who were prepared to compromise and talk to the royalists. The result of this meeting, held at Khamir in May 1965, was a conference in Ta'if, Saudi Arabia, in August, attended by more than 200 republican and royalist delegates. The message to both Egypt and Saudi Arabia seemed clear: a substantial number of the Yemeni elites were prepared to work out a compromise without Egyptian and Saudi participation.

Evidently the pace and direction of the meetings affected Egypt and Saudi Arabia: President Nasir and King Faysal met in Jidda (also in August) in order to work out their own plan for a settlement of the conflict. Their joint proposal, announced two days later, was detailed, comprehensive, seemingly explicit, and included provisions for a plebiscite on the form of government, a cease-fire, withdrawal of troops, etc., as well as subsequent conferences to implement them. And, much to the surprise of many, the first of these conferences, at Harad (November) actually took place, and the cease-fire held. Attended by neither al-Sallal (who clearly disapproved) nor the imam, it did have representatives of all parties.

The optimism which first prevailed was soon dispelled, however, when it became obvious to the attending Yemenis that the Jidda Agreement had eliminated both the republic and the imamate, and that the delegates were there solely to choose a governmental form which was neither. The delegates were soon deadlocked over the form of government, the technicalities of the plebiscite, and the form of any transitional government.

Other events soon changed the mind of President Nasir about coercing the republicans into accepting the agreement; the change in Egypt's policies naturally resulted in a change in Saudi policy as well. The first of these events was the largest sale of military equipment in many years to Saudi Arabia by the U.S. and the U.K. Since it included many types of sophisticated equipment, including jet aircraft, it seemed designed to improve significantly Saudi Arabia's military strength and its ability to re-export material at a critical juncture in relations between Egypt and Saudi Arabia, as well as in Yemen.

Second, the USSR decided to supply the republic with military equipment and advisors independently of Egypt; evidently, this gave some of the republic's leaders the confidence and ability to resist Egypt's pressure to compromise with the royalists. At the same time, however, the promise of Soviet support independent of Egyptian control seems to have convinced the Egyptian president that only by keeping the initiative in the defense of the republic could the threat of Soviet penetration and intervention in Arab affairs be limited.

In other words, the actions of outside powers had immediate repercussions and effects upon the policies of the participants in the Yemeni civil war; in this case, they undermined what had seemed to be the first real joint effort to bring outside intervention to an end. For the long term, however, the most important side-effect was the increasing perception among the Yemenis themselves that they were becoming pawns in the political games of others.

Negotiations and other maneuvres of various kinds continued throughout the following two years; most of them can be characterized as desultory and primarily designed to gain a public relations or indirect military advantage in the Yemeni theatre. It was not until 1967 that meaningful negotiations involving Egypt once more took place, and then directly as a result of the Egyptian defeat in the "June War" of that year. The magnitude of the defeat, and its consequences, made the Egyptian presence in Yemen untenable. At the Khartoum Summit Conference (August 1967), President Nasir agreed to withdraw all Egyptian forces from Yemen before the end of the year—thereby guaranteeing his receipt of Saudi subsidies for his severely damaged economy. The last Egyptian troops were withdrawn from Yemen before the end of November.

Unfortunately, this did not result in increased Saudi security, nor did it accomplish Saudi goals in Yemen: Syria, Algeria and the USSR stepped in to fill the weapons and financial requirements of the republic.

Once again external events impinged upon and directly affected the policy options of the participants, this time developments in South Yemen. At the same time that the two major outside participants appeared willing to compromise, a new set of circumstances arose which forestalled a settlement: the British withdrew from their South Arabian holdings (the Crown Colony of Aden and the Aden Protectorates), and handed over the reins of power to the National Liberation Front—no friend of Saudi interests in southern Arabia, and considerably more radical in its orientation than the republicans of North Yemen. The Saudis saw themselves required to make another effort to dislodge the republicans, and essentially agreed to fund one last effort on the part of the royalists to accomplish this end. When it failed, for the usual constellation of reasons (see below), King Faysal decided that it would be more prudent and rational to seek an accommodation with the republicans of Sana'a, clearly a more moderate group than the NLF.

For the next two and one-half years, the two sides settled into a rough stalemate—though not the classic "hurting stalemate." The royalist effort was undermined by its own inconsistencies with respect to goals and tactics, its internal rivalries, its operations in the relatively isolated and difficult mountain fastnesses of the north, and its subordination to Sunni (Saudi) financial and military assistance. The republicans, on the other hand, were plagued by sectarian and ideological differences and rivalries, not to mention conflicts within their ranks over the relationships with their foreign advisors and suppliers.

Apparently the primary, if not the only, point of agreement among a significant and presumably majority element on both sides was the opposition to any further foreign intrusion or manipulation of the Yemeni conflict for external purposes. There were, as late as the end of 1968 and early 1969, still significant opportunities for the royalists to defeat the republicans (e.g. the siege of Sana'a, which was resisted by a combination of republican and Soviet actions). This effort seems to have been the last effort which the Saudis were prepared to fund; when the usual list of royalist problems enabled them to "snatch defeat from the jaws of victory," the heart seems to have gone out of both the Saudi and the royalist effort. In March of 1969, the imam's deputy, Prince Muhammad ibn Husayn, the strongest and most able leader of the royalists, resigned his position and abandoned the cause. In the meantime, of no small importance, the moderate and almost exclusively Zaydi republicans had managed to defeat the Left (mostly Shafi'i) decisively in a battle for control of the republic. It does not seem inappropriate to suggest that the final compromise, worked out with Saudi encouragement in the Spring of 1970, was in part easier to achieve precisely because it was overwhelmingly Zaydis discussing the issue with Zaydis.

It would not be possible at this point to list all of the many factions which characterized both sides; this would require a detailed listing of the tribes of Yemen and their many sub-units and the changes-of-side which occurred between 1962 and 1970. It is quite likely that no one could (or ever did) have this information. The important point is that the constellation on each side, because of the nature of the tribes in Yemen, really consisted of many dozens of individual "nations" which saw their interests affected by the many cross-currents which characterized the war, and changed their allegiance(s) accordingly.

This important fact leads to a few hypotheses concerning the ending of civil conflict based on the Yemeni experience:

H1:   The larger the number of factions within each side, the greater the opportunity to reach a compromise solution, since each side's factions will find it easier to find someone on the other side with whom to undertake discussions and negotiations.

H2:   The larger the number of "players" who are recognized as part of the game, the easier it will be to develop at least transitional peace arrangements, since there will always be someone with whom to discuss/negotiate.

H3:   Political figures who do *not* have complete political security, i.e., who do not have unalloyed support either in the military or in the civilian sector, but who have enough to remain active players, will be more prepared to enter into compromise arrangements in order to protect whatever influence, power, or perquisites might still be available in any post-settlement arrangement.

3. The Military Balance in the Field

Although it would be utterly fallacious to argue that weapons alone cause conflicts, they are nevertheless one of the factors which need to be analyzed if one is to understand civil conflicts. Clearly, the types, amounts, and capabilities of weaponry will be an important factor in the decision to continue or terminate a conflict. In the case of Yemen, it is definitely the case that the winning side, the republicans, had access to more sophisticated weaponry and more of it.

When the conflict began in 1962, the typical weapon of the Yemeni combatant on both sides was a World War II Mauser, a Springfield, or, almost as often, a single-shot rifle of pre-World War I vintage. With the onset of the civil war, and the subsequent participation of a number of states with access to much more modern weaponry, the types and level of sophistication of the weapons used in the conflict increased dramatically. Within just weeks and months, the number and variety of semi-automatic and automatic weapons introduced significantly affected the fighting (and the outcome of some battles).

In addition, entirely new types of weaponry were introduced: mortars, machine-guns (various calibres), bazookas, grenade launchers, recoilless rifles, and major artillery pieces. For example, by mid-1964, even the royalists were receiving 81mm mortars, 75mm recoilless rifles, 105mm and 155mm howitzers of Russian and Chinese origin. Although at the outset only the Egyptians and their republican allies were equipped with Soviet (and Bloc) weaponry, by 1964 by far the largest part of the military equipment being used was of "Eastern" origin. This is not to suggest that Western weaponry was not used: since Saudi Arabia, Jordan, and Iran were primarily responsible for the small arms and lighter equipment being used by the royalists, much of it *was* of Western origins.

Inevitably, considering the terrain and the ebb and flow of the conflict, the forces of one side or other overran the supply depots, caches, villages, forts, etc. of the other side. This meant that by war's end there was an incredible mixture of weaponry on both sides. One must add, however, that the preferred weapon of the tribal forces associated with both sides was the AK–47 (Kalashnikov) in its many versions—primarily because of its firepower and reliability (a function of the simplicity of its design). In fact, the biggest problem was not so much weaponry as supplying ammunition of the proper calibre and manufacture to the levies, tribesmen, mercenaries, and soldiers allied with one's side. More than one battle was lost or won based upon which side had an adequate amount of ammunition.

The Yemeni civil war, however, was not fought solely on the ground. This was partly due to the terrain, which made armored personnel carriers (APCs) and tanks as well as jeep-mounted recoilless rifles less than useful on many occasions. The terrain indeed practically guaranteed that airpower would be employed; although there was some use of fighters, the most important weapon available to the republic which the royalists did not have was the bomber, specifically the Su–7 fighter bomber, Tu–16 medium jet bombers, and especially the Il–28 light jet bomber, which proved useful in maneuvering around the mountainous valleys of the north. It is difficult to be precise on such matters, of course, but it seems legitimate to argue that the airstrikes of the Egyptians against royalist strongholds in the northern mountains were a major factor in weakening the strongpoints which the royalists created as base camps, supply centers, or command centers (including the location of the imam).

Briefly, then, the Egyptians were able to monopolize the skies; further, their ready access to APCs and some tanks to cover their movements along major roads and tracks on many occasions gave them a significant advantage. The same may be said for their use of artillery. On the other hand, their dependence upon hardware often left them vulnerable to the effective guerrilla tactics used by the tribal warriors of the imam, who knew the mountains and effectively exploited the defiles, passes, and treacherous conditions to their advantage. At the same time, the use by the Egyptians of poison gas delivered by light jet bombers seems to have succeeded only in totally alienating many Yemeni elements (republican as well as royalist) from the Egyptians. (The use of gas was always officially denied; however, it was acknowledged on the ground in Yemen, and plentiful evidence was provided by correspondents and neutral observers.)

The intuitively attractive concept of the "hurting stalemate" does not provide much explanatory power in the case of the Yemen conflict. It would be fair to characterize a number of distinct periods in the development of the conflict as essentially stalemates; they were, however, periods during which time the parties obtained new sources of support (weaponry), re-cemented or re-invigorated various support systems (diplomatic, military, etc.), or engaged in desultory negotiations in order to "score points" in the international community or with potential allies or significant powers. Neither side, in these situations, felt compelled by the situation (or its projection into the near future) to negotiate an end to the conflict seriously. Neither side, in other words, was suffering sufficiently—in terms of casualties, economic costs, or whatever other criteria might be deemed relevant—to negotiate a settlement seriously; both believed that an extension of the conflict would lead to their eventual victory.

In sum, the types and quantities of military equipment available to the two sides demonstrated great discrepancies, but the republicans had access to far more, more varied, and more sophisticated equipment. However, in the final analysis, equipment and access to it were not the deciding factors in the conflict or its eventual settlement.

4. The Role of Third Parties

Third-party intervention and participation in the Yemeni civil war was basically of two types: (1) aid and assistance to the combatants and (2) mediation efforts.

The role of Egypt, and the "progressive" forces which were its allies and supporters in defense of the republic, and the role of Saudi Arabia, and the "conservative" forces which were allied with it in defense of the imamate, have been covered above and need no further review. In an effort to be complete, however, it is probably relevant to add that no potentially important third party failed to become involved, either directly or indirectly.

For example: one of the "superpowers" of the time was involved on each side; all of the "progressive" regional states at the time were involved (Egypt, Iraq, Algeria, Syria); all of the "conservative" regional actors were involved (Saudi Arabia, Jordan, Iran, Morocco). However, the majority of European states chose not to get involved directly, with the single exception of Great Britain, presumably because of its extensive regional interests at the time (in the Gulf states, including Oman, as well as South Yemen).

Only two external parties attempted to mediate the conflict: the United States and the United Nations. Neither was successful; as the brief summary which follows shows, neither was really interested in playing the role of neutral mediator or arbiter.

A. *The United States*

The U.S. had recognized the republic in December 1962 as a result of a complex of motives, including (a) the desire of the Kennedy administration to demonstrate its support for progressive rather than conservative monarchical regimes; (b) the desire to exercise a moderating influence on the republic at a time when it began to receive Soviet military assistance; (c) the desire to give President Nasir an opportunity to withdraw gracefully, which it was presumed would be possible as a result of the American decision (to recognize the republic), which it was assumed would be followed by a similar decision on the part of other governments; and (d) the assumption that the American decision would cause supporters of the imamate to limit or even end their assistance since all (Saudi Arabia, Jordan, etc.) were dependent almost entirely upon the United States for their military equipment.

The American decision did not result in all of the expected consequences; although the United Nations and some 50 countries followed the American lead, Great Britain did not. And Saudi Arabia, which clearly feared the consequences of expanded Egyptian influence and a strong republican government in Yemen, was unwilling to cease its aid. Furthermore, President Nasir did not withdraw his troops, since he interpreted the events in the light of his experience with Syria in the United Arab Republic. He believed that the disintegration of the first attempt at Arab unity was not due to a failure of leadership or commitment on the part of Egypt, rather it was due to the treachery of imperialist Western powers in league with Arab reactionaries; it was, therefore, unthinkable to permit these same forces once again to stand in the way of bringing progressive government and ideas to the Arab world.

Despite their mutual antagonism and recriminations, Egypt and Saudi Arabia first expressed a desire to end the conflict by early 1963; since their opinions over the most effective means were at variance, it was decided that only a neutral mediator might be able to bring about an effective agreement.

The United States first attempted to fill this role, and at the same time brought in the United Nations for the same purpose. President

Kennedy sent former Ambassador Ellsworth T. Bunker to the area to undertake the necessary negotiations, which were intended to produce a disengagement agreement between Egypt and Saudi Arabia. Bunker, because of his circumspect and practiced methods, was able to get the two countries to agree on a vague program which would be implemented by the United Nations. On the other hand, since he failed even to meet with any representatives of the royalists, they were understandably reluctant to accept the United States as a neutral mediator.

B. The United Nations

The UN sent its own emissary, Ralph Bunche, then Undersecretary for Special Political Affairs. He also made no effort to speak with any royalist representatives, and indeed his actions were seen as so one-sided that the Saudis even refused him permission to enter the country.

The Egyptians and the republicans, after their consultations with the U.S. and UN emissaries concerning mediation, apparently decided that the visit of the two "mediators" was an opportunity to prove the extent of their control, as well as the justness of their cause. As a result, the Egyptians dispatched additional troop units and equipment to Yemen at the same time that the republicans launched a campaign against two major towns in the eastern regions which had long been in the hands of the royalists. Using aerial and armored forces, the Egyptians drove the royalists out; immediately thereafter, the republicans and Egyptians conducted Bunche to the area to demonstrate the extent of republican control in the east. Mr. Bunche returned to Cairo, indicating that he had been most impressed by the "seriousness of purpose" and the strength of the republic. (Shortly thereafter, of course, the royalists were able to return to the two strongholds.)

The result of the two visits was a decision by the United Nations Secretary General, U Thant, to create a United Nations Yemen Observation Mission (UNYOM) to oversee the agreement for which Bunker had laid the cornerstone: the phased withdrawal of Egyptian troops in return for a cessation of all aid on the part of Saudi Arabia to the royalists and a prohibition on the use of Saudi territory as a staging post for royalist incursions and attacks on republican positions. The two countries agreed, in addition, to permit UN observers access to all areas of the country necessary to insure compliance.

U Thant selected as UNYOM commander Major General Carl von Horn, formerly of the Palestine Truce Supervisory Organization. Von Horn spent a week discussing his and the UN's role in Cairo, Jidda, and various cities in Yemen, and prepared a less-than-optimistic but complete report on what he believed would be necessary to carry out the UN mandate. Accordingly, in July of 1963, UNYOM officially began operations. However, it was evident from the outset that the size of the mission (200 men), combined with the nature of the terrain, made it impossible for UNYOM to carry out the duties assigned to it (i.e., to attest to no further Saudi aid and the phased withdrawal of Egyptian troops). Within two months, von Horn submitted his resignation, complaining that UNYOM's work was hampered by incompetence in the UN Secretariat, neglect and dismissal of his reports and suggestions concerning the safety of his men, and the unwillingness to provide adequate funds for equipment, maintenance, etc.

One of von Horn's most revealing complaints about the UN's policies with respect to Yemen was that the UNYOM was prohibited from having any contact with the royalists. It is difficult to imagine a more unrealistic directive: the chief of a UN mission designed to help bring about the end of a civil conflict being prohibited from making contact with one of the parties to the conflict.

One is forced to entertain at least two conclusions:

(1) The U.S. was not interested in acting as a neutral mediator; rather, from all appearances, the U.S. had made up its mind concerning the conflict and its outcome in late 1962. Then, when the anticipated conclusion failed to develop, U.S. policy seems to have been designed to force reality to match preconceived notions.

(2) The UN was no more interested than the U.S. in determining the facts of the situation, or in behaving in an even-handed (neutral) fashion. In fact, it appears to have been completely subordinate to the United States as far as its policies and assessments were concerned.

Some minor powers managed, at least in part, to bring the major outside participants to participate in negotiations. President Ahmad Ben Bella of Algeria and President Abd al-Karim al-Arif of Iraq acted as intermediaries between President Nasir and Prince Faysal in bringing about the talks held at Erkwit, in November of 1964. The Crown Prince of Kuwait helped to mediate between these same figures and bring about the Jidda Conference.

(NB: The United Nations mission under von Horn consisted of personnel from Sweden, Ireland, the U.S., Guatemala, Britain, and Canada; it was, however, materially assisted and dependent upon a mobile reconnaissance unit of some 122 Yugoslavs, whose movements and reports were controlled by a political commissar who got his orders from his government, which in essence got its orders from the Soviet Union. One consequence, of course, was that the reports and the activities were extremely prejudicial to the interests and actions of the royalists.)

5. The Post-Conflict Polity

It has been suggested that the nature of the polity which is created through the resolution of a civil conflict will affect its chances of "success." There are at least two problems of verification with this thesis:

(1) Setting a standard of longevity without a renewed outbreak of violence; in other words, how much time must pass before any political violence takes place and yet have the new system be declared a "success"?

(2) What kinds of actions merit consideration as a "resumption of violence"? Do assassinations count? What kinds of domestic violence—rebellions, riots, etc.—count? Does passive resistance to government policy count? What if the government does not control all of the territory of the polity, yet there is no overt violence between the government and those who control the other areas?

The civil war in Yemen and its resolution present some interesting alternatives to other civil conflicts on a number of characteristics. For example: the Compromise of 1970 clearly integrated the former rivals into the new polity (which was still called the Yemen Arab Republic). Some important members of the royalist entourage (though *not* members of the old imamic family) were included in the new government, and one prominent royalist was included in the new three-member Republican Council, the highest executive organ of the new state. Moreover, royalists were integrated at lower levels into the administrative agencies and bureaus of the new government, at least in part because these individuals (qadis and sayyids) had education and expertise which the republic could use.

Another issue which intuitively seems relevant is the disarmament of participants—both in terms of actual weaponry as well as psychological orientation (i.e., to the use of weapons in order to resolve socio-economic and political issues). As far as the actual equipment is concerned, the issue never arises in Yemen since the average Yemeni male has always carried a weapon. It was not until the late 1970s that the three major cities were able to prohibit the public carrying of firearms; in the remainder of the country, it is quite common to see individuals carrying weapons (automatic rifles, especially). The only difference between the pre-civil war period and its aftermath is in the quality (type) of weapons being carried. In other words, no effort whatsoever was made to disarm the losing side; to have attempted to do so would have meant a resumption of the conflict (perhaps even along different lines).

The second issue, is, of course, a bit more difficult; since an eight-year civil war has the inevitable tendency to promote the use of arms as a mechanism to cope with various types of social, economic and political disagreements, how does one judge whether or not the participants have abandoned the psychological tendency to employ weapons as a mechanism for conflict resolution? One side-effect of the civil war was perhaps inevitable: the inclination of the armed forces to participate in politics. Although many of the cabinets since 1970 have been dominated by civilians (especially technocrats), there is little doubt that the Yemeni military has become the most important domestic player in the political arena. On the other hand, its role has been in the nature of a background condition, the framework within which the civilian technocrats and political figures carry on the "game of politics."

This is not to suggest that there has been complete domestic peace since the end of the civil war. A complete summary of events since that time requires acknowledgement of two sets of circumstances in which old disputes and differences flared anew.

(1) There were two political assassinations in 1978; in both instances it was the president of the republic who was killed. The perpetrators were never found; their motives have always been unclear. It would appear, however, that both assassinations had more to do with Yemen's foreign relations, especially with South Yemen, than with domestic intrigues, political differences, or conflicts.

(2) The old political Left, which had been largely decimated in the late 1960s when the republicans fought each other for control of the republic, emerged in the 1970s as the National Democratic Front. It attracted a number of other, smaller groupings with a va-

riety of grievances against the republic and its policies, and was funded by the People's Democratic Republic of Yemen (PDRY), i.e., South Yemen, governed at the time by a radical Marxist regime. After numerous skirmishes and disruptive activities on the part of the Front, the government decided upon a frontal assault on the positions and activities of the Front, and in 1982 essentially eliminated it and drove its few remnants into exile in the PDRY.

On the other hand, especially since the defeat of the NDF, the Ali Abdullah Salih regime has encouraged the development of civilian institutions at both the local and national level, and since the mid-1980s, there have been free elections to the resulting variety of bodies.

By the end of the 1980s, the Ali Abdullah Salih regime had succeeded in integrating nearly all elements of the society into the political system; the only outstanding exceptions were the al-Wazir family, and most of the Hamid al-Dins. Indeed, the old qadi families and many of the sayyid families had already been integrated and become an integral part of the intelligentsia of the new system. Even the tribal elements of the north had been more or less included (though occasional incidents of opposition to governmental policy and administration were still a feature of the system in the late 1980s).

One of the most important criteria by which to judge the successor regime to a civil war would seem to be its ability to meet "new challenges," i.e., cope with the variety of social, economic as well as political problems which any government must confront and attempt to resolve. The Ali Abdullah Salih regime has had to confront a particularly thorny and varied set of "challenges" during its twelve years in power (as of 1990).

In the foreign arena, the primary challenges came from various efforts from Saudi Arabia and the PDRY either to weaken or seriously alter the government's policies on a number of issues (both domestic and foreign). This included two wars with the PDRY (1972 and 1979), as well as numerous campaigns in the northern areas of the country to establish the government's legitimacy and control.

In the domestic arena, the primary challenges were in the economic sphere, due to the fundamentally weak economy and its dependence upon foreign subsidies, loans, and aid packages, and in the political sphere where the government sought to gain legitimacy and establish its authority over various domestic groups (e.g. the tribes) and regions, as well as provide the population with the goods and services which it demanded. Perhaps the most important challenge, however, was the search for legitimacy, that is, to move beyond simply military might as the basis for the regime. In this sense, the regime has done considerably better than most post-civil war systems: it has supported the creation of various popular organizations at the local and national level, and permitted, even encouraged, free elections to these bodies.

At the international level, in 1990 it succeeded in putting what appears to be a permanent end to the differences with the PDRY by entering into a unification agreement, creating a united Republic of Yemen, in which new state there will be political parties and free elections (which include the participation of women both as candidates and voters).

An overall assessment would have to be that the regime had succeeded very effectively at coping with a large number of thorny and rather varied challenges.

Conclusions and Commentary

Some assessment of these various factors and the information included above seems appropriate.

The first and possibly the most important question is: what is the primary reason for the ending of the conflict? What factor was most important in the thinking and behavior of the participants in deciding to end the war?

In the answer to this question, we need to distinguish between the motives and behavior of the outside intervenors, and the motives and actions of the Yemeni combatants.

The actions of Egypt and Saudi Arabia appear to have been motivated by a number of factors: (1) their perceptions of the consequences of the victory or defeat of their particular side in the Yemeni conflict upon the political situation in the Arab World; (2) their perceptions of the consequences of the victory or defeat of their ally upon their own situation/position in the Arab World; (3) the economic costs of continuing to support their client/faction in the Yemeni conflict; (4) their perceptions of the consequences of the conflict and its outcome on the position of the Soviet Union and Great Britain in the Middle East in general, and in the Red Sea region in particular. Last and, it would appear, least: (5) their relations with the side they supported in Yemen itself.

The actions of the Yemenis themselves are perhaps a bit more clear, and it may be argued, eventually significantly affected the policies and actions of their supporters. Clearly, Yemeni motives and policies changed during the conflict, from the assumption of completely defeating the opponent to the position that negotiations with the opponent were the only feasible and possible outcome to the conflict.

What was it, in the final analysis, that made it possible for the Yemenis to come to an agreement among themselves, and directly or indirectly make the departure of their various allies and supporters from the Yemeni theatre of operations the only feasible choice?

Five factors appear to be a reasonable summary.

(1) The behavior of the Egyptians, which succeeded in alienating increasing numbers of Yemenis, most especially those in the republican camp. Their military actions and policies had already thoroughly alienated the royalists; pronounced cruelty and barbarous practices in field operations led to retaliatory actions by the tribesmen, which only further infuriated the Egyptians, producing a spiral of vicious behavior which meant that only rarely were prisoners taken.

Their actions and policies toward their Yemeni allies eventually produced the impetus toward settlement with the royalists: an almost complete unwillingness to permit differences of opinion within the ranks of republicans; their unwavering support (until the very end) of the incompetent and slavish Abdullah al-Sallal; and their countenancing a variety of disgraceful policies designed to stamp out flexible approaches to the conflict. This included the assassination of Muhammad al-Zubagri and the incarceration of such respected figures as Ahmad Nu'man when these individuals would not accept the uncompromising and fruitless policies of their Egyptian allies. The republicans increasingly turned on the Egyptians, considering them unrealistic, arrogant, and meddlesome in the extreme, and decided to use other (often secret) means to come to terms with the royalists.

(2) The policies of the Saudis. Although the essence of reaction and opposition to progressive forces because they provided military and

financial aid to the royalists, it is interesting that they were viewed with considerable suspicion by the royalists. What motives could a Sunni political system/state have for providing aid to a Shi'a cause? The fact that the imam and some of his advisors appeared to be subservient to Saudi interests and goals raised considerable suspicion among some of the traditionally strong supporters of the imamate/royalist cause. Within the living memory of many participants in the conflict, Saudi Arabia had taken the oasis of Najran and the province of Asir—both of which are considered integral parts of Yemen by Yemenis.

It should be noted, however, that there were considerable differences between the two Saudi monarchs during whose tenure the Yemeni civil war took place. Until November 1964, the king of Saudi Arabia was Sa'ud ibn Abd al-Aziz, whose reputation was substantially tarnished by his profligate and unsophisticated ways and policies; he was replaced by his brother Faysal ibn Abd al-Aziz, whose political skills were substantially greater than those of Sa'ud. (One quick indicator: King Faysal never demanded the return to the throne of Imam Muhammad al-Badr, presumably because he recognized the futility of this as a goal; his purpose was to have a reasonably sympathetic buffer state created in (North) Yemen to counter the position and policies of the South Yemenis.)

(3) The presence of the Europeans (of various nationalities). What motives drove Christian (and atheist) Europeans to participate in a conflict thousands of miles from their homelands? What did they hope to gain? To re-create their past empires in the Middle East? To humiliate Islam? To control resources which the Yemenis did not even know they had?

(4) The mercenaries. Clearly such persons were not to be trusted, since their loyalty and assistance were available for purchase; what would happen if the other side offered to pay more? Foreign mercenaries were only good as trainers in the use of sophisticated military equipment, since their advice on tactics was either irrelevant to the Yemeni context, or was possibly even designed to undermine or weaken the cause.

The obvious conclusion is that one of the most venerable hypotheses in the social sciences appears highly appropriate if not fully confirmed by the Yemeni civil war: an external threat or danger tends to submerge internal conflicts.

The Yemeni conflict, however, leads to a rather more specific hypothesis concerning foreign intervention:

H4:   Intervention by foreigners in a domestic conflict will produce a reaction among the indigenous population, in one or more of the following ways: (a) opposition to the continued presence of the foreigner; (b) growth in nationalist sentiment, i.e., a re-assertion of the particularistic features of the society and its culture which distinguish it from that of the intervenors (or any other system); (c) a concomitant growth in xenophobia, generally; and (d) an increased effort to use the indigenous culture as a basis for a settlement of differences in order to avoid further intervention and actions by the foreigner.

H5:   A civil conflict in a polity is likely to be resolved without a division of the polity into separate successor states because both sides to the conflict, expecting to win after the war, prefer to inherit the population, territory, and resources of the entire state rather than accept only some portion thereof.

Because Yemen is characterized by so many clearly distinguishable geographic as well as ethnic divisions, and because for such a long period of time it was possible to characterize the conflict as a stalemate, there was a *de facto* division of the country. The republicans controlled the so-called "triangle" bounded by the three major urban concentrations of Sana'a, Ta'izz, and Hudaydah; the royalists controlled the north, northeast, northwest, and most of the eastern regions.

In fact, the distribution of political power after the compromise which ended the civil conflict very much resembled the *de facto* division existing during the stalemate; however, this is misleading. First, the royalists did not exist as an organized political force governing the areas theoretically under their control; rather, the "authorities" in these areas were the autonomous tribes—the same tribes which had insisted upon their autonomy under all previous governments and rulers.

Second, although the central government could not and did not control even 50% of the territory of the state during the night-time hours, it *was* increasingly able to show its control over access to the things which the population of all regions wanted: schools, clinics, roads, and piped water systems. As it demonstrated that it was able to deliver such services, and that significant decisions with respect to the supply of an increasing range of goods and services were being made in the urban centers, the areas over which it could not exercise direct control began to shrink. The tribal authorities simply could not compete.

Third, at least with respect to the eastern regions, the discovery of oil in what was long one of the most independent of areas resulted in a dramatic expansion of governmental authority.

The point, of course, is that governmental authority and power may not be solely a function of military prowess; in Yemen, the ability to provide the things the population wants is a far more important factor in the government's efforts to obtain legitimacy than its ability to field adequate police forces.

This leads to a few additional hypotheses:

H6: The successor government after a civil war must be able to demonstrate and provide a clear increase in the kinds of goods and services which the population believes it is entitled to or demands (no doubt at least in part to make up for the deprivations endured while the conflict was still in progress) or else face a renewed outbreak of civil violence.

H7: The conclusion of a civil conflict will not only raise expectations among the victors, who will expect to benefit concretely somehow from the sacrifices and costs paid—in status, prestige, jobs, income, access to goods and services, etc.; it is likely to raise the expectations of the defeated parties even higher, since there is no further justification whatever for the deprivations and losses associated with defeat or the conflict itself.

H8: A successor regime which cannot make peace effectively with its former opponents' supporters and allies will find itself in serious difficulty (economic and political), including the possibility of renewed conflict instituted by precisely these parties.

In the case of Yemen, the biggest problem was with the Saudis: since so many of the northern tribes were tied to the Saudis as a result of their acceptance of money and weapons, they were used to intervening in domestic policy. And, since the government was dependent upon Saudi financial (budgetary) assistance during these same years, the new government was considerably circumscribed in its policy options. It was not until Yemen began to export oil from its newly discovered fields that its government was able to exercise greater independence in both domestic and foreign policy without incurring the wrath of the Saudis, usually displayed through endemic resistance to governmental authority by such tribes as the Sufyan.

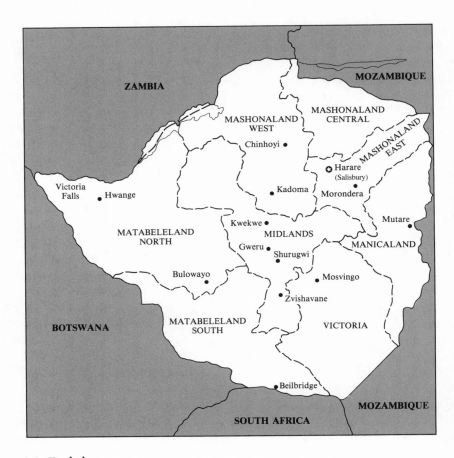

6.1 Zimbabwe

124

The End of the Zimbabwean Civil War

Stephen John Stedman

There is always something new coming out of Africa.—Pliny

At a time when Africa has become out of vogue for American political science, it has become a remarkable laboratory for the study of conflict resolution. At present in Africa three countries (Uganda, Zimbabwe, and Namibia) are reconstructing after civil wars—the latter two ended by negotiation, one country (Sudan) has reached agreements to end civil violence only to find itself in the throes of civil war again, and four other countries (Angola, Ethiopia, Mozambique, and South Africa) have undergone negotiations in the last year to end violence and bring about new political orders.

In this chapter I examine the Zimbabwean civil war and reconstruction.[1] It is a particularly compelling case to study because it is one of the few cases in the world of a mediated, negotiated settlement of a civil war. In the first section of this chapter I provide a general historical overview of the case. I then examine the successful negotiated termination of the Zimbabwean civil war of the 1970s and conclude by discussing events in Zimbabwe since the war ended in April 1980.

Historical Background

In the last sixty years the territory encompassing present-day Zimbabwe has had four different names—Southern Rhodesia, Rhodesia,

Zimbabwe-Rhodesia, and its current name—a fact that tells much about the lines of conflict in the country. The "self-governing" colony of Southern Rhodesia was a hybrid possession of the British Empire, somewhat akin to Bernard DeVoto's description of Texas—half horse and half alligator. Nominally under the control of the British, yet *de facto* ruled by its white settlers, Southern Rhodesia was very much the product of its namesake, Cecil Rhodes, who once said that if it had been in his power, he would have "colonized the stars." Rhodes, through force and chicanery against its African inhabitants, had established a foothold in the territory in the late 1800s. Rhodes' British South African Company had consolidated its rule there through a charter granted by Britain. A key turning point in the country's history took place in 1922 when its white settlers were given the opportunity to vote on the future of their new home. Their choices were to continue under the charter, join the Union of South Africa, or opt for self-government.

The majority of whites chose self-government in 1923. Now formally annexed to Britain, but with power devolved to its white settlers, Rhodesia achieved the anomalous status of "self-governing" colony. During its history a white minority that never amounted to more than five percent of the population ruled over and systematically oppressed the black majority in Southern Rhodesia. Southern Rhodesia's 1923 constitution, unlike that of South Africa, committed its peoples to a "color blind" franchise (O'Meara 1975, 8). Property and educational requirements, however, prevented almost all blacks from political participation. The whites extended their disenfranchisement of Africans to social and economic affairs. The most important resource to the people of Rhodesia was arable land, which from the beginning of the twentieth century had gradually come under the possession of the small European population. In 1930 the Land Apportionment Act legally segregated the holding of land, by giving Europeans the right to purchase in the most desirable agricultural regions. The remainder of the land was distributed to Africans. Ten percent of the land was set aside for those Africans with the resources and desire to compete in Rhodesia's Darwinian economic environment of the 1930s. The remaining 90 percent of African land was committed to communal farming in areas called the Tribal Trust lands.

This system of land rights was further codified in 1969 with the passage of the Land Tenure Act. The Act, which Rhodesians waved as a banner of their racial enlightenment, "equally" divided the land into 45 million acres for blacks and 45 million acres for whites. Given the discrepancy in farming populations between the two groups, this "equal" distribution provided the average white farmer 6,100 acres compared to seven acres for the average African farmer. This again tells only part of the story, for the most fertile, rich land was distributed to the whites, while the Africans were left parcels of arid, barren soil (Austin 1975).

The inequality in land holdings mirrored other important discrepancies between blacks and whites in Rhodesia in terms of jobs, wealth, health services, government expenditure on students, and access to education. In most cases such inequalities were reinforced through laws designed to deprive the black population of basic human rights. Far from seeing the system they had constructed as an affront to human dignity, most Rhodesians saw their relationship with the Africans as a "partnership" between "the black horse and the white rider" (Godfrey Huggins quoted in O'Meara 1975).

The white community, self-contained amidst an ocean of blacks, forged a world view that denied the intelligence and humanity of the African people. Most whites knew blacks only in the context of master and servant. In the 1950s a few whites, most of them members of families that had lived in Rhodesia since the 1920s, attempted to include blacks in the political process through a gradual reform of the election roll. This movement ended abruptly in the late 1950s as whites who had emigrated to Rhodesia during the post-World War II years came to dominate white politics. Such whites formed the nucleus of the racial supremacist Rhodesian Front, which would find its leader in Ian Smith. Smith and the Rhodesian Front dominated white politics in Rhodesia from the early 1960s on. One study estimated white liberals who opposed Smith never constituted more than 20 percent of the electorate (Hancock 1984).

The influence of new whites coming to Rhodesia cannot be underestimated. The bulk of the European population in Rhodesia were newcomers and, unlike their Afrikaner compatriots south of the border, could not claim the legitimation of "being African too." For most whites, the Rhodesian identity was forged in a compressed amount of time, perhaps thirty years. In the 1969 census, for example, there were 130,613 whites not born in Rhodesia as compared to 92,934 born in Rhodesia. When those whites under the age of twenty are subtracted from each category, giving us white adults eligible to vote, the numbers become even more dramatic: 115,362 European adults born outside of Rhodesia to only 29,785 Europeans adults who were Rhodesian born. Of those not born in Rhodesia, 49,585 came from South Africa, 52,468 came from the United Kingdom, and another 10,000 more or so came from various former crown colonies that had achieved independence (Rhodesia, Central Statistical Office 1971).

In the early 1960s Britain began pulling out of its African colonial possessions and gradually turning over power to the African populations. When formal British decolonization began to accelerate, the white minority government led by Prime Minister Ian Smith rebelled against the threat of British pressures for majority rule and unilaterally declared its independence (UDI) from Britain in 1965.

In the ensuing years a guerrilla war sporadically erupted against the white government of Rhodesia. The various liberation movements, however, were split by ideological and ethnic divisions. The three important actors were two parties with military strength—ZANU (Zimbabwe African National Union), founded by Ndabaningi Sithole and eventually led by Robert Mugabe, and ZAPU (Zimbabwe African Peoples Union), led by Joshua Nkomo—and a political party with a wide constituency—the ANC (African National Council) eventually led by Bishop Abel Muzorewa.

In the early stages of UDI Britain sought to negotiate with the Rhodesians on the terms of formal decolonization. Twice, in 1966 and 1967, in talks on the battleships *Tiger* and *Fearless*, British officials and Ian Smith failed to gain agreement on the question of independence. The British position, opposed bitterly by the white Rhodesians, was labelled NIBMAR (no independence before majority African rule).

In 1971 an agreement was reached between Sir Alec Douglas Home and Ian Smith that was to lead to the formal independence of Rhodesia—an agreement that put the likelihood of majority rule into the twenty-first century. The British, however, stipulated that the agreement had to pass a test of support from the black population of Rhodesia. To investigate the acceptability of the proposals the British formed the Pearce Commission, which was responsible for canvassing African opinion on the agreements. This marked the first time that Africans in Rhodesia were consulted regarding the future independence of their country. Since most of the black nationalist leaders (Nkomo, Sithole, Mugabe, and countless others) were in prison or in exile, the task of organizing opposition to the proposals fell on the shoulders of Abel Muzorewa, a United Methodist Bishop. The opposition campaign was a stunning success: the Pearce Commission reported that the overwhelming majority of Zimbabweans opposed the terms of the agreement, thereby sinking the Smith-Home pact.

The guerrilla war that had begun in 1965 had taken little toll on white Rhodesia until 1972. At the end of that year ZANLA (ZANU's army—the Zimbabwean National Liberation Army), using sanctuary in neighboring Mozambique, began implementing a strategy based on the politicization of the countryside and hit-and-run terrorist tactics against "soft" targets such as schools and farms. While the decision to intensify the war against the Rhodesian government posed a real security threat for the whites, two factors contributed to change the military situation in favor of the revolutionaries. First, the collapse of the Portuguese authorities in Mozambique in 1974–75 opened a 600 mile-long sanctuary for Zimbabwean guerrillas. Second, the draconian anti-terrorist activities of the white security forces drove tens of thousands of rural Zimbabweans into refugee status across the border in Mozambique. These refugees provided a pool of young and willing prospective guerrilla fighters against the white regime. By 1972 many Africans concluded that, "Whites must be led down the garden path to the place of slaughter. Morality does not come into it" (Zvobgo, quoted in Flower 1987a, 126).

Rhodesia's geography and the pattern of white settlement in the country produced a way of life and a regime susceptible to guerrilla war. The most recent census at the time (1969) showed a European population of 228,296 and an African population of approximately 5.4 million. While Rhodesia is a country of about 153,000 square miles (roughly the size of Montana), a little over 71 percent of the European population (163,182) lived in the four cities in Rhodesia with populations of over 45,000 (Salisbury, Bulawayo, Umtali, and Gwelo).[2] Salisbury alone contained 42 percent of the European sector. Another 31,000 Europeans lived in small towns and villages, which left approximately 33,500 Europeans in spread-out farming areas far removed from urban centers and other farms. The 1969 census put the number of Europeans who were "Economically Active . . . in Agriculture, Livestock Production, and Hunting" at 7,396 (Rhodesia, Central Statistical Office 1971). The amount of farming lands that were apportioned to Europeans in 1969 for farming amounted to 45 million acres (Bowman 1973, 12) or about 6,100 acres per farming European. Each isolated farm, not easily defended, became a target for guerrillas.

While the agricultural sector employed less than 4 percent of the European population, it was crucial for Rhodesia's economy. In 1975, for example, agriculture accounted for a little under 11.5 percent of the Gross Domestic Product (Rhodesia, Ministry of Finance 1975). Much of Rhodesia's agricultural crop was tobacco for export, bundled in disguised crates and shipped to a network of middle-men, all in a vast charade to beat international sanctions that were imposed in 1965 and 1968. While the Rhodesian government publicly maintained a stoic indifference towards such sanctions, the Rhodesian business community was reeling from their effects (Minter and Schmidt 1988, 220–225).

Other aspects of Rhodesia's demographic profile stand out: 85,000 Europeans were either under the age of fifteen or over the age of sixty—too young or too old to fight in a guerrilla war. The Rhodesian Army did not use women for combat duty, which meant that its recruiting pool was somewhere around 60,000 to 70,000 white men. Eventually, the Rhodesian Armed Forces drew on the African population for their fight, but nonetheless all European males aged eighteen to sixty were subject to draft by the end of the war in 1980. As the war continued and more and more males were called and recalled to duty, the economy suffered tremendously because of the loss of skilled white labor and management.

At the end of 1972, however, only a few within Rhodesia's intelligence and military command understood the full implications of a counterinsurgency war against black guerrillas. The war against the guerrillas from 1965 to 1972 had been successful, but had also bred overconfidence within the Smith government (Flower 1987a, 112). The opening up of the Mozambican front and the change in black strategy had turned the military situation around. Ken Flower, head of intelligence under Smith, writes about that time as a transformation from "a winning position . . . [to] the stage of the 'no-win' war, which lasted from December 1972 to 1976" (Flower 1987a, 119). From 1972 on, a serious split emerged within the Rhodesian government over the nature and severity of the guerrilla threat. Intelligence professionals like Flower argued for the need for political settlement, while politicians within the Smith regime believed that the war was winnable (Flower 1987a; Moorcraft and Mc-

Laughlin 1982, 25). In the middle between the two groups was the Rhodesian military, which needed the experience of combat to sway it from Smith's point of view. Few of these splits, however, were evident to those outside the government. To its own citizens and to the world outside, the Rhodesian government seemed a bastion of unity.

After the Pearce Commission had ruled that the Home-Smith agreement was not approved by most Zimbabweans, the British sought to wash their hands of the affair. Three times they had negotiated with Ian Smith, three times their efforts had come to naught. Smith had developed almost a mythical reputation among the British for his negotiating style. As Lord Blake put it more bluntly, "For Ian Smith negotiation was not a matter of compromise, but of wearing down one's opponent till he concedes all the points at issue" (Blake 1977, 362). Smith, himself, described his delaying tactics as "pulling the wool over the eyes of the British" (*The* [London] *Times*, May 8, 1978).

While Smith and others felt little need for give and take with Britain, this was not so concerning Rhodesia's relations with South Africa. Smith was an enormously popular figure with many white South Africans, but was disdained by their leaders because of his obstinacy in the face of their advice. When Smith was contemplating UDI, Hendrik Verwoerd, then Prime Minister of South Africa, had counselled against such a course. When John Vorster replaced Verwoerd, he referred to Rhodesia as "the Achilles heel of Southern Africa" and urged Smith to reach some kind of settlement. Incidents between Rhodesian forces and ZIPRA (ZAPU's army) near the South African border in 1967 had prompted Vorster to provide the Rhodesians with 2,000 paramilitary police, helicopters and pilots. More importantly, South Africa was Rhodesia's economic lifeline to the outside world for military supplies and equipment, food, and oil. By 1976 a Rhodesian intelligence briefing admitted that "Rhodesia is totally dependent upon South Africa for military and economic survival" (Flower 1987a, 132). Smith thus had to walk a narrow line in his battle to thwart majority rule. He could try to appeal over the heads of the South African leaders directly to their followers for support, but doing so risked alienating "the only leaders who could pressurize us" (I. Smith 1987).

To complete the story of social and political chasms in Rhodesia in the early 1970s it is necessary to look as well at the splits among the black leaders who were fighting for Zimbabwe. Such splits were mostly muted until the early 1960s when disputes over the capabilities and strategies of the leaders led to public fighting between the supporters of Joshua Nkomo, who went on to found ZAPU, and the supporters of Ndabaningi Sithole, Robert Mugabe, and Herbert Chitepo who led ZANU. While the split originated over the ability of Nkomo to lead the nationalist movement, more layers of difference were added. Nkomo, although always stressing the national character of ZAPU, found his strength in the areas around Bulawayo in Matabeleland, where an ethnic group that comprised 15 percent of Zimbabwe's population—the Ndebele—lived. Later, ideological, strategic, and logistical differences would also emerge: ZANU chose a guerrilla strategy and aligned itself to China and locally to Mozambique while ZAPU downplayed guerrilla tactics, received arms, training, and advice from the Soviet Union, and based itself in Zambia. Political parties proliferated even further in the early 1970s as ZANU splintered into different wings, one backing Sithole and one supporting Robert Mugabe. Further confusion was added when Bishop Muzorewa formed the African National Council, an umbrella group within Rhodesia formed to fight the Smith-Home agreement in 1972.

The various black partners (or rivals, depending on the particular day) posed a problem for any potential mediator. Regional leaders such as Kenneth Kaunda, President of Zambia, and Julius Nyerere, President of Tanzania, often found themselves exasperated at what Masipula Sithole labelled "struggles within the struggle" (Sithole, 1977). When unity was achieved briefly in 1974 Sithole (brother of Ndabaningi Sithole) eloquently described the coalition of the different nationalist factions:

We must state at this point that the said declaration of unity united sheep, foxes, hyenas, and leopards. The sad assumption was that the four would realize that they had many things in common: They were animals and their common enemy in the bush was the lion. All that was needed for unity was to bring them around a table, sign a piece of paper singing *"Ishe Komborera Afrika!"* (Lord Save Africa), and all would be well. Yet we know that the interests of leopards, hyenas, foxes, and sheep do not necessarily coincide, even given their common fear of the lion. (M. Sithole 1977, 108)

At the end of 1974, because of strategic changes by ZANLA and more importantly, the collapse of Portuguese authorities in neighboring Mozambique, the struggle in Rhodesia intensified into a full-fledged guerrilla war. As described earlier, two issues originally drove the conflict: majority rule and land redistribution. As the war progressed new issues emerged: Who would rule during the transition to a new government? Who would supervise a cease-fire? Who would create a new constitution?

Between 1974 and 1979 there were three efforts to mediate a settlement in Rhodesia. In 1974 Kenneth Kaunda, President of Zambia, Rhodesia's neighbor to the west, and John Vorster, the President of South Africa, the powerful state to the immediate south of Rhodesia, had attempted to bring the black nationalist leaders of Zimbabwe and Ian Smith, Rhodesia's Prime Minister, to the bargaining table. Although the efforts of Kaunda and Vorster did not lead to a settlement in 1975, their plan became the blueprint for two other attempts to solve the conflict—the efforts of Vorster and Henry Kissinger in 1976, and the initiatives of David Owen and Cyrus Vance in 1977 and 1978. The Kaunda-Vorster plan called for the Front Line Presidents—the Presidents of the black countries bordering on Rhodesia—Kaunda of Zambia, Machel of Mozambique, Khama of Botswana, and Nyerere of Tanzania, who served as the regional patrons of the black nationalist movements to pressure the diverse movements into unifying as a single negotiating voice for the black majority of Rhodesia. In turn, South Africa, the country that Rhodesia depended on for its survival, promised to pressure Rhodesia into accepting a transition to majority rule.

The Kissinger-Vorster effort led to a British-run conference on Rhodesia, held in Geneva in the autumn of 1976. Before the conference started in October, Kissinger had won a commitment to majority rule from Ian Smith. But Kissinger had done so by promising conditions to the whites that did not have the support of the black movements or the Front Line presidents. The conference lasted for about three months without gaining approval on a single issue. This experience set the stage for the next attempt to solve the war, the Anglo-American initiatives of David Owen and Cyrus Vance. These leaders studied the Kissinger mediation and the Geneva conference, and decided that the parties in conflict were too far apart to reach agreement on their own. Instead, the British and Americans would put forward proposals which would develop a new constitution, establish a transitional government which would carry out free and fair elections, and implement a cease-fire between the warring parties. The principal reasons for the failure of the Vance-Owen initi-

atives were, first, an insistence that the armed guerrillas of the nationalist movements would compose the national military during the
transition, a proposal that the white military characterized as a demand for their surrender, and second, the alternative that Ian Smith
developed away from the negotiating table, known as the internal
settlement.

In 1976 ZAPU and ZANU, then led by Robert Mugabe, formed
the Patriotic Front (PF).[3] The two movements, under the pressure
of their regional allies, entered into the alliance in 1976 in order to
present a unified bargaining face to the Rhodesians and any potential
mediators. The coalition omitted two black political leaders without
military support: Ndabaningi Sithole and Bishop Abel Muzorewa.
Sithole had originally been one of the top leaders of ZANU, but had
been ousted in a party coup in 1974. Sithole claimed political support
in Zimbabwe, but was hampered because of his ethnic Ndau origins.
The Ndau of eastern Zimbabwe constituted only 4 percent of the
Zimbabwean people. Muzorewa, a Shona-speaker, claimed much
more extensive support within Zimbabwe, including the following
of the African National Council.

As the war intensified between the black guerrilla armies and the
armed forces of the white regime in Salisbury, Ian Smith entered
into talks with Muzorewa and Sithole over the formation of a new
government. Smith ceded majority rule to the blacks, but insisted
that the white minority be given a disproportionate number of representatives in the national legislature and a blocking mechanism to
veto any legislation it deemed odious. On March 3, 1978 Smith,
Muzorewa, and Sithole announced the signing of what came to be
known as "the internal settlement." The agreement pledged the
participants to a government by coalition until an election could be
held to determine the leadership of the country. Smith and the whites
were gambling that ceding the trappings of dominance but not yielding its substance would attract substantial numbers of guerrillas away
from Mugabe and Nkomo. More importantly, the new coalition
hoped that the agreement would lead to the removal of international
sanctions and the recognition of the government's legitimacy by
world actors.

The new government stumbled through 1978 unable to win recognition from international actors and ineffective in winning guerrilla
desertions. As the war intensified the government of Zimbabwe-Rhodesia prepared its white and black voters for its first elections to be

held in April of 1979. In what British conservatives described as a referendum on the new constitution of the country and in what others described as a sham election, Muzorewa won a landslide for Prime Minister with a reported 63 percent of the population voting.

At the beginning of 1979 all parties to the Rhodesian conflict were committed to alternatives away from the negotiating table. As one American diplomat noted, "Rhodesia had seemingly inscribed itself on the permanent agenda of the world's political-ethnic conundrums—Northern Ireland, Cyprus, the Middle East, South Africa—unamenable to human persuasion or reason" (Davidow 1984, 13). Yet by the end of the year an agreement between all parties would be reached at Lancaster House, and after a harrowing cease-fire and election, Zimbabwe would be granted independence in April of 1980.

The Military Situation

As early as 1977 the Rhodesian Central Intelligence Office believed that Rhodesia was losing the war to the guerrillas. In April of 1977 Peter Walls, head of Rhodesian armed forces, estimated that 2,350 armed guerrillas had infiltrated into the country. In January 1978 the estimate had climbed to 8,000 ZANLA guerrillas inside Zimbabwe with ZIPRA force levels in Zambia over 8,000. Gross Domestic Product for 1977 was −7 percent; defense expenditures exceeded a million dollars a day; the inability of the Rhodesian regime to provide basic services to its farmers led to the decimation of livestock; and white emigration, the indicator that mattered the most to Ian Smith, totaled almost 11,000 for the year. Casualties for guerrillas, Rhodesian soldiers, and civilians in 1977 alone surpassed the totals in each category for all the years from 1972 to 1976 combined. Figures 6.1 and 6.2 and Table 6.1 provide evidence on war deaths, guerrilla infiltration into Rhodesia, white flight, and general breakdown of the country.[4]

The objective military situation led to different subjective assessments among the actors. As stated above, the Rhodesian military and intelligence establishment had concluded that the white military situation was desperate, and that Salisbury needed a settlement to the war. Ian Smith, however, was often buoyed by temporary successes of the Rhodesian military, such as their highly destructive raids into Zambia and Mozambique, and believed that the war could be won.

Figure 6.1 Deaths in the Zimbabwean Civil War, 1973–1979

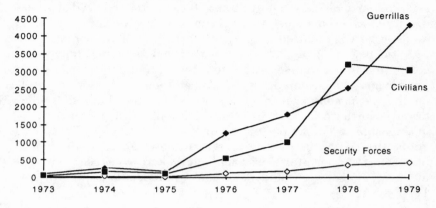

Figure 6.2 Comparison of Guerrilla Strength and White Flight

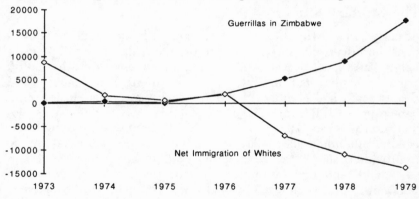

His belief was predicated on the assumption that eventually Britain and the United States would recognize Abel Muzorewa and lift sanctions against the regime. In any event, Smith made clear his preference for fighting on under any circumstances; Smith believed that even a losing war and possible death was preferable to Patriotic Front rule. Bishop Abel Muzorewa believed that the military situation was not desperate; he assumed that in due course most of the guerrillas would desert ZANU and embrace his leadership.

On the Patriotic Front side, ZANU and ZAPU perceived things differently. Most in ZANU, and especially Robert Mugabe, believed

Table 6.1 Indicators of Social Collapse, Rhodesia 1972–1979

A. Tourism (Visitors to Rhodesia—in thousands)						
1972	1973	1974	1975	1976	1977	1978
339	244	230	244	140	104	88

B. Ages of Men Eligible for the Draft			
Until 1976	July 1976	Jan. 1977	Jan. 1979
18–30	18–34	18–50	18–59

C. Percentage of Rhodesia under Martial Law				
Sept. 1978	Nov. 1978	Dec. 1978	Sept. 1979	Dec. 1979
intro.	50	70	90	95

D. Schools Closed in Rural Black Areas	
July 1977	Nov. 1978
300	986

E. Cattle Dips in Operation in Rhodesia	
1972	1978
8,000	1,500

that they were winning the war, and that they would defeat the Salisbury regime in short order. ZAPU, on the other hand, believed that the Patriotic Front would eventually win the war, but at a prohibitive cost. Nkomo and his military leadership felt that ZANU's guerrilla strategy could never bring victory. At some point in the war a transition to conventional war could be necessary, which ZAPU's leadership assumed would cause a much larger regional conflagration. Finally, both of the Patriotic Front's patrons—Zambia and Mozambique—were absorbing heavy costs for their support of the Front, and preferred a settlement to the prolongation of the war.

Two elections in 1979 created an opportunity for mediation of the war. First, Bishop Abel Muzorewa was elected Prime Minister of Zimbabwe-Rhodesia. For the first time in fifteen years, someone other than Ian Smith would be the chief decision maker in any possible negotiations. The election of Muzorewa was embraced by both General Peter Walls and Ken Flower, effectively isolating Smith in the government. Two months later, the people of Great Britain elected Margaret Thatcher Prime Minister. Thatcher, whose electoral campaign had stressed recognition of the Muzorewa government, caused all the antagonists to rethink the situation. In particular, the two elections provided a credible threat and inducement to bring all parties to a settlement conference. The Muzorewa government needed recognition and most participants believed Thatcher could give it to them. The leverage of recognition provided a means for Britain to influence the Muzorewa regime directly—no longer would Britain have to rely on South Africa for pressure against the Salisbury government. Recognition, when combined with active support for British mediation from Zambia and Mozambique, provided the means to prompt Patriotic Front moderation.[5]

After winning the Prime Minister's office and appointing Lord Carrington as Foreign Secretary, Thatcher decided in June 1979 to proceed with another mediation attempt. British officials had studied the past failures of mediation and concluded that the previous proposals had *substantial* flaws that *in and of themselves* sufficed to sabotage any possible agreement. In the case of the Kissinger effort, the fatal flaw concerned Kissinger's "package deal," in particular, the provisions on white control of Defence and Law and white veto over the Council of State and the Council of Ministers (Renwick 1981, 7). In the Anglo-American initiative, the stipulation that during the transition period the armed forces would be based on the guerrilla armies precluded white acceptance. Any new initiative would have to take from the previous talks a core of a settlement, yet avoid these specific problems.

The British study of past efforts concluded that Smith would fight any proposed agreement, and therefore, it would be crucial to isolate him from the rest of the Salisbury delegates. On the Patriotic Front side, the British believed that Mugabe would also fight any settlement. But the British recognized that Mugabe's reluctance did not stem from ideology or principle. As one diplomat stated, "Mugabe was convinced that he could win outright and he feared risking the gains he had already won. Mugabe was convinced that he would win an election, but was unsure he would have a chance to win an election. He believed in armed struggle, *because of Smith*" (British Diplomat A. 1987). In order to pressure Mugabe the British once again needed the help of the Front Line Presidents. As for Nkomo, he "didn't need a lot of pressure—he was the weak link in the Patriotic Front. Lancaster House was his last chance" (British Diplomat A. 1987).

The British plan was put into action in August at the Commonwealth Meeting in Lusaka. Under Lord Carrington's supervision a Commonwealth working party consisting of Kaunda, Nyerere, Jamaican Prime Minister Michael Manley, Commonwealth Secretary General Shridath Ramphal, Australian Prime Minister Malcolm Fraser, and Nigerian Foreign Minister Major General Henry Adefope, hammered out a joint Commonwealth position on Rhodesia:

The resultant communiqué, approved by all the heads of government, affirmed their commitment to genuine majority rule, noted that the internal settlement constitution was defective in certain important respects and accepted that it was the British government's responsibility to bring Zimbabwe to legal independence. It recognized that the search for a lasting settlement involved all the parties to the conflict and appropriate safeguards for minorities; that the government formed under the independence constitution must be chosen through free and fair elections properly supervised under British government authority and with Commonwealth observers present; and that it was the British government's intention to call a constitutional conference to which all the parties would be invited . . . The recognition that it was Britain's responsibility to propose a solution was an essential element of the Lusaka communiqué. No less important was the commitment to fresh elections. These were the natural corollary of a new constitution and the key to offering all the parties an alternative to continuing the war. (Renwick 1981, 14)

The British had a clear idea of what they wanted going into the talks. Lord Carrington's strategy for the Lancaster House meetings emphasized four factors. First, Carrington would use what he called the second class solution—British recognition of Muzorewa and removal of sanctions—as a carrot with Muzorewa and as a stick with the Patriotic Front. As stated earlier, the British had hinted to Muzorewa that if the PF was responsible for the failure to reach a settlement, Muzorewa would gain recognition. The attractiveness of the second-class solution is that it established a bargaining game whereby the first party to walk away from the table would lose: the game, therefore, had a dynamic built into it, so that both parties feared being the first to repudiate the negotiations. In order to put the utmost pressure on the Patriotic Front, on each issue the British would turn first to the Salisbury delegation and then, armed with their acceptance, would put matters to the Patriotic Front on a "take-it-or-leave-it" basis.

Second, Carrington realized that, although this first factor was a powerful leverage, it was not enough. It was crucial that both parties believe that they could win a fair election. If any party believed that it could not win, it would have reason to walk away from a settlement. Moreover, the parties had to believe that the British would run fair elections and that both parties would abide by the results, regardless of their outcome.

Third, the British had determined beforehand that within the two delegations, they would have to work to isolate those members who were opposed to a settlement: Ian Smith and Robert Mugabe.

Fourth, Carrington realized that Britain lacked sufficient leverage with the Patriotic Front, and therefore needed the help of the Front Line Presidents to pressure Mugabe and Nkomo, especially Mugabe.

Lancaster House

The Lancaster House Constitutional Conference on Rhodesia began in September 1979. At the introductory session of the meetings Lord Carrington set the tone for what would follow. Emphasizing that the conference had the backing of the Commonwealth, Carrington stressed that Britain was determined to carry out its role as decolonizer. He made it clear that the conference was a "constitutional" conference, that since the constitution was the most important issue and cause of the war, it would have to be addressed first: "it is essential to the prospects of success that we should first seek agreement on our destination—which is the independence constitution. If that can be achieved it will be necessary to decide the arrangements to give effect to that agreement." Moreover, he stated that "it is illusory to think that any settlement can fully satisfy the requirements of either side" (United Kingdom 1979, Minutes Introductory Session).

Carrington also stated themes that would recur throughout the meetings: 1) Britain was acting on a mandate of the Commonwealth; 2) Britain was serious about asserting its decolonizing responsibilities; 3) the constitution was the key to the settlement, and only when that was solved, would the conference proceed to discussions about arrangements; 4) Britain had long experience as a decolonizing power, which provided it with experience at dealing with the sticky issues involved in the conference; 5) agreement would not come from the parties, but instead would demand compromises on all parts; 6) independence did not mean that one side would win, but that all sides would have an equal chance to win an election; 7) the British proposals would form the basis of the working document—other parties' suggestions would be considered but only insofar as they dealt with the British document.

The Constitution

From the start, Carrington's dictatorial power was evident. He made clear that the only working document would be the British proposal he put forth. While welcoming any revisions to these proposals, Carrington emphasized that no other documents would be discussed. The agenda of the conference was decided in the first meetings. Both the Patriotic Front and the British tabled proposals. The British plan consisted of three issues: 1) proposals for a new constitution, 2) the plan for a transition period before elections, and 3) the arrangements for the cease-fire. The Patriotic Front's proposal envisioned first discussing the transitional period—arrangements and a temporary constitution—and then moving on to the topics of the independence constitution and cease-fire.

Carrington argued forcefully that the constitution be settled first:

the only way to end the war is to remove the reasons for it. . . . The approach of the British Government has been to discuss the best way to achieve a solution with their friends and allies and the parties involved. It was clear from these discussions that the root of the problem lay in the constitution. If the conference could agree on the constitution, it would remove the causes of the war, once agreement on the constitution was settled, agreement on other matters could come more easily (United Kingdom 1979, Minutes 1st Plenary).

Muzorewa seemed to bridle at the suggestions that the constitution was inadequate, and insisted that "the people of Rhodesia have already decided on the constitution" (United Kingdom 1979, Minutes 1st Plenary). Carrington prevailed, however, as neither side wanted to waste negotiating capital so early in the proceedings.

The three sides tabled proposals for the new constitution. The British proposal basically accepted most of the formalities of the new constitution of Zimbabwe-Rhodesia, but eliminated the discriminatory provisions that Smith had forced on Muzorewa, most importantly the blocking mechanism of the whites in government. The British proposals still contained important safeguards for protecting minority interests. The most important of these safeguards was an extensive bill of rights guaranteeing individual freedoms, the guarantee of an undetermined number of white seats in a 100-person legislature for a period of seven years, remuneration for any land that might be redistributed, and the honoring of pension rights for white public officials.

The Patriotic Front spent the early meetings insisting that no agreement on the constitution could be reached until the arrangements for the transition were known. Mugabe said it was essential to spell out the transitional arrangements to insure that progress towards independence was irreversible. On this matter, however, there could be no compromise on the British part. The British had learned from Geneva that there would be no end in sight to the conference if the parties were allowed to renegotiate clauses at later dates in the proceedings. The British insisted that all matters having to do with the transition and cease-fire would be addressed, but only after agreement was reached on the constitution.

Having lost the procedural battle, the Patriotic Front took aim at the specific components of the constitution. At the sixth plenary session Mugabe reproached the British on minority representation in Parliament:

The British proposals variously call this minority 'European' and 'white.' The Patriotic Front certainly wants to see everyone in Zimbabwe represented in the legislature, but I am puzzled that the British Government should want the new republic to start off with a constitution which divided the people. All people who live in Zimbabwe should consider themselves as citizens of that country. Is it possible to call a section of the community European? Surely there can be no such thing as a European in Africa? Similarly the term 'white' could cause problems. Is the conference being asked to work out a chart of shades of colour and then agree the percentage by which each shade should be represented? This is a racial approach and repugnant to our delegation.
CARRINGTON:
It was accepted that the ideal solution is that the people should think of themselves as citizens of Zimbabwe rather than black or white, Shona or Matabele. The crux of the issue is how this is to be achieved. The political realities of the past cannot be ignored. Nor can the hopes and fears of the people.
MUGABE:
I wish to underline the fact that the war of liberation has been waged to destroy the racial basis on which society in my country

has been constructed. The minority has acquired certain rights and privileges to the exclusion of the majority. The war has been waged against this exploitation. The British want us now to retain vestiges of that system. (United Kingdom 1979, Minutes 6th Plenary)

Ian Gilmour, Carrington's second in command, then answered that it had been agreed at Lusaka that it would be in Zimbabwe's best interests for the whites to stay and that the provisions in the constitution would be necessary for them to remain. He also pointed out that the civil war had made the arrangements necessary only temporarily. The plenary came close to dissolving into open rebellion as members of the Patriotic Front battered the British arguments on racial and regional representation. At the end of the meeting the discussion turned to the guarantee of civil servant pensions. Edison Zvobgo, Mugabe's press officer, pointed out that such civil servants "might be regarded as public officers by some people, but by others as mercenaries." Mugabe went a step further: "If this is to be a retrospective blessing by the British Government for treasonable conduct, this should be clearly stated" (United Kingdom 1979, Minutes 6th Plenary). When no progress was made at the next plenary on September 18, it was agreed that it might be best for the conference to work in bilateral meetings away from the negotiating table. The British would negotiate separately with each team.

The first showdown of the conference within the delegations came in the Salisbury team. In meetings from September 19 to 21, Ian Smith argued vociferously against the dilution of the white safeguards and insisted that any constitution had to have a blocking mechanism for the whites. Muzorewa and others supported the compromises put forth by the British. The African members of the delegation had never had any fondness for the white veto, and Carrington and his aides had made it clear to the white members of the delegation that, while protective measures would be placed in the constitution, the blocking mechanism had to go. If not, Carrington added, the country would never gain recognition.

In a bilateral meeting on the nineteenth, Carrington presented the Salisbury delegation with specific numbers. Twenty seats out of a 100-person Parliament would be reserved for whites, and seventy votes would be necessary to amend the constitution. Eight of the twelve-man Salisbury delegation including David Smith, spoke in favor of changing the constitution. Ian Smith, however, refused to back down, and for more than an hour argued with Carrington that the mechanisms were necessary "to maintain white confidence and morale." On the morning of the twentieth in a meeting of the four white delegates, Smith found that he had no support. The key apparently was a telegram from General Peter Walls that underscored the need for a quick agreement.

This first showdown came to an end on the morning of 21 September. For two and a half hours Ian Smith argued his position. He had backed off his insistence on the white veto; his insistence now was based on " 'maintaining standards,' by retaining the dominant position of white officials in the commissions for defence, the public service, the Army and the police" (*The* [London] *Observer*, September 23, 1979, in Baumhogger 1984, 1059). One Muzorewa delegate said that Smith's arguments were not "practical, but philosophic in nature" and that David Smith, after listening to Ian Smith go on, finally stood up and said, "enough is enough." (UANC Delegate A. 1987) Muzorewa then called for a secret vote on whether to accept the constitution: the tally was eleven to one in favor. That evening the Salisbury delegation publicly announced their acceptance of the new constitution. But they also tried to pressure Carrington by insisting that sanctions be removed, since they had fulfilled their part of the bargain ("Statement by the Government of Zimbabwe Rhodesia," in Baumhogger 1984, 1060).

Carrington then turned to the Patriotic Front. The PF held out for two weeks in disagreement with the British proposals. The Patriotic Front had accepted the twenty seat representation for whites, but still raised objections over land, pensions, citizenship, protected rights, and form of constitutional government. On October 1 a British diplomat, Derek Day, briefed representatives of the Front Line Presidents on the stalled talks. Later that day these same representatives met with Mugabe and Nkomo to relay Front Line dissatisfaction with the progress of the negotiations. The representatives emphasized that, since the Front had accepted the difficult issue of special representation for the whites, the other less important issues should not halt the proceedings.

On October 3 the British tabled the revised constitution in specific detail. It failed to grant any concessions to the Patriotic Front. Within two days Muzorewa had granted his delegation's acceptance. On October 6, Ian Smith flew back to Salisbury to rally Rhodesian Front support for his rejection of the constitution. While at home Smith raised the issue of whether the constitutional changes had to be ratified by the Rhodesian Parliament. The British in conjunction with the Salisbury delegation immediately squashed this possibility by contacting the highest ranking judge in Rhodesia, who gave an impromptu ruling that ratification was inappropriate in view of the circumstances.

On October 9 the Patriotic Front again tried to stick by its positions. Carrington's responses on that day are revealing of the British intention to arbitrate and not mediate a settlement. For example in responding to Patriotic Front demands for an executive presidency, Carrington states, "the British Government *reached its decision* only after very careful consideration of all the arguments." Other statements read like a judge's decree: "The Patriotic Front say . . . the British Government does not take that view." "There can be no question of the British Government or Parliament accepting such a provision . . ." "The Patriotic Front have also reiterated their objections to the principle of dual citizenship. In our view their fears are misplaced . . ." "The British Government regards it as essential that the Declaration of Rights be specially entrenched." "The British Government cannot accept those changes" (regarding land); on public service, "The British Government regards it as eminently reasonable that . . ." (United Kingdom 1979, Minutes 11th Plenary, emphasis added).

When the Patriotic Front suggested "agreeing to disagree" and moving on to discuss the transitional arrangements, Carrington put his foot down. Considerations of transitional matters could not be taken before the constitution was settled. It was not good enough to "agree to disagree" and leave it. There must be agreement. The British Government had taken into account all sides and had presented a constitution as "the only basis on which it is now possible to reach full agreement at this conference" (United Kingdom 1979, Minutes 11th Plenary). Matters would not be allowed to be reopened now or in the future. Carrington finished by reasserting Britain's duty to *arbitrate*: "When the Conference cannot agree, when the parties cannot agree, we have an obligation to make clear what in our mind is fair and reasonable and we have done so" (United Kingdom 1979, Minutes 11th Plenary). Carrington then asked the Patriotic Front to provide a "definitive reply in two days" as to whether they would accept the constitution as presented by the British, and left to attend the annual Conservative Party convention in Blackpool.

The PF could swallow all of the concessions that Carrington demanded, save one: what to do about land. One ZAPU delegate stated what was mentioned in many interviews: "The land issue was the hardest to accept, because it involved such visceral feelings and our mobilization had depended on land, thus we decided we had to make some kind of stand" (ZAPU Delegate A. 1987). But what kind of stand? Hardliners including Mugabe threatened to walk out of the conference. Josiah Tongogara, ZANLA's top commander, warned that Mozambique would take away ZANLA bases. Mugabe insisted, and Nkomo told him if ZANU walked, it walked alone. The Patriotic Front would have to break: Zambia would take away ZAPU's bases.

Two days later at the next plenary session, the Patriotic Front refused to respond. Carrington publicly set another deadline. According to Jeffrey Davidow, Carrington also approached the PF in a bilateral session and presented them with a British offer to cover some of the expense of reimbursing farmers for land redistribution. This offer "was pocketed by the Patriotic Front's leaders, and did not lead to an immediate change in their stance" (Davidow 1984, 62).

The intransigence of the PF prompted both a search by third actors for some kind of face-saving measure for Mugabe and Nkomo, and a hard line from the British. On October 15 Carrington publicly stated that the conference, with or without the participation of the Patriotic Front, would resume the next morning to begin talks on the transition period. He added that until the guerrillas had accepted the constitution, he would be forced to move on with only the Salisbury delegation. At this, Shridath Ramphal, the Secretary General of the Commonwealth, publicly rebuked Carrington: the British mandate from the Lusaka meeting was for an "all-parties" conference. Kenneth Kaunda backed Ramphal, calling Carrington's actions "not helpful" and "negative." The Front Line Presidents in a special summit session backed the Patriotic Front, as did Nigeria's President Shagari. On the other side of the issue, South Africa sent its Foreign Minister, Pik Botha, to London to pressure Carrington into getting on with things and recognizing Muzorewa's government.

Between October 15 and 18 the United States, in response to initiatives by Ramphal and Carrington, gave ambiguous support for a fund that would help Zimbabwe bear the economic burden of pensions and compensation for land. In the words of one ZANU delegate: "With the United States offer of aid we had something we could sell to the people. The Front Line States told us, 'You have a promise from the United States; if you feel like you have something you can sell to the electorate, then take it" (Mubako 1987). On the eighteenth the Patriotic Front announced that, pending their satisfaction with the transitional arrangements, "there will not be need to revert to discussion on the constitution" ("Statement by PF," in Baumhogger 1984, 1113).

The Transitional Arrangements

Turning to the details of the transition period, Carrington insisted that it would be handled with the existing Rhodesian military and police forces under direct British supervision with no role for any U.N. officials or peacekeeping force, and in a two month period. The British wanted to keep their risk to a minimum. First, the British had no intention of giving their or anyone else's troops the job of stepping between the two armed adversaries. They went to great pains to emphasize that any cease-fire would have to be largely self-enforcing. Instead of peacekeeping forces, the British plan called for a small contingent of Commonwealth troops (no more than 300) to monitor the cease-fire. Since the British knew that the Salisbury regime would balk at United Nations involvement, they had ruled out such a possibility. Second, Britain, while willing to take over power during the interim, wanted to minimize commitment of resources and so decided that a British governor would use the existing police and bureaucracies to run the country. Finally, the time element was crucial for maintaining the illusion that the election was "up for grabs." As one British official said, "We felt most strongly about a short transition period. If anyone found out who lost before the election, then it was all over" (British Diplomat A. 1987).

On October 19 Carrington presented his general view on the transition. Once again donning the mantle of legitimacy vested at Lusaka, he demanded that both parties accept the principle that "there had to be free and fair elections, properly supervised under the British Government's authority, with Commonwealth observers present." Nkomo immediately asked for clarification on the term "British Government's authority." Carrington replied that "this refers to our responsibility for the conduct and supervision of the elections." Mugabe then answered that the Patriotic Front had their own proposals, and would need to wait to see the specifics of the British plan. Muzorewa announced that the Patriotic Front proposals were absolutely unacceptable, and that after all, "free and fair elections have already been held in Zimbabwe Rhodesia" (United Kingdom 1979, Minutes 13th Plenary).

The plan was equally onerous to both Muzorewa and the PF. For Muzorewa, "the advent of a British governor with full legislative and executive power could only mean the relinquishment of power by the bishop and his cabinet, a bitter pill for a newly elected government" (Davidow 1984, 69). Mugabe and Nkomo objected on four grounds. First, relying on the existing police to keep the peace offered no protection whatsoever. They felt that only a police force comprised of both Salisbury and Patriotic Front officers would work. Second, since the transition government did not incorporate any of the liberation movement's political or military personnel, the guerrillas were not granted legitimacy or equality. Their minimal demand was equal recognition. Their maximum position demanded a full integration of the armed forces with the guerrillas forming the core of the army. Third, the PF felt that the short time period was insufficient: they wanted the opportunity to move mass numbers of people from their refugee centers back into Zimbabwe. Fourth, the Patriotic Front, fearing that the Salisbury regime would try to rig the elections, demanded a full registration of voters—an arduous task that would take longer than two months.

Carrington, as he did during the discussions on the constitution, sought Muzorewa's acceptance before that of the Patriotic Front. For tactical reasons Carrington needed Salisbury's approval to keep pressure on Mugabe and Nkomo. This time, however, the British were not as confident of the outcome. As Jeffrey Davidow has argued, "obtaining from Muzorewa his agreement to step aside and transfer power to a British governor proved to be the single most difficult task confronting Carrington" (Davidow 1984, 69). This point was emphasized by one of the British diplomats at Lancaster House: "To ask a government to get out of the way and let you run it is a tough business" (British Diplomat A. 1987).

In the case of Muzorewa and the request that he stand down, the British confronted a split delegation. On the one hand, Ian Smith chose the issue to make one last stand: he argued that if Muzorewa gave in, then the path would be clear for a Patriotic Front takeover of the government. Sithole, as leader of the opposition, however, desired new elections and saw that if Muzorewa stepped down, it would increase his chances of electoral success. Muzorewa's own deputies were adamantly against the concession; their concern stemmed from their own interests, for if Muzorewa lost power, then they would lose power. Since the proposals were put as a package, however, there was much that appealed to the white members of Muzorewa's faction, especially Peter Walls who found appealing the provisions calling for reliance on the existing security forces.

Unlike their experience in accepting the constitution, the decision on whether Muzorewa would stand down was his alone. The British worked on two tracks. The first appealed to the Bishop's ethics and tried to convince him that stepping down was the "right" thing to do, that it was necessary to give everyone an equal chance to lead a new Zimbabwe. The second track aimed at Muzorewa's interests and attempted to convince him that his loss of position would be temporary, that he would win another election and regain his position in a matter of months (Carrington 1987). Finally, one has to take into account Muzorewa's realization that there was a real possibility that the PF might not, in Davidow's words, "gag and swallow" the transition conditions. If so, the door would be open for British recognition, but only if Muzorewa first accepted the British terms. The British privately were telling the Bishop that acceptance of the transition by the Front was unlikely. On the twenty-eighth of October when a response was requested by the British, Muzorewa, after a night of prayer, acceded to their demands to step down. From interviews with him and others in his delegation I am convinced that he did that as the "fair" thing to do. But I am equally convinced that Muzorewa was completely certain that he would be reelected and would soon regain his leadership spot.

During the time Muzorewa deliberated, Lord Carrington had sent his Minister for African Affairs, Richard Luce, to visit the Front Line Presidents. While the move was in part to inform them of the proceedings, it was also undertaken in order to build up a reserve of legitimacy for the British proposals. This legitimacy was obtained just in time for the eight plenary sessions held between October 26 and November 1. In plenary on October 26 the Patriotic Front presented a stinging analysis of Britain's plans for the interim period. Their anger focused on the British choice of using existing police and administrators, who, the Patriotic Front argued, could not possibly be impartial. For the guerrillas the plan was a recipe for violence and bloodshed. Having criticized the British plan, the Front then repeated their proposals: a six month period before the election; security forces and police made up of both the regime's and the PF's forces; a United Nations peacekeeping force and police force; an electoral commission; and an interim government formed on a power-sharing basis with equal numbers of Patriotic Front leaders on one side and British and Salisbury leaders on the other.

At the eighteenth plenary on October 27 Ian Gilmour, acting on behalf of Lord Carrington, responded point by point to the Front's proposals. The result was a heated discussion between Gilmour and various members of the Front's delegation, but no concessions on the British part. This prompted Nkomo and Mugabe to test the British mandate. On October 28 they met with Michael Manley, Jamaican Prime Minister and one of the authors of the Lusaka communiqué, and Shridath Ramphal. This meeting was preparatory to a showdown on the British handling of the negotiations. While the Commonwealth set up a special meeting in London for October 30 to discuss a Patriotic Front call for change in the British plan, the Front also went to the public with their case. Edison Zvobgo told the press: "After our talks today it is fairly clear that our position is regarded as very sound by the Commonwealth. Does Britain really expect Nkomo and Mugabe to sleep in Salisbury guarded by Bishop Muzorewa's men? We might not even see the end of an election. Why should they not just kill us?" (The [London] Guardian, October 29, 1979).

The next evening as High Commissioners and representatives of thirty-nine Commonwealth states were seeking a mandate from their superiors for a vote on Tuesday, Carrington and Manley met with Margaret Thatcher. They said that many Commonwealth leaders felt that the Patriotic Front's concerns were legitimate, a sentiment also signalled to Carrington by American Ambassador to Great Britain, Kingman Brewster, on behalf of the Carter Administration. Carrington acknowledged privately that the British were willing to bend on some issues.

The next day the Patriotic Front was denied a public victory over Carrington. After listening to Ramphal and the Commonwealth's Committee on Southern Africa, the representatives of the thirty-nine states failed to endorse Patriotic Front demands for U.N. participation, and refused to condemn the negotiating efforts of the British. In a very lukewarm statement, the diplomats "expressed concern" rather than criticism. However, there was general agreement that the two month election period was too short and that there should probably be a strengthening of the Commonwealth observer team to the elections.

While Carrington had maintained the mandate of the Commonwealth, it had been made clear to him that the British would have to give up ground to the Patriotic Front. The conference, now going into its eighth week, was starting to unravel. Both the British and the Patriotic Front turned to a brinksmanship style of bargaining. At the end of plenary on November 2, the British had asked for a definitive answer from both parties by November 5 on the full forty-two-point proposal for the transition period. November 5 was a significant deadline, because the British Parliament that week was to begin to debate on whether to continue sanctions against Rhodesia. When the deadline came, Muzorewa accepted fully the British proposals. The Patriotic Front refused to commit themselves and gave the British a list of concerns that they wanted addressed. That Muzorewa had accepted and the Front had not, put enormous pressure on Carrington and Thatcher from the Conservative Party to recognize Muzorewa's government and to lift sanctions. When another plenary session on November 6 failed to elicit PF acceptance, Carrington decided to up the ante the next day.

As the twenty-eighth plenary began on November 7 Carrington informed both delegations that the British had introduced into Parliament an enabling bill that would set in motion the necessary paperwork for Rhodesia to be returned to British authority. While this inflamed the Front, Carrington refused to relent. At the end of the brief plenary Carrington demanded an answer to the transitional arrangements the next day. Carrington added that if he did not receive one, he did not know how he could continue the conference. Carrington did not tell the Patriotic Front that Ian Gilmour was also to inform Parliament that, while most sanctions would remain in force, the Thatcher government had no intention of renewing them.

The Patriotic Front did not attend the plenary that had been planned for the next day, November 8, and Carrington did not receive an answer. Carrington took the opportunity to castigate the Patriotic Front in public. The Patriotic Front claimed that it was a misunderstanding caused by the failure of their request for postponement to reach Carrington. In lieu of the plenary meeting, Mugabe and Nkomo had met with Kenneth Kaunda, who had flown to London in hopes of breaking the deadlock. Kaunda's concern had been intensified due to a series of Rhodesian attacks on ZAPU bases in Zambia and economic and transportation targets within that country, purportedly to minimize ZAPU infiltration into Zimbabwe in anticipation of an election. Zambia, already reeling from three such attacks in October, was further dealt a blow when the Muzorewa government on November 5 decided to use food as a weapon and halt maize shipments into Zambia.

From November 8 to 10, the British and Patriotic Front castigated each other for their stubbornness. While the bickering continued between the delegations, Carrington, Kaunda, and Thatcher thrashed out possible compromise agreements. First, Carrington decided and made public that there would be a Commonwealth monitoring force of around 1,200 soldiers to supervise the cease-fire. While Carrington had been loath to discuss the cease-fire before an agreement on the transition, the sharing of this information would make it easier for the PF to understand what was coming if the negotiations proceeded. Second, the British would lengthen the interim period from two months to twelve to thirteen weeks. Since part of the Front's objections to a short interim period was their concern to resettle refugees in camps in Mozambique and Zambia, the British government would undertake assistance in helping such resettlement.

The Kaunda intervention helped to bring the parties together. In plenary on November 14, Carrington and Mugabe discussed areas of agreement and disagreement. The Patriotic Front had accepted a British Governor who would rely on the existing Rhodesian administration, an Election Council and British Election Commissioner, and a party-list system of voting. Areas of disagreement included the full registration of voters, the nature of the police force, the length of the transition, the formation of a cease-fire commission, and the composition of the peacekeeping force. Carrington then spelled out the compromises the British would make: the lengthening of the cease-fire, an addition of more than 100 staff members to the Election Commissioner, and a Commonwealth monitoring force rather than a peacekeeping force. Carrington rejected a cease-fire commission: "The role of the military forces on both sides will be to maintain the ceasefire, for which they will be equally responsible to the Governor" (United Kingdom 1979, Minutes 33rd Plenary).

A series of bilateral meetings between the British and the Patriotic Front went late into the night of November 14. The Front had accepted all of the British proposals, but hedged because they believed that the language of the agreements still provided differentiated status to the two armies.

The next day in plenary Mugabe read a statement to which Carrington quickly agreed: "In the light of the discussions we have had as a result of President Kaunda's proposals to the Prime Minister, if you are prepared to include the Patriotic Front forces in paragraph 13 of the British paper, we are able to agree on the interim proposals, conditional on a successful outcome of the negotiations on the cease-fire" (United Kingdom 1979, 34th Plenary, Conference paper CC(79)76, November 15, 1979). The added sentence read, "The Patriotic Front's forces will also be required to comply with the directions of the Governor" (United Kingdom 1979, Conference Addendum 1, November 15, 1979). The final concession was a symbolic one. The sentence formally granted Nkomo and Mugabe what they had been fighting for—the acknowledgement that they were equal to the existing administration.

The Cease-fire

Carrington felt that the problems of reaching an agreement on the cease-fire would be greater than those encountered during the previous negotiations. But he also felt that his strategy of proceeding issue by issue was paying off and was providing the momentum he had hoped to achieve. On November 16 the British tabled their general proposals. The next plenary session fell into the pattern of the previous two months: the Patriotic Front tabled their own proposals, Mugabe and Nkomo expressed displeasure at how the British were running the conference, and then Carrington asserted that "a conclusion is needed within a few days" (United Kingdom 1979, Minutes 35th Plenary).

The Patriotic Front proposal once again differed dramatically from the British outline. First, it envisioned the demarcation of different parts of the country to be under the control of the guerrillas and the Security Forces. The British rejected this out of hand, feeling that such a process would result in the discussions' being prolonged indefinitely, with little prospect of ever reaching agreement. The heart of the Front's plan called for a peacekeeping force that would enforce the cease-fire. The British argued that the cease-fire had to be self-enforcing with the responsibility for maintaining the peace with the respective armies. Finally, the Front believed that during the cease-fire, a start should be made in integrating the armies and police forces. The British countered that the interim period would be used for all concerned to get their electoral message across, and not to begin the making of a new Zimbabwe.

On November 22 Carrington tabled the full proposals for the cease-fire. The most important feature of the plan was that it would take place in two stages. First, the Salisbury troops would be deployed to their main bases. Second, when the monitors had reported that the troops were at their bases, the Patriotic Front guerrillas would have to gather at assembly points throughout the country where they would then be fed and monitored by the Commonwealth force. The time span for these two stages was seven to ten days.

At the same plenary that Carrington submitted the full proposals, he also took time to respond to events taking place in the region at that moment. On November 16 South Africa had announced that it would not accept "chaos" in Rhodesia. Between November 16 and 19 Rhodesia bombed five road bridges in Zambia and destroyed the last remaining rail bridge that linked Zambia to the outside world. The destruction of all transport routes out of Zambia put the country on the edge of economic collapse. Kaunda countered by mobilizing his country for war. The East German and Soviet embassies in Lusaka took rare action and officially warned South Africa to keep their forces out of Zimbabwe if the Patriotic Front came to power.

At the time Rhodesia's motives were thought to be a search for leverage on Kaunda, to force him to put greater pressure on the Patriotic Front. In fact the bombings had not been ordered by Salisbury's military commanders. Rather the actions were undertaken by lesser officers temporarily out from beneath the control of their elders preoccupied at Lancaster House. For these junior officers, the destruction of economic targets did not constitute a major escalation; the bombings were a way of turning on the heat at Lancaster House (Flower 1987b). For Kaunda, however, the action was at the threshold of crossing a tacit limit that could change the conduct and scope of the war.

Carrington issued two ultimatums at the November 22 plenary. First, he demanded that both sides accept the British cease-fire proposals by November 26. Second, he urged that "as an immediate measure to reduce the danger of a further escalation of the conflict . . . an agreement should immediately be concluded in order to avoid any further increase in tension between Rhodesia and Zambia." The

agreement would include Rhodesian word that cross-border operations into Zambia would cease and Patriotic Front word that there
would be no further movement of personnel from Zambia into Rhodesia. Carrington stated that he had already received cooperation
from President Kaunda, who had been in touch with Margaret
Thatcher that day, and that he expected word from both delegations
on this proposal by the following morning.

The plenary quickly dissolved into heated argument. Mugabe and
Nkomo were irate that Carrington was drawing a similarity between
the two forces and their actions. As to Carrington's deadline on the
cease-fire, Mugabe demanded that the Salisbury delegation publicly
state their unwillingness to talk directly with the Front, or the talks
would not proceed. Tongogara, in a more problem-solving way, expressed his frustration with not talking directly with the Salisbury
delegation, because "These are the two forces in conflict; my delegation cannot secure an agreement with Britain." He then added
that it would prove difficult in the future for the two sides to sit
down and talk in Salisbury, if they were not prepared to talk in
London. The conference ended when Mugabe and Nkomo pulled
their delegations, Nkomo warning Carrington "not to come the following Monday and expect an answer from my delegation without
discussions—the chairman will not get one" (United Kingdom 1979,
Minutes 37th Plenary). The two rebel leaders gave an impromptu
press conference, "still shaking with anger . . . Asked what will happen when the Monday deadline comes, so far as the Patriotic Front
is concerned, Mr. Mugabe said there could be no question of toeing
the line. Lord Carrington, he said, 'Can go to hell' " (*The* [London]
Guardian, November 23, 1979).

Carrington's ultimatum prompted Mugabe to fly to Dar Es Salaam
to meet the Front Line Presidents, where Mugabe publicly stated
that he would not allow his soldiers slaughtered on the way to the
assembly points and "General Walls gaining at Lancaster House what
he failed to achieve on the battlefield" (quoted in Smith and Simpson
1981, 139). After the meeting in Dar Es Salaam, the Front Line
Presidents, through their representatives in London, lobbied Carrington hard on three issues: the length of the cease-fire, the need
for close monitoring of the Rhodesian forces, and the need for particularly close watch on the Rhodesian Air Force to prevent it from
bombing the assembly points. Carrington grudgingly met the latter
demands but refused to concede a longer cease-fire period.

This was the only time where Carrington's emphasis on arbitration had to yield to a softer approach. What is intriguing is that while Carrington and his staff, and the Patriotic Front's legal advisers were playing a hard bargaining game on the issues of the cease-fire, an informal coalition was formed between the Patriotic Front's military leaders and the British military advisers, who both felt that the stakes were too important to leave for the civilians. One ZAPU delegate remarked, "The only give and take negotiations were over the military transition and cease fire. . . . There were negotiations then only because the British military were frightened; they had to listen if we said you can't do something in twenty-four hours, for example. . . . Everyone was interested in saving lives and it was a matter of finding the best way of doing things" (ZAPU Delegate A. 1987). Simbi Mubako, ZANU's member of the Patriotic Front's legal team, went so far as to mention Tongogara's role in moderating the cease-fire negotiations:

I remember him saying (about the number and location of the assembly points), "This is not a point on which to break the conference." You see the military people knew the situation on the ground; they knew what they could live with; what they could get away with. For example, he knew that so many would be able to be kept out of the assembly points and he knew that we could send the majibas (teenage scouts) into the assembly points and keep our best fighters out and in the villages to work on the election. The lawyers were much more theoretical because we didn't know what could happen on the ground." (Mubako 1987)

An important piece of information that was shared between Tongogara and the British was that he could reach any of his troops by relay in four days (Davidow 1984, 81–82). This dramatically undercut the Front's bargaining position on the need for a long cease-fire period.

The PF gave partial acceptance on December 6, but made full approval conditional on the longer cease-fire period and additional assembly points. Just when agreement seemed imminent, the PF's conditional acceptance threatened to bring down the whole settlement. The conference had become "bogged down over precisely how, where, and when the war would end . . ." (Smith and Simpson 1981, 148).

Carrington was forced to cash in on the momentum that had built to this point by reporting to the press that a settlement was only days away and that, given all that had been accomplished so far, the

Patriotic Front could not possibly turn their backs from the negotiation. Relying on brinksmanship, Carrington then named Lord
Soames Governor of Zimbabwe and dispatched him to Salisbury.
Both moves provoked the PF's most belligerent responses to that
date, with Mugabe's press secretary, Edison Zvobgo, informing the
British press that Lord Carrington "can go to hell," and that
"Thatcher can jump in the Thames." Zvobgo concluded the impromptu press conference by "brandishing the British maps [of the
assembly points] and giving a shake of his head into camera for each
of the television networks there: 'The answer, Lord Carrington, is
NO . . . NO . . . NO' " (Smith and Simpson 1981, 150).

Just when the edifice was about to collapse, Samora Machel came
to Carrington's rescue. Samora Machel passed a message to his chief
aide in London, Fernand Honwanna to give to Mugabe. Honwanna
informed Mugabe that the war was over and that, "if he [Mugabe]
did not sign the agreement, he would be welcomed back to Mozambique and given a beach villa where he could write his memoirs"
(Davidow 1984, 89). After a final face-saving gesture by the British
in granting the Front an additional assembly point, the Lancaster
House Accords were signed on December 21, the one hundred and
second day of the conference.

The End and Beginning

The signatures at Lancaster House only signalled a commitment to
a peaceful transition. The next two months would be more harrowing
for the participants than any other time in the conflict. In the words
of Lord Soames, the British Governor, "It was a tinderbox, but, hap-
pily, no one struck a match" (Newhouse 1983, 78). The fuel for the
fire was everywhere. In the first two weeks of the cease-fire, 22,000
guerrillas marched to assembly points. ZANU and especially ZAPU
kept most of their best fighters out of the camps as a failsafe measure
in case the country exploded. The British, fearing the possibility of
a coup from disgruntled white soldiers or a reneging on the case of
the Salisbury regime, went out of their way to be tough on ZANU
in order to appease Muzorewa and Walls. In a not-very-subtle move
the South African Army moved three divisions to the Zimbabwean
border as a reminder of what they would do in the event of "chaos."
Amidst threats by the British that they would disqualify ZANU be-

cause of voter intimidation, Mugabe feared that his suspicions of a double-cross might come true.

Two of the three individuals who were moderating influences on ZANU at Lancaster House were unable to play that role during the election campaign. Tongogara, in advance of the ZANU delegation, had flown to Mozambique a week earlier than the signing in London in order to ready his troops for the cease-fire. While in Mozambique he died in an automobile accident, which, amidst rumors of assassination, brought everyone's nerves to the edge. Then Mugabe, before leaving London, announced that ZANU would run on its own in the election and not in coalition with ZAPU. This stunned Nkomo, as his strategy throughout the previous two years had been predicated on coming to power in conjunction with Mugabe. But Mugabe, confident of victory on his own, discarded his less powerful partner.

British pressure kept building on ZANU until Mugabe had a direct talk with Soames. The talk was prompted in part by two assassination attempts against Mugabe. Soames privately reassured him that no party would be disqualified from the election. Britain's public posturing against ZANU, however, prompted Julius Nyerere two weeks before the scheduled elections at the end of February to say that he would only recognize the winner if it was Mugabe. This greatly angered Soames and his staff, because the whole election period and cease-fire hinged on the believability of a free and fair election in which any of the parties could win and which the other parties would abide. Nyerere's statement threatened the confidence of the white Rhodesians, because it was an implicit threat that if ZANU did not win the election, the war would continue.

At Lancaster House, the British had an idea of a feasible settlement. But when the conference succeeded they were really not prepared to implement the agreement. A member of Soames' staff described the transition as "a gigantic game of bluff, keeping just enough Rhodesians obeying the Governor long enough to pull it off" (British Diplomat A. 1987). Britain's formal status of decolonizer became crucial at this point, for enough white Rhodesians in the administration saw the British presence and authority as legitimate.

After the election of February 27–29 but before the announcement of the election results on March 4, the British, knowing that Mugabe was to win, contacted Machel and arranged a meeting in Mozambique between Mugabe, Flower, and Walls. Machel's aide Fernand Honwanna "understood that if Mugabe won, he would need the British and a modus vivendi with Walls" (British Diplomat A. 1987). At the meeting Mugabe offered Walls the command of the new Zimbabwean army, a job he accepted.

On March 4, 1980, the election results were announced. Mugabe and ZANU had won fifty-seven out of one hundred seats, Nkomo had gained twenty seats, and Muzorewa three. To a stunned nation Soames, Mugabe, and Walls went on television that evening. Soames began by announcing his duty to hand over power in an orderly fashion. He was followed by Peter Walls, who appealed "to you all for calm, for peace. No hatred. No bitterness." The last speaker was Robert Mugabe: "Let us join together. Let us show respect for the winners and the losers. . . . There is no intention on our part to victimize the minority. We will ensure there is a place for everyone in this country. I want a broadly based government to include whites and Nkomo" (Quoted in Flower 1987a, 267–268). On April 18, 1980, Zimbabwe was granted formal independence from Great Britain.

Reconstruction

Upon taking power Mugabe issued a plea for racial reconciliation in Zimbabwe. He immediately undertook measures to instill confidence in those whites who chose to remain in Zimbabwe. Such measures included keeping Peter Walls as head of the armed forces, maintaining Ken Flower as head of the Central Intelligence Office, naming Ken Norman, a white farmer, as Minister of Agricultural Affairs, and announcing that ZANU-PF fully intended to abide by the Lancaster House constitution.

Reconciliation, however, opposes revolution. The former implies coming to terms with one's enemies, a preference for forgiveness over retribution, a willingness to maintain continuity amidst change, and taken to its logical extreme a partnership between old adversaries at the expense of one's old allies. Revolution involves transformation, a powerful rejection of the past, a reversal of fortunes between haves and have-nots. One often thinks of revolution as having losers and winners, and reconciliation as having all winners. This is an intellectual error. Both reconciliation and revolution have winners and losers, only the aggrieved party differs. In the case of reconciliation, the most bitter proponents of fundamental change lose, in revolution they triumph. Such is the case of any negotiated settlement to civil war.

The negotiated settlement was not favored by all concerned. Those who viewed Lancaster House as a sell-out had four options: exit, the choice most preferred by hard-line whites; grudging acceptance combined with a willingness to seek political change within the political system; the rejection of the agreement and willingness to choose violence in opposition; and finally, acquiescence to change, either because of loyalty to Mugabe or ZANU, or because of feelings of powerlessness to fight undesirable change.

While Robert Mugabe emphasized his commitment to revolutionary socialism, he chose continuity over change on the most important issue facing Zimbabwe: land. Having decided that the country's white farmers were crucial to Zimbabwe's economic survival, Mugabe embraced this community, while rejecting the hundreds of thousands of land poor who believed that a triumph in the war would result in the redistribution of the white farmers' land. The policy of reconciliation practically disenfranchised two formerly crucial constituent groups of Mugabe: the land poor and the freedom fighters—the latter euphemistically labeled "ex-combatants."

While Mugabe professed his desire to work with members of the white government and ZAPU, some within these groups hedged their bets. Mugabe forced Walls to resign several months after independence when it was revealed that Walls had urged the British government to initiate a coup against Mugabe when he won election in April. An assassination attempt against Mugabe and leading ZANU officials failed during the summer.

Violence did not end with the settlement of the civil war. Its bases, however, fundamentally changed. The first major challenge to the post-independence regime came not from renewed clashes of whites against blacks, but rather directly from ZAPU, ZANU's partner in the Patriotic Front. Radicals within ZAPU, seemingly with Nkomo's active encouragement, refused to accept the new Zimbabwe, and hid large stocks of weapons at properties in the countryside bought by Nkomo. All of this occurred before a national army had been forged between ZANLA, ZIPRA, and the Rhodesian Army.

The problems between ZIPRA and ZANLA and their respective political wings dominated Zimbabwean politics for much of the decade after Lancaster House. Essentially a political fight between the two movements, the struggle had overtones of ethnic warfare. This was inevitable, given that Nkomo and ZAPU became increasingly based in Matabeleland, home of the Ndebele people of Zimbabwe. The first major outburst of violence took place in the fall of 1980, prompted by an incendiary speech by a ZANU Minister, Enos Nkala, himself an Ndebele, in Matabeleland. Camps of ZIPRA followers, not yet disarmed, attacked groups of ZANLA soldiers in the region. At another instance of fighting between the two armies, a newly constituted brigade of soldiers, integrated from ZIPRA and ZANLA, was brought in to quell the violence.

This competition between ZAPU and ZANLA took a different turn in 1981–1982. Disaffected remnants of ZAPU's armies, possessing stocks of weapons not turned in to the national army, initiated hit-and-run terror attacks against civilians, white farmers, and government representatives in Matabeleland. Mugabe's government, which at first used little force to stop this incipient insurgency, chose harsh, indiscriminate aggression against the region in the hopes of eliminating these guerrillas, now referred to as "bandits" or "dissidents" by the régime. The culmination of the terror came when the government unleashed the Fifth Brigade—an all-Shona brigade trained by North Koreans—against the insurgents. Most reliable accounts believe that approximately 1,000 Ndebele civilians died during the brigade's slash-and-burn campaign through Matabeleland. Even then the guerrillas refused to go away. Attacks on white farmers increased in the next years. The violence ended when ZANU and ZAPU reached a unity agreement in 1988 that merged the two parties and gave a few cabinet positions to ex-ZAPU leaders.

While Mugabe and ZANU-PF honored the Lancaster House constitution, they angered many of their allies and supporters by keeping intact security legislation (the Emergency Powers Act) from the Smith régime, which it used to detain, harass, and torture suspected enemies of the state. It must be remembered that ZANU's policy of repression was not simply the legacy of the security state it inherited, nor was it the paranoid terror of a régime which came to power through violence and saw enemies lurking behind every stone. Moreover, the violence was not the tribally based blood bath predicted by Rhodesian whites, an image embraced by some of the "keenest" Western reporters at the time. ZANU's "paranoia" resulted primarily from the real threat that South Africa posed to an independent Zimbabwe. Zimbabwe's independence came at a time of intense regional destabilization by the South African government. In the summer of

1990, in reaction to changes in South Africa, Zimbabwe finally repealed the emergency legislation put in place by the Smith régime.

One must be careful about the lessons one draws from the Zimbabwe case. Jeffrey Herbst argues that Zimbabwe's demographic profile provided for an easy abatement of the white/black conflict. What Herbst calls a tacit economic bargain set the parameters of racial co-existence in Zimbabwe. Whites who chose to remain would live in affluence, but would not have direct involvement in political decision making. A gradual dwindling of the white population would gradually cede white land holdings to the régime (Herbst 1990, 221–227).

As Herbst suggests, Mugabe and others in ZANU have continued to voice the goals of revolutionary socialism and transformation to obfuscate what have been mostly pro-capitalist and pro-Western economic policies. Land, never a serious issue for the party in the 1980s, remained a problem that has worsened due to African population growth. The government can speak proudly of its commitment to equalization of educational opportunities and health care. In the case of the former, however, the government faces a stiff challenge from producing hundreds of thousands of school graduates with few opportunities for employment ahead of them.

Notes

1.   This chapter draws heavily from Stedman 1991.

2.   After independence the names of three of these cities changed to Harare, Mutare, and Gweru. Bulawayo stayed the same.

3.   Sithole had been leader of ZANU until 1974 when he was overthrown by members of the Executive Committee. For two years a fierce battle raged for control of ZANU, and Robert Mugabe was chosen by the ZANLA guerrillas as their "spokesman." Mugabe won the support of those guerrillas because of his refusal to countenance any negotiations with Smith. By 1976, Mugabe had not fully consolidated his leadership within ZANU and could not afford to be conciliatory towards any settlement.

4.   Figures are from Wilkinson 1980; Cilliers 1985; and Martin and Johnson 1981. In terms of the breakdown in civilian deaths into whites and Africans, Wilkinson states that at the beginning of 1979 the cumulative figures were 310 white civilians killed and 3,845 African civilians killed (Wilkinson 1980, 114).

5.   The leaders of Zambia and Mozambique were prepared to work for a settlement due to the extensive costs inflicted on their countries by the

war. As I stated earlier, Zambia had initiated the search for peace in 1974, and Mozambique had signalled its willingness to work for a settlement in 1978. Tanzania, as a Front Line State, expressed its willingness to work for settlement, but it had less leverage than Mozambique and Zambia and had incurred lower war costs as well.

SEVEN

The End of the American Civil War

Stephen John Stedman

We must remember, it is the most difficult process in the world to make two people of one.—John Calhoun, 1838

Over 620,000 soldiers died in the American civil war, a staggering amount comparable to many of the most gruesome prolonged wars in the world over the last ten years. The number of American dead in that war approximates the number of American dead in all of America's other wars combined. One would imagine that such a war would interest scholars of comparative politics, and political science writ large. After all, America, long discussed in terms of its exceptionalism, underwent problems of political development similar to those of other countries, and the most important solutions to those problems were forged in civil war, not through civil society. Yet few works place the American civil war in comparative perspective, in contrast to the millions of pages devoted to American study of the war.[1]

This is a small attempt to rectify that situation. In this chapter I describe how the American civil war ended in order to gain insight into the comparative problem of civil war termination. In particular I address the following components of the ending of the war: 1) the decision of the Confederate military in opposition to its civilian leadership to surrender to the Union armies of Grant and Sherman; 2) the relationship between Southern motives for going to war, the course of the war, and the failure of the South to pursue a strategy of partisan, guerrilla war in 1865; and 3) the relationship between Northern motives for the war and the policies the North pursued toward the defeated South from 1865 to 1877.

Spring 1865: Political Intransigence and Military Surrender

In early 1865, after four years of a bloody war, the Confederate States of America found itself near military collapse. Towards the end of 1864 Southern morale suffered shattering blows. Union General William T. Sherman's march through Georgia and the Carolinas proved that the Union could raid with impunity the heartland of the Confederacy; attacks by Union General Philip Sheridan destroyed the Confederate hold over the Shenandoah Valley in Virginia, a crucial region for the feeding of Confederate troops and the defense of the Confederate capital in Richmond; finally, Abraham Lincoln's re-election crushed any hopes for Northern acquiescence to a peace favorable to the South. By January 1865 Confederate generals literally were watching their armies disappear—that month alone a staggering eight percent of Southern soldiers deserted.

In March of 1865, General Robert E. Lee visited Confederate President Jefferson Davis to discuss the possibility of some form of negotiated surrender. Lee had concluded that the end was near and preferred a negotiated surrender on Northern terms to the continuance of the war by remnants of the Confederate armies. He believed strongly that if the conflict were to evolve into a guerrilla partisan war, the consequences would be worse for the South than for the Northern armies of occupation. Jefferson Davis, however, refused to consider any talk of surrender, and Lee departed, having found Davis "pertinacious in opinion and purpose" (quoted in Ballard, 1986, 27).

Jefferson Davis wrote a letter to a friend about this meeting, stating, "We both entered into this war at the beginning of it; we both staked everything on the issue, and have lost all which either public or private enemies could take away" (Davis to Bragg quoted in Ballard, 1986, 28). On April 4 Davis proposed to his cabinet "a war of persistent guerrilla-type harassment" and pledged "never to give up." The proposal found little sympathy among his subordinates, most of whom agreed with Confederate Secretary of War John Breckinridge, who "hoped the Confederacy would surrender as a country and not 'disband like banditti' " (Ballard, 1986, 38). One pro-Union

Confederate senator was convinced that "Davis would make no peace 'so long as he shall be supplied with the resources of war' " (Ballard, 1986, 57–58). This senator suffered from overoptimism. In early April Union troops threatened Richmond, prompting the Confederate government to flee for its very survival. When Davis received the confirmation of Lee's surrender at Appomattox, he still refused to accept the inevitability of defeat. On April 11, to a query about whether Lee's surrender meant the end of the war, Davis replied, "By no means. We'll fight it out to the Mississippi River" (Ballard, 1986, 59).

At the time of Lee's surrender at Appomattox the Confederacy still possessed two large armies: one under the command of Joseph Johnston in North Carolina and the other under Kirby Smith in the Trans-Mississippi. Johnston had recently taken command of the army in North Carolina, "with a full consciousness on my part . . . that we could have no other object, in continuing the war, than to obtain fair terms for peace" (quoted in Ballard, 1986, 24). On April 13 Johnston, General P. T. Beauregard, Davis's cabinet, and Davis himself met to discuss Confederate alternatives. Both Johnston and Beauregard urged negotiations, and all of the cabinet, except Secretary of State Judah P. Benjamin, concurred. Davis refused the advice of those around him, but knew that he was isolated. He approved a meeting between Johnston and William T. Sherman, believing that such talks would prove to his underlings that Northern peace terms would hold little attraction for them.

When Johnston met Sherman the Union general passed on the news that Abraham Lincoln had been assassinated. Sherman, without consulting his superiors in the North, established his own terms for Southern surrender. Sherman, who by his own words had made Georgia "howl," preferred a lenient peace, and developed terms he believed would have met Lincoln's approval. They included the recognition of present state governments in the South, the reestablishment of federal courts in those states, and the guarantee of constitutional rights and amnesty for all Southerners who had fought or aided the Confederate war effort. Sherman's terms, which did not even address the question of slavery, established the prewar status quo as a settlement.

The Southern cabinet, now in Greensboro, North Carolina, met to discuss Sherman's offer. Predictably, Davis believed that a guerrilla war was still preferable to a settlement that did not provide for

Southern independence. His cabinet, however, was adamant: in the words of Stephen Mallory, then secretary of the navy, guerrilla warfare "would be more disastrous to our own people than it could possibly be to the enemy" (quoted in Ballard, 1986, 104). After Breckinridge refused to support moving to the Trans-Mississippi to continue the fight, Davis, believing that Sherman's superiors would themselves reject Sherman's terms, agreed to the settlement.

Davis had calculated correctly; while Johnston waited for word from the Confederate government, Sherman informed him that his offer had been overturned in Washington, D.C. Andrew Johnson, the Union's new president, and Edwin Stanton, the Union secretary of war, had chastised Sherman for overstepping his authority by including political terms of settlement in the military surrender. Sherman was allowed to offer the conditions Grant gave Lee at Appomattox—a purely military surrender with stipulations providing for soldiers under arms. Johnston, instead of waiting for a new reply from Davis, took upon himself the task of surrender, and on April 26 abandoned the fugitive Confederate government.

As late as May 2, while on the run and with only a limited cavalry guard, Davis insisted that a small force could be mustered to continue the struggle. One soldier with Davis's entourage wrote later: "We looked at each other in amazement and with feelings akin to trepidation, for we hardly knew how we should give expression to views diametrically opposed to those he had uttered" (quoted in Ballard, 1986, 122–123). Eyewitnesses described Davis's delicate mental balance:

Poor President, he is unwilling to see what all around him see. He cannot bring himself to believe that after four years of glorious struggle we are to be crushed into the dust of submission.

Mr. Davis seemed overwhelmed with a sense of the national calamity; he at times exhibited some impatience and irascibility, but I never witnessed in a man a more entire abnegation of self, or selfish considerations. He seemed to cling obstinately to the hope of continuing the struggle in order to accomplish the great end of Southern independence—his whole soul was given to that thought, and an appearance of slackness upon the part of others seemed to arouse his indignation. I think the very ardor of his resolution prevented him from properly estimating the resources at his command. (quoted in Ballard, 1986, 112, 126)

Days later, the remaining Confederate armies in the Trans-Mississippi surrendered on their own, and Union patrols captured Davis and shipped him to prison in Maryland where he awaited his fate at the hands of the victors.

Some Issues and Questions

This story only marks the end of the first stage of the termination of the American civil war. The fate of the South in the period after defeat and the policies pursued by the North will be addressed later in the chapter. For now, however, this story of the Confederacy's last days is rich in nuance for the discussion of civil war termination. First, the issue of surrender pitted Jefferson Davis, who believed that the Southern cause was national independence and therefore uncompromisable, against many of his cabinet and military leaders who were either unwilling to bear the costs of guerrilla war to achieve such independence or defined the conflict differently than Davis and could see that some of their concerns could be met by lenient terms from the North. Second, it was Davis's generals—and not Davis or his cabinet—who surrendered. Third, Davis's desire to fight a protracted war prompted little or no elite or popular support at the time.

This story raises a number of questions. First, why did some participants on the Southern side see unconditional surrender as unacceptable? That is, why did Jefferson Davis, even after obvious military defeat, refuse to surrender? Why did he view the draconian costs of continuing the war as preferable to surrender? Second, how did those Southerners who were willing to surrender define the issues at stake, so as to allow them to surrender? Third, when some of the Southern leadership desired to fight a guerrilla partisan war, why did the will of the people continue to crumble?

According to Beringer et al. (1986), answers to these questions are to be found in comparison to other wars. Drawing on the example of Paraguay's war against Brazil, Argentina, and Uruguay from 1865–1871, when Paraguay lost over fifty percent of its population and eighty percent of its fighting men, they argue that had the South been convinced of the righteousness of its cause, it could have made itself unconquerable to the North. By continuing the war by different means, the South could have won its independence against an overstretched Northern occupying force.

This failure of the South to fight a protracted, guerrilla war resulted from a lack of agreement about why it went to war in the first place, and the fact that the coalition that comprised the Confederacy contained latent splits which became manifest when the costs of the war became prohibitive.[2] In the words of Beringer et al.:

the Confederates lacked a feeling of oneness, that almost mystical sense of nationhood. They lacked a consensus on why they fought or what they stood for. The Confederate nation was created on paper, not in the hearts and minds of its would-be citizens. These differences reflected a national will that did not equal the demands placed upon it. (Beringer et al., 1986, 64)

The natural counterpart to this interpretation holds that although the Northern coalition also had differences about the goals of the war, such differences waned in importance as the Northern people, leaders, and armies came to understand that, in the words of Lincoln, this was "a people's contest": a total war that demanded tremendous sacrifice to achieve a non-negotiable principle—in this case, "one nation indivisible." To paraphrase Phillip Paludan, the North, unlike the South, learned "what the war meant" (Paludan, 1989, 58). The incredible costs of the conflict tended to galvanize Northern commitment while weakening that of the South.

James McPherson (1988) argues that a crucial part of this process of defining the stakes in the struggle and the willingness of the North to fight a total war was an element of "contingency." That is, at crucial times in the course of the war events conspired to harden Northern determination and strike at the Southern will to fight. In McPherson's interpretation the preexisting sense of nationalism on both sides does not matter so much as how the war affected that sense of nationalism.

Ante-Bellum America: Grounds for Conflict and Extent of Polarity

The debate between McPherson and Beringer et al. is significant for what the arguments hold in common. They agree that the South's loss of the war was not due to the North's overwhelming capabilities and resources. They agree that many on both sides lacked the will to fight such a war. Moreover, they agree that factional differences existed on both sides of the war. These similarities between the two competing interpretations suggest a further puzzle. If so many on both sides lacked the will to fight the war, and there existed factional differences on both sides concerning the motivations for war, how and why did the war, as costly as it was, come about in the first place?

Most arguments on the origins of the war can be reduced to the question of whether the war was prompted by the slavery issue or whether that issue was symbolic of a deeper political, economic, cultural, and ideological conflict. This debate relates to the fundamental question of ante-bellum polarity and the extent of differences between North and South. I would like to suggest that while important differences existed between the sections, ultimately there were important similarities—similarities that had a great effect on the course of the war and its outcome.

Many of the older scholarly (and often partisan) treatments of the war portray an ante-bellum South that possessed a fundamentally separate (as opposed to distinct) cultural identity rooted in political and economic visions incompatible with those of the North. They argue that the civil war was in essence fought between different nationalities. Beringer et al. (1986) dispute this: the South was not a separate nation and had few of the attributes of imagined community associated with nationalism. On this point they elaborate upon a line of argument developed by David Potter. As Potter elegantly argues, the thesis of competing nationalisms founders on the shoals of common sense. If these regions had been so hostile and incompatible, how then do we account for the sixty years of co-existence that preceded the conflict and the relatively short period of hostility between regions after the conflict? As he points out, for every belief and interest that would suggest a fundamentally hostile separation, one can easily point to beliefs that all participants in the war held in common, as well as cross-cutting economic interests that joined some Northerners and Southerners (Potter, 1968, 98–100).

To explain an antagonism which sprang up suddenly, and died down suddenly, the historian does not need to discover, and cannot effectively use, a factor which has been constant over a long period, as the cultural difference between the North and South has been. He needs to identify a factor which can cause bitter disagreement even among a people who have much basic homogeneity. No factor, I would suggest, will meet this need better than the feeling, widespread in the 1850s in the South, that the South's vital interests were being jeopardized, and that the region was being exposed to the dangers of a slave insurrection, as a result of the hostility of antislavery men in the North. Applied to the sectional crisis, such a view of the sources of friction would make possible the explanation of the Civil War, without making impossible the explanation of the rapid return to union after the war. No cultural explanation will do this. (Potter, 1968, 103)

McPherson also pays homage to Potter by developing an explanation of the civil war that stresses the development of a faction within the North, the New England abolitionists, that desired the revolutionary transformation of the South's society, polity, and economy. Drawing on the work of Arno Mayer (1971), McPherson asserts that the South seceded to preempt this revolution, and therefore has much in common with the counter-revolutionary movements that had swept through Europe in the late 1840s.

The historical narratives of McPherson (1982; 1988), Potter (1968; 1976), and Donald (1978) tacitly argue that the civil war resulted from the inability of American political institutions to resolve conflict as the country's society changed. These scholars portray the road toward civil war as one of failed compromise, bargaining processes of incomplete information about intentions, radical factions in the North and South that each side thought of as representative of the other side, misperception among the actors, and the gradual loss of commitment to negotiated settlement and constitutional union.

The institutions for resolving conflict in the United States in the 1800s can be differentiated into those governing competition within the nation as a whole and those bounding competition over the slavery issue. The former, of course, consisted of the Constitution and the American political party system: both were supposed to function to protect sectional interests without plunging the nation into sectional conflict. On the other hand, the institutions governing slavery in America comprised a set of rules, norms, and expectations produced by historical compromises over a sixty-year period. These compromises included the prohibition of the African slave trade, the secure recognition of the South's right to slavery, and the tacit acknowledgement that the North would not comply with the fugitive slave clause of the Constitution but that the clause would not be enforced so as to avoid civil disobedience. The single most important inviolate rule was the 36–30 line established in the Missouri Compromise of 1820 that would determine whether new territory would be admitted to the Union as free or slave states.

Potter and McPherson begin their analysis of the causes of the civil war with the United States's war with Mexico in 1848.[3] By opening up new lands for annexation, the Mexican War forced Northern and Southern politicians to confront anew the slavery question, which had been dormant for almost thirty years after the Missouri Compromise of 1820.

The spoils of the Mexican War—new territories in California and New Mexico—forced the slavery issue back on to the national agenda. The Compromise of 1850 crafted a series of compromise measures that permitted California to enter the Union as a free state. But one of these measures required the federal government to enforce, the Fugitive Slave Act and to return slaves who had escaped to the North back to their Southern owners. In states such as Massachusetts, where for all intents and purposes the Act had lain dormant for years, federal authorities tried to enforce the Act. Abolitionists such as William Lloyd Garrison reviled the United States Constitution as a pact with the devil, asserted that there was a higher law than the Constitution, and organized to prevent federal enforcement.

This proved to be the first abandonment of constitutional law as the compromise that made possible a union of states. The decision of Northern radicals to disobey and circumvent the law was mirrored by Southern radicals, as "filibusterers" set sail to the Caribbean in the hope of annexing Cuba, Nicaragua, and other points south as new slave states for the Union.

The Compromise of 1850 prompted South Carolinians for the second time—1832 and the Nullification Crisis being the first—to threaten secession from the Union. For the second time other Southerners had little spirit for secession and failed to support the South Carolinians. But if these other Southerners did not believe the Compromise of 1850 was worth leaving the Union for, neither were they satisfied with the half-measures taken to keep the Union as one. In the words of David Potter, the Compromise of 1850 should more accurately be called the armistice of 1850 (Potter, 1976). The decade of the 1850s would see repeated battles over the slavery issue, a civil war in the new state of Kansas that was a preview of the larger war to come, and a gradual escalation of rhetoric, hostility, and fear about the intentions of Northern and Southern leaders. It must be emphasized, however, that the decade of the 1850s was also a decade of searching for political solutions to the problem of slavery and its extension—evidence that secession was pursued only after other possibilities had been exhausted.

The status of new prospective states in the 1850s constantly threatened the delicate equilibrium between North and South, and led to major repudiations of the larger institutional arrangements concerning slavery. The first major repudiation occurred in the writing of the Kansas-Nebraska Act in 1854 when Stephen Douglas deliberately junked the key focal point of compromise, the 36–30 provision of the Compromise of 1820:

by permitting Southerners to maneuver him into outright repeal of the Missouri Compromise, Douglas, as many Northerners believed, came close to tampering with the Constitution. Of course, the Missouri Compromise was not part of the written Constitution, but it was an agreement that had almost constitutional status, having been observed loyally for more than three decades and having acquired, as Douglas himself declared in 1849, respect as a "sacred thing which no ruthless hand would ever be reckless enough to disturb." (Donald, 1978, 61)

The Kansas-Nebraska Act instituted the rule of "popular sovereignty" for determining whether a territory would enter the Union as a free or slave state and set off a rush towards Kansas. Northern abolitionists, Missourians, and Southerners poured into Kansas to provide votes for the Kansas they desired. Although the numbers favored a free state, Southerners turned to violence and crass manipulation of laws to ensure that Kansas would enter the Union as a slave state. The result was "Bleeding Kansas": a civil war to precede the larger conflagration between the states.

What had been a trickle of defection from the institutional compromise upholding the Union became a veritable flood: in strategic terms, as each side witnessed the other's abandonment of the rules of bounded competition, the other defected as well. The final episode that destroyed the régime governing slavery came in 1857 with the Dred Scott decision and the assertion by a Southern-dominated court that Congress had no power to regulate slavery in the territories and that slavery in the Northern states was conceivable: slaveholders could spend time in those states with their slaves, who by force of law would remain slaves.

The régime that regulated slavery in the United States had collapsed with no immediate prospect of replacement. What is more, however, the collapse had also irreparably damaged the larger régime that mediated political life in the country as a whole. The Constitution was defiled as a bargain with the devil and seen to be a lesser law than that of God; the Supreme Court was seen as a biased tool for the South to impose its will on the North; political parties that had been national up until 1854 were now sectional parties; and violence—justified by a higher end—had become an appropriate means to force change.

McPherson traces the disappearance of national political parties directly to the Kansas-Nebraska Act. In their wake rose the Republican party with its stated ideology of "free men, free labor, and free soil," which Southerners perceived as a direct threat to their interests. McPherson argues that many in the South believed that the party of Lincoln desired to transform the American polity, society, and economy fundamentally and that such a transformation demanded violent opposition. This was not entirely misperception: vocal, visible Northerners, calling for just such a revolutionary transformation, played an active role in the founding of the Republican party. The Southern error was to mistake the rhetoric of the few as representative of the motives of the whole: Lincoln and many in his party were more than willing to live with the continuation and protection of Southern slavery.

This perception of the Republican party as a revolutionary party helps to explain one of the paradoxes of the American civil war: in 1861 both sides went to war professing conservative, counterrevolutionary aims. The Confederacy believed that it represented the essence of what the founding fathers had intended America to be, and argued that it was fighting to preserve America from the revolutionary transformational zeal of Northern abolitionists and Republicans. Lincoln and most Northerners, on the other hand, saw their war aims in much the same way: a conservative response to save the threatened Union.

The reasons that individuals on both sides fought in and supported the civil war vary and cannot be subsumed under one issue. The Union and the Confederacy should be seen as coalitions of factions with different motivations for fighting. In the Confederacy one must distinguish between the die-hard "fire-breathing" secessionists of the seven states that seceded first and the leaders of the remaining states (Arkansas, North Carolina, Virginia, and Tennessee) that joined the Confederacy after the attack on Fort Sumter. One must also distinguish between the landed upper classes of the South and the yeoman farmer. While both poor and wealthy whites saw gains from slavery, such gains accrued disproportionately to the latter, a fact that placed limits on the willingness of the former to bear the burdens of the impending war.

For the die-hard secessionists of the South the central issue at stake in 1861 was slavery, in particular whether the peculiar institution would be afforded the protection required for it to survive. Steven Channing's study of the politics of secession in South Carolina (1974) argues convincingly that secession was the product of fear: a fear of a future without slavery or a future where slavery was an institution without protection. Having built a system based on dominance and submission, violence and cruelty, Southerners feared a domestic uprising of the victims of the system and also believed that the federal government would do little to protect slavery against the incitements of Northern abolitionists who would provoke such an uprising.[4] Such fears seemed reasonable given John Brown's insurrection at Harper's Ferry in 1860 and the near-canonization, as McPherson calls it, of Brown by many Northerners.

Why the South Lost the War

Upon taking the office of president of the Confederacy, Davis knew that "Southern nationalism at the beginning of 1861 was still a fragile and weak organism" (Escott, 1978, 32). Unlike other Southerners who had supported secession as a bargaining ploy to gain concessions from the North and expected either no war or a short war to come, Davis expected "a long and bloody" war. He knew that if the South was to triumph in such a struggle, it had to be unified in its purpose, and that his job as president of the Confederacy was to define that purpose. Davis also knew that the Southern states were a precarious, unstable coalition and that many within the coalition would not fight such a bloody contest for slavery. He therefore looked to define the Southern cause without recourse to slavery, and to do so, "the first step in developing Confederate nationalism was to establish independence as the South's primary goal" (Escott, 1978, 38).

Herein resided one of the first and fundamental contradictions of the Confederate war effort: the meaning of independence was different for ruler and ruled. For Davis, independence was tied to nationhood—a concept tied to the American Revolution: the South was fighting for a separate nation. Such a motive cannot be compromised: one is either a separate independent nation or one is not. Independence, in the discourse of most Southerners, however, was not an independence of nation. Rather, independence in the ideology of the American political culture of the day harkened to notions of individual rights and, by extension, to the states as the protectors of those rights. Individual independence is a matter of degrees and involves various trade-offs. National independence is an either/or matter; either there would exist a Confederate States of America or there would not.

Davis was at a distinct disadvantage in attempting to inculcate a feeling of Confederate nationalism. For over sixty years the United States of America had created a common history, common mythology, and common traditions. Davis could not appeal to a common historical Southern identity, and instead identified the Southern cause as a conservative American one—the upholding of the American Revolution against a revolution being made in the North:

At a time when many Southerners were reluctant to leave the Union, Davis identified Confederate goals with the history and traditions of the United States. The key to the effectiveness of his ideology was its claim that the Confederacy was the true embodiment of American democracy. . . . Repeatedly he sounded his main theme: that the new Southern nation was the true heir of the founding fathers and existed to continue the work which they had begun. As a supplement to this, he tried to demonstrate that the United States had fallen away from its heritage and become a land of fanaticism, executive usurpations, and tyranny. (Escott, 1978, 170)

Reid Mitchell in his study of civil war combatants illustrates the difficulties of fighting for Southern independence while claiming the mantle of American national legitimacy:

The flag presentations, the patriotic speeches, the parades all celebrated the war, and they were all elements of a political culture common to the North and the South.

The most important reference point for this political culture was the American Revolution. Both the Union and Confederate armies kept the Revolution before their eyes in systematic fashion, by celebrating its past events at appropriate times. Soldiers were reminded of their Revolutionary heritage, the heroism and purity of their forefathers, and their own duty to emulate them. Both armies customarily observed Washington's Birthday, when the Farewell Address was sometimes read aloud to the assembled troops. But the most significant holiday on both sides seems to have been the Fourth of July. . . .

In general . . . Confederate symbols were pathetically reminiscent of the old American symbols, just as the Confederate constitution copied the United States constitution, and as Confederate ideology was a parody of American ideology. It is quite understandable that Confederates, with their common American heritage, should continue to use the old symbols, but the power of borrowed symbols to compel loyalty is severely limited. However, the Confederates had no choice: they had to use American symbols because they regarded themselves as the true Americans. And historically, their claim to American symbols was hard to dispute . . . (Mitchell, 1988, 20–22)

The South had enormous advantages in terms of size and geography that would have made it difficult to subdue if the North had had to occupy it. The war, however, was fought with huge armies in pitched battles, and there was the expectation on both sides that one overwhelming victory by either side could determine the war. Since the war was fought in such a fashion, the morale of both sides hung in the balance of each military battle. It was the North, however, that first understood the total nature of the war, and that a protracted conventional war effort was necessary to prevail. The South, on the other hand, entered the war believing that it would be a short one, and its confidence was bolstered by easy victories in the first battles of 1861.

Southern hopes also rested on foreign recognition and aid. Confederate leaders believed that cotton—a commodity needed by the mills of England—would provide necessary leverage on Britain to gain its support. But Britain was only one among five major powers in Europe, and had as much at stake economically with the North as it did with the South. Three kinds of pressures prevented Britain from recognition of the South. First, British society was divided on the question of recognition: while much of the upper classes desired to see America's democratic experiment come crashing down, the working classes tended to sympathize with Northern goals and purposes. In essence the British working class saw the Union as a progressive force attempting to eliminate the remnants of aristocracy in the South. Second, the war did not provide a straightforward economic sanction: while Britain had been dependent on Southern cotton, the effects of a shortage of the material were not felt until late 1862. Moreover, the British had much trade with the industrialized North, and imported wheat and grains from its farmers. Third, Britain had to calculate the effects of its recognition upon its relations with its European rivals. British fear of involvement in a war with the Union led to a policy of non-involvement until the Confederacy had established itself as a de facto nation and had militarily defeated the Union. It is noteworthy, here, that British recognition and assistance might have brought such a result, and held out hope for the Confederacy throughout much of 1862 when the war was unquestionably favoring the South. It was not until the battle of Antietam in late 1862 that Britain decided to put the recognition issue aside, a move that was reinforced by Lincoln's Emancipation Proclamation.

The course of the war favored the South in the first two years. Military victories and possible foreign recognition provided much optimism to the Southern cause. What is striking, however, is how in a relatively short time, the Southern war-fighting morale was shattered. After victories in the west and in Maryland and Pennsylvania, the South came face-to-face with the price of "independence." Doubt arose about whether that price was worth it, and what the war was about.

Beringer et al. (1986) argue that it was precisely the lack of separate identity—the foundation of nationalism—that spelled doom for the Southern war effort. And if we accept the theorists of cultural identity who argue that war against a mutually defined enemy often strengthens or creates the mystical feeling of "imagined community" (Coser, 1964; Anderson, 1983), the lack of such a feeling on the part of the South is even more striking.

This view helps to explain Jefferson Davis's refusal to surrender and the preference of most Southerners for reunion with the North to a protracted war for Southern independence. What does this suggest for understanding how civil wars end? I would like to put forward two explanations of Davis's behavior and what they might mean for war termination. First, one could look to what Davis assumed the consequences of Northern victory to be. It is possible that Davis truly believed that a Northern victory would end in utter subjugation of the South, or in his words, "slavery." The costs of defeat might be so draconian that the stakes were nothing less than survival. Second, one could posit that Davis's preferences were non-compromisable, or lexicographic; that is, before Davis would be willing to consider the utility of various outcomes, his one overriding preference— Southern national independence—had to be met.[5]

Perhaps a greater mystery than Southern secession was the Northern resistance to Southern assertions of independence. First and foremost, although the slavery issue prompted the South's drive for autonomy, most Northerners did not fight to eliminate slavery. Abolitionists were a decided minority within the North, many Northerners were as prejudiced as their Southern counterparts towards blacks, and it "remains unclear how the North, with all its Negrophobia, could eventually consent to the sudden liberation of four

million slaves on American soil, and, shortly thereafter, to their enfranchisement" (Fredrickson, 1981, 151).

Lincoln primarily went to war to preserve the Union, and his
actions were guided by political expedience in order to keep the
Northern coalition together. As Eric Foner observes,

Lincoln fully appreciated, as he would observe in his second inaugural address, that slavery was "somehow" the cause of the war. But he also understood the vital importance of keeping the border slave states in the Union,
generating support among the broadest constituency in the North, and weakening the Confederacy by holding out to irresolute Southerners the possibility that they could return to the Union with their property, including
slaves, intact. In 1861 the restoration of the Union, not emancipation, was
the cause that generated the widest support for the war effort. (Foner, 1988,
4)

To further understand that abolition of slavery was not the primary
motivation of Northerners in 1861, one need only point to the Crit-
tendon-Johnson Resolutions of Congress in July 1861, which limited
"the war to conservative goals: the preservation of the Union and
the restoration of the rule of law ante-Sumner" (Paludan, 1989, 87–
88).

The demands of fighting the war effectively prompted Lincoln
(with much reluctance) to embark on emancipation—the first step
for those radicals in the North who wanted a revolutionary transformation of the South. Even emancipation was a compromise, however. It was only binding on Southern slave states not under Union
control—a move by Lincoln to minimize hostility among those border
slave states that had stayed in the Union: Missouri, Kentucky, Del-
aware, and Maryland.

Lincoln faced a dilemma that would confront the North throughout the war and during reconstruction. On the one hand, Lincoln
came to believe that the means and methods of war would have to
become total. He fully supported Grant and Sherman who sought to
insure that the South would be so militarily defeated that it would
never again contemplate secession. On the other hand, Lincoln did
not believe in the total war goals of revolutionary transformation of
the South's institutions. He believed, as did Sherman, in a "lenient
peace." The North unified behind the goal of militarily crushing the
South and its spirit of rebellion. But once having accomplished that
goal, severe differences existed whether to build a new South based
on the remaining vestiges of the past or based on new political, social,
and economic classes and arrangements.

Reconstruction

Reconstruction, or the policies to pursue towards those regions of the South that were conquered, split the Northern coalition that had successfully fought the war. As long as the war was being fought, the coalition between Northern radicals, moderates, and conservatives remained intact.

As Eric Foner observes, most of the early reconstruction policies were pursued out of military necessity or out of political considerations towards ending the war as quickly as possible. Emancipation, the policy that destroyed the South's peculiar institution, was itself a product of strategic considerations: "It is probably most accurate to say that Lincoln, neither an egalitarian in a modern sense nor a man paralyzed, like so many of his contemporaries, by racial fears and prejudices, did not approach any policy, even emancipation, primarily in terms of its impact upon blacks; for him winning the war always remained paramount" (Foner, 1988, 6).

Lincoln saw reconstruction as a means to end the war as quickly as possible and as early as 1863 developed a policy which he believed would signal leniency to the South and therefore induce their surrender. His plan called for pardons of all Confederates willing to take an oath of loyalty to the Union and and the readmittance of reconstructed state governments into the Union when ten percent of a state's population voted for reconstruction. The plan called for the protection of Southern property, with the exception of slaves, who were to remain emancipated.

Lincoln's plan won few adherents in either the North or the South. Within the Union Republican radicals believed that the plan did not go far enough. These individuals, like Thaddeus Stevens, believed that nothing short of a political, economic, and social transformation should be the price of Southern defeat. Such a transformation could only be brought about by vanquishing the planter class that prompted the rebellion:

The whole fabric of Southern society must be changed and it can never be done if this opportunity is lost. The Southern states have been despotisms, not governments of the people. It is impossible that any practical equality of rights can exist where a few thousand men monopolize the whole landed property. . . . If the South is ever to be made a safe republic let her lands be cultivated by the toil of the owners or the free labor of intelligent citizens. This must be done even though it drive her nobility into exile. If they go, all the better. (Stevens quoted in Sewell, 1988, 189)

On the other hand, many Northern Democrats felt that Lincoln's refusal to reestablish slavery proved that he had used the war to expand its aims beyond those for which the Union originally fought. The Democratic party's slogan during this period was, "The Union as it was, the Constitution as it is, the Negroes where they are."

Nor did Lincoln's policy achieve its intended effect in the South. Beringer et al. (1986) argue that Lincoln's terms actually stiffened Southern resistance at that time because of the impression that the ten percent rule was despotic and proved Northern intent to run roughshod over the people of the South. (Of course, given Jefferson Davis's preferences for independence, it is not clear that any more lenient terms would have gained Southern acceptance.)

Lincoln was a firm believer in reconciliation and his goals were essentially conservative (Fehrenbacher, 1987, 117). Reconciliation is necessarily a policy of compromise, entirely antithetical to the fulfillment of revolution. The seeds of conflict within the North over the course of reconstruction were present even before Andrew Johnson took over the presidency.

Johnson's policies towards the South after 1865 were essentially those of Lincoln's. Johnson offered a lenient amnesty program for Southerners who had been involved in the war effort, and emphasized that it was the task of the defeated state governments to reconstruct themselves. Congress, where a coalition of radical and moderate Republicans ruled, felt that it was the responsibility of Congress to set the terms of reconstruction. The radicals in Congress were assisted in this battle with Johnson when many of the former Confederate states elected unrepentant leaders who had actively supported secession in the first place. Public opinion in the North was easily set in motion against Johnson as violence against Northerners and freedmen in the South became known. In this battle Congress held the trump card, as it could decide whether or not to seat those Southerners who were elected to office during self-reconstruction.

Johnson's self-reconstruction plan failed because of the lack of repentance on the part of those Southerners who rallied to his plan and the widespread feeling among Northerners that 350,000 deaths deserved some show of submission on the part of the South. Moreover, the states treated freedmen as second-class citizens, who, while no longer slaves, had no protection or rights under the law. Laws were immediately passed that would keep slavery in everything but name.

As opposition to Johnson's plan grew, Congressional Republicans had an alternative in hand. Northern Republicans saw reconstruction as an opportunity for forging a coalition with the freedmen and former Southern Whigs, thus establishing the Republican party as a national party. To do so would require electoral suffrage for the freedmen, and temporary restrictions against former Southern leaders from participating in state politics. Congress, over Johnson's inept opposition, soon passed a constitutional amendment that gave the freedmen the vote, a change that would have been unthinkable three years previously. Republicans assumed that the political sphere would be the key to the successful integration of the black into society. No measures were taken to provide the ex-slaves with financial assistance and land; no economic integration into society paralleled their political integration into society.

The threat of black suffrage to white supremacy in the South served to galvanize white resistance to reconstruction measures:

The acceptance of emancipation, of course, did not commit Southerners to a policy of racial equality. Rather, they assumed that the free Negroes would be an inferior caste, exposed to legal discrimination, denied political rights, and subjected to social segregation. They had every reason to assume this, because these, by and large, were the policies of most of the Northern states toward their free Negro populations, and because the racial attitudes of the great majority of Northerners were not much different from their own. White Southerners were understandably shocked, therefore, when Radical Republicans, during the Reconstruction years, tried to impose a different relationship between the races in the South—to give Negroes legal equality, political rights, and, here and there even social equality. . . . Now for the first time white Southerners organized a powerful partisan movement and resisted Republican race policy even more fiercely than the civil population had ever resisted the invading Union armies during the war. (Stampp, 1980, 268)

The rise of the Ku Klux Klan and other similar organizations during radical reconstruction should be seen as the partisan warfare that had been missing at the war's end. Indeed, the number of deaths during some of the years after Appomattox, to the best of my reading, were sufficient to qualify as civil war under Small and Singer's criteria (1982). For example, McPherson states that in 1868 alone there were 200 political murders in Arkansas, a substantial number in Georgia, and 1,000 political deaths in Louisiana (McPherson, 1982, 544). Obviously these figures suffer from imprecision, but suggest that in a fundamental sense the civil war did not end in 1865.

Having been provided with the vote, ex-slaves proved adept at the arts of political organization and, in conjunction with former Southern Whigs, were able to win the state houses and U.S. congressional seats of the Southern states. But with the rise of militant white opposition, the success of radical reconstruction would depend on the protection of Northern troops and the ability of these newly elected governments to rule. In this they were hampered by the sheer costs of the destruction of the civil war, a national recession, and a Northern ideology that felt it anathema to assist the South to rebuild economically.

Radical reconstruction failed for a number of reasons. William Gillette points to the following: 1) administrative incapacity and the failure to protect pro-Union Southerners and freedmen from violence; 2) Northern policies that were the product of political trade-offs and therefore incoherent in their application to the South; 3) a constitutional tradition that restricted policies such as land redistribution and economic help to the freedmen, which would have enabled the newly freed slaves to compete fairly with Southern whites; 4) the use of law as a "panacea," or the belief in the North that social attitudes and limits to conflict in the South could be legislated; 5) racism in the North that accounts for the ease with which former radical Republicans turned their backs on the freedmen as political partners. Finally, what is unstated in Gillette's book, but seems apparent is that there was a real desire among Northerners "to get on with it"; that is, a real impatience with reconstruction as a social experiment and a real desire for national reconciliation (Gillette, 1979, 365–370).

Reconstruction proved the limits of the radicals' revolution. The free soil, free labor ideology of the Republican party demanded the end of slavery in the South. The ideology demanded equal rights and the vote for the freedmen as the best insurance that they would survive and prosper after the war. But the same ideology balked at providing the freedmen the governmental support and continued protection that were necessary to achieve the revolutionary transformation of the South.

Another striking aspect of the limits of the revolutionary ideology of the Republican radicals concerns the punishment of the secessionists. It is important to note the lack of direct retribution against those who made the rebellion. Only one Confederate was tried for war crimes—Henry Wirz, the commandant of the Andersonville prisoner-of-war camp. While Jefferson Davis was arrested and spent two years in federal prisons, he was never brought to trial for treason and was paroled in 1867. The only action taken against the leadership of the rebellion was the temporary forfeiture of rights of voting and office holding. David Donald (1978, 175–183) attributes this lack of retribution or punishment of the Southern leaders to a strict belief in constitutionalism among politicians of the North.

In 1877 Northern whites made their peace with Southern whites, as reconstruction ended and national reconciliation began. Such a reconciliation necessarily meant that someone would lose. Radicals in the North abandoned the black freedmen of the South, in order that one nation would come together again. It did not take long for the North to embrace the new ideology of social darwinism that would justify Southern segregation of the freedmen. As George Fredrickson has so succinctly put it, "this last act of the drama of national consolidation that had begun with a struggle to preserve the Union and destroy the 'slave power' can be seen for what it really was—a Northern betrayal of the blacks who had been emancipated and promised full citizenship" (Fredrickson, 1981, 191).

Concluding Observations

The policies pursued by the North towards the defeated South were neither coherent nor consistent. In the first three years after the war, two visions of a reconstructed South competed for prominence in the North. The visions differed on the extent to which Southern social, economic, and political institutions would have to be radically transformed in order for the South to be incorporated again into the Union. Andrew Johnson's policy of presidential reconstruction preferred limited change. If fully implemented, the South would be rebuilt by the aristocratic planter class that had initiated the war in the first place. While blacks would no longer be slaves, Johnson's policies would insure them inferiority and subordination to their former owners. The policy of radical reconstruction, advocated by the extremists of the Republican party, envisioned a new order in the South, built by the newly freed ex-slaves and those whites who had opposed the Confederacy. By granting political rights to the freedmen, radical reconstruction would eradicate the power of the former aristocracy. This eradication would in turn mean a Southern economy built on the free-labor, free-soil ideology that was part and parcel of the North's vibrant industrial order.

Both Johnson and the radicals' plans for reconstruction were based on assessments of their political interests. Johnson believed that his personal political ambitions were best served by a quickly reconstructed South. He hoped to forge a coalition of Southerners and Northern Democrats, that would isolate the radical wing of the Republican party. The radical Republicans, for their part, believed that their future power depended on creating a new political force in the South based on the freedmen and ex-Whigs. To accomplish this necessarily meant circumscribing the participation of those Southerners who had supported the war.

The institutional strength of the radical Republicans prevented Johnson from fully implementing his policies. Johnson's unwillingness to compromise on his program pushed moderate Republicans to embrace the radicals: within three years one of the most dramatic swings of political ideology had occurred in the United States. In 1865 radical demands for suffrage and equal rights for blacks were extreme positions in the North. By 1868 such demands enjoyed overwhelming political support: the extreme had become the mainstream. But, as has been argued earlier, even the policies of radical reconstruction were piecemeal, not uniformly applied, and hostage to political considerations in the North throughout the period of radical ascendancy.

The two competing programs of reconstruction in the North had clear views of what a new South should look like. Two dimensions of the policies were crucial. The first dimension, discussed by Henry Kissinger in his study of the peace after the Napoleonic Wars, concerns the retrospective or forward-looking aspect of the peace. Kissinger asserts that victors can either "crush the enemy so that he is unable to fight again . . . [or] deal with the enemy so that he does not wish to attack again." In Kissinger's analysis,

a retrospective peace is the expression of a rigid social order, clinging to the only certainty: the past. It will make a 'legitimate' settlement impossible, because the defeated nation, unless completely dismembered, will not accept its humiliation. (Kissinger, 1957, 138–139)

The second dimension is one of totalization: the victors can assume that the prior war was caused by specific, limited grievances or they can assume that the cause of the war lies in the very nature and character of the opponent's political and social institutions.

The war aims of the North as represented by Lincoln, Sherman, and Grant attempted the strange amalgam of crushing the enemy so that the South would be unable to fight again, with a view of the war that saw Southern grievances as limited, albeit uncompromisable. Thus Lincoln pursued a combination of policies that would attempt to destroy the will of the South to fight again, with the attempt to establish a legitimate social order that did not involve a revolutionary transformation of Southern society. The radicals, however, hoped to crush the South and then, through political and social engineering, create a newly transformed South, whose new institutions would be the basis for a new legitimate order. The crucial difference between the policies concerned the audience for considering whether a new order was legitimate: the defeated whites who had waged war against the North or the ex-slaves and opponents of the Confederacy who had waged war alongside the North.

For the political and social engineering of the South to have been successful, the North would have had to provide much economic aid to rebuild the South and ongoing federal protection to the newly formed governments.[6] Even with such assistance, radical reconstruction would have involved a long-term commitment from the North. Neither the assistance nor commitment were forthcoming, and the North once again faced a decision between reconciliation among whites or continued social engineering of the South. The North chose reconciliation, a policy by definition at odds with revolutionary transformation. By 1877 North and South reached a rather limited bargain: the South would never again consider secession or institute slavery, the North would abandon the freedmen and accept a white supremacist South. One must not forget that a policy of reconciliation, as much as a policy of revolution, has its losers.

Notes

1. The most noted exception is the chapter on the civil war in Moore, 1966. Paul Kennedy's recent tome (1988) discusses the Civil War and argues that the North won because of preponderant military and economic power. As I point out here, that interpretation is at odds with most recent American scholarship on the war, including that of Beringer et al., 1986, and McPherson, 1988.

2. Beringer et al., 1986, dismiss the explanation that there was no model for fighting a guerrilla war at that time. They point out that Southern officers

were familiar with Clausewitz's writings on Napoleon's Spanish campaign and the ability of partisans to harass and defeat larger armies. The argument that such a model was not available is contradicted by the experience of some Southerners who fought that style of war (Fellman, 1989).

A second argument on why the South did not fight a guerrilla war is that such a fight would have contradicted Southern concepts of honor. A recent biography of one of the South's partisan fighters makes clear that he believed that "Southern honor" was incompatible with the demands of guerrilla warfare (Ramage, 1988).

3. To understand the lack of connection between separate cultural identities and the onset of the civil war, consider the differential effects of the Mexican War on American politics and society of the time. In terms of the web of meaning that surrounded American lives in 1848 the Mexican War marked the culmination of the American mystical feeling of imagined community. While the war did much to consolidate a single feeling of nationhood throughout the states (Johannsen, 1985), it also began a process of destroying the balance of institutions that made the Union possible.

4. An interesting comparison of the role of fear in perpetuating domination can be drawn from South Africa today (Hugo, 1988).

5. For a discussion of lexicographic preferences, see Elster, 1978. To give another example of such a preference, imagine a voter who places the abortion issue above all others. The preference is lexicographic, if in terms of voting she/he first chooses a candidate on how the candidate stands on the issue of abortion rights. If all candidates support her/his position on abortion, she/he will then go on to choose among them based on positions on other issues. If only one candidate has the correct position on abortion, that candidate will receive the individual's vote.

6. An interesting parallel exists between the reconstruction of the South and the reconstruction of Germany after World War I. Keynes, among others, argued that if German militarism were to be replaced by new democratic institutions, then the Weimar government would have to be assisted rather than punished for the previous war.

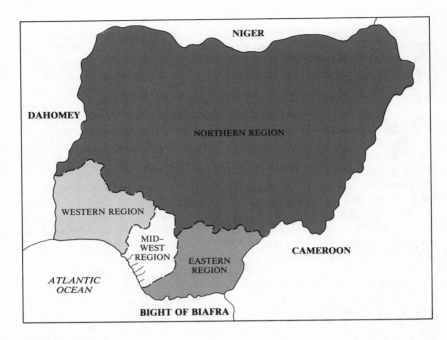

8.1 Nigeria

The Ending of the Nigerian Civil War: Victory, Defeat, and the Changing of Coalitions

James O'Connell

Introduction: The Sources of Conflict

It is difficult to be precise about the causes of war. War results from a series of decisions in which events take on the meaning that persons and groups give them.[1] In the Nigerian case there were underlying reasons for the drift towards conflict, rooted in the geographical and ethnic shape of a huge colonial-made state and in its pace and pattern of political and economic development. There were more immediate sources in the political patterns of interaction between the ethnic groups after independence. These patterns were heavily influenced by the federal structure fashioned for independence, by the uneven spread of skills among the peoples, and by the location of oil.

At independence (1960) Nigeria had a federal constitution that ran in the face of received federal theorizing: one federal unit (the Northern Region) was larger in size and in population than the other two federal regions or states (the Eastern and Western Regions) added together. The situation was not immediately improved when the Northern and Eastern politicians combined to break the Western Region into two states (Western and MidWestern Regions) in 1964. However, though the move against the West and its dominant Yoruba groups created strains in the contest for political power in the federation, the basic cleavage within Nigeria had long been between

North and South. The majority Far Northern Muslim peoples (Hausa, Kanuri, and Fulani) had taken to modern education more slowly than the Middle Belt (the southern and mostly non-Muslim part of the North) and Southern peoples who were mostly becoming Christian and sending their children to mission schools. Under British rule the Northerners had retained the traditional social structures of their emirates, and they feared a federation in which the federal administrative structures as well as the commercial and industrial life of the country would be controlled by Southerners.

At several times during the constitutional negotiations before independence the Northern leaders had threatened to secede from Nigeria, and only their land-locked situation had prevented them from seeking to implement that threat. The Southerners in the independence negotiations had accepted reluctantly a federation that left the huge Northern Region intact—a solution which was strongly supported by the British administration—in return for independence's not being delayed. They also felt that their skills would bring them crucial post-independence power and they might eventually re-shape the independence settlement. A certain political stability seemed assured at independence since the first federal government was a coalition between the Northern ruling party (which provided the prime minister) and the Eastern ruling party (which provided the finance minister—and later the governor general/president as well), while the Western ruling party went into constitutional opposition. In that way the danger of a North-South split appeared to be averted.

Independence politics quickly revealed the strains of a new and artificial country with insufficient time to create a minimum sense of nationhood out of several hundred ethnic groups. More seriously, constitutionalism—good law and a respect for the rules of the game, not least in not pushing opponents to the wall—had not matured in the insecurity of colonial and early independence politics. Capable leaders might have overcome some of the problems, but the Nigerian leaders who had been formed in the politics of agitation did badly with the politics of governing: many proved to be incompetent in running a state with modern requirements; most were tribalist or communal in outlook and loyalties; and too many of them were pervasively corrupt.

The Drift towards Civil War

A series of crises tested the strength of the political system. Under-lying all the crises was a revolution of rising expectations, especially among the Southern communities, that created bitter competition among the elite members of the main ethnic groups and that put immense pressure on politicians to deliver rewards to their followers. Slow economic growth led to a general strike in 1964 that almost halted the modernizing sectors of the Southern economy, disrupted transport between South and North, and seriously frightened the federal government. Meanwhile a mismanaged change of vice-chan-cellors at the University of Lagos displayed the venomous compe-tition of the Yoruba and Ibo intelligentsia for public service posts and undermined social trust.

The moves against the Western Region's government, which in-cluded installing a Northern allied government in the place of a properly elected government and which saw a regional election bla-tantly falsified, damaged confidence in just administration of law. A federal election in 1964 that brought an artificially large Northern majority into parliament deprived Southerners of the hope of chang-ing the country's government through the ballot box. Previously a falsified national census had consolidated the Northern right to a plurality of seats in the lower and more powerful house of parliament.

The violence that erupted against the rigged Western Region elec-tion at the end of 1965 finally brought discontent to a head in the South and created an atmosphere of violence in which Southern officers, mostly Ibo, carried out a coup in January, 1966 that toppled the federal and regional governments. Those officers who initiated the coup did not manage to gain power. The army high command, however. moved into the vacuum and took over control of govern-ment. Significantly the army high command which was predomi-nantly Southern and Ibo had to contend with a rank-and-file who were mostly from the Northern Middle Belt.

The Northerners were not monolithic because they divided broadly into Far Northerners who were Muslim and Middle Belt groups who were becoming Christian and spreading Christianity among their communities like their Southern counterparts. They had little affection for the 'old politicians' and waited cautiously to see how the new regime would turn out. Southerners were mostly eu-phoric. However the army high command—the commander-in-chief,

General Ironsi, was an Ibo—made a series of inept political decisions that culminated in an unfortunate decree that appeared to abolish the former federal structure. Northerners believed that they were about to lose whatever political power they still possessed in the country, that a horde of Southerners would move in to take over posts in the North and impede the progress and prospects of Northerners, and that public resources would be denied to Northern communities.

Two events brought the country to a greater crisis. In May, 1966, shortly after the unification decree, riots broke out in the Northern areas against Ibos who were seen as symbols of Southern domination and who as petty officials and traders were resented by the less modernized Northerners (O'Connell, 1967). A great part of the several hundred thousand Ibo population in the North fled home to the East, although many had little to which to return. In consequence, a great number still remained in the North, and many returned from the East once law and order were apparently restored.

Significantly Ironsi had not dared to use his army to protect his fellow Ibos. Discontent kept simmering among all groups of Northerners. Then in July, 1966 the Middle Belt rank-and-file of the army rebelled, turned their guns on their Ibo officers and on their Eastern comrades, and broke the federal army. They immediately constrained Northern officers to take over the running of the country; and they made the most senior Middle Belt officer, Brigadier Yakubu Gowon, army commander and head of state. The broken rump of the Easterners in the army headed for their own Region and reconstituted themselves in military order under the direction of the Ibo military governor of the Eastern Region, Brigadier Odumegwu Ojukwu.

The first instinct of the Northern army officers and men was to have the North secede from the rest of the country. Federal civil servants persuaded them to change their minds and reconstruct the Nigerian federal system by creating more states out of the existing four regions. The Eastern representatives opposed the result, as did important political elements in the Far North. In September a veritable pogrom against the Ibos in the North was launched which betrayed many signs of organization and which killed some six thousand Ibos, mostly poor people since by that time the well-to-do had read the signs of the times and had left the North. Northern politicians and collaborators in the administration had cynically unleashed massacres of men, women and children in order to break the unity of the federation and to connive in a most perverse way with their counterparts in the East who possessed the same objective.[2]

The killings shocked and stunned the country. The federal government had an uneasy conscience about the killings, was desperately trying to re-organize a disorderly army, and was lost in indecision and procrastination. The Eastern leader, Odumegwu Ojukwu, in consultation with his advisers and with the agreement of practically the whole Ibo intelligentsia and people, had no hesitation about what he wanted to do: he wanted his region to secede from Nigeria and to retain entire control over its revenues, including its oil revenues. He built up Ibo unity around the solidarity and fear of his people; he initiated a world wide drive to secure sympathy on the grounds of the massacres to which they had been subjected; and he set about enlarging his military forces and equipping them. He took administrative step after step until by April, 1967 the federal writ did not run in his region and it was in virtual secession. He said that he was willing to compromise on a form of external association with Nigeria but he refused any solution that did not give his area full political sovereignty.

Civil War: Legitimacy, Numbers, and Arms

Gowon, the federal leader, who was also seeking to buy arms abroad tried to conciliate the Eastern leadership. But, under pressure from his own hawks, he offered little that was imaginative to the Easterners, while Ojukwu and his advisors were unwilling to accept any compromise that retained the unity of the state. The country moved inexorably towards civil war. In May, 1967 Ojukwu formally declared the secession of his region and established the Republic of Biafra. Some two months later the federal government sent troops across the regional boundary to end the secession. The war would involve both bloody military struggle and starvation for Eastern civilians. It did not end for two and a half years.

On a number of occasions before the war began as well as during the war's progress, Ojukwu might have secured reasonable peace terms, that is, terms that conceded greater financial and resource rights to the region and left it relatively intact territorially. Concessions could be wrung from the federal side because the government was not sure that it could win the war and because it recoiled from the costs likely to be involved in pursuing it. But Ojukwu had calculated that he could carry the secession through—a calculation that he maintained long after it was manifest that he had lost the war. It is also true that he and his people feared any solution that gave the federal army control over the Eastern Region. He skillfully rallied his people, using the fear of 'genocide' that shaped Ibo psychology after the Northern killings and telling them that to fail to resist the Nigerian onslaught risked widespread massacre.

During the war the federal troops gradually won territory from the secessionists. They regained initially the areas of the Eastern minority ethnic groups, especially those of the Ibibio and the Ijaw, who collaborated with the invading forces. These minorities formed close to two-fifths of the population of the former region; and they had in great majority opposed secession, which they saw as a Biafran captivity. Towards the end of the war the federal forces controlled large tracts of territory in which the soldiers treated civilians in a humane and considerate way. Though there had been several massacres during the war by federal troops, these had proved to be the exception and not the rule.[3] In fact, the war was mostly fought along the main roads on which the federal troops advanced behind their artillery fire. The villages in which most people lived were fortunately away from the roads and remained relatively safe except for the dire famine situation in many areas. During the war no guerilla action materialized in the areas taken over by the federal troops. Also, though Ojukwu promised that in the event of a conventional military defeat, his people would fight on as partisans, no effort to do so was made.

In military terms the Nigerian army won the war because it had more troops, better equipment and greater supplies. These advantages offset the shorter command lines of the Biafrans and their more homogeneous forces. At the outset of the war, when the British who were traditional military suppliers to Nigeria showed some reluctance to sell arms to the federal government, the latter turned to the Soviet government which sold them planes and other equipment— and which supported the federal side throughout the war. The British quickly changed their policy and supplied the federal side abundantly and—from a British viewpoint—profitably. The Biafrans failed initially to buy equipment and ammunition from government and official sources, and their inexperienced private buyers bought badly and expensively. Moreover, Biafran foreign exchange began to run out quickly. Their situation changed dramatically when France intervened to supply war materials in late 1968. But France only gave enough aid to prolong the war and not enough to enable the Biafrans to win it.[4] The French government realized that, if it stepped up supplies beyond a certain point, the British and the Soviets would escalate their help since both were by then heavily committed to a federal victory. The French calculation appeared to be that, by making the progress of the war difficult and prolonged, the fissures—ethnic and personal—in the federal side as well as the uneven quality of the federal military leadership would cause the federal effort to falter and the Biafrans would be able to negotiate a favorable settlement. The French failed to understand how desperately many of the federal groups looked on military and political failure and underestimated the key role of the Middle Belt troops and officers in the conduct of the war.

By January, 1970 the civil war was for practical purposes over. The Biafran army had almost exhausted its ammunition; transport had practically run out of fuel; military morale had broken and soldiers and others were turning towards messianic cults in the futility of magical hopes; it had become impossible to recruit or to conscript new troops; the main food growing areas had been taken over by the enemy; and deaths from malnutrition, especially among children, were multiplying. In particular, the will-to-resist which had depended so heavily on fear of large-scale federal massacres evaporated as people realized that the troops had behaved well in the places where they had taken over and that in any case the troops were mostly Middle Belt soldiers from peoples who had been very little involved in the Northern pogrom as well as Yoruba soldiers from a people who had not been involved at all.

Yet the end came quickly and unexpectedly. At the start of January, 1970 Colonel Obasanjo's Third Division cut through the Biafran lines from the south and linked up with the First Division at Umuahia. This manoeuver not only cut the remaining enclave in two but cut off the Biafran forces from their last food-producing areas. There was now no denying that the end had come. Ojukwu, who had issued a defiant statement less than two weeks earlier, fled on January 10 to the Ivory Coast. Two days later General Philip Effiong, the Biafran chief of staff, surrendered unconditionally.

It may be asked why the Biafrans accepted Ojukwu's decision to continue the war when its tide had turned utterly against them. Apart from the fears of the result of defeat that continued to be held almost until the end, they also misjudged the strength of the federal coalition and hoped against hope that its will to win would peter out or that divisions between Yorubas and others would weaken it. In a sense they hoped that a 'hurting stalemate' could be established and continue long enough and take sufficient toll of the enemy to enable them to achieve their basic aims. The Ibos also overestimated the importance of international humanitarian opinion, which they thought might halt the federal advance, and misjudged the worth of a popular sympathy in Western countries that was not on the whole shared by governments.

Why did the Nigerian federal government win? It won for a cumulative set of reasons: it retained the legitimacy of the internationally recognized government, leaving the secessionists at a disadvantage in arms buying as well as lack of recognition; it obtained general African support among countries that were nearly all afraid of their own colonial boundaries' coming under pressure; it derived enough revenues from petroleum and crops to carry on the war and acquire sophisticated weaponry, while the secessionists were blockaded by the small federal navy and ran short of funds for buying arms, mechanical spare parts, and food; it was able to recruit and equip a much larger army than the Biafrans; its peoples were relatively united behind the war, while the Ibos had to cope with significant dissent from Ibibio, Ijaw/Kalabari, Ogoja, and other groups; and the Ibo intelligentsia held back from personal commitment to the fighting and expected the less well-to-do and unemployed to risk their lives.

Above all, the federal side won because the Middle Belt peoples, especially the Tiv, Idoma, and other Northern minority groups which provided the bulk of the federal infantry, needed the federation desperately. If the federation were to fail, they would face, on the one hand, the danger of Hausa-Fulani domination as the Northern region became a country in the break-up of Nigeria and, on the other hand, the fate of being left in a country bereft of the oil revenues. They used the federal resources; they collaborated with the other pro-federal groups; they fought bravely; and they overcame opponents who also fought bravely and whom they came greatly to respect in the course of the war.

The Shape of the End: Neither Nuremberg Trials nor German Miracle

In the final outcome there was no settlement with the secessionists. They were overwhelmed militarily. But inherent in the way that the federal government had rallied its own side were terms that offered a degree of conciliation and assurance to the vanquished. The new twelve-state system ended the hegemony of the old North and re-distributed power evenly throughout the federation.[5] Nonetheless the Ibos suffered immediate disadvantages. First many of their areas and all their main towns were devastated.[6] Second, Ibos who had fled federal posts were for the most part not reinstated; businesses were destroyed and could not quickly be re-established; the East-Central state (the new Ibo state) could not quickly afford to take on staff—though it did open the Nsukka university quickly after the cease-fire. Third, Ibos were prevented for many years (and in measure still are) from returning to the main Ibo commercial and manufacturing town, Port Harcourt, which lay outside the boundaries of their new state and in the Rivers state whose peoples hated and feared Ibo clannishness and entrepreneurship. Finally, the Ibos had only one state and state ruler among the twelve officials who with Gowon made up the majority of the ruling council of state. As a result they carried much less proportionate weight in the post-war Federal Military Government than their numbers in the country should have given them. Moreover, not only did the East Central Administrator, Ukpabi Asika, exercise little influence in federal councils but he displayed no great initiative in restoring the economic life of his state. Fortunately however his lack of initiative was more than compensated for by the energies of a people who had lost a war but not their dignity and their ambition to better themselves.

However, an endemic lack of capital bedeviled Ibo efforts for years. Influential federal civil servants had resented Ibo competition in earlier years and blamed their elite counterparts for being part of the cabal that had started the secession. They openly declared that there would be no 'German miracle' for the Ibo areas. Ordinary Ibos began to re-build their lives as best they could, and their communities quickly began to display the resiliency that had made them a powerful modernizing force within Nigeria. The elite exhibited for a time the schizoid reactions of those who had been forced back into accepting citizenship of the state which they had rejected; who suf-

fered the humiliating complex of defeat; and who were glad enough
to have survived the uncertain end of a way that might have destroyed them. But they also soon set about making new or old careers.

However if there was going to be no 'German miracle,' there were
also going to be no 'Nuremberg trials.'

General Gowon implemented his pledge of a general amnesty on January
15, 1970, and, aside from a handful of junior army officers who allegedly
collaborated with the Biafran invasion of the Midwest, there were almost
no war-related detentions. High ranking Biafran officers, such as General
Philip Effiong, reverted to their prewar rank in the Nigerian army, were
placed on immediate indefinite leave, and later retired. The only civilian
leader known to have been arrested was Ojukwu's chief economic adviser,
Dr. Pius Okigbo, and that, according to his associates, was the result of a
local and not a federal order. By mid-1971, Dr. Okigbo had been released
and was running a consulting firm in Lagos with a large contract from the
federal government. (Stremlau, 1977, 371–372)

Some further remarks are worth making. First, in the aftermath
of the war there was an extraordinary lack of enduring bitterness. It
is true that Ibos regretted having lost the bid to secede as well as
the opportunity to obtain some justice for the Northern pogroms,
and federal groups resented the losses that the Ibo leadership had
brought on them and on the country. But to those who had witnessed
the bitternesses of Ireland or Spain fifty years after civil war, African
capacities for setting aside hatred were deeply humane and utterly
remarkable. Second, inter-community or inter-ethnic wars among
many African groups in the nineteenth century displayed a willingness to leave groups with basic social and economic integrity. In
Nigerian politics parties appeared to have lost that tradition as they
pushed opponents to the wall, but in the ending of a bitterly fought
civil war that tradition of clemency reappeared.[7] At the end of the
war both sides showed mostly relief and a will to get back to living
ordinary life again.

The end of the war—like much of its course—was riddled with
ambiguities between stated means of action, the logic of actions undertaken and faces presented to the outside world. This was true
nowhere more than in the food blockade during the war in which
the federal government made relatively half-hearted efforts for a long
time to impede secular and religious relief efforts. When the federal
government eventually stepped up its food blockade in an effort to
starve the rebel enclave into submission, it never openly admitted

it because of the Western outcry over the starving civilian population, especially the children. The federal government had mostly lost the international propaganda battle ever since the Ibo massacres in the North and resented the pressures put on it to lift a blockade that it saw as vital to shortening the war as well as to winning it. Moreover, they could point to the blockade of Germany during both world wars that had evoked no equivalent condemnation. They attributed Western attitudes partly to Biafran propaganda and partly to the general belief in the West that the participants in the civil war were throwing lives away in a bloody conflict that was being fought over issues of little real worth and to no purpose.

However, bowing to foreign pressure towards the end of 1969, the federal government agreed to permit a land corridor across its territory to enable food to be delivered to the rebel-held areas. The government refused to permit other routes. Ojukwu had been having arms delivered in some relief planes and was using relief planes generally as a cover for arms planes. He refused the land route as he also refused daylight plane deliveries. His government was willing to sacrifice lives for the prestige of sovereignty as well as to prevent the delivery of food from harming the will to hold out.[8] The difference between the leaderships in this respect was that Ojukwu was willing to sacrifice his own people whereas Gowon and his advisors were at least dealing with a rebel people—and yet with a people that they wanted to re-integrate into their own country.

The one good side of the food controversy was that it continued to focus world attention on the last days of the war as it moved inexorably towards a federal victory. In consequence, it spurred the federal government to step up efforts to deal with hunger immediately after the war ended. It also strengthened the hands of those on the federal side who were determined to prevent sporadic massacres or large-scale looting with the end of the war. Moreover, these efforts offered an essential conciliation to the Ibo intelligentsia and people as they acknowledged that they had lost the war but that peace need not be impossible. They remained for a long time secessionist at heart but accepted that they had failed to carry their secession through. They also realized that with the end of the war and the creation of the new states the ethnic groups, whom they had carried unwillingly into secession and on whose land nearly all the oil was, were about to acquire new state structures as well as federal support that made any new attempt at secession impossible, at least in its Biafran shape. Yet there was much political loss for Nigerians in that the representatives of an able people accepted their country for purely pragmatic reasons and had no wish or intention to create charismatic affection for or emotional loyalty to the political entity within which they lived.

The Nigerian civil war made clear—as have other civil wars—how difficult it is for outsiders, whether governments or other groups, to intervene effectively within a country.[9] The Commonwealth Secretariat took an early initiative to bring the sides together but was simply shrugged aside. The Organization of African Unity (O.A.U.) made several efforts to mediate and on several occasions (meetings at Addis Ababa and Kampala, among others) got representatives of the federal government and Biafra around a table. Individual heads of state, especially Haile Selassie, the Ethiopian emperor, undertook personal efforts to find peace formulae.

All these efforts foundered on two intransigencies: the Nigerian leadership was unwilling to accept any solution that did not retain Nigerian unity, a federal structure, and a unified army; and the Biafran leadership was unwilling to settle for anything short of sovereignty and its own army. The Nigerians were willing to bargain about the shape of the federation—though they were hampered by having set up three states in the old Eastern Region, some boundary revisions could almost certainly have been negotiated—and they were willing to re-work the allocation of oil and other revenues between the federal center and the states. Apart from sovereignty the other sticking point for the Biafrans was the future of their army as well as their refusal to have federal troops on their soil. The Nigerians, while insisting on a single army, were willing to concede that for a time after the end of the war foreign troops might be stationed in the Eastern states, but the Biafrans while they thought they could prevent a federal victory did not take up this offer. The Ibos had been traumatized by the massacres in the North as well as by incidents in other areas that had threatened their lives and caused them to flee (O'Connell, 1969). Both elite groups and the common people shared a terrible fear that endured almost to the end of the war and that made agreements requiring trust hard to make.

Outside negotiators had no influence on a settlement in the war. There was finally no settlement but a federal victory. In a crucial sense, outside negotiators can operate only when each side to a conflict is willing, no matter how initially hesitant, to meet the other part of the way. They can also operate best if they can explain each side to the other and remove misconceptions. Another cause of the intransigence in the Nigerian war was the extreme lucidity with which each side saw the other—the leadership groups had served in the same army, had gone to the same secondary schools and most knew one another personally and even intimately—and realized that each was pursuing incompatible goals. Yet the mediation efforts did have some effect in that they helped to convey to the federal leadership how much future Nigerian international status depended on humane treatment of the vanquished at the end of the war.

Peace and the Re-forming of Coalitions

The settlement that emerged out of the war has already lasted some twenty years. There is no indication that the immediate causes of the civil war have continued to endure or that it could be fought again along the same lines of division. What is the explanation? Civil wars are not fought all over again once the termination of the war not only prompts the dissolution of the political alliances around which it was fought with little hope of their being re-formed but also creates new alliances. In the Nigerian case the Ibo leaders had used regional resources—political, administrative, and economic—to mobilize a secession. They challenged the whole country, and they cowed the Eastern minorities into initial submission.

Once they had lost, they no longer had the capacity to mobilize resources for renewing the war. But once they could no longer do that, the alliance opposing them was no longer needed and a new system of alliances began to take shape. Crucial to the new political equilibrium was the twelve-state structure of the federation. It ended the old hegemony of the North as well as impeding the renewal of the civil war. In other words, if the Ibos had lost control of a region, so had the Hausa-Fulani. With time the latter were to show that they could build political alliances without the need for the former regional apparatus. But this time they had to negotiate alliances and could not mostly dictate them as in the past, and ironically they eventually had to negotiate with—among other Ibo leaders—Odumegwu Ojukwu when he had been permitted to return to the country after exile and had become active in civilian politics.

Not only had the Ibos lost the capacity to fight the war again but in threatening to secede they had obliged the federal rulers just before the war to announce the creation of new states. Even though the Ibos in the hope of greater gains in carrying through a successful secession had rejected this re-shaping, they could still in the post-war situation make the best of the new structures; they could develop new alliances in the new federal politics; and they could glean some satisfaction from the way in which their old enemies, the Hausa-Fulani, had also in good measure lost politically in the outcome of the war.

Once the war ended, those problems that underlay the build-up of conflict—as distinct from the immediate causes of the war—remained. Ethnic distrust, lack of good political leadership, difficulties in creating constitutionalism and strains of rapid social change were complicated after 1970 by an unbalanced, oil-rich economy whose resources were not easily translated into general economic growth and social development. Moreover, the old North-South divide has proved difficult to overcome.[10] In sad irony, once the Ibo secession had been eliminated and Ibos had not moved back to the North in great numbers, Muslim Northerners experienced several fundamentalist religious upheavals. Sometimes Christians were the targets, but often Muslim extremists fought against one another in fratricidal strife as the tensions that had led to the Ibo pogroms were now unleashed within socially divided Far Northern communities.

In recent Nigerian politics the defence of Islam—and Christianity in reaction—has become a form of code for strains between Far Northern and Southern groups. The educational gap between Far Northerners and Southern peoples makes Islam an effective political ideology and organizing principle that appears to avoid the taint of ethnicity and yet enables claims to be put forward that benefit particular ethnic groups. The Iranian revolution has also influenced Muslim groups to politicize their religion and to adopt a harsher and more fundamentalist line than Nigerian Islam has been accustomed to take.

This religious cleavage which mimics the old North-South division could in the long run prove more serious than confrontation between straightforward ethnic alliances since it threatens new and cherished modernizing social identities as well as embittering and widening ethnic cleavages. Moreover, if Far Northern groups threatened to secede, Southerners would have less incentive to resist; the federal coalition in the civil war was determined not to lose Southern oil resources, and there is no comparable resource in the North. However, were the Far North to go, the Southern groups might quickly find that the secession principle turned into a fission principle that would benefit few in the longer run. The Northerners may be given pause by the potential loss of access to the oil resources that they once sought to prevent the seceding Ibos from taking with them as well as the discredited ideology of secession in a country and continent that have good reason to fear it. What these considerations suggest, finally, is how far Nigeria has moved from the sources of its first civil war and how strongly the post-war situation has rendered a recurrence of that particular conflict most unlikely.

Notes

1. For that reason it makes better sense to talk about the sources of war.

2. Participation in the killings by certain army units added greatly to the casualties.

3. One of the worst took place at Asaba, a MidWestern Ibo town on the Niger, and was a reprisal for an attack on federal troops after a cease-fire.

4. De Gaulle personally played an important role in the French decision to intervene. His motives seem to have been mixed: he disliked the size of British influence in anglophone West Africa and hoped to extend French influence, and he saw economic opportunities for France in post-war co-operation with an oil-rich and grateful Biafra (Cronje, 1972).

5. Ibo leaders had argued for some such state structure during the independence negotiations and in the subsequent era of civilian politics.

6. For example, the capital of the Eastern Region, Enugu, which I visited during the war, had not suffered much from shell-fire or fighting. But every stick of furniture had been removed; every movable object had been looted; and every door in every house had been broken down. The entire place looked uncannily and eerily like a doll's house without furniture.

7. Great personal credit needs to be given to the federal leader, Yakubu Gowon, who exercised his considerable influence consciously and consistently in favor of clemency.

8. A considerable part of Biafra's foreign exchange for buying weapons came directly or indirectly from relief-linked operations. The relief agencies, for example, paid landing fees for planes bringing in relief aid!

9. In his study of the international aspects of the war John Stremlau devotes a long chapter section to discussing with considerable insight the limited effects of outside diplomatic interventions (Stremlau, 1977, 372–387).

10. The most recent army split and attempt at a military coup (1990) was led by some Southern officers who wanted to split Nigeria into two states, leaving a Far Northern state landlocked and without access to oil revenues. They did not mobilize much support, but they had hoped to capitalize on the existing North-South strains.

9.1 Greece

The Doomed Revolution: Communist Insurgency in Postwar Greece

John O. Iatrides

The Greek communist insurgency of the late 1940s has been viewed as one of Europe's major civil wars of the twentieth century (Laqueur, 1976, 286). For a brief moment it appeared to have the strength not only to overthrow by force the Athens government and replace it with a revolutionary regime, but to influence as well the emerging East-West conflict in favor of the Soviet Union (Acheson, 1969, 219). Yet such perceptions proved faulty. During the time when the communists could have seized control of the country, they remained largely ambivalent and on the defensive. By 1947, when the insurgency finally got under way, the government had already mobilized a superior force and the defeat of the communists was merely a matter of time.

In fact, the insurgents were never able to field an army capable of victory while their opponents, united in their fear of communism, were determined to crush the revolution. Political and military circumstances enabled the Athens government and its foreign supporters to avoid all dialogue and reject out of hand all possibility of compromise. Thus, although fundamentally political in its origins, the conflict in Greece remained strictly a contest of armed strength in which the two sides were overwhelmingly uneven, and the stage was quickly set for a winner-take-all outcome.

Serious fighting lasted less than two years. Afterward, those of the revolutionaries who were not killed or did not escape abroad lan-

guished in prison, while their families and supporters remained har-
assed and powerless for decades. In short, the relatively quick end
of the Greek civil war, the total victory of the government side and
the complete banishment of the losers resulted from the basic weakness, poor tactics and bad timing of the insurrection, and from the
vastly superior power of the domestic and foreign forces that opposed it.

Postwar Greece in Revolutionary Upheaval

Greece emerged from the Second World War a crippled and polarized nation. About ten percent of the population had perished as a
result of the Axis invasion and the four-year occupation which followed; many more were left maimed, emaciated and broken for life.
Widespread destruction, pillaging and neglect had paralyzed a traditionally weak economy and severe shortages of every kind continued long after the occupiers had left. The vast majority of Greeks
were hungry and destitute and their suffering was made more painful
by the knowledge that others had enriched themselves in black mar-
ket and collaborationist activity (Thomadakis, 1981). Liberation had
brought little promise of quick recovery, particularly since the government seemed incapable of securing and distributing desperately
needed relief supplies. To make matters worse, sharp political divisions threatened to perpetuate instability and lawlessness which
would inevitably block the way to economic recovery. Thus the political crisis would have to be addressed first.

There was universal agreement that there could be no return to
the prewar system of government. The fascist trappings and police-
state methods of the regime of John Metaxas (1936–1941) had discredited the state machinery and had tarnished seemingly beyond
repair the image of King George II, who had been the late dictator's
willing accomplice. But there was violent disagreement on what
should take the place of the institutions of the recent past.

Greece's traditional parties had been basically clientelist followings of prominent personalities without a social program worthy of
the name. In the aftermath of years of passive acquiescence to the
dictatorship and enemy occupation they were disorganized, demoralized and out of touch with the vast majority of Greeks. Most old-
school politicians appeared to envision a return to the pre-Metaxas
days of an Athens-centered and paternalistic parliamentary govern-

ment (Legg, 1987; Petropulos, 1981). This was clearly the goal of British policy as well and the basic reason for Britain's direct and decisive involvement in Greek affairs throughout the war and post-liberation years. And although there was debate among British officials concerning the return of the Greek king, Prime Minister Churchill considered the monarchy's early restoration the best guarantee that Britain's interests in Greece and the Eastern Mediterranean would not suffer in the uncertain days ahead (Churchill, 1953, 102–16, 283–325).

But Greece's wartime legacy also included a new and powerful mass political movement whose vision clashed openly with the wishes of the bourgeois parties and of the British government. Built around the principal resistance organization (EAM) and its military arm (ELAS) and controlled by the communist party (KKE), this populist movement condemned in the same strong terms not only the hold-overs of the Metaxas dictatorship and Nazi collaborators but also the king and the country's traditional power holders. In vague leftist language it advocated sweeping purges, radical reform, social justice and the establishment of a "peoples' democracy." Its size, militancy and organization surpassed anything the country had ever seen before (Stavrianos, 1952; Woodhouse, 1981).

During the war the growing political divisions had led to violence, as in the mutinies of the Greek forces in the Middle East (Stavrianos, 1950) and the clashes between rival resistance bands in October 1943 (Hondros, 1983, 175–87; Woodhouse, 1982). And although in the fall of 1944 EAM had reluctantly entered a government of national unity under the prominent Liberal Party leader, George Papandreou, a few weeks after liberation serious fighting broke out in Athens—in December 1944—when EAM refused to abide by a British-sponsored formula for the disarming of the resistance bands. This so-called Second Round lasted until early January 1945, when superior British troops, rushed to Athens from Italy, drove ELAS out of the capital and compelled the communist leadership to accept the disarming of ELAS and agree to a package containing steps for resolving the more fundamental causes of the crisis—the Varkiza accord (Iatrides, 1972, 320–24; McNeill, 1949; Richter, 1980).

Despite such an inauspicious beginning, revolution and all-out civil war were not inevitable in postwar Greece. Without a clear plan of action and possibly discouraged by Moscow's aloof attitude the communists had failed to exploit their military advantage in the final days of enemy occupation: instead of seizing power before Papandreou's government and its British escort could return from exile, they joined it as its junior partner. The horrors of the Second Round, which many Greeks blamed on the communists, cost EAM much of its popular support and brought some unity among its opponents, collectively self-anointed the "nationalists." The Labor government continued to commit Britain's prestige and depleted resources to propping up the Greek authorities and even the United States, however reluctantly, was beginning to take an interest in Greek problems. Finally, the Varkiza agreement offered reasonable prospects for national reconciliation and stability. In particular, beyond the disarming and disbanding of the resistance forces, it provided for a popular referendum on the crucial question of the king's return, to be followed by elections for a parliament to replace the one banished in 1936. Thus the basic framework for the peaceful settlement of the key political issues appeared to exist.

It was not to be. Before the end of 1945 political tensions began to rise again and with them the level of violence. The government, chosen by the British from the ranks of the "nationalist" political elite, had neither the authority nor the means to suppress lawlessness and introduce a credible program of economic recovery. More often than not, real power belonged to the state apparatus, largely the remnants of the Metaxas and occupation regimes, which regarded the veterans of EAM/ELAS as agents of Slavo-communism and attacked them in the name of national survival. Something approaching a "white terror" began to sweep Greece.

On the opposite side, several thousand ELAS cadres had defied the Varkiza agreement and, ignoring orders from their superiors, remained armed and in hiding all across the country but especially in the regions along the Balkan frontiers. They were gradually joined by others who had at first surrendered their weapons and were now fleeing right-wing persecution. Another 5,000–6,000 armed Slav-speaking Macedonians, who had collaborated with Tito's partisans during the war, continued to roam across Greece's poorly guarded northern borders. At first scattered, disorganized and on the defensive, these men in the mountains of Greece posed a threat to the weak and demoralized Athens government whose police was insufficient and ill-trained to fight guerrillas in the countryside and whose regular army was as yet virtually nonexistent. By 1947, the government authorities had lost effective control over more than half of the country's rural regions.

For more than a year after the Second Round the KKE showed no signs of contemplating armed revolution and did nothing to encourage its followers to join the bands in the mountains. Its chief, Nikos Zahariadis, who had spent the war years imprisoned at Dachau, appeared eager to consolidate his personal authority over the party and to intensify its confrontational but basically non-violent tactics against the government (Richter, 1987; O. Smith, 1987). In early 1946 a KKE delegation travelled to Moscow to seek the Kremlin's endorsement and support for armed revolutionary struggle in Greece but was advised instead to continue the political effort, at least for the time being (Iatrides, 1981; Partsalidis, 1978). In February of the same year, before the Kremlin's response had been received, the party's central committee adopted a set of cryptic and ambivalent decisions and warned the government that unless the persecution of leftists was halted the party would boycott the approaching parliamentary elections and there would follow "tragic consequences" for the nation. In all probability, preparations for armed confrontation which the party called "armed self-defense," were also stepped up (KKE, 1988, 241–54; Richter, 1987; O. Smith, 1987). On March 30, 1946, one day before the elections, a guerrilla band carried out a successful attack on the garrison of a small village at the foothills of Mt. Olympus. Although an isolated act, in retrospect this operation could be regarded as the first battle in the civil war.

All through 1946, politicians of various persuasions, united in their fear of the communist-led movement, rotated cabinet posts and looked to Britain and increasingly the United States to rescue the country from its domestic and foreign enemies. The elections of March 31, which were supervised by American, British and French observers, changed little. Boycotted by the KKE and others of the Left, they produced a clear victory of the conservative and largely pro-monarchy Populist Party led by Constantine Tsaldaris; state institutions remained in the same anti-communist hands as before (Mavrogordatos, 1981). The government's inept handling of Greek territorial and reparations claims succeeded in antagonizing friends and enemies alike and added fuel to the tensions that were mounting between Greece and its Balkan neighbors. In September, a popular referendum returned to Athens King George II, in whom many Greeks saw a symbol of continued allied support and of security from communist revolution. When he died in April 1947, he was succeeded by his younger brother Paul. With his German-born wife,

Frederica, the new monarch tried to personify the nation's struggle to survive (Frederica, 1971, 95–140).

As if to underscore the point that the battle lines were now firmly drawn, in the fall of 1946 the KKE established a common command structure for the guerrilla bands, which were collectively named the Democratic Army, to be led by "General" Markos Vafiadis, a veteran communist. Reversing its earlier policy the party now launched a vigorous recruitment effort in the rural areas—the larger cities were under effective government control—and a network of training and supply centers was created with the help of the communist regimes to the north, especially Yugoslavia. A year later (September 1947) the KKE announced the transformation of the Democratic Army into a "force which will ensure the establishment of a Free Greece in the shortest possible time, starting with all the northern regions" (KKE, 1988, 263). The party was promptly banned and most of its leaders, whom the government now charged with sedition, fled to the mountains. In December, a "Provisional Democratic Government" was proclaimed in the Greek mountains with Markos as premier and minister of war. To earn credibility and foreign recognition the Democratic Army employed heavy concentrations of troops and some artillery to attack several large towns in the north (Florina, Grevena, Konitsa) where the seat of the communist government might be established. Although repulsed, the ferocious fighting and heavy casualties were a severe test for the Athens government and its foreign advisors (O'Ballance, 1966, 146–78; Woodhouse, 1976, 203–59).

The insurgents received no official recognition. Nevertheless, they were publicly heralded by Moscow and other communist regimes as heroic democratic fighters pitted against "monarcho-fascists" in Athens. And they continued to rely on munitions and supplies of every kind made available to them primarily by Yugoslavia and to a lesser degree by Albania, Bulgaria and other members of the Soviet bloc (United Nations Security Council, 1947; Howard, 1949; 1966). By 1947 relations between Greece and its Balkan neighbors were all but broken, as charges and countercharges were traded at various international fora and especially at the United Nations, where the Greek civil war and its regional character emerged as a major irritant in the growing East-West division (Coufoudakis, 1981).

During 1947 and much of 1948 the level of violence continued to rise and no region could be considered safe from attack. The insurgents, who by the summer of 1948 numbered about 28,000, took advantage of the long and virtually unguarded frontier and the rugged terrain to move about unobserved, suddenly attacking garrisons of mostly isolated and poorly defended settlements, often benefiting from vital intelligence provided by local sympathizers. As long as they operated essentially as independent guerrilla units they were highly effective and appeared capable of pursuing their tactics indefinitely and with devastating results (Iatrides, 1981; Murray, 1954).

At first the government's security forces were woefully inadequate for the task at hand. A newly formed regular army, trained and equipped by British advisers for traditional border defense and conventional warfare, lacked the numerical strength, the appropriate weapons and the spirit to go after the guerrillas. Morale was seriously low as the political loyalty of more than a third of all recruits was uncertain while many young men sought to escape service altogether. Large numbers of field officers lacked combat experience and, afraid to take the initiative, settled for defensive tactics and much long-range fire which was ineffective and wasteful. At times the stationing of troops was more a matter of politics than military planning: influential politicians sought to have the major towns in their own districts protected before anybody else's.

During 1947 the army's effectiveness slowly improved and the air force also began to come into its own in reconnaissance, bombing and troop support (Campbell, Downs and Schuetta, 1964). A large number of small-scale operations designed to locate and encircle the guerrillas gave the government forces much-needed experience but proved largely ineffective: the bands took evasive action and gradually returned to their bases once the sweep had ended. But if 1947 saw little military success of the government side, developments in Greece, the Balkans and the international arena soon thereafter turned the tide. As the government's fortunes steadily improved, and as its authority was gradually reestablished everywhere except the most remote and inaccessible areas, the insurgents were led to their defeat and destruction.

During the Second World War, beyond contributing emergency relief, the United States had refused to become embroiled in Greek problems, which it viewed as part of Britain's military responsibility (Amen, 1978, 15–56; Iatrides, 1980; Wittner, 1982, 1–69). After the war there was a growing realization in Washington that Greece and much of Europe would need assistance to rebuild its ravaged economy. But American officials insisted that the Greeks had to put their political house in order first and show their ability to benefit from outside economic support. In the spirit of the Declaration on Liberated Europe contained in the Yalta accords, and to promote the establishment of stable government in Athens, the United States played a leading role in the supervision of the Greek elections in March 1946. By the end of that year Washington had concluded that Greece needed not only economic assistance and diplomatic support but political and technical advice if it was to survive. In March 1947, responding to Britain's announcement that it would soon discontinue aid to Greece and Turkey, the United States proclaimed the Truman Doctrine. The deeper causes of Washington's new-found dynamism can be traced to its alarm over Soviet aggressive behavior across a broad front extending from Germany to Eastern Europe and the Middle East. An immediate beneficiary of the policy of "containing" the Soviet Union was destined to be Greece, in whose escalating civil war the Truman administration saw Moscow's hand (Acheson, 1969, 194–201, 212–26; Jones, 1955; Kuniholm, 1980, 399–424).

The American involvement in Greece in the late 1940s and early 1950s was all-pervasive and its impact on Greek developments decisive. Massive economic assistance and American direction of virtually every sector of state activity produced a measure of political stability, improved public services and confidence to most Greeks that their crisis would be overcome. Officials in Athens and Washington soon agreed that recovery and development were not possible unless firm governmental authority was first established over the entire country. This, of course, required the defeat of the insurgents and the annihilation of the political force they represented. Such an outcome would insure the survival of Greece as an outpost of the western world and serve as proof positive that Soviet expansionism could be contained. Thus the focus of the American assistance program became the military effort against the communist insurgents. In effect, the Greek and American governments adopted the dictum which Churchill had proclaimed during the Second Round of December 1944: no peace without victory (Couloumbis, Petropulos and Psomiades, 1976, 115–25; Fatouros, 1981; Pollis, 1981).

In retrospect one can only speculate what might have happened had the United States not intervened. Left to themselves, it is highly unlikely that the Greeks would have been able to end their civil war through negotiation and compromise: after 1946 the ideological divisions and mutual suspicions were too strong, the public mind too inflamed, the political leadership in Athens too demoralized, and the bloodletting too widespread. Without substantial outside help neither side was capable of clear military victory, especially since the British had neither the resources nor the political will to support the Greek government to the bitter end. The fighting could have continued for many years until mutual exhaustion had dictated some kind of temporary truce. However, from the outset the insurgents had enjoyed the sympathy and support of the communist regimes to the north, and especially Yugoslavia. Had the civil war remained stalemated for some time, these regimes, and perhaps Moscow behind them, would have found it difficult to resist being drawn into the conflict and to withhold assistance in sufficient amount as to give the insurgents the upper hand. Significantly, until 1948 and before his break with Stalin, Tito's "Balkan federation" scheme included a Greek component as well. Therefore, especially had the British withdrawn their limited military presence in Greece as they apparently had decided to do, Greece, or at least its northern regions, could have followed the other Balkan states behind the "iron curtain" before the United States could intervene.

This is not, of course, what happened. British troops and missions remained in Greece, giving the Athens government material and psychological support. In September 1947, at the insistence of the Americans, the Greek government underwent radical change. Tsaldaris relinquished the premiership to the octogenarian leader of the Liberal Party, Themistoclis Sofoulis, but stayed on as deputy premier and minister of foreign affairs. From then on key appointments needed the approval of the American embassy and economic mission, whose specialists served with all major departments. The military effort was supervised by an American military mission under a seasoned combat officer, General James Van Fleet (Van Fleet, 1967), and several hundred officers were assigned to the more important military commands. Although the matter was given serious consideration in Washington, American combat troops were not sent to Greece (Iatrides, 1981, 215–16; Jones, 1989, 79–94). Britain was persuaded to continue its military presence, even if diminished, thus staking the reputation of both principal western powers on the defeat of the Greek communist insurgency.

By the spring of 1948 the government forces had greatly improved in strength, equipment, training and, above all, in spirit. A series of carefully planned and well executed operations swept across the entire country and in hard-fought battles dislodged the Democratic Army from its principal strongholds. Even though by that fall the insurgents had managed to reinfiltrate some of the same areas along the northern border, the end was in sight. Except in remote mountainous regions where the insurgents had concentrated their units, the government had reestablished its authority over the country. In the process, it deprived the insurgency of whatever popular support remained. Families of the insurgents and unarmed supporters moved across the border into Albania and Yugoslavia, where many were to settle permanently. Others were relocated to more distant lands, including the Soviet Union.

In the spring and summer of 1949 the Democratic Army's main force was encircled on the Grammos-Vitsi range along the Greek-Albanian border and after ferocious shelling, bombardment from the air (including napalm) and, finally, hand-to-hand combat, it was mauled and dispersed. Many of the survivors were taken prisoner while others managed to flee into the communist states and to exile which for most was to prove permanent. As a military force and also as a political movement the communists were finished.

If the outcome of the civil war was primarily determined by the strengthening of the government side, it was also significantly influenced by the tactics of the insurgents. The Democratic Army had been effective as long as it operated as a loosely structured guerrilla force and did not attempt to seize and hold territory. But in late 1947, to achieve its political goals, it switched to basically conventional warfare, deploying large, poorly coordinated units with little artillery and no air support against sizeable towns defended by well-equipped government forces. Although individually its troops fought well and gave the Athens government a serious scare, the insurgents were not adequate to this new task. Markos was sacked and Zahariadis took personal command; several Democratic Army commanders were court-martialled and executed. But Zahariadis could do no better. As a consequence of these major setbacks the insurgents' morale suffered badly, especially since public sentiment in heretofore friendly areas was now turning decisively against them; the government's tactic of wholesale relocation of villagers also deprived the insurgents of valuable information and support. Their reserves dwindled, leading to forced recruitment and to the assignment of front-line combat roles to large numbers of women, resulting in higher casualty rates for the insurgents.

Although the evidence is unclear, Markos' dismissal may also have been connected to the Stalin-Tito feud and to Yugoslavia's expulsion from the Cominform in June 1948. According to some accounts, Markos not only had opposed the switch to conventional warfare but had also objected when the party leadership took Moscow's side against Tito and declared itself in favor of "autonomy" for Greek Macedonia, a position which was anathema to an overwhelming majority of Greeks (Eudes, 1972, 241–356; KKE, 1987, 299–316). Whatever its specific policies and tactics, at the most critical turning point of the civil war the KKE leadership became badly (and openly) divided with disastrous consequences for its Democratic Army which was gradually cut off from its reserves and supply bases in Yugoslavia. The Stalin-Tito feud thus dealt a severe blow to the insurgents while strengthening the resolve of the Athens government to avoid concessions and to secure total military victory. If compromise was not a realistic possibility before the summer of 1948, for the government it was totally out of the question after that point. In just over a year the insurrection would be crushed.

Once the fighting had ended and the surviving insurgents were in prison or abroad, the government attempted to appear magnanimous and conciliatory, offering amnesty to those of the Democratic Army rank-and-file who were not accused of "common crimes." But although the character of the government changed—Sofoulis died in June 1949—the state's attitude toward the now-defeated insurgents remained basically the same: only "nationalists" were regarded as true and trustworthy Greeks. The KKE remained outlawed until 1974 and for decades to come its followers and sympathizers who remained in Greece lived in hiding or under the watchful eye of the police and other internal security agencies. The nation's sense of identity, its culture and especially its educational systems at all levels had been permeated by a fanatically anti-communist spirit which would not fade until the 1970s (Tsoucalas, 1981). Thus, the military defeat of the communists was followed by their political banishment for another generation.

The Primary Actors

Lack of effective leadership across the entire political spectrum was undoubtedly a major factor both in causing the civil war and in determining its outcome. In the absence of systematic studies of the

Greek leaders, institutions and processes in the 1940s, this key issue can only be reviewed here on the basis of impressionistic observations.

Because of the chronically fragile nature of Greece's political institutions, strong personal leadership was critically important even in times of relative stability and prosperity. At the moment of liberation from the Axis occupation only the most resourceful, broad-minded and pragmatic political leadership could have produced the sense of national unity, public confidence and spirit of toleration needed to harness the country's depleted energies to the task of relief and reconstruction. The constitutional and policy issues which required prompt and authoritative answers touched on the most fundamental aspects of the Greek state and society; benign neglect would only aggravate an already explosive situation. Because of the severe shortage of vital supplies and economic resources, for most Greeks governmental action—or inaction—spelled the difference between relative comfort and hope on the one hand, and hunger, misery and desperation on the other. Lacking a national political forum of any kind, with country-wide networks of clientelist party machinery in total collapse, and without widely accepted bureaucratic institutions to serve as transmission belts between the public and the government, key decisions had to be made entirely at the very top and quickly. In a state that had not developed a strong tradition of parliamentary government and executive accountability, this situation placed the nation's heavy burden on very few shoulders. Political leadership could literally save or doom the country.

In a nation of politicians, would-be leaders were in abundant supply and during the interwar years many had acquired respectable reputations and recognition. In the Venizelist-republican ranks such men as Stylianos Gonatas, Nikolaos Plastiras, Panayiotis Kanellopoulos, George Papandreou, Sofoclis Venizelos (son of the leader) and Themistoclis Sofoulis (Venizelos' successor as head of the Liberal Party) had established themselves as prominent national figures. The conservative-royalist camp boasted of such notables as Constantine Tsaldaris, John Theotokis and Petros Mavromihalis, as well as a galaxy of lesser but still promising personalities. But in the aftermath of the Second World War none seemed to possess the qualities needed to handle the nation's crisis. Although the reasons for such individual and collective failure are a matter of debate, certain generalizations appear to be valid.

Whatever their talents and capabilities, all these men had remained under the shadow of their illustrious and domineering leaders who had regarded their respective parties as their personal domain. With the partial exception of Sofoulis, they had not acquired the self-confidence, independent vision and managerial skills to govern a troubled nation. When Venizelos and Panages Tsaldaris died in 1936, the issue of leadership succession shook both camps to their core. Moreover, the Metaxas dictatorship condemned them all to total inaction and sent many to prison or internal exile. The enemy occupation which followed made matters worse. In short, the events of 1936–1944 had stunted the growth of political leadership. In their minds, these men had continued to live in the world of the 1920s and 1930s and when liberation came they were not equal to the task. As U.S. Ambassador Lincoln MacVeagh, who knew them all well, observed from Athens in October 1946:

Lack of leadership is certainly what principally ails this country at the present time—leadership which can see beyond political problems which are not only local in character but also completely out of date. The five-year Metaxas dictatorship seems to have effectively prevented the rise of a new generation of politicians to take the place of the oldsters, who have now come back into the saddle, for lack of other leaders, and who still think in terms of the old struggle between Royalists and Venizelists, entirely missing the meaning of developments in Europe and the world which World War II and the rise of Russia have brought about. Small men, old men, and men entirely lacking in a sense of realism which the situation requires, are what we are having to deal with now.

As for the other prominent actor on the political stage of Greece, MacVeagh concluded: ". . . the King who has been brought back as a 'solution' for the problems which the politicians will not tackle is the same old muddled indecisive figure that he always was" (MacVeagh, 1980, 703–4). In fact, the sullen personality and sterile mind of King George II made him totally unsuited to be the monarch of the unruly Greeks. He felt a total stranger among his subjects, whose institutions and culture he regarded with disdain and whose language he could hardly speak, and he lived for the days and hours he could spend with his own kind, in England. More the symbol than cause of division, he remained until his death the convenient target for the alienated and added fuel to the fire simply by trying to keep his throne.

The totally inadequate economic resources at hand and the magnitude of the recovery problem added to the passivity and indecision of Greek politicians and made them turn to Britain and the United States for salvation. Coupled with a tradition of subservience to foreign influence, this attitude invited external manipulation and restricted even further the freedom of Greek authorities to take initiatives that might have fostered political compromise and averted civil war. Instead, they sought, received and carried out a steady stream of rigid instructions emanating from the British and American embassies and all but eliminating the possibility for accommodating even the more legitimate demands of the Left.

Finally, in the course of the enemy occupation and resistance most bourgeois politicians had developed a pathological fear of communism, in which they saw the negation of everything they treasured. For all their feuding, they were united in their conviction that genuine cooperation with the KKE and its principal organ, EAM, would lead to the enslavement and destruction of the Greek nation. In their eyes, communist leaders belonged in jail, not in the cabinet. All through the civil war the "nationalist" leaders remained convinced that negotiations with the insurgents were out of the question. Offers of amnesty and leniency were conditional on the willingness of the insurgents to surrender and place themselves at the mercy of the government.

The communist leadership of the 1940s differed from that of the bourgeois parties. Largely a nation of poor but land-owning peasants, tradition-bound, church-oriented and yet fiercely individualistic, Greece offered little fertile ground for a communist movement. Nevertheless, in some respects the KKE leadership labored under the same handicap as its bourgeois opponents, except more so. It was accustomed to obeying the commands of its Moscow-picked chief and when he was gone, a form of collective leadership contributed to sluggishness, disunity and lack of resolve. Always a very small and often persecuted party, the KKE had never been involved in the governing process and even its parliamentary life had been short and catastrophic. After the national elections of January 1936, the KKE's fifteen deputies gave the party the chance to play the part of power broker between the deadlocked and quarrelsome Liberal and Populist parties. Although secret dealings with both bourgeois parties proved inconclusive, their revelation sparked a violent reaction from the army leadership—under General Alexander Papagos, the communists' nemesis in the civil war—which threatened a military takeover unless the communists were kept out of the government. This communist "scare" opened the way to the Metaxas dictatorship and produced the myth that the country had been saved from communist revolution. Until the war came to Greece, the KKE was struggling to survive as an underground organization, decimated and demoralized by the clever tactics of Metaxas' security police which convinced many communists that they had been betrayed by their comrades.

Moreover, throughout its troubled existence the KKE had tried to steer a course between the dictates of Greek nationalism and the orders of the Comintern, particularly as they affected the future of Macedonia (Kofos, 1964). For the Slav-dominated international communist movement, the KKE was the unwanted waif, to be used and abused in the interests of more important comrades such as the Bulgarians. Thus, in addition to their image as bomb-throwing revolutionaries, the KKE leaders carried the stigma of being willing tools of Greece's foreign enemies to the north. The "anti-nationalist" label, which the KKE could not shed, undermined its popularity and during the period of occupation and resistance compelled it to seek cover behind the broadly based and clearly patriotic EAM coalition.

With party secretary Zahariadis imprisoned at Dachau and others languishing in Greek jails, the burden of KKE's wartime leadership fell upon a small circle of veterans of the proletarian struggle: George Siantos, Yiannis Ioannidis, Dimitris Partsalidis, Petros Rousos and Chrissa Hadjivasiliou. Long years of underground and largely fruitless work, punctuated by party splits and purges, imprisonment and torture, had produced a generation of colorless and dispirited plodders who nevertheless continued the struggle. Cut off from the international communist movement and under the watchful eye of domestic and foreign adversaries, they sought to strike a delicate balance between fighting the foreign occupiers and preparing for the day when political power might at last be their reward. For all their dogma, discipline and personal courage, they were unsure of their strength and of the opportunities before them. Despite EAM's impressive achievements, at the moment of liberation they were no more confident that they were fit to govern the nation than their bourgeois detractors. Their frame of mind is suggested by the fact that for decades many seasoned communists believed that Siantos—who died in 1947—had been an agent of the Greek and British authorities all through the resistance and postwar years.

Unquestionably the central figure in the Greek communist insurgency was Nikos Zahariadis. Born in Asia Minor in 1903, he became a labor organizer and professional revolutionary in Istanbul and fought in the Russian civil war, joining the Soviet communist party. He went to Greece for the first time in 1923 and rose quickly through the ranks of the party's youth organization and was named to the central committee's bureau. In 1929 he was sent to Moscow for training and returned to Greece in 1931 as secretary of the KKE whose leadership he promptly purged on instructions from Stalin. Five years later the Metaxas dictatorship placed him in solitary confinement where he remained until the German invaders sent him to Dachau.

When he returned to Greece in May 1945 he was 42 and had spent a total of ten years in that country, most of them in prison. By ideological indoctrination, personal experience and outlook he was much more a Soviet agent than a Greek. Imperious and short-tempered, he took personal charge of the party and quickly turned its direction to a bold and unrelenting confrontation with the government authorities. No less than his ideological opponents, he had no use for the art of political compromise. With the help of Markos, who had proven himself as a guerrilla leader during the occupation, Zahariadis built up the party's military structure and by the spring of 1947 he launched an all-out insurgency. While it is certain that he received encouragement and promises of support from Belgrade it is not clear what signals and assistance he received from Moscow itself (Eliou, 1979–1980; Stavrakis, 1989, 127–202).

Under his firm and harsh leadership the party performed aggressively and with a clear sense of revolutionary purpose. But Zahariadis made two errors which, together, were to prove fatal to his movement. First, his sense of timing was wrong: by the time he was ready to order the party rank-and-file to battle, the Athens government was strong enough to fight back and the chances for a successful communist revolution in Greece had come and gone. And despite ambiguous signals he apparently remained confident that in the end Stalin would somehow insure the victory of the party in Greece. His strategy wrecked the party, whose ranks were decimated, and cost the country dearly.

Third Parties

The Greek political crisis of the 1940s was first and foremost a domestic affair. Nevertheless, without foreign involvement on both sides of the insurgency there would have been no civil war. Without substantial support from the communist regimes, and the confidence that much more would soon follow, the Greek communists could not have gone beyond the stage of widespread banditry. And without propping up by Britain and the United States the postliberation governments in Athens would not have been able to survive. It hardly needs saying that, in deciding to become involved, outsiders were motivated not by any genuine sympathy for their Greek client but by the fear that their client's defeat would harm their own special interests in the region.

The reputation of the Balkans as Europe's powder keg was not, of course, entirely undeserved and the Second World War did nothing to improve matters, at least as far as Greece was concerned. Albania had served as the springboard for fascist Italy's attack in October 1940 and successive Athens governments continued to consider themselves technically at war with Tirana as late as the 1980s. Bulgaria had received Nazi Germany's permission to annex Greek Thrace, whose population it proceeded to brutalize or expel. Although on the surface relations with Yugoslavia had been much better, the territorial and other aspirations of the two states continued to be a source of friction. After the war, Greek demands for reparations, frontier adjustments, and for "Northern Epirus" (Southern Albania) sharpened divisions even more. Thus, when Greece's three neighbors established communist dictatorships, an ideological dimension was added to traditional feuding as the "iron curtain" came to coincide with the northern borders of Greece.

During the years of occupation and resistance Tito's partisans had sought to establish controlling influence over Slav-speaking guerrillas in northern Greece. Although the move had not been particularly successful, it had planted the seeds for cooperation in the future. As already seen, in the postliberation period veterans of the EAM and ELAS, fleeing from government harassment, had found refuge in the neighboring communist states, especially Yugoslavia. By 1946, refugee settlements—for example, Boulkes, north of Belgrade—had become bases of political indoctrination and military training. In addition to clothing, shelter, food and medical supplies, Soviet bloc countries made available to Zahariadis' agents quantities of weapons, including artillery, which played a significant role in the arming of the Democratic Army. It is also safe to assume that the Tito government gave encouragement and advice which influenced the KKE leadership in opting for all-out civil war.

In fomenting and supporting the insurgency the Tito regime had hoped to achieve two basic goals: first, to destroy Greece as the last outpost of British—and later American—influence in the Balkans and, second, to set the stage for the establishment of a communist "federation" in the region under Belgrade's aegis. If the Greek comrades, with Tito's help, could topple the government in Athens, they could safely be expected to bow to his wishes. Similarly, for Enver Hoxha's regime in Albania and Georgi Dimitrov's in Bulgaria, supporting the Greek communist insurgency was the most convenient way of neutralizing and perhaps destroying their enemies in Athens, thereby adding to their own security.

But even before the Tito-Stalin split in mid-1948, which proved disastrous for the Greek insurgents, the three communist regimes in the Balkans acted with considerable caution and restraint. The supplies provided were never sufficient in quantity or quality to tip the scales against the forces of the Athens government. The heavy weapons, mechanized transport and even aircraft the insurgents' high command expected never materialized. Instead, throughout the civil war the Democratic Army faced serious shortages of every kind and had to economize and improvise constantly. Equally significant, despite the many public words of support, the communist regimes would not extend official recognition to the insurgents. Perhaps there was little confidence that the Greek communists could win. More probably, Belgrade, Sofia and Tirana were afraid of international consequences, especially after stern warnings from Washington and London. And after the summer of 1948, Tito's regime had every reason to wish to see the communist insurgency in Greece defeated.

That the Moscow-dominated international communist movement wished to maintain a safe distance from developments in Greece is also forcefully demonstrated by the attitude adopted by the newly created Cominform. Not only was the KKE not invited to join, or even attend the organizational meeting—near Warsaw, in September 1947—but it had to learn of this momentous development through press reports (Eliou, 1979–1980, Jan. 12, 1980). When the Yugoslavs spoke at that meeting in favor of support to the Greek insurgents, the Soviet delegation pointedly ignored the subject altogether (Swain, 1989, 47). Elsewhere, the French and Italian communist leaders had expressed their disapproval of the KKE's resort to full-scale insurrection. Soon after, when Tito began pressing the Bulgarians for a Balkan federation with Greece as a member, Stalin ordered Tito and Dimitrov to appear before him and condemned the idea, setting the stage for Yugoslavia's formal expulsion from the Cominform (Djilas, 1962, 171–86).

In the absence of solid proof, Moscow's own involvement in the Greek civil war can be evaluated only on the basis of circumstantial evidence (Stavrakis, 1989, 127–202). Certainly the image of the Soviet Union as the greatest military power in postwar Europe, combined with developments in the continent's eastern half, must have made it for the KKE a beacon to be followed to ultimate victory in Greece as well. For Zahariadis, who had spent his life serving Stalin's cause, the success of communism in its struggle against the Athens regime was bound to have the Soviet leader's endorsement. Conversely, it is difficult to believe that Zahariadis would have disobeyed had Moscow given the KKE explicit instructions to refrain from taking up arms against the government.

What little is known suggests that in response to repeated appeals for assistance, Moscow's few direct messages to the KKE leadership were ambiguous and temporizing, allowing room for hope that assistance might still come (Stavrakis, 1989, 127–202; O. Smith, 1987, 175). In the aftermath of his "percentages agreement" with Churchill in October 1944 and with much more important developments elsewhere, Stalin may have been stringing the KKE along to see what it might do, while avoiding further complications with Britain and the United States. However, as the level of violence intensified in Greece and the Democratic Army took to the field, Stalin's attention was fixed not on Greece but on Tito, whose ambitious schemes Stalin was determined to crush. Thus, even if the Soviet leader had any sympathy for the KKE, it was lost in the upheaval of his break with Yugoslavia. That the KKE dutifully took Moscow's side against Tito was irrelevant and once again the Greek communists discovered that they were the least important and most expendable among the faithful.

To be sure, the Soviets missed no opportunity to denounce the Greek government publicly as a reactionary regime bent on harassing and killing its nation's democrats and threatening its Balkan neighbors. At the United Nations Moscow and its satellites sought to condemn not only Greece but also Britain and the United States for their support of the authorities in Athens. But this flurry of diplomatic activity had more to do with the tactics of the emerging East-West conflict across Europe and beyond than with the situation in Greece.

Furthermore, in the 1940s Anglo-American influence in the United Nations was strong enough to neutralize Soviet efforts to exploit the international organization for Moscow's own purposes. For all the debates, investigatory commissions and reports, the role of the United Nations in the Greek civil war was to remain mostly symbolic and largely vacuous (Howard, 1966).

In particular, the efforts of Herbert Evatt, Australia's foreign minister and president of the U.N. General Assembly during 1948–1949, to bring the Balkan states together for purposes of mediation and conciliation, proved frustrating and ineffective. Openly opposed by the United States, the Evatt initiatives foundered because mutual suspicions and hostility in the Balkans proved intractable as long as the major powers themselves could not agree on a formula to end the conflict. In the spring of 1949, as the Greek army was preparing to attack the remaining communist strongholds, cautious Soviet intimations to the United States that the major powers might cooperate in enforcing a solution to the Greek crisis were turned aside: Washington viewed any prospect for compromise as a victory for the insurgents since it was bound to destroy morale in Athens. Moscow, possibly concerned that an emboldened Greek government might invade Albania and bring down the Hoxha regime—as Athens had secretly proposed to Washington and London—apparently suggested to the Democratic Army that it might suspend its activities, at least temporarily, as a gesture of good will and moderation. Nothing came of these moves and although the United States would not approve an invasion of Albania, Greek government troops crossed into Albanian territory in pursuit of retreating insurgents (Kontis, 1984, 382–88).

In the highly polarized and supercharged climate of the late 1940s, a crisis which came to be regarded as a focal point of the East-West conflict could not be settled through international mediation. In the United Nations and elsewhere no neutral ground could be found as each side demanded a settlement on its own terms. Under those conditions the Greek civil war could only end with the total defeat of the weaker side.

By any standards, the most influential third parties in the Greek civil war were Britain and the United States. Motivated by traditional power considerations affecting the Eastern Mediterranean and the Middle East, and by a growing fear of Soviet expansionism in both those directions, during the Second World War British officials had shepherded the Greek government in exile as well as the resistance movement. They succeeded in preventing the leftists from gaining control, particularly during the December 1944 crisis, and installed anti-communist forces in positions of authority in Athens. Military and economic assistance as well as continuous and direct involvement in the management of Greek affairs had made British officials the key decisionmakers in everything but title.

The experience proved costly and frustrating: Britain could save its Greek clients from drowning but could not make them stand on their own feet. In February 1946, as he prepared to leave his post in Athens, the British ambassador reported to his superiors that in his considered opinion, the only real solution to the problem was "to allow an elected Greek government to apply (after a plebiscite) for membership of the British Commonwealth" (Richter, 1986, 421–25). Although the ambassador's suggestion to grant Greece dominion status was dismissed as impractical, one Foreign Office official declared:

I still think that *colonial* treatment whether by us or by some trusteeship group is the only method which offers any hope of nursing Greece towards solvency and political stability. "Dominion status" is meantime impossible because . . . Greece is a backward, extravagant and irresponsible country whose vanities are made greater and whose difficulties are therefore accentuated because for both us and the USSR Greece has strategic importance. (Richter, 1986, 425)

One year later the Labor government informed the United States that Britain could no longer carry the burden in Greece (and Turkey). By February 1947, growing American concern over developments in Europe and the Middle East gave the British every reason to believe that Washington would not allow Greece to be lost to the Soviet camp. Moreover, Britain's recent role greatly facilitated America's entry in Greek affairs: the institutions and practices of foreign control were already in place and could be expanded as needed (Anderson, 1981, 176–84).

As already indicated, the Truman administration decided to go to the aid of the Greek government because it became convinced that the insurgency was a concrete manifestation of Soviet aggression which threatened not only Greek but American interests. In late August 1946 the American embassy in Athens reported that the KKE was controlled by Moscow; a month later Ambassador MacVeagh commented that "in final analysis" the Soviet Union was responsible for the armed struggle in Greece (Iatrides, 1987, 232–33; United States Department of State, 1969, 226–27). In March 1947 Mac-Veagh told a congressional hearing on the Truman Doctrine that "the fellow to blame was the fellow who controls the little countries to the north of Greece, the fellow who is backing them, right square back to the Moscow Government" (United States Senate, 80th Congress 1973, 40). And in October 1947, after visiting Greece, a senior U.S. army official reported to his superiors, "The Soviet Union must be recognized as solely responsible for the existence of serious internal strife in Greece. . . . In essence the struggle in Greece is simply one phase, though an important one, in the worldwide struggle between the United States and the Soviet Union" (Iatrides, 1987, 236).

Such a perception of the character of the Greek crisis called for an all-out rescue mission and the total defeat of the communists since America's security interests and reputation as defender of the free world were now at stake. The appropriations which President Truman requested for Greece would be the beginning of a program of massive economic and military assistance that would continue into the 1950s. Moreover, American officials soon echoed their British colleagues' lament that Greece was a "backward, extravagant and irresponsible country." In February 1947 the first head of the economic mission reported that Greece was not really a state "in the Western concept," that its civil service was a "depressing farce," and that its government was in the hands of "a loose hierarchy of individualistic politicians, some worse than others" (Iatrides, 1980, 51). Gen. James Van Fleet, who headed the military mission, and other American officials thought that Greece needed a strong-man government which would not compromise with the insurgents (Iatrides, 1980, 64–65).

While the Department of State continued to insist on a broadly based government of moderate politicians, it presided over the establishment of an elaborate system of direct American control of Greek affairs that was unique and unprecedented. Thus, in an attempt to separate the responsibilities of the embassy from those of the economic and military missions, the Department produced the following list of fields of activity in which the ambassador was to have the upper hand:

(a) Any action by the United States representative in connection with a change in the Greek Cabinet; (b) Any action by the United States representatives to bring about or prevent a change in the high command of the

Greek armed forces; (c) Any substantial increase or decrease in the size of the Greek armed forces; (d) Any disagreement arising with the Greek or British authorities which, regardless of its source, may impair cooperation between American officials in Greece and Greek and British officials; (e) Any major question involving the relations of Greece with the United Nations or any foreign nation other than the United States; (f) Any major question involving the politics of the Greek Government toward Greek political parties, trade unions, subversive elements, rebel armed forces, etc. including questions involving the holding of elections in Greece. (Iatrides, 1980, 65)

As might be expected, as a result of these arrangements and for the duration of the civil war, Greece was in effect governed by the various American missions in Athens and their superiors in Washington. One particular consequence of this situation was that compromise or even serious dialogue with the insurgents was simply not considered, as the means for their total defeat were now available.

The Military Balance

The key military aspects of the civil war have already been outlined; only a brief recapitulation will be attempted here (Iatrides, 1981).

At first grouped into roaming independent bands, by the fall of 1946 the insurgents were brought under a centralized headquarters created by the KKE and commanded by "General" Markos. In the spring of 1947 Markos' Democratic Army could count on about 17,000–20,000 "regular" troops, with another 5,000 in reserve or training abroad. During that year and the first half of 1948 its monthly recruitment rate was perhaps about 1,000, mostly young farmers from small mountainous villages in the north. In 1948 recruitment became increasingly by force and included for the first time large numbers of women who soon represented at least twenty percent of the total combat force. A hierarchy of communist "political commissars" and an elaborate bureaucratic system of internal security relying on informants of the worst kind suggests that the KKE and its military cadres had little confidence in the loyalty of their troops.

The Democratic Army's strength peaked at about 28,000 in May 1948, and fell rapidly afterward due to the heavy fighting and reverses of that summer. Significantly, KKE leaders had estimated that to accomplish its objectives the Democratic Army would need a combat strength of 50,000–60,000, heavy weapons, modern transport and some air support. However, by the following spring it had risen only to about 25,000 men and women under arms and about two-thirds of that force took part in the final operations in the summer of 1949 on Grammos-Vitsi. Of those, perhaps 5,000 escaped to Albania and exile. According to government sources, during the four years of fighting the insurgents suffered 38,421 killed, 23,960 captured, and 21,544 surrendered on their own. In all, during 1947–1949 more than 100,000 men and women fought in the ranks of the insurgents.

Some of the original guerrillas had retained their personal weapons—mostly old rifles and pistols—from their days in the resistance movement. In 1946–1947 they added to their arsenal weapons and equipment, including light mortars and machine-guns, anti-tank guns and wireless sets, taken from government troops. In 1947–1948 the Democratic Army received from the neighboring communist regimes—mostly through Yugoslavia—quantities of rifles, mortars, heavy machine-guns, grenades, panzer-fausts, mines and a few artillery pieces. Perhaps ten percent of the insurgents' arms, including most of the heavier weapons and mines, were provided by foreign sources. The endless variety in the weapons' origin, vintage, type and caliber was to plague the insurgents all during three civil wars. As one American study concluded, the Democratic Army's supply system "except in the border area, could not support sustained combat operations and failed entirely under the demands of protracted engagement" (Murray, 1954, February, 56). The static, positional tactics which the insurgents employed after 1947 revealed their weakness as a conventional military force and doomed them to destruction. In short, the Greek communists never acquired an army strong enough to accomplish what they set out to do.

For the government forces 1946–1947 was a painful period of growth and adjustment. While a new army was being organized, trained and equipped under British supervision, a hastily formed National Guard and special "rural security units" of armed civilians, all undisciplined and incompetent, were no match for the fast-moving insurgents. Their conduct turned many against the government, while part of their equipment was seized by the communists. By the spring of 1947, when a number of successive anti-guerrilla operations were undertaken, the army's strength had reached 120,000, with an additional 50,000 in the National Guard and 30,000 in the gendarmerie. Badly conceived and poorly executed, these operations failed to destroy the insurgents, who returned to the "cleared" areas as soon as the army had moved on. Nevertheless, the government forces gradually took the initiative and the movement of the insurgents' units was restricted to ever-shrinking areas.

In 1948, with growing American support and direction, the army grew to 147,000, with another 51,000 in the National Guard, 26,000 in the gendarmerie, 14,000 in the rebuilt navy and 6,500 in the newly formed air force. Tens of thousands of armed civilians assisted the authorities in their districts. Equally important, the government forces were supplied with new and more powerful weapons, including much-needed pack howitzers (and thousands of mules), heavy mortars, recoilless rifles, rocket launchers, flame-throwers, napalm, reconnaissance planes and dive-bombers, and modern field communications equipment. These weapons proved extremely effective against the bunkers and fortified positions which the insurgents attempted to defend in 1948 and in the final battles in 1949. American officers were involved in the preparation of operations and evaluated their execution, often very critically. Finally, in January 1949 the Americans requested and secured the appointment of General Alexander Papagos to the newly created post of supreme commander with virtually dictatorial powers in matters pertaining to the war effort. By then the superiority of the government forces over their opponents was overwhelming.

The defeat of the insurgency was achieved at a very high cost. According to official figures the government forces suffered 8,440 dead, 29,496 wounded, and 5,446 missing; uncounted numbers of civilians were also killed or injured as a direct result of the civil war in which land mines were used extensively by both sides. More than 700,000, or about one-tenth of the total population, were forcefully uprooted from their villages, many never to return. Thousands of actual or suspected communists languished in concentration camps on barren islands, while more than 25,000 children were taken by the insurgents out of the country. The physical damage was no less extensive as whole villages were demolished, roads and bridges blown up, power and telephone lines destroyed and mountainous areas made impassable by land mines.

Death and destruction are, of course, the mark of civil war. What distinguishes the Greek case from most other conflicts in recent decades is the very rapid change in the military balance which in turn determined the winner-take-all outcome. Within the span of about a year the insurgency lost the military and political momentum as the goals it had set for itself became clearly unattainable because of the domestic and foreign factors outlined above. During the same short period the government's strength and resolve grew steadily and total victory became a virtual certainty.

As long as the insurgents held the military initiative and their goal appeared to be the establishment of a communist regime in Greece, the government was too frightened and politically weak to seek a compromise. And once the government side had received the American commitment of support and began to secure the material means to defeat the enemy, it had no incentive to make concessions. Except for propaganda statements, neither side communicated to its opponent a willingness to reach a settlement based on compromise; foreign factors also strongly militated against a negotiated settlement. On the contrary, the brutality displayed by both sides was a clear indication that peaceful resolution of the conflict was not being contemplated. In short, what has been termed a "hurting stalemate" that might have produced a settlement through compromise was never reached and the civil war was fought to its bitter end.

The Outcome

The Greek civil war ended in the early fall of 1949 with the insurgents' crushing defeat and their destruction as a political movement. Although the victors soon reverted to their traditional infighting and the Populist Party faded into oblivion—to be replaced by Papagos's new conservative "Rally"—the communists remained for decades banished and stigmatized as enemies of the nation. With most of the KKE leadership scattered in exile and violently split, and while veterans of the Democratic Army languished in prisons, a fanatically anti-communist spirit continued to permeate Greek politics and culture and to characterize the actions of every agency of the state for decades to come. The insurgents' defeat could not have been more total or its consequences more lasting.

The reasons for such a decisive, winner-take-all outcome were many and complex, as earlier portions of this study have shown. But the most critical factor was the fundamental weakness of the insurgency as a political movement and also as a military force, resulting in a dramatic imbalance between the two sides in the civil war. This domestic imbalance was further accentuated by the very different roles played by the foreign patrons of the Greek protagonists.

For all their early successes as guerrillas, once the civil war began the insurgents never acquired a strong popular base. Generally perceived as revolutionaries serving their foreign masters, they could not rid themselves of the anti-nationalist label; the more they fought, the more feared and hated they became. As a result, they were not able to build up their strength to the point where victory over the government forces might be a realistic possibility.

To be sure, Zahariadis' delay in ordering his followers to the mountains and the failure to procure military equipment in sufficient quantity and quality contributed significantly to the inherent weakness of the Democratic Army. Without massive support from abroad the KKE could not possibly hope to topple the government; and despite the many pleas and promises, such support never came. On the contrary, at a critical moment the Stalin-Tito feud disrupted even the relatively modest support network on which the Democratic Army had come to rely by the summer of 1948.

Nevertheless, at the root of the communists' problem was the fact that the vast majority of Greeks, however disillusioned with the ruling elites in Athens, could not bring themselves to lend support to what they perceived as the nation's enemies. And once the benefits of American assistance became apparent and the defeat of the insurgency came to be viewed as inevitable, most Greeks rallied behind the government. This substantial measure of national unity against the insurgents improved the morale and effectiveness of the government forces, now greatly expanded and equipped with all that was needed to defeat the enemy. In addition, the United States and Britain appeared determined to prevent outsiders from changing the balance between the two sides, thus insuring that the government forces could finish the job. By contrast, the Soviet Union seemed unwilling or unable to rescue a communist insurgency which it had not inspired or actively supported. Once the civil war had started, if there was a period during which the outcome was truly in doubt, that period was very short indeed.

In a negative sense Moscow contributed to the long-term outcome of the civil war in yet another way. Many of the KKE leaders who managed to escape abroad eventually reached the Soviet Union where they were settled under conditions of virtual house arrest. Even for lesser cadres travel was severely restricted and all "political" activity was strictly forbidden. After 1953, Stalin's successors considered them as no more than a burden to be tolerated. Coupled with their own bitter divisions and feuding, this enforced inactivity away from their homeland prevented the Greek communists from continuing their political struggle in any form.

After the 1950s the climate in Greece began to change and a more moderate political center began to emerge. The Cyprus problem, which strained Greek relations not only with Turkey but also with Britain, the United States and the Atlantic alliance as a whole, damaged the fortunes of the conservatives and led to a reorientation of Greek politics. The gradual lessening of East-West tensions also contributed to a mellowing of political passions in Greece. But it was only after the fall of the colonels' junta in 1974 that the KKE was legalized and some of its cadres began to return from the Soviet Union and other countries of Eastern Europe. By then, a new generation of communist leaders had emerged. Thus, if the Greek communist insurgency had been doomed from the start, its final chapter could not be written until forty years after the guns were silenced.

PART III

Theoretical Issues and Problems

The Causes of Peace
Robert Harrison Wagner

Because of the division of intellectual labor between students of domestic and international politics, the causes of civil and interstate wars tend to be studied separately.[1] However, the justification for this division of labor is not as clear as it is commonly believed to be.

Writers in the Realist tradition have taught generations of students that international politics is fundamentally different from domestic politics.[2] It is different because there is no government at the global level, and therefore no institution to enforce agreements or restrict the means people use for accomplishing their objectives. Domestic politics, however, takes place in an environment in which governments try, with considerable (though not complete) success, to do both. Kenneth Waltz has tried to capture this distinction by saying that international politics is characterized by anarchy, while domestic politics is characterized by hierarchy (Waltz, 1979).

Violence, however, occurs in both. But how can the use of force in the domestic arena be consistent with a hierarchical order? Waltz says:

The difference between national and international politics lies not in the use of force but in the different modes of organization for doing something about it. . . . A government has no monopoly on the use of force, as is all too evident. An effective government, however, has a monopoly on the *legitimate*

I would like to thank Jack Levy, Roy Licklider, and Paul Pillar for their comments on earlier versions of this paper.

235

use of force, and legitimate here means that public agents are organized to prevent and to counter the private use of force. Citizens need not prepare to defend themselves. Public agencies do that. (Waltz, 1979, 103–104)

Thus "hierarchy" seems to mean simply that there are public authorities, and they are expected to have some success.

But this definition of "hierarchy" applies only to "effective" governments. Citizens sometimes succeed in defending themselves against the authorities, and public authorities sometimes divide into warring factions. The result may be ineffective government, but it is still part of domestic politics. As Waltz has written:

The threat of violence and the recurrent use of force are said to distinguish international from national affairs. But in the history of the world surely most rulers have had to bear in mind that their subjects might use force to resist or overthrow them. If the absence of government is associated with the threat of violence, so also is its presence. (Waltz, 1979, 102–103)

Indeed, Waltz writes, violence may be more prevalent in some domestic political systems than in the interstate system. Therefore ". . . no durable distinction between the two realms can be drawn in terms of the use or the nonuse of force" (Waltz, 1979, 103).

Thus the distinction between domestic and international politics does not really coincide with the distinction between political behavior that is constrained by government and political behavior that is not, in spite of what Realists say. It would seem to follow that an understanding of the causes of war among states might be relevant to an understanding of the causes of war within states. Moreover, if one focuses on politics that is not constrained by institutions, while leaving to others the study of politics that is constrained, one is unable to investigate why institutional constraints are sometimes effective and sometimes not. And if one is interested in understanding the role of political institutions as a means of preventing war at the global level, an investigation of the causes of domestic peace might be a promising place to begin. As Inis Claude wrote in his classic book on the management of force at the global level, ". . . the prevention of civil war is the function of national government most relevant to the problem of ordering international relations . . ." (Claude, 1962, 269). Thus the division of labor between students of domestic and international politics may have inhibited an understanding of both.

The purpose of this paper is to follow these suggestions and see where they lead. Since the focus of the discussion will be on war, whether at the interstate or domestic level, it will be useful to begin by considering what a war is.

War

A war is a contest, in which organized groups of people use weapons that were designed to wound and kill each other, and destroy each other's property. Contests in the use of force occur when the use of force is opposed by the use of force. Not every contest in the use of force is conventionally recognized as a war, however. If one group uses force against another, the result will not be considered a war unless the victim not only decides to resist, but also does so with just enough success that the conflict lasts a while and produces a significant number of casualties. Therefore a war cannot be the result of the actions of only one group, and a war as conventionally defined need not have been intended by any of its participants.[3]

Contests in the use of force can take more than one form. To understand the forms they can take, it will be helpful to consider what force can be used for if it is unopposed. Using force means doing physical harm to people or their property. It includes, therefore, killing people, physically hurting or injuring them, and harming them by doing damage to third parties or to things that they value. One man may use force against another, or threaten to do so, either in order to remove another's resistance to his will (as when one man kills another in order to take his property), or in order to induce another to conform to his will (as when one man tortures another in order to induce him to reveal information).

It will be important to bear in mind that, while force is often the most effective means of getting one's way, it nonetheless has important limitations even when it is unopposed. Killing people prevents one from profiting from their cooperation. Harming people, or threatening to kill or harm them, may be less effective as a means of inducing their cooperation than the use of positive inducements.

Another important disadvantage of the use of force, however, is that its intended victim may use force to resist it. A man can use force to kill another man who is trying, or may try, to kill him; he can try to destroy the means available to the other to use force against him; or he can try to induce the other not to use force by harming him, or threatening to harm him if he does use force. These three methods of using force against the actual or threatened use of force, if not immediately decisive, can lead to three types of contest in the use of force. I will call them *mortal combat, counterforce duels*, and *contests of punishment*, respectively.

Mortal combat is a contest in which the combatants try to kill each other. A counterforce duel, on the other hand, is a contest in which the combatants try forcibly to disarm (or disable) each other. The one who succeeds will then be able to use force against the other without opposition. The outcome of mortal combat leaves nothing to be decided. A counterforce duel, on the other hand, only decides who gets to use force without opposition; it does not decide what form the subsequent unopposed use of force will take, or how effective it will be.

Both mortal combat and counterforce duels can lead to decisive outcomes if they are continued long enough, but they can also be stopped if the contestants agree to do so. A man engaged in mortal combat who believes he will be killed can offer to be disarmed instead; if the other agrees, the fight will stop. Someone who believes it likely that he will be disarmed in a counterforce duel can offer to disarm himself voluntarily, and may ask for some compensation for saving the other from the necessity of continuing the contest. Thus both these contests can be ended either by negotiation or by fighting to a decisive conclusion.

A contest of punishment occurs when each adversary tries to bend the other to his will by using force to injure or harm him until he does. If the means of punishment are being used up in the contest, then contests of punishment can end in the same two ways as mortal combat and counterforce duels, since if a contest of punishment is continued indefinitely, one party may exhaust his means of punishment before the other does, and will thus be unable to oppose the other's use of force against him. If the means of punishment are not used up in the contest, however, then a contest of punishment can only be ended by the voluntary action of the contestants, and therefore by negotiation.[4] Moreover, while mortal combat and counterforce duels can lead to decisive outcomes if continued long enough, they may instead end in stalemate, and thus be indecisive. In that case they, like contests of punishment of the latter sort, can only be ended if the parties to the contest decide to end them.

There is no reason, however, why contests in the use of force must be symmetrical. One adversary may be trying to kill the other, while the second is trying to induce the first to stop by harming him or destroying things of value to him. Moreover, a counterforce duel may be followed by a contest of punishment, or by an asymmetric contest in which one side continues to try to disarm the other, but the latter now tries to induce the former to quit by harming him. Finally, both mortal combat and counterforce duels are usually unpleasant in their own right, which provides a motive for ending them before they reach a decisive conclusion. Thus most contests of force include elements of a contest of punishment, whatever the primary form of the contest may be, and a stalemated counterforce duel may be indistinguishable from a contest of punishment.

It is the potentially decisive character of mortal combat and counterforce duels that makes it plausible to speak of "winning" and "losing" such contests. Note, however, that mortal combat is decisive only if one's aim is merely to kill one's adversary, and one or the other side succeeds in doing that. Counterforce duels are decisive only in determining who gets to use force without opposition; they do not determine the outcome of the unopposed use of force (which, as emphasized above, may be disappointing).[5] And they may not even be this decisive if they lead to stalemate, or if they are followed, not by the unopposed use of force by the victor, but a shift by the loser to a strategy of opposition by punishment (as when the loser of a conventional war shifts to guerrilla war against the winner instead of accepting defeat).

Contests of force between or among groups are rarely examples of mortal combat (though they obviously include many instances of mortal combat), since whole groups do not normally try to exterminate each other.[6] Conventional interstate wars among the great powers have rather been counterforce duels, in which states sought to disarm each other by killing members of each other's armed forces and destroying their weapons, or demonstrating their ability to do that convincingly enough that the enemy's forces agreed to surrender instead.[7] Terrorism, guerrilla wars, and some scenarios for fighting nuclear wars, on the other hand, are all examples of contests of punishment. The US government tried to find and disarm its enemy in Vietnam, but found itself participating in a contest of punishment instead.

Note, however, that states, to achieve their objectives, need not be able to disarm their adversaries completely; they may only need to drive the adversary's military forces from particular pieces of territory that they control.[8] Moreover, even if a state has demonstrated its ability to disarm its adversary, it may choose not to do so, but to use its victory on the battlefield to extract concessions from its adversary instead (as did the victorious allies in World War I).

Weapons, numbers, organization, and territory are all important in determining who has an advantage in contests in violence. This fact provides a motive for cooperation in the use of force: by pooling their resources and organizing, individuals can gain an advantage over other individuals in contests in the use of force. It also provides an opportunity for a division of labor: some people can specialize in contests in violence, and offer to support others in them, in exchange for other things of value (including some of the resources that are needed to make or acquire instruments of violence).

But disagreements can be expected to arise among people who decide to help each other in violent contests. And disagreements will arise between specialists in violence and those to whom they sell their services. How are these disagreements to be settled? Perhaps they will also be settled by the use of force. While this is possible, however (as when thieves fight over how to divide up a pile of loot), it tends to make the coalition less effective in the use of force. While fighting among themselves, its members cannot direct their energies against their opponents; and those who are weak in the struggle over dividing up the spoils may elect to join the opposing side instead. Thus the need of individuals and groups to cooperate in the use of force can be a motive for settling differences among them in a nonforceful way. War and peace can therefore each be a cause of the other.[9]

In summary, then, wars are contests in the use of force. They occur when attempts to use force are contested, but in a way that is not immediately decisive. Thus wars will not occur if (1) no one tries to use force as a means of getting his way; (2) force is used (or threatened) but never contested; or (3) contests in the use of force are always decided quickly and without many casualties or much damage. Peace, therefore, may be associated either with the avoidance of the use of force, or its unchallenged or effective use.

Wars are fought by groups and not by individuals. Thus how contests in the use of force are decided, and whether they will be decided quickly, depends on what coalitions exist and whether they will persist. The difference between domestic and international politics is sometimes said to be that in the domestic arena the use of force by the state is not subject to serious challenge, while in the international arena one state's use of force can be effectively challenged by other states. A state, however, is itself a kind of coalition, and its ability to defeat its domestic opponents decisively cannot explain its ability to hold itself together. Thus the supremacy of the state can at best be only a partial statement of the conditions for civil peace. If so, then the domestic and international arenas may not be so different after all, and the literature on interstate war may be relevant to understanding the conditions for civil peace.

The Causes of International War

Wars are unpleasant, and much of the study of them has been motivated by the practical question of how to prevent them (or whom to blame for them). As a result, the study of wars of all sorts focuses overwhelmingly on how they begin, rather than how they end. Once a war has begun, however, ending it often becomes a practical problem in its own right. The small literature on the endings of wars, therefore, tends to ignore the question of how wars begin.[10] Yet if one is interested in what determines whether adversaries are at war or at peace, it seems reasonable that one should investigate both how wars begin and how they end, and expect some systematic relation between the two. Any condition that caused a war to begin, one might think, will cause the war to continue until either the condition ceases to exist or the adversaries are unable to continue fighting. And there is the possibility that if the condition disappears before either adversary is unable to continue fighting, the war will nonetheless end.

If so, then another effect of separating the study of the beginnings of wars from the study of their endings will be that the object of one's study becomes poorly defined. There is a huge literature, for example, on the origins of World War I. But what was World War I? It was the whole military contest that took place from the first shot that was fired until the armistice. If the war had ended much earlier, or taken a different course, then the war whose origins one is seeking might have been a very different war from the one that has been studied so much. Much of the literature on the causes of war tacitly assumes that, once begun, a war takes its own autonomous course until it reaches a decisive conclusion (usually equated with the victory of one side or the other). A closer look at the way wars end, however, teaches us that this need not be true, and often is not true:

groups that decide to begin a war can decide to end it.[11] Thus, if one wants to explain the occurrence of a war as customarily identified, explaining its beginning cannot really be separated from explaining its ending, and everything that happened in between.[12]

The idea that the causes of war and the causes of peace are intimately related has been most eloquently defended by Geoffrey Blainey, who wrote:

For every thousand pages published on the causes of wars there is less than one page directly on the causes of peace. And yet the causes of war and peace, logically, should dovetail into one another. A weak explanation of why Europe was at peace will lead to a weak explanation of why Europe was at war. A valid diagnosis of war will be reflected in a valid diagnosis of peace. (Blainey, 1988, 3; see also Wittman, 1979)

Blainey meant these statements to apply to war and peace among states. But there is no reason why they should not also apply to war and peace within states.

According to Blainey, the relation between war and peace is simply that

Wars usually end when the fighting nations *agree* on their relative strength, and wars usually begin when fighting nations *disagree* on their relative strength. Agreement or disagreement is shaped by the same set of factors. Thus each factor that is a prominent cause of war can at times be a prominent cause of peace.

Therefore "[w]ar itself," he writes, "is a dispute about measurement; peace, on the other hand, marks a rough agreement about measurement" (Blainey, 1988, 122). Unfortunately, Blainey did not make entirely clear what these remarks meant, or why he thought they were true. Some clarification is therefore necessary before we can properly evaluate them.

Blainey's main thesis, I suggest, can be reconstructed in the form of the following simple argument, which I will call Blainey's Argument:

1. In order for a war to occur, at least two states must be willing to fight.
2. No state will fight unless its leaders believe that the expected consequences of fighting are better than the expected consequences of not fighting.
3. Any outcome of war can also be achieved without war if all the potential combatants agree to it.

4. All leaders prefer no war to war if the expected outcome of both is the same.

∴ No war will occur unless the combatants have different expectations of its outcome.

Interpreted in this way, Blainey's claim is to have identified conditions that are *necessary* for war, and therefore *sufficient* for peace.[13] Since the word "cause" ordinarily means a sufficient condition for something, Blainey's book might have been better titled *The Causes of Peace*. This argument implies that one of the causes of peace is convergent expectations of the outcomes of wars. If potential antagonists disagree about the consequences of a war between them, then a war may occur, but need not; if they agree about the outcome, however, then a war will not occur. At the beginning of a war, therefore, the antagonists must have different expectations of its outcome; but if the progress of the war causes their expectations to converge, then the war will end even if both sides are able to continue fighting.

Unfortunately, this is not, as it stands, a valid argument. For suppose the combatants are uncertain of the outcome of war, but their expectations are identical. If one or both the combatants are risk-acceptant, then there may be no compromise outcome that they both prefer to the lottery associated with war.[14] Thus at the very least the conclusion to Blainey's Argument must be changed to read:

∴ No war will occur unless the combatants are uncertain about the outcome of war, or disagree about what it will be.

This amended conclusion is obviously still consistent with the spirit of Blainey's discussion.

Unfortunately, however, the argument is still not valid. For suppose two combatants have identical and certain expectations of the outcome of war between them, but there is a range of possible agreements that both would prefer to fighting the war. Then it may not be common knowledge which agreements each prefers to war and which it does not. Thus one may hold out for an agreement more favorable to itself than the outcome of war, believing that the other would be willing to accept it. The other may then decide that the expected outcome of war is preferable to the expected outcome of bargaining.

Moreover, suppose it were common knowledge which agreements each side preferred to war and which it did not. Bargaining over the terms of an agreement would still take time, and if the combatants believed they were far apart in their expectations of the outcome of bargaining, they might decide that the expected outcome of war was preferable.

Finally, suppose both sides expect the war to be a contest of punishment in which neither will be able to disarm the other, and therefore they expect the military contest alone to be indecisive. Then fighting is bargaining, and each must compare the value of an agreement now with its expectation of what agreement the other will be willing to accept after further fighting. The fighting can end, therefore, only when the combatants have convergent expectations of the outcome of bargaining.

If it is to be valid, then, Blainey's Argument must be further modified, so that its conclusion reads:

∴ No war will occur unless (1) the combatants are uncertain about the outcome of war, (2) the combatants disagree about what the outcome of war will be, (3) the combatants are uncertain about the outcome of bargaining, or (4) the combatants differ greatly in their expectations of the outcome of bargaining.

This is now a valid argument, since if none of the hypotheses stated in the conclusion is true, the combatants must prefer negotiating to fighting. It can be summarized by saying that anything that contributes to the convergence of expectations of the outcome of war and the outcome of bargaining makes peace more likely.[15]

Even if the argument is valid, however, the conclusion may still be false if one or more of the premises is false. The first premise is a consequence of the way "war" has been defined, and therefore is not open to much dispute. The second is a weak rationality assumption, which is perhaps more controversial. One important reason for questioning it is that the expectations of leaders and followers may differ. Thus leaders may be willing to accept an agreement as an alternative to war, but realize that it would be rejected by their followers. This, however, is not so much a fundamental objection to Blainey's analysis as it is a reason for modifying it to take into account the relations between leaders and followers. It implies that wars will be harder to end if followers as well as leaders on both sides must have convergent expectations of the outcome.

The third premise seems quite plausible as long as it makes sense to distinguish between the effects of war and its outcome. This requires that political leaders be self-interested, and therefore care only about their own side's gains and losses. Then the damage done to the other side by war will be neither a gain nor a loss to them. If, instead, each takes satisfaction in the suffering of the other side, then in order for the third premise to be true it would be necessary for the agreement that is accepted instead of war to incorporate the infliction of punishment on one or both sides. This seems unlikely, and if it were possible then the truth of the fourth premise would become questionable.

The fourth premise is also not very plausible if the expected outcome of war is the physical extermination of one side and that outcome is the goal of the other side. Note, however, that political absorption is not the same as physical extermination. Physical extermination is not a very common motivation for the use of force among states; it may, unfortunately, be more common as a motive within states.

A more serious problem with the fourth premise is that states may want to fight in one war in order to enhance the credibility of their commitment to fight in others. If war is avoided, their reputation for fighting will not be enhanced, and thus the fourth premise may be false. Even so, however, the point of cultivating a reputation for fighting is to influence the expectations of one's adversaries about the consequences of their using force in other contexts. Thus the reason why the fourth premise is false with respect to one conflict may be that it is true of another.

It may at first appear that one or another of these premises must be false if there is an incentive to attack first. But an incentive to attack first really implies that, since the outcome of war depends on who begins it, it is not possible for the adversaries to have convergent expectations about the outcome unless they also know who will attack first. Thus an incentive to attack first may make it more difficult to avoid war by making it more difficult for states to have convergent expectations of the war's outcome. On the other hand, as I have already emphasized, once someone has attacked and therefore acquired any advantage associated with attacking first, the incentive to attack first cannot explain why the war does not end immediately.

There are, then, important circumstances in which one or more of these premises may be false. It seems likely, however, that these premises will often be true. And when they are true, convergent expectations of both the outcome of war and the outcome of bargaining will make peace easier to achieve. Even then, convergent expectations will be a sufficient condition for peace, not a necessary condition, and therefore there may be peace even when there is no consensus as to the expected outcome of war.

Thus Blainey is right when he says that "[e]xpectations . . . seem to be a crucial clue to the causes of war and peace" (Blainey, 1988, 55). It is important to keep in mind, however, what sorts of expectations are relevant. When he says that war occurs when states disagree about their relative strength, and therefore that war is a "dispute about measurement," he seems to have in mind factors that influence the outcome of a counterforce duel. But at other times he refers to expectations about the outcome of bargaining, as when he says that war is a "dispute about bargaining power" (Blainey, 1988, 117). These are not the same, and both are important. For substituting agreement for war requires that the combatants agree not only on the subsequent course of the war if fighting continues, but also on how to divide up the gains from stopping it. This, however, can only be decided by bargaining. And bargaining leads to agreement only when all parties prefer some agreement to the expected outcome of further bargaining, which may not be true if they differ greatly in their expectations of what the outcome of further bargaining will be.

Even though Blainey claimed that the causes of war and peace were the same, and that if one understood why wars ended one would also understand why they began, his book is about the beginnings of wars and not their endings. The study of peace negotiations by Pillar (1983), however, provides strong support for his ideas (at least as I have interpreted them).[16] One of the main themes of Pillar's book is the difference between expectations concerning the future course of military operations and expectations concerning the future course of negotiations, and the importance of the convergence of both as a precondition for the negotiated settlement of wars.[17]

Let us follow Blainey, then, and say that anything that contributes to convergent expectations of the outcome of war makes peace more likely. What does this imply about the causes of peace? According to Blainey, it implies that the surest cause of peace is war itself, since the best way of measuring the relative power of states is to have them test their power in war against each other. Thus decisive wars are followed by long periods of peace, since the information they provide about the power of states lasts long after them. Over time, however, this information becomes out of date, and the probability of war therefore increases. Similarly, Blainey concludes that a lop-sided distribution of military power is a potent force for peace, since this promotes consistent expectations of the outcome of war (Blainey, 1988, 108–119).[18]

These inferences have two problems in common, however. First, they seem more relevant to counterforce duels than to contests of punishment. Contests of punishment are contests of will. It is not clear how the outcome of one contest of punishment bears on the outcome of another where the stakes may be valued differently. And in contests of punishment, the distribution of military force between the antagonists, while not irrelevant, is not decisive in determining the outcome (as the war in Vietnam illustrates).[19]

Second, even with respect to counterforce duels, these inferences do not take into account the effect of shifting coalitions on the out-comes of wars. If there are more than two possible participants in a war, then even if there are convergent expectations of the military outcome of every possible war, there cannot be convergent expec-tations of the effect of State A's attempted use of force against State B unless it is also known who will support State A and State B, and therefore which of all the possible wars in which State A and State B fight on opposite sides will actually occur. And once a war has begun, it may not end until it is clear whether states that have not yet joined will still do so, and under what circumstances those that have joined might be induced to quit. Thus it is not clear how wars can be decisive enough to lead to long periods of peace, since the outcome of some particular war need not provide information about the outcome of another war with different participants.[20] For the same reasons, in a world of more than two states, the concepts of "equal" and "unequal" distributions of power are not even well-defined, since if states are evenly matched when considered indi-vidually, there must be some coalitions that are superior to others, and vice versa.[21]

Let us consider the second problem first. It is as relevant to un-derstanding the causes of domestic peace as it is to the causes of international peace. Since it has been discussed most extensively in the literature on the balance of power, however, that is the place to begin.

Peace and the Balance of Power

Traditionally, the concept of the "balance of power" was associated with the idea that weak states would find it in their interest to join together to prevent the hegemony of powerful states. This, it was thought, was the main means by which the independence of states could be protected in what Realists would now call an anarchic system. Thus the emphasis of traditional balance of power theory was on system stability (meaning the nonelimination of the members of the international system) and not peace, and the relation between the balance of power and peace has been controversial.

In recent years the idea of the balance of power has come to be associated with the distribution of power among states. In debates about what distribution of power is desirable, there often seems to be a conflict between the goals of peace and stability. Stability, it is argued, requires equality of power, since equality maximizes the probability that all states will be able to defend themselves. Inequality of power, on the other hand, as Blainey suggested, makes convergent expectations of the outcome of war more likely, and therefore maximizes the probability of peace.[22] But as we have seen, "equal" and "unequal" distributions do not have a clear meaning in a world of more than two states, where one has to take into account not only the power of individual states, but also alliances among them.

It is precisely because the possibility of shifting alliances makes it difficult to anticipate the outcomes of wars that Kenneth Waltz has claimed that what he calls "multipolar" international systems are more prone to war than bipolar ones (Waltz, 1979, 161–193). But no one, including Waltz, has ever stated clearly how to recognize a bipolar international system. It is clear that in a bipolar system, two states are much more powerful than the others. What is not clear is how much more powerful they have to be, since in every system in which the three most powerful states are not exactly equal and there is no tie for second place, there must be two states that are more powerful than all the others. Much of Waltz's discussion of the significance of bipolarity seems to assume, not a particular distribution of power among many states, but a system of only two states.[23] Thus Waltz does not really tell us what distribution of power in multiactor systems minimizes uncertainty about alliances.

Blainey has rightly emphasized the importance of convergent expectations of the outcomes of wars as a cause of peace, and Waltz has rightly emphasized the fact that uncertainty about who will ally with whom makes for uncertainty about the outcomes of wars. Let us see if we can combine these clues with the logic of traditional balance of power theory to draw some conclusions about the relation between the distribution of power and international peace.

Suppose that the military resources of each state could be represented by a single index number, the resources of states could be combined and used against others in war, and the military outcomes of wars were determined entirely by the ratio between the military forces assembled on each side, so that, in a counterforce duel, equality of forces would lead to stalemate, and superiority would lead to victory.[24] Consider, then, a system of five states in which each state has the same quantity of military resources as every other state, so that the system can be characterized by the vector (60, 60, 60, 60, 60). Then any combination of three states could defeat the other two, if they could agree on how to divide up the military resources of the defeated states. And any two states could defeat a third, if no other state came to its aid.

Suppose, on the other hand, that the same quantity of resources were distributed as follows: (150, 100, 20, 15, 15). Then no state would join the first in attacking the others, since as soon as the first acquired an additional unit of resources, it could defeat any combination of other states, including its former ally. For the same reason, if the first state attacked any one of the others, all the others would have to come to its assistance, since only a combination of all the other states could successfully oppose the first. Finally, the second or third states would not want to attack the smaller ones, since while they did so the first would be free to join in, and thus to increase its power. This, then, is a system in which all uncertainty about alignments has been eliminated, as a result of the fact that one state is on the verge of dominating it. It is a system that might be called "bipolar," since two states are much more powerful than any of the others. Its distinctiveness, however, is the result of the fact that one state is so powerful that it is on the verge of being able to defeat any combination of other states. In the previous system, by contrast, every state has a long way to go before it becomes a threat to all the others, and therefore some states can lose a lot of resources before others have an incentive to come to their aid.

In these examples, however, the only uncertainty is the result of the interdependence of the choices of the actors; once the participants in a conflict are identified, the outcome of war can be predicted, and thus by Blainey's Argument need not be fought. Thus systems with the properties of these examples might be stable or unstable, but in either case they should be completely peaceful.[25] But if there is uncertainty about the outcomes of wars, there will also be uncertainty about when any state is on the verge of hegemony, and thus about what sort of opposition to an attempted use of force a state may expect.

Many people have claimed that a state that controls all of Europe will be close to hegemony in this sense, and concluded that both England and the United States have a vital interest in preventing any state from controlling the European continent.[26] Many people in both countries have also disputed this claim, however. And if the leaders of Germany had been absolutely confident that the leaders of England and the US would adhere to this principle prior to World War I and World War II, their behavior might have been quite different. Since in both cases a lot could happen before Germany was close to dominating the continent, it was difficult for the leaders of the US and England to communicate what their response to that possibility would be.

After World War II, however, the Soviet Union was sufficiently close to dominating Europe that this possibility had to be faced prior to the use of force by the Soviets, rather than after it as in the case of Germany, and steps had to be taken to communicate how the US and England would respond.[27] Moreover, since World War II, the size of the US contribution to the defense of Europe, as well as the existence of the US nuclear deterrent, has facilitated the formation of an opposing force. These are facts that have helped make Waltz's concept of "bipolarity" seem plausible in spite of its ambiguities.[28] Thus a plausible alternative to "bipolarity" as the distinguishing feature of post-World War II international politics is that, unlike the hegemonic wars that preceded it, World War II was fought in such a way that one of the defenders against the previous claimant to hegemony was placed in a near-hegemonic position itself, that is, World War II ended with Soviet troops in the middle of Europe and poised to advance further to the West. As a result, the sort of uncertainty about who would ally with whom that Waltz argues was one of the causes of World War II has been minimized.[29]

The lesson of the simple examples discussed above, therefore, is that when all states are far from hegemony, the interest of each state in preventing the emergence of a hegemonic state is not sufficient to prevent weak states from being preyed upon by stronger ones; when one state is on the verge of hegemony, however, it should expect to be opposed, as balance of power theory has traditionally claimed, by all the other states in the system. If potentially hegemonic states are always successfully opposed, then the international system may be stable.[30] If hegemony is to be prevented without war, however, then there must be convergent expectations of the outcome of a hegemonic war. And if such a war is to be a counterforce duel, then, as Blainey has rightly said, this will most likely be true if the challenger expects to be met by an overwhelming concentration of force. But if there is room for disagreement about when the challenger will have reached the point of hegemony, then there may not be convergent expectations concerning who will join the opposing coalition, and therefore there may be uncertainty about the outcome of a potential hegemon's attempted use of force.

Thus the belief that there must be a conflict between the goal of stability, which requires equality, and the goal of peace, which requires inequality, is the result of trying to analyze systems with more than two actors by using the logic of two-actor systems. In principle, both stability and peace could be achieved in multi-actor systems, if attempts to use force were always expected to be opposed by overwhelmingly superior coalitions.

This is unlikely in multi-actor international systems, however, for two reasons. First, sufficiently large opposing coalitions have an incentive to form only when doing so is necessary to prevent another state or coalition from acquiring a position of hegemony. When states that are far from hegemony use force, other states may have an incentive to join them, or may have no incentive to oppose them and thus choose to sit on the sidelines instead. And second, the very reason why, if there is to be peace, states contemplating the use of force must expect to be opposed by overwhelmingly superior force, namely, uncertainty about the outcomes of wars, is also one of the reasons why this requirement may not be met: there may not be a convergence of expectations concerning when any particular state will have achieved a position of hegemony.

Let us now consider what all this implies about the relation between the distribution of power within states and domestic peace.

The Causes of Domestic Peace

In the literature on international politics, a system in which states agree to cooperate so that the use of force is always opposed by overwhelming force is called a collective security system. We have just seen why a collective security system is not a reliable way of preventing international war, and the limitations of the balance of power mechanism as an alternative.[31] In Claude's summary of the literature on the management of force at the global level, the only alternative to the balance of power and collective security as a means of avoiding war is world government (Claude, 1962). Claude points out that writers on international politics customarily equate "government" with an organization that has a monopoly on the ability to use force (Claude, 1962, 223–242). Government can therefore prevent war by guaranteeing that the use of force will always be opposed by overwhelming force.

Claude, however, disagrees with this conception of the relation between governments and domestic peace. He says, in the passage quoted at the beginning of this paper:

. . . I would argue that the prevention of civil war is the function of national government most relevant to the problem of ordering international relations, that governments cannot and do not perform this function by relying primarily upon either police action against individuals or military action against significant segments of their societies, and that governments succeed in this vitally important task only when they are able to operate an effective system of political accommodation. (Claude, 1962, 269)

Yet governments do use force against dissident groups, and Realist students of international politics are not alone in emphasizing the importance of the expected use of force by governments as a deterrent to political opposition and domestic violence.[32] Moreover, political accommodation that takes place in a context in which violence is a likely alternative means of getting one's way is quite different from the sort of political accommodation that is normally practiced in stable democratic societies.[33]

Claude's objection has greater force if restated in the following way: the requirement that governments be able to oppose the attempted use of force with overwhelming force is unlikely to be met if governments must act against large, well-armed, and well-organized domestic groups. For even if governments are likely to win such confrontations, there may be sufficient uncertainty about the outcome that civil war is possible. And the question is not how governments are able to defeat their domestic opponents, but how they are able to guarantee domestic peace.

Claude also points out that governments are themselves just collections of individuals, and the ability of a government to defeat

organized domestic opponents does not guarantee that it will remain
united in opposition to them. As he says:

> . . . in a case of deep conflict within the civilian body of a society, organized
> forces of rebellion may be built up while the organized forces of the state
> may break down; these are likely to appear as two aspects of the same
> process. (Claude, 1962, 237)

Civil wars are not always just conflicts between the government and
its opponents; they are also often conflicts within the government's
armed forces.

Taken together, these objections imply that if civil peace is the
result of the expectation that the use of force will be opposed by
the government with overwhelming force, then the government's
opponents must not expect to be able to organize a large force in
opposition to it, and the government must be expected to remain
united in its use of counterforce. Seen in this way, government is
just a component of a collective security system. The problem, then,
is to understand why such a system is possible within states but not
among them.

As Claude points out, one answer that is given to this question by
the proponents of world government is that, to be effective, government must be able to impose controls on individuals, and not just
subordinate units of government (Claude, 1962, 243–255). Claude
objects to this answer, however, on the ground that it falsely equates
the problem of preventing civil war with the problem of controlling
crime. The appropriate analogy, he says, is rather with the problem
of accommodating the demands of large dissident *groups* (Claude,
1962, 255–271).

While Claude is right in calling this answer naive as a contribution
to the problem of preventing war at the global level, however, he
is too quick in rejecting it as at least part of the explanation of the
ability of governments to control domestic violence. Claude's objection amounts to saying that those who argue that governments
control violence by controlling individuals assume that individuals
will never organize into large groups that might challenge the force
available to governments. And in this, of course, he is correct. But
in making this objection he overlooks the fact that governments often
have an advantage over their potential opponents in precisely this
respect, by virtue of the fact that the force available to governments
is already organized, whereas its opponents must first organize themselves before they can challenge the government. And in trying to

accomplish this, dissidents must cope with all the problems of collective action that the literature on collective goods and the Prisoner's Dilemma has made clear to us in recent years.

This casts a somewhat different light on Waltz's statement that "[t]he difference between national and international politics lies not in the use of force but in the different modes of organization for doing something about it," cited at the beginning of this paper (Waltz, 1979, 103). The idea that the force available to the government is overwhelmingly more powerful than the force available to its opponents is no better defined than similar statements about the distribution of military power at the global level, since in both cases the distribution of power depends on what particular coalitions will face each other. The advantage the government has is, rather, often an organizational one, with the result that it need not face all its potential opponents at one time. Thus one important difference between international politics and domestic politics within many (but not all) countries is that at the global level it is much easier to put together coalitions for the use of force.

Note that this is exactly the opposite of what is usually said about the effect of anarchy on the achievement of common objectives: since at the global level there is no government to enforce agreements, it is usually argued, cooperation is more difficult among states than within them. And this may well be true in many areas. But in the domestic arena, the government is not available to enforce agreements to use force against itself; rather governments act so as to make such agreements more difficult. At the international level, on the other hand, two facts facilitate the organization of coalitions for the use of force. First, the number of independent actors is much smaller, and the organizational problems correspondingly easier to overcome. And second, the effect of each government's contribution to the outcome is much greater, and therefore the direct benefit to each government from participating is more likely to exceed the cost. (Moreover, there is no organizational problem at all to be overcome before one government can use force against another.)[34]

One might object that this line of reasoning is at most relevant to the question of how the government maintains its supremacy over its potential nongovernmental opponents, but has no bearing on the question of how the government maintains its unity. Yet the same reasoning can be extended into the government itself. Consider members of a platoon contemplating mutiny. If the platoon leader issues a command and an individual private is the only one who disobeys, the private is in trouble. If, on the other hand, no one obeys, the platoon leader is in trouble. Thus expectations about who will support whom are crucial in determining whether force will be met by overwhelming force. And potential dissidents within the government are often at a disadvantage in concerting their actions as compared to defenders of the government. Modern totalitarian states have shown us how far it is possible to go in preventing the use of force against the state by making it difficult for the opponents of the government (or the ruling clique within the government) to organize.

These same states have also recently shown us, however, how fragile such ways of suppressing conflict can be. Moreover, the organizational advantage of the state authorities can often be compensated for by the existence of other ties that facilitate communication, such as those of race, religion, ethnicity, or geography (especially when reinforced by federalism), when they coincide with the incentives that exist to use force against the government.

In addition, as I pointed out earlier, the idea that convergent expectations of the outcome of war are the result of expecting that force will be met by overwhelmingly preponderant force is most appropriate to wars that are expected to be decisive counterforce duels. It is not clear what "preponderant force" means in the context of a contest of punishment in which it is not possible for one side to disarm the other. Because contests of punishment cannot be settled on the battlefield, it is often difficult to change either side's expectation that further conflict will lead to a better outcome than the one the opponent is currently willing to accept, and therefore it may be difficult to prevent such conflicts, or bring them to an end once they begin.[35] Small forces skilled in terrorism or guerrilla warfare have often been able to avoid being disarmed, and to make life very unpleasant for their enemies, especially if they have a foreign sanctuary and source of supply. And, since foreign support can be crucial in sustaining the minimum level of force necessary to wage a contest of punishment, the expectations of the anti-government forces will be influenced not just by the force available to the government, but also by the expected actions of foreign governments.

Thus Claude is right in stressing the limitations of the idea that domestic peace is the result of the preponderance of force available to the government as compared to its adversaries. The alternative, however, is not, as Claude suggests, simply political accommodation of those contemplating the use of force, which Blainey's Argument implies will in any case often be possible only if there are convergent expectations of the result of opposing force with force. Rather the alternative is the creation of a situation in which the use of force, even if unopposed, is less attractive than alternative means of getting one's way. These alternative means are, of course, chiefly economic exchange and the use of a system of rules for making collective choices.

Contests in violence are the result of using force to oppose the use of force. Such contests will not occur if force, even when unopposed, is an inferior means of achieving one's goals. When open markets and competitive political institutions exist, most people will prefer working for a living to armed robbery, buying what they need to stealing it, hiring people to work for them to using forced labor, taking people to court to using force to redress a wrong, and engaging in political activity (or moving to another jurisdiction) to rebellion, even if the probability is small that the use of force would be met by force; and the government itself will prefer to help people enrich themselves and then tax them, rather than use the force it controls to confiscate the property of its citizens arbitrarily. Then it will not be difficult to arrange that anyone whose preferences are different from these will be apprehended and disarmed by the forces of the government. In these circumstances domestic peace is a property of a complex equilibrium in which the superior force available to the government enforces the maintenance of markets, courts, and political institutions, which in turn reduce the government's need to use force. Thus what sustains peace is not simply superior force, but the entire equilibrium of expectations of which force is only one component.[36]

As Waltz emphasized, states do not have a monopoly on the use of force; they may, however, have a "monopoly on the *legitimate* use of force." This Weberian phrase is often repeated, but seldom defined. One possible definition is that it simply stands for the complex equilibrium just discussed.

In an environment in which the prevailing equilibrium implies greater rewards to the use of force relative to its alternatives, however, there will also be incentives to try to oppose force with force. And then it will be possible that two adversaries each prefer to engage in a contest of force to allowing the other to use force unopposed, in which case armed conflict can be avoided only if they have convergent expectations of the outcome of such a contest and also expect to be able quickly to agree on a mutually preferred alternative.

From Civil War to Domestic Peace

As Blainey (1988) has emphasized, many discussions of the causes of war are really discussions of the causes of conflict. But conflict is ubiquitous, while war is not. Eliminating conflict would, of course, eliminate war. But eliminating conflict would be impossible, and therefore it is fortunate that it is not necessary to do so in order to avoid war.

Similarly, many discussions of the endings of wars focus on the problem of changing the goals of the combatants. For example, Randle says:

The struggle to preserve or to gain ideological or power political values is evident in the stages just before a declaration of war, and that struggle continues throughout the war and during all phases of the negotiations for peace. Indeed, the struggle may be intense enough to prevent agreement upon even minimum terms of a settlement. In fact, all cases where belligerents refuse to consider a movement towards peace or are unable to agree upon peace terms after negotiations have begun can usually be ascribed to such intensely espoused ideological or power political values. . . . if the parties are to achieve even a partial settlement, the war must become *deideologized*. The values that the leaders of the states or factions had hoped to gain must be *devalued*. . . . the competition for values must diminish in intensity below a certain level before peace will be possible. (Randle, 1973, 11)

Since war itself usually has the opposite effect, such reasoning makes the ending of wars seem exceptionally difficult. As Ikle wrote:

Whatever the obstacles to an arrangement that would have prevented war, the use of violence itself engenders new obstacles to the reestablishment of peace. Fighting sharpens feelings of hostility. It creates fears that an opponent might again resort to violence, and thus adds to the skepticism about a compromise peace. . . . more is expected of a settlement because both the government and the people will feel that the outcome of the war ought to justify the sacrifices incurred. (Ikle, 1971, 107)

Because the goals of the participants in civil wars are believed to be especially hard to compromise, civil wars, some claim, are harder to end than international wars. And if war makes conflict more intense, then it may seem unlikely that the participants in a civil war will be able to coexist thereafter, and either partition or the recurrence of civil war may seem more likely.

Most civil wars are not ended by negotiation, a fact that seems to confirm this pessimistic reasoning (Modelski, 1964b; Pillar, 1983, 16–26). One might think, then, that it would be useful to find a way to foster negotiated settlements of civil wars. Thus Modelski wrote:

As a method of terminating internal war, settlement has a number of features to commend it to the student of politics. Settlement reduces the amount of violence and serves as a clear landmark beyond which the renewed use of violence becomes illegitimate. Settlement takes account of a wider range of interests and mirrors more accurately the state of political forces in society. Settlement, above all, is a rational way of ending a period of violence and the appropriate method for inaugurating a period of domestic peace. (Modelski, 1964b, 149)

But Blainey's Argument implies that this reasoning may be mistaken. Wars will end when the combatants have convergent expectations about the outcome of further fighting, regardless of the goals that led them into war in the first place. Moreover, because war conveys information about the consequences of using force, war itself can be a potent cause of peace, and civil war can therefore make a subsequent civil war less likely.

We have seen, however, that Blainey was unclear about the relation between negotiation and the outcome of war. Let us therefore examine more closely the implications of Blainey's Argument, as I have restated it, for understanding the role of negotiation in ending civil wars.

As Pillar has emphasized, whenever the victor on the battlefield cannot achieve its objectives merely by eradicating its opponent or expelling it from a piece of territory, the victor requires the loser's cooperation, and therefore the termination of war must lead to at least tacit bargaining (Pillar, 1983, 38–39; see also Kecskemeti, 1958). Moreover, even adversaries who have been decisively defeated in counterforce duels may retain the capacity to engage in contests of punishment in the form of guerrilla warfare. Thus if one looks closely enough one can usually find evidence of bargaining between adversaries even when one of them accepts defeat on the battlefield and surrenders its forces. The role of the outcome of the military contest is then to determine who can do what to whom in the bargaining that follows.[37] This is why bargaining cannot begin until the combatants have convergent expectations of the outcome of battle, and agreements may not be kept if these expectations change.

Since wars are fought by organized groups, however, a distinction has to be made between wars that lead to the dissolution of one or more of the combatants (whether temporary or not), and wars that leave the organization of the participants intact (though their military forces may be destroyed). In the latter case, all the participants retain their identity as well- defined adversaries in the bargaining process. In the former case, the losers on the battlefield may still retain the capacity to resist the actions of the victors, but the victors may not confront an easily identified bargaining partner.

The endings of World Wars I and II illustrate this distinction. World War I ended when Germany and its allies concluded that further fighting would lead to their defeat. They agreed to an armistice that preserved the military advantage of the victors, and this military advantage then influenced the relative bargaining power of the participants in the peace negotiations that followed. This outcome was possible, however, only because the victors were not interested in using their military advantage to end the political independence of the losers. In World War II, on the other hand, the victors on the battlefield did not want to leave the political identity of the losers intact while they determined their future, and thus, while the losers retained some ability to resist the demands of the victors, the victors did not confront a single, well-organized bargaining partner while determining the fate of the defeated countries.

Pillar tries to capture this difference by saying that World War I ended by negotiation, while World War II ended by "capitulation" (Pillar, 1983, 18–23).[38] But if so, these two wars provide little support for the idea that negotiation is a way of shortening wars, promoting compromise settlements, or fostering conditions in which war is unlikely to recur, since the outcome of World War I is not preferable to the outcome of World War II in any of these respects.

If this is the difference between negotiation and capitulation, then we should expect negotiated settlements of civil wars in only two cases: wars of independence in which the rebel forces succeed in disarming the forces of the established government, and civil wars of any sort in which no combatant is able to disarm the others, or, in other words, civil wars that lead to a stalemate. Since rebels fighting for their independence only need to avoid defeat in order to achieve their objectives, cases of the first type ought to be rare. Thus we should expect most cases of negotiated endings to civil wars to be characterized by military stalemate. It is not surprising, then, that Modelski concluded that "stalemate is easily the most important condition of a settlement" (Modelski, 1964b, 143), or that Zartman has emphasized the importance of a "mutual hurting stalemate" as a precondition for making a conflict "ripe for resolution" (Zartman, 1985, 224).

We have already seen, however, that a military stalemate merely transforms a counterforce duel into a contest in punishment, in which war becomes indistinguishable from bargaining. Thus in deciding whether to accept some proposed settlement, there are two ways in which a party to a stalemate might expect to do better if it continued fighting instead: it might be able to overcome the stalemate and achieve a military advantage, or its opponents might, after further suffering, decide to settle for less. A negotiated settlement therefore requires that all parties to the conflict prefer the terms of the settlement to the expected outcome both of further fighting and of further bargaining.[39] It may take a long time to achieve the necessary convergence of expectations, as the wars in Korea and Vietnam illustrate. Thus, while a stalemate may require that a war, if it is to be ended, must end in a negotiated settlement, there is no reason to believe that the existence of a "mutual hurting stalemate" implies that the war will end promptly. Modelski, in arguing for the merits of negotiated settlements of internal war, wrote that "a stalemate can always be contrived by international action" (Modelski, 1964b, 143). It is important to recognize that this is as likely to prolong the war as it is to shorten it.

But do negotiated settlements make subsequent conflict less likely? In thinking about this question, we must not confuse compromise with a change in the objectives of the parties to the compromise. Negotiated settlements reflect the relative bargaining power of the participants in a conflict, which is based on their expectations of the consequences of rejecting the settlement. Of course, after wars are over the objectives of the adversaries may change. But this is not guaranteed by the achievement of a negotiated settlement, and if the expectations that supported a settlement change but the objectives of the adversaries do not, then war may break out again. The fact that a civil war has occurred implies that the organizational advantage of government has been overcome. Thus one of the disadvantages of a negotiated settlement may be that, because no combatant is able to disarm its adversaries, a settlement requires that all the adversaries retain some semblance of their organizational identities after the war, even if they are disarmed. While such an agreement may facilitate the ending of one civil war, it may also facilitate the outbreak of the next.

More important than the way civil wars end, then, is the nature of the political arrangements created after they are over. In light of our previous discussion, we might distinguish loosely among three types of possibilities, which I will call a *balance of power*, the *supremacy of the state*, and a *monopoly of the legitimate use of force*.

As we have seen, the term "balance of power" is often used to refer to a particular distribution of power among potential combatants which is claimed to promote peace; when used in this way, a balance of power usually means an equal distribution of power, a term whose meaning is not clear in multi-actor systems. By "balance of power" in this context, however, I mean instead the expectations of the consequences of using force that led to the settlement that ended the preceding civil war, based on the capabilities of the adversaries that were demonstrated in that war, whatever their distribution might be. As Blainey pointed out, if these expectations persist in the aftermath of the war, then war can lead to peace, since none of the adversaries believe that it is likely that a renewal of the war will lead to a significantly different outcome.

There is no reason why a balance of power in this sense should not lead to domestic peace for long periods of time, so long as the lessons of the previous war are commonly believed to remain approximately valid. Obviously, however, this method of keeping the peace is as fragile at the domestic level as at the international one, since many things can happen that will lead antagonists to expect a more favorable outcome from the attempted use of force.

By "supremacy of the state" I mean a situation in which no one can expect to be able to organize a military force capable of challenging the forces available to the established government. This type of outcome will often require not only the disarming of all but one faction in a civil war, but also efforts to destroy the organizational identity of the losers, and inhibit the organization of dissident groups in the future (including possible dissident factions within the ruling elite). Finally, by a "monopoly of the legitimate use of force" I mean the complex equilibrium described above, in which the ability of the government's forces to overcome dissidents is guaranteed not just by the difficulties potential rebels face in coordinating their actions, but also by the fact that there are nonforceful means of collective choice that most people would prefer to forceful means even if forceful means had some prospect of success. (These last two types of outcome are best thought of as extreme points on a continuum, and any particular political system may contain elements of both.)

The last outcome, of course, is not only likely to be the most stable, but would be considered by many to be the most desirable on other grounds as well. It is not, however, an outcome that is easy to achieve as the result of a negotiated settlement of a civil war, for the simple reason that it may be inconsistent with the maintenance of the balance of power that provides the incentive for accepting the settlement. Adversaries in a civil war must be concerned about how any agreement they reach will be enforced if their opponents choose not to keep it, and thus will be reluctant to abandon the option of forcibly resisting violations of the agreement. But unless they do so, there is little chance of creating a monopoly of the legitimate use of force.[40]

Pillar lists both the Russian civil war and the American civil war among those that did not end by negotiation (Pillar, 1983, 18–21). One led to the supremacy of the state, and the other ultimately to a monopoly of the legitimate use of force. What determines which outcome emerges from a non-negotiated ending to a civil war? I do not know how to answer this question. But it seems likely to me that two related factors are important: the fragility or permanence of the coalition that wins the civil war, and the residual bargaining power of the losers. (The studies in this volume of the civil wars in the United States and Nigeria provide some support for this idea.)

In thinking about war, everyone tends to confuse the outcome on the battlefield with the political settlement that follows.[41] We have seen that Blainey himself is guilty of this confusion, despite his statement that war is a dispute about bargaining power. There is also, as we have seen, a tendency to equate bargaining (and compromise) with negotiation between equals. Thus it is easy to overlook the fact that even total victory on the battlefield may leave the losing side with significant bargaining power, and therefore be disappointing to the victor. These confusions are the basis for the common belief that a compromise settlement of a civil war is impossible, as exemplified by the following passage from Pillar:

Stakes are usually less divisible in civil wars than in other types of war; the issue is whether one side or the other shall control the country. . . . each side in a civil war is a traitor in the eyes of the other and can never expect the enemy to let it live in peace. The struggle for power becomes a struggle for survival as the options narrow to the single one of a fight to the finish. As a result, few civil wars end through negotiation. . . . (Pillar, 1983, 24)

This reasoning in turn is the basis for the belief that civil wars tend to be intractable, and that fostering negotiated settlements would be desirable.

It should now be clear that the reasoning behind these conclusions is mistaken. While there may be no room for compromise over who will control the country, there are many possible compromises over the way in which the country will be controlled.[42] The problem in settling civil wars may therefore not be the absence of possible compromises, but the difficulty of finding a way of enforcing a compromise that does not violate its terms. And a negotiated settlement may make this more rather than less difficult. Thus the complete victory of one side on the battlefield is not necessarily inconsistent with the achievement of domestic peace, stability, and justice, and an effort to foster a negotiated settlement instead need not promote such conditions, or even reduce the bloodshed by shortening the war. Indeed, it is possible that one reason why domestic conflicts seem more intractable than international ones is that the ever-present possibility of intervention by outsiders makes it difficult to arrange for a situation in which all combatants are simultaneously pessimistic about the possibility of improving their position by further fighting, and thus one or the other prefers to continue the war rather than end it.

Civil War and International Peace

We have seen that the literature on international war has something to say about the causes of domestic peace. What does thinking about the prevention of civil war tell us about the prospects for international peace?

Claude wrote that

In the final analysis, it appears that the theory of world government does not *answer* the question of how the world can be saved from catastrophic international conflict. Rather, it helps us to *restate* the question: How can the world achieve the degree of assurance that inter-group conflicts will be resolved or contained by political rather than violent means that has been achieved in the most effectively governed states? This is a valuable and provocative restatement of the question—but it ought not to be mistaken for a definitive answer. (Claude, 1962, 271)

The discussion above does not enable us to give a complete answer to Claude's question. It does enable us, however, to identify the most important parts to the problem. They are many factors that will affect the utility of the *unopposed* use of force, relative to its alternatives, on the one hand, and the convergence of expectations about the outcomes of *contests* in the use of force on the other. Discussions of the effects on the probability of war of various forms of interdependence, including economic interdependence, confuse these two factors. It is often only in retrospect that the costs of war can be seen to outweigh any possible benefits, since war itself is associated with divergent expectations of the consequences of the use of force. There may be occasions, however, where the gains from the unopposed use of force seem great relative to the gains from trade; and the belief that the other side expects war to be costly can lead to the expectation that the use of force will not be very effectively opposed.[43]

In the most stable societies, these two sets of factors are components of a complex equilibrium, in which the expectation that most people will find the unopposed use of force an inferior alternative reinforces the expectation that those who do use force will be opposed by overwhelming force, and vice versa. The force that is exercised by governments is only one component of such an equilibrium. It alone is not sufficient to produce it. What is not clear is whether it is necessary if such an equilibrium is to exist.

Notes

1. Compare, for example, Blainey (1988) and Rule (1988). A recent exception is Goldman (1990).

2. For a recent discussion of the Realist tradition in the study of international politics, see the essays in Keohane (1986).

3. For a discussion of some of the implications of these points for the empirical literature on the causes of international war, see Most and Starr (1983).

4. These distinctions expose an ambiguity in the concept of a "war of attrition." Mearsheimer (1983), for example, distinguishes between wars of

attrition and blitzkriegs; as he uses the terms, however, both are examples of ounterforce duels. An exchange of limited nuclear countervalue attacks, on the other hand, would also involve the attrition of each side's forces, even though the weapons are targeted at population centers and not at each other.

5. The outcome of the recent war between the US and Iraq provides a striking illustration of this fact.

6. Though many people assume that this is what a nuclear war would entail.

7. This is what Clausewitz meant by saying that "[w]ar is nothing but a duel on a larger scale" (Clausewitz, 1976, 75). This has sometimes been misinterpreted to mean that war is similar to the stylized contests in which gentlemen once defended their honor by dueling with swords or pistols, and thus might, like that custom, fall out of fashion. See, for example, Mueller (1989, 11), and Pillar (1983, 28–29).

8. Clausewitz acknowledged this fact as well (Clausewitz, 1976, 69).

9. The possibility that external threats might induce contending factions to compromise their differences is a perennial theme in the literature on international politics. The study of the civil war in Yemen included in this volume suggests that this factor may have been important in the termination of that conflict.

10. An important exception is Ikle, 1971, 106–131.

11. See especially Pillar (1983).

12. For example, even if an incentive to attack first helps explain why a war begins, it does not explain why, once it has begun and the owner of the first-strike advantage is identified, the war does not end immediately.

13. Thus Blainey's work is consistent with Bruce Bueno de Mesquita's contention that the study of the causes of war should focus on necessary rather than sufficient conditions (Bueno de Mesquita, 1981).

14. Consider a situation in which two people have tickets to a lottery in which there is a 50% chance of winning $1000, but they can each instead have some fraction of $1000 for certain if they can agree on how to divide it between them. If one is risk-neutral, then he will not accept less than $500 as a substitute for the lottery ticket. But if the other is risk-acceptant, then he will demand more than $500. There is therefore no division of the $1000 that they both prefer to the gamble.

15. The first two premises in this argument might tempt one to say as well that anything that increases the cost of war will make peace more likely. But if the leaders of State A believe that the cost of war will make the leaders of State B prefer not to contest their use of force, they may decide to use it. And if each mistakenly believes this of the other, then war may be more likely. This is important to bear in mind in thinking about the effect of nuclear weapons on the probability of war.

16. See also the discussion in Kecskemeti (1970).

17. Since bargaining occurs only if the bargainers have divergent expectations of its outcome, bargaining is necessarily associated with what game theorists call incomplete information. At the time Pillar wrote, however, bargaining theory, like the rest of game theory, rested on the assumption that all features of the bargaining situation were common knowledge. Thus Pillar had to wrestle with the problem of fitting an analysis of rational behavior with incomplete information into a framework that assumed complete information. Subsequent developments in game theory have made possible the analysis of rational behavior with incomplete information, and thus provided a foundation for further investigation of these problems.

18. Wittman (1979), like Blainey, emphasizes the relevance of understanding why wars end for understanding why they begin. Wittman claims, however, that there is no relationship between the distribution of power and the probability of war. But this is because he assumes that the distribution of power only affects the probability that one side or the other will win, whereas Blainey's claim is that the combatants' estimates of the probability of winning are more likely to be consistent if the distribution of power is very unequal. Wittman recognizes that inconsistent expectations make war more likely.

19. As Mearsheimer (1983) has emphasized, even if a war is expected to be a counterforce duel, one side or another may believe it has discovered a strategy that enables it to win quickly and cheaply in spite of the balance of forces.

20. This problem is all-too-briefly discussed by Blainey (1988, 119–120), who does not clearly distinguish between expectations concerning the outcome of a war among some combination of states, and expectations concerning which combination of states will fight.

21. This problem is discussed in Wagner (1986).

22. See especially Claude (1962, 11–93).

23. In discussions of bipolarity, this ambiguity is often hidden by statements to the effect that a bipolar system is a system with only two Great Powers, where "Great Power" is an undefined term.

24. This sort of system, as well as the following example, is discussed in Wagner (1986).

25. In order to focus on the issue of system stability rather than peace, I assumed in my article on the balance of power that the outcomes of wars could be known with certainty, but resources could only be transferred by war; I thus avoided the issue of whether peaceful settlements could substitute for war (Wagner, 1986). Niou and Ordeshook, in their various explorations of the same problem, assume that potential victims can always avoid war by preemptively transferring resources to the attacking states; they also assume that the outcomes of wars can be anticipated with certainty (Niou and Ordeshook, 1989; Niou, Ordeshook, and Rose, 1989). Neither set of assumptions is adequate for examining the causes of peace.

26. See especially Spykman (1942). One must be careful not to confuse the word "hegemony" as used in the balance of power literature with the notion of "hegemony" in the literature on "hegemonic stability." In the balance of power literature, a hegemonic state is one that is able to defeat, in a counterforce duel, any combination of other states. It is not clear what "hegemony" means in the literature on hegemonic stability.

27. The emphasis in the US on deterrence after World War II is therefore not solely the result of the development of nuclear weapons.

28. Nuclear weapons, on the other hand, have led to extensive debates about what kind of contest of force a war in Europe would be, and therefore what configuration of forces would be adequate to deter the Soviet Union.

29. This interpretation is reinforced by the dramatic effects of the recent collapse of the Soviet military position in central Europe. For a fuller discussion, see Wagner (1991).

30. This is not enough to guarantee that all systems will be stable, however. See Wagner (1986) and the work of Niou and Ordeshook.

31. Because of uncertainty, the difference between collective security and the balance of power is not as clear-cut as the discussion here might imply. The need to communicate to potential hegemons that they will be opposed by overwhelming force can be hard to distinguish from the view that "peace is indivisible" and aggression everywhere must be prevented. Thus the idea of collective security and the logic of the balance of power are often confused, and both have been invoked as justifications for US foreign policy since World War II.

32. See the discussion of this subject in Rule (1988). The extensive literature on the Prisoner's Dilemma as a metaphor for social life in an anarchic environment has reinforced the idea that the cure for war is to give a monopoly in the use of force to government.

33. Blainey's Argument implies that war can (almost) always be avoided by political accommodation, even in the absence of political institutions. But accommodation may require convergent expectations of the consequences of non-accommodation. It is because these expectations may differ that accommodation is not always possible.

34. On the other hand, I have shown how the inability of states to enforce agreements about how to divide up the spoils of victory can make international systems stable that would otherwise be unstable (Wagner, 1986).

35. The war in Vietnam, the Iran-Iraq war, the Palestinian question, the Lebanese civil war, and the conflict in Northern Ireland are all examples of the problem of ending contests of punishment when counterforce duels are not decisive.

36. For an interesting recent attempt to identify the conditions for the existence of such an equilibrium, see Goldman (1990).

37. Consider, for example, the relation between the outcome of the war in the Persian Gulf between the US-led coalition and Iraq, and the bargaining

that is currently going on over future Iraqi policy on various issues, including treatment of the Kurds.

38. Though he notes that "the line between capitulation and negotiation can be fuzzy," partly because of "the lack of a generally accepted definition of negotiation" (Pillar, 1983, 15). An illustration of this fuzziness is Kecskemeti's statement, contrary to Pillar, that both World War I and World War II ended by "capitulation" (Kecskemeti, 1958, 5–8). This apparent disagreement is the result of the fact that Kecskemeti focuses on the outcome of the contest of military forces, which in both cases ended in the surrender of the losing side, while Pillar focuses on the process leading to the ending of a state of belligerency, or the final settlement of the war. Confusion between these two aspects of military conflict is pervasive in the literature on both civil and international war.

39. Note that these expectations are interdependent.

40. Consider, for example, the situation created by the recent termination of the civil war in Nicaragua. Among the civil wars that Modelski counts as ending in a settlement are the Chinese civil war of 1927–36, the civil wars in Laos in 1953–57 and in 1960–62, and the 1958 rebellion in Lebanon (Modelski, 1964b, 150–153). These are not encouraging examples.

41. For another discussion of this point, see the chapter by Jane E. Holl in this volume.

42. See the discussion in the paper by Harvey Waterman in this volume.

43. These lines were written before the recent invasion of Kuwait by Iraq, which provides a nice illustration of the point.

When War Doesn't Work: Understanding the Relationship between the Battlefield and the Negotiating Table

Jane E. Holl

There is a persistent, intuitive belief that decisive success on the battlefield confers victory in war. This observation seems so obvious as to be trite, yet history records many cases in which belligerents' claims to battlefield streamers were far more secure than the objectives for which those battles were fought. Prominent cases spring to mind: America's war in Vietnam; the Soviet Union's failed effort in Afghanistan; the Israeli adventure in Lebanon.

Clearly, however, if war were such a consistently unprofitable enterprise we might reasonably expect to observe fewer instances of it. We suffer from no lack of material for study, however; indeed, there are a number of examples since the Second World War in which decisive military success delivered unambiguous victory in war: Israel's Yom Kippur triumph; Britain in the Falklands; the United States in Grenada and Panama. In certain cases, war does work, but the conflicting evidence regarding how successful warfare is suggests that there may be no clear or consistent relationship between activity on the battlefield and the achievement of war aims.

This chapter investigates how the process of waging a civil war might shape the process of terminating that war. More specifically, it seeks to develop an understanding of how the battlefield situation in civil war affects the ability of the belligerents to reach accommodation in a negotiated settlement.

269

The central argument of this chapter is that even though wars are all about the use of force to resolve contentious issues, over time a civil conflict often develops to the point where the military activity between the belligerents is not the deciding, or even the most important, factor in resolving the war. Moreover, belligerents often fail to recognize this tendency, with the consequent effect that they incur unnecessary costs (in terms of resources and lives) that may, in turn, undermine their efforts to achieve specific war aims in negotiated settlements. Remarkably, how a civil war is fought can have little to do with how it ends.

Any attempt to understand how battlefield developments factor into civil war termination raises questions regarding the use of force as a policy instrument. However, the complex relationship between the decision to use force and the efficacy of that choice lies beyond the scope of this effort.[1] We seek to know how the process of warring can influence the way in which belligerents in a civil war seek to end a conflict. While it is clear that the antecedent conditions of warfare matter in civil war termination—as they invariably must in all wars—understanding how they do is not the task of the present effort.

War and Political Purpose

One can think of the relationship between the application of force and its political purpose as ranging on a continuum from the extreme of the perfect coincidence of military and political objectives to the complete disarticulation of the two. In the first instance, if political aims have been translated clearly into battlefield objectives, the military effort in a war will more likely conform to a larger, coherent policy designed to achieve a set of objectives thought otherwise not obtainable. In these cases, the progress of the war represents a tangible index of the achievement of strategic aims, and if the war can be brought to an end through decisive military engagement the political objectives of the war also will have been achieved. The Union's decisive defeat of the Confederate army in the American Civil War illustrates this relationship, as does the outcome of the Spanish civil war in this century.[2]

At the opposite extreme, however, military accomplishments hold little political significance. This condition seems particularly true of long, protracted wars where, over time, the political value of military achievements becomes harder to fix. Either or both sides may be uncertain whether holding certain terrain or defeating particular units achieves the objectives of the war. Lebanon's painful case makes the point. For long periods of time in that conflict, none of the many competing factions could claim military superiority, and hence a dominant political position, with any degree of authority.[3]

In these situations, the disarticulation of military instrument from political purpose works to impede efforts to bring the conflict to a conclusion. Warfare becomes little more than witless destruction. The inability of one or another side to establish clear military dominance seems to reflect a situation in which few incentives exist, aside from war weariness or resource exhaustion, to settle. If neither side can impose its will through force, neither does either side feel compelled to capitulate.

Perhaps because these wars do not end through decisive military victory, the battlefield achievements matter less in shaping either the terms of the settlement or the postwar order. The notion of a 'hurting stalemate' captures the essence of this disjuncture (Zartman, 1989; Modelski, 1964b, 143–144). Settlements of these kinds of conflicts are often brought about by third parties that intervene decisively either on behalf of one of the belligerents, or as bipartisan mediators.

Clausewitz (1976, book 1, chapter 1) correctly observed that the most critical aspect of military activity is the degree to which it accurately reflects political objectives, and that it is this association that links success on the battlefield with victory in war. This fundamental relationship between the application of force and war outcomes anchors our effort to understand the conditions under which the battlefield influences efforts to terminate a civil war.

Civil wars seem particularly suited to a study of how the battlefield-negotiation relationship can matter in war termination efforts for several reasons, all originating from the degree to which political and military objectives are more or less tightly or loosely connected. First, because irreconcilable differences over issues of governance generally precipitate a civil war, there are, at least at the outset of this kind of conflict, clear notions of just what the violence is supposed to achieve: the physical destruction of the opposition either by killing them outright or by destroying their means—if not always their will—to resist by inflicting a military defeat. Indeed, by a margin of over two to one, civil wars tend to end through decisive military achievements (Pillar, 1983, 18–26). In these cases, focusing on the military effort and its relationship to the achievement of war aims gives us a relatively straightforward understanding of how these wars end. As with many international conflicts, clear military success unambiguously conveys political victory.[4]

However, a number of interesting cases illustrate that civil wars can be concluded through negotiated settlements (contrary to the expectation that these zero-sum conflicts must end in victory for one side and defeat for the other).[5] In these analytically more interesting cases, we can examine how the act of fighting itself influences the belligerents' pursuit of the objectives sought.

Second, a civil war is characterized by organized violence occurring within the established political borders of a state. This is not to suggest that civil wars are characterized by well-trained and coherently structured militaries opposing each other; indeed, civil wars rarely present such a case. Rather, to distinguish civil war from the random, and often extensive, violence that frequently occurs in unstable states, 'organized' violence refers to the fact that the contending military efforts are focused (more or less) on an objective in opposition to each other.

Indeed, in civil wars, more so than international conflict, the character of the opposing militaries can vary greatly. The central government often can lay claim to the national military which is usually better organized, equipped, and trained than its adversary. Insurgents' groups, on the other hand, possess more political than military organization and thus may lack the experience to mount effective opposition. In consequence, their military effort is usually more loosely organized, inconsistently and inadequately trained, and poorly equipped—often relying on a hodge-podge of weapons and munitions that confound unit training and complicate sustained resupply. This variance will have implications for efforts to terminate a civil war as the conventions for ending war presume a level of organization and authoritative competence within the opposing sides that will permit negotiations (or even capitulation) and render agreements meaningful. Thus, civil wars characterized by asymmetries in military organization may prove particularly difficult to terminate in ways other than through decisive military victory.

Regardless of the relative extent of organization of the belligerents, however, the inhabitants of the war-torn state are affected in direct and profound ways by the concentration of force. The exposure of the general population to intense and directed violence magnifies the importance of war termination efforts; no doubt the searing experience of civil violence will affect efforts to end that violence.[6]

Finally, it seems plain, particularly in civil conflicts, that warfare will have an enormous impact on the postwar order of the state in which the war occurs. Thus, the nature and duration of the battles can retain their significance long after the smoke has cleared. In civil wars the manner in which the war is fought may assume particular salience for the timing and character of the settlement. If, for example, one side made use of unusually brutal tactics or subjected the civilian population to indiscriminate violence, war termination efforts may be impeded. Belligerents are not unmindful of the fact that, in the aftermath of a civil war, they may be forced to bear the responsibility for their violent acts without the security of their arms. If the consequences of their brutality appear grave enough, they may endeavor to forestall a conclusion to the war until such time when memories of particular atrocities have faded or other factors work to mitigate the effects of their deeds. Indeed, expectations of recriminations following a settlement may be so abhorrent that the belligerent acts to prevent the war from ending by reducing the intensity, frequency, or duration of military clashes with its opponent, thus causing the war to linger on interminably. This possibility notwithstanding, a civil war conducted at relatively low levels of violence could also present a number of points at which negotiations might begin, thereby enhancing efforts to terminate the conflict.

In sum, civil war offers an exceedingly appropriate context in which to uncover those points during armed conflict that might make ending the violence more or less possible. This analysis of the state of the military struggle does not convey the ability to predict points at which a civil war will end, particularly since, as noted, important military asymmetries between the belligerents characterize the conflict. Rather, it seeks to develop a fuller appreciation of how the activity on the battlefield interacts with other factors within the larger political context of civil war to influence the conclusion of the conflict.[7]

As noted above, there are a number of cases of civil wars that have been concluded through negotiated settlement. But as with interstate conflict some of these settlements did not reflect the relative distribution of power between the belligerents (or even the military balance that resulted from pitched combat); weaker parties did much better in settlement than they had over the entire course of the war, and belligerents that dominated the military contest were unable to realize the fullest measure of their victories. These seemingly incongruous situations owe their occurrence to the fact that over the course of the war conditions giving rise to other considerations emerged, and the military balance between the belligerents became a less important factor informing the final shape of the settlement.[8]

At least four reasons can account for the diminished importance of the military instrument in the war termination process. First, the effects of warfare are different in civil wars where possible compromise solutions exist than in conflicts where they do not. In the former, the war might be settled in a number of possible ways; therefore, escalation is generally less profitable—yielding relatively small gains for its costs.[9] In the latter case, successful escalation creates even further incentive for increased levels of violence, and the war can only be brought to an acceptable end when one side establishes clear military dominance.

Second, the intensity or duration of combat may matter less because a belligerent may come to value the shape of the settlement far more than the costs of continuing to disagree, thus making that party less sensitive to the costs associated with prosecuting the conflict.[10] In other words, though extreme or prolonged exposure to violence may induce "war weariness" and cause a belligerent to seek a way out of a conflict, strong desires for a particular outcome may dominate and thus cause the war to go on.

Third, decision-makers tend to evaluate battlefield activity more prospectively than retrospectively, and this tendency affects efforts to terminate a civil war. Runners do not quit races because of how far they have come, but because of how far they have yet to go. Though decision-makers are often moved to seek peace in situations where they have experienced military setbacks, they may also do so in situations where they have the tactical upper hand.

Finally, the actual fighting between belligerents may be less influential in the final settlement of a civil war because, over time, wars tend toward a greater degree of internationalization, which introduces additional factors external to the immediate conflict, which, in turn, may reduce the relative importance of the military contest (Rosenau, 1964). Greater internationalization may expose or amplify factors such as reputational concerns or the effect the war is having on extrinsic economic interests. These factors, or a reconsideration of a belligerent's absolute war costs, can come to subvert the importance of the relative military balance and dominate the war termination calculus. Indeed, greater internationalization often leads to third-party mediation between the belligerents; many civil conflicts terminated through negotiations have been the result of the active participation of third-party intermediaries (Deutsch, 1968, chapter 13).

The following discussion examines each of the four reasons outlined above in more detail.

The Battlefield and War Termination

The effects of warfare are different in civil wars where possible compromise solutions exist than in conflicts where they do not. Clearly, not all civil conflicts can be ended through compromise settlements. Indeed, in most cases it appears that civil wars are genuinely zero-sum; that is to say, one side achieves gains only at another's loss. A war over who governs a particular state is the most obvious example. Compromise solutions are usually not possible in these kinds of wars because neither side is willing to consider power sharing arrangements with its opponent. In consequence, the total destruction of the opponent is generally the objective sought by belligerents, with the effect that these types of civil conflicts are characterized, at least for a time, by considerable levels of violence and are remarkably resistant to negotiated settlements (Modelski, 1964b, 141–142; Ikle, 1971, 95).

Every effort to increase the intensity of such a civil war entails costs to the party that undertakes the escalation. 'Successful' escalation results when a belligerent realizes a net gain from the endeavor—a situation in which the costs imposed on one's adversary yield an advantage that exceed the costs one incurs by escalating.[11] Because a successful attempt to intensify the conflict widens the margin of difference between the belligerents, the behavior encourages future escalation. It now takes less power (relative both to one's former level and to the power of one's opponent) to widen further the advantage over one's adversary. Because the belligerents recognize no common ground for compromise, strong incentives exist to exploit military successes; consequently, negotiated settlements to these total civil wars may prove elusive.

All civil wars do not present conditions under which successful escalation encourages a belligerent to intensify the conflict further, however (Pillar, 1983, 160–172). In certain civil conflicts, possibilities for compromise such as partition, separation, or power-sharing do exist, and it may not always be politically profitable to escalate, even if the escalation is militarily 'successful.' Because the parties are generally aware of potential compromise settlements, after the initial phases of conflict the level of violence tends to become more measured, its momentum more controlled. Here, escalation is not as profitable as in civil wars less amenable to negotiated settlements because of the comparatively small advantage to be gained relative to one's position without escalation. In these situations the belligerents generally acknowledge that acceptable compromises exist; thus, intensifying a conflict simply to drive the settlement further in one's favor makes less sense because great effort yields only small gains. The advantage achieved through escalation in these kinds of civil wars represents only a marginal improvement over the position previously held. In other words, the effort required to achieve an improved position is significantly greater than the margin of advantage the additional gain conveys.

In conflicts where a range of possible compromise solutions exists, ending the war involves negotiating the distribution of the dissatisfactory aspects of compromise until a mutually acceptable point is reached. Once the belligerents accept the notion that the war can conclude without the extermination or expulsion of the adversary, the warring parties develop what may be characterized as a certain level of indifference regarding the settlement—a number of possible distributions of gains are more or less acceptable to both parties; consequently the costs of continuing to disagree are magnified.[12] One may escalate successfully, but the gains from that escalation will be comparatively slight (unless a massive effort is undertaken to drive the settlement point to one's extreme position), since the difference between acceptable settlement positions is relatively narrow. Marginal gains are increasingly seen as not worth the marginal costs.

Finally, there is the mixed case, where one belligerent believes room for compromise exists while its opponent does not. In these situations, the adversary with the limited objective might easily find itself waging war at a higher level than would otherwise be the case in order to counter its more ambitious opponent effectively. Consequently, the level of combat in these conflicts will tend to exceed the value that the belligerent pursuing limited war aims assigns to its objectives. This conclusion illuminates the dilemma inherent in conflicts of asymmetrical motivation and leads us to the second reason why the battlefield activity of the belligerents may come to be less influential than other factors in shaping the final settlement of a civil conflict (George, Hall, and Simons, 1971, 218–219; Mack, 1975, 175–200).

The intensity or duration of combat may be excessive because belligerents value the shape of the settlement more than the costs of disagreement.   In war generally, and in civil war specifically, a belligerent attempts to influence the type of settlement reached by manipulating the costs to its opponent of continuing to disagree. These disagreement costs mount over time, and the cumulation of costs can come to play an important role in formulating a basis from which a belligerent might seek an exit from a civil war. The actual effect the costs of warfare have on the warring parties depends, in part, on whether a belligerent places more importance on achieving its objectives than on the effort it expends in doing so (Pillar, 1983, 169–172).

A belligerent more concerned with the shape of the settlement will be willing to undertake less-efficient military actions and incur higher costs than would otherwise be the case. If its opponent is similarly motivated, the war will be intense. If its opponent is more concerned with the costs of the war than with the precise arrangements under which it could be brought to an end, however, that opponent will tend to relax its expectations regarding the issue under dispute and consider a wider range of possible solutions.

Escalation can serve the war termination interests of belligerents with markedly diverse motivations. To the belligerent that values settlement more than lives and resources spent in its pursuit, escalation, regardless of its success, serves usefully to amplify disagreement costs. These higher costs may serve to prompt its adversary to undertake initiatives to settle. To the combatant more concerned with the mounting costs of the war, escalation may be undertaken as a final push to establish a more favorable basis from which to pursue a non-military solution.

For parties enmeshed in a civil war, knowing the inclination of one's opponent is a useful, but not necessary, element of the escalation calculus. Decision-makers have expectations not only regarding their opponent in war, but also regarding how war functions as a medium of interaction.[13] Leaders tend to believe, intuitively, that they have strong incentives to perceive both their opponent and the combat situation correctly. The supposition is that a complete understanding of the adversary and one's relative position in war will suggest a dominant operational strategy to achieve one's objectives (Kecskemeti, 1970, 105–115; Jervis, 1976, 109–110). For example, combatants implicitly believe that one's opponent desires to be in a superior, or at least tenable, position at the end of a conflict. The persistence of this belief reveals an often-unarticulated expectation that the opponent will undertake strategies in the conflict that reflect some reasonable understanding of the distribution of power between the adversaries. Furthermore, expectations regarding the desire to survive a war imply that one's adversary is operating in the domain of gains with respect to the final settlement. We may safely reserve cases of belligerents' voluntarily entering a war with every expectation of losing for theatre.

This conclusion may not always be warranted, however. If an opponent believes himself to be in the domain of losses (that is, he only expects to be worse off than he is now), it still may be rational for him to engage in or escalate a conflict. Extensive research has demonstrated that individuals tend to become risk acceptant when they perceive themselves to be operating in circumstances where they will incur a loss. For example, when faced with the certain loss of $100 or an 80% chance of losing $150 (and a 20% chance of losing nothing), most elect the gamble (Kahneman and Tversky, 1979 and 1984). The same logic can be applied to belligerents at war. If a belligerent believes its position is hopeless, there is little more to lose by taking additional risks. Indeed, there may be surprising gains to be made.

Thus, in some situations it may be possible to perceive accurately the intentions and motivations of one's opponent, because the manifested behavior can be explained from a perspective of either gains or losses. These situations do not, however, leave one without a course of action, i.e., forced into immobility until the situation is clarified. In these cases, a strategy of preponderance—that is, overmatching force to the objectives sought—allows a belligerent a good chance of realizing its objectives irrespective of its opponent's intentions or motivations. The strategies one pursues may not be the most efficient, but their costs can fall within an acceptable range given the potential gains to be achieved and the uncertainty regarding the opponent's motivations.

While it is usually the incumbent regime that can lay claim to resources that would allow it to adopt a strategy of preponderance, the insurgent side—usually less well equipped and manned—is not necessarily without the means to emerge victorious. Clearly superior forces can be offset with more limited resources, provided one makes ingenious use of the intangible aspects of warfare.

Political will is one of the most critical intangible aspects of warfare that influences the conduct of a civil war and the war termination process. The ability of a party to wage war consists in the association of two factors: the tangible resources available and the strength of its political will to commit those resources to the achievement of the war aims. An important question, then, is if a group is moved to armed conflict, does it have not only the means to wage war, but also the political will to use those means in pursuit of the defined objectives? Part of the answer to this question lies in knowing just how powerful a belligerent is.

A belligerent's power capabilities—subject to some objective measurement—include the human and material wherewithal available for commitment to a conflict. Supportive population, monetary and other forms of aid, the size of the organized military, among other examples, are surrogate indicators of a combatant's power. However it is measured and valued, one's capacity to wage war depends on available human and material resources, and these resources are objectively limited and knowable. While one recognizes that the potential exists for third parties to resupply belligerents continually (suggesting that resources in a civil war might be effectively unlimited), the point here is that there are objective and subjective components to warfare. 'Resources' is used here to capture the objective component.

In contrast, political will is a difficult, if not impossible, phenomenon to measure with any degree of exactness or reliability. Its role in war, especially civil war, however, is undeniable (Clausewitz, 1976, chapter 2; Howard, 1979).

Political will can be thought of as a party's willingness to bear costs in pursuit of the objectives of a conflict. Hence, political will reflects the value placed on achieving the war aims—i.e., the level of costs deemed acceptable to incur on behalf of those objectives. Appreciating the role of political will in war enables us to understand better the relationship between a belligerent's power and the war outcome.

The value that a party associates with war objectives calibrates the application of its power capabilities in the war. For groups pursuing limited political objectives, the use of the military to achieve those objectives is politically constrained. Indeed, over the course of the war, that group's valuation of war objectives often changes, with a corresponding influence on the level of resources committed to the conflict, particularly as costs mount. If costs rise to generally unanticipated levels, a reconsideration of the war objectives results. While sacrifice does initially create value—a fact which no doubt accounts, in part, for a certain amount of sustained support for the war—at some point mounting sacrifices engender a reconsideration of the war objectives.

If a serious disjuncture develops between the value that a belligerent assigns to the stated goals of the conflict and the costs incurred or anticipated, then one of two things occurs: either the objectives are re-evaluated and determined to be worth the costs, or the costs are determined to have exceeded the value of the objectives, in which case serious opposition to continued warfare will emerge from within the group and political activity to terminate the conflict will begin.

Conventional notions of military victory in war imply that if an opponent's military capability to wage war has been virtually destroyed, any desire on its part to continue the fight does not matter, because the means to that end no longer exist. However, if we think of political will as the commitment or willingness to bear costs in pursuit of specified war objectives, then the strength of that commitment functions either to unleash or constrain the war effort. Thus, if a belligerent is no longer willing to bear the costs associated with continued struggle, then the power of that belligerent to wage war, no matter how great, becomes essentially irrelevant.

This relationship between will and capability offers an explanation for how more powerful combatants can lose wars to less capable adversaries. Political will is a critical factor in the termination of conflicts in which one contestant is committed totally, while its opponent pursues a more limited objective. For the adversary that perceives itself to be involved in a total war, the importance of the shape of the settlement establishes a much higher cost threshold, one that may extend virtually to the whole of its objective power capability. This considerable tolerance for costs associated with pursuing vital objectives will dwarf that of its opponent, despite the fact that the opponent's objective power capability may be far greater. Consequently, a belligerent perceiving itself to be involved in a limited war will cross its unacceptable cost threshold relatively early compared to its opponent who is committed to total military victory, and the costs of continued combat will weigh more heavily for the belligerent pursuing limited objectives than for its opponent.

In general, the higher the political will, the greater the costs that can, and will, be borne. Conversely, the higher the costs of the war, the greater the need for strong political will to continue to absorb those costs. Some combatants may be forced to limit the costs of the conflict so as not to exceed the tolerance of the political will, while simultaneously taking steps to bolster the political will to ensure that the costs being incurred or anticipated will be supported.

In sum, then, different valuations of the shape of the settlement and the costs of disagreement between adversaries mean that abhorrence of war will not provide a basis for accommodation—belligerents will not necessarily cease fighting or seek alternate solutions simply because war is nasty business. In those civil conflicts where a belligerent confronts an opponent more concerned with the shape of the settlement than with the costs associated with that settlement, the military activity will weigh more heavily to the party pursuing limited objectives until such time as the costs are seen to be acceptably limited. But rarely will a belligerent be willing to quit the contest altogether. Instead it will undertake to drive the intensity of violence down to a level that allows it to gain time for negotiations that produce some version of a settlement that is acceptable. Such de-escalation can work to undermine the degree to which the military contest influences the ending of the war.

Decision-makers tend to evaluate battlefield activity more prospectively than retrospectively, causing them, under certain battlefield circumstances—regardless of recent success or failure—to seek peace.
During the course of a civil war, decision-makers continually reassess the value of continuing the conflict. If they decide to continue, they face further decisions regarding the level of violence to maintain.

The degree of military activity forms the basis for adversaries' expectations as they consider these decisions. Because combatants attempt to influence the shape of settlement through manipulating the costs of the war, they expect changes in the behavior of their adversaries to be the result of changes in their fortunes. But changes in behavior are less the result of changes in fortune than they are the result of changes in expectations (Jervis, 1976, 145–154 and 181–187). If an insurgent expects the incumbent to dominate certain aspects of the conflict, the insurgent's behavior will not change just because the existing regime does, in fact, dominate. It will change, however, if the insurgent expects the incumbent to prevail and it does not, or if the insurgent expects to prevail and it does not. These expectations apply in a similar way to both sides of a conflict.

Thus the 'critical battle' is not necessarily the one in which one side achieves a decisive victory unless it is also the one that causes the belligerents to revise their expectations of the future course of the war (Pillar, 1983, 201–203). Therefore, manipulating the costs of war by increasing the level of violence in the war through escalation will not necessarily cause an adversary to capitulate or seek a negotiated settlement, especially if such escalation were expected.

What, then, is the relationship between the static situation on the battlefield and the belligerents' expectations regarding future developments? Four different relationships seem possible: A belligerent has experienced recent victories and expects his fortunes to improve; a belligerent has experienced recent setbacks, but expects his fortunes to improve; a belligerent has experienced recent victories but expects his fortune to decline; or a belligerent has experienced recent setbacks and expects his fortunes to decline further still. All of these possible relationships have implications for war termination.

A belligerent will be least willing to settle a conflict if he has experienced recent setbacks but expects his fortunes to improve. Certainly no belligerent wants to initiate or conclude negotiations at what it perceives to be its lowest point. Conversely, a belligerent will be most inclined to settle if it has experienced a recent victory but expects its fortunes to take a turn for the worse. In this position, one will be anxious to exploit a relatively advantageous position while it is still possible (Pillar, 1983, 245).

The two remaining relationships present interesting issues for war termination. If a belligerent has experienced recent setbacks and expects things to continue to decline, the natural tendency would be to recognize the objective power balance and capitulate. The interesting question is why belligerents in this position ever receive any consideration at the conclusion of a war which they have lost badly. One explanation could be that their adversaries misperceive the extent to which their opponent has become disabled. A second explanation is that these "loser" groups often fare better in war settlements than they "should" because the victor has certain incentives to grant minor concessions in order to avoid incurring the costs associated with having to contend further with the loser's residual fighting capacity (Kecskemeti, 1958). A final reason is that the imposition of draconian terms of settlement may result in greater instability in the postwar order than does an outcome in which the losing side's sources of power simply are reduced to acceptable levels.

If a belligerent has experienced recent successes and expects that things will only improve, it will be inclined to press the war effort more toward total victory. The interesting question then becomes, when would a belligerent in this position ever agree to settle or, indeed, seek a settlement on terms less than could be achieved through clear military victory, which appears to be at hand?

Pressure to settle the conflict short of clear military victory can come from within the victorious side by groups motivated by a number of political reasons or those just weary of the war. Alternatively, pressure to constrain one's effort toward total victory can come from the international environment (Randle, 1970). In the absence of such pressures, however, the tendency will be for the victorious power to press ahead for a more complete military victory. Nevertheless, perhaps the ultimate interests of the tactically superior belligerent are better achieved through the attrition of its opponent's power rather than the complete destruction of every basis of that power.

Whatever the belligerents' perceptions of the future course of the conflict, it would appear that prospective evaluations of battlefield activity are more important than retrospective ones in determining the prospects for peace. Interestingly, success on the battlefield does not ensure the pursuit of victory, just as battlefield failure does not necessarily enhance the opportunity for a negotiated settlement.

The military aspects of a civil war may be less influential in the final settlement because, over time, these wars tend toward a greater degree of internationalization.   The interests, incentives, capabilities, and opportunities of belligerents combine in complex ways during war. Wars focus actors' interests, and this phenomenon is true not only for those immediately party to a conflict, but also to certain uninvolved groups or states. While many states, particularly those in geographical proximity to the conflict or those with close economic or cultural ties to the combatants, have significant interests in a war, the opportunity to act on those interests and the incentives for doing so—particularly if action may bring unwanted involvement in the war—may not exist.

As civil wars approach their concluding stages, however, the potential costs to outsiders wishing to register their interests in the outcomes are markedly less than earlier in the conflict because clearer notions of just what sort of outcome the war will have may be emerging; third parties can join the war with a greater certainty of the consequences. Therefore, over time, the opportunities increase for external actors to assume a larger role in its settlement. Consequently, factors other than the military balance between the belligerents can become important elements shaping a potential settlement.

Western style democracies tend to think of war and peace as mutually exclusive conditions in the international environment. But peace is not solely the absence of war, just as the occurrence of war does not necessarily mean the disruption of a generally stable peace. Two factors are critical in determining whether or not the ending of a civil war will, in fact, lead to the creation of an environment in which an enduring peace adheres: first, an appreciation of how the belligerents' view of warfare as a means of resolving disputes informs both the war effort and the recognition of opportunities for peace; and second, a genuine understanding of the belligerents' general and specific tolerance for conflict.

Tribal, familial, or nationalist quarrels have given certain regions in the world a tradition of violence which, in some cases, is centuries old. These deep-seated tensions have, in many cases, been exacerbated by conventions of the state system—political boundaries have been imposed that coincide with neither cultural realities nor long-standing endowments of power and authority within a region. Much of the political landscape of twentieth century Eastern Europe, the continent of Africa, and the Middle East reflects this artificiality. Rather than functioning to contain and ameliorate disputes, the often-capricious political enfranchisement of certain cultural and ethnic groups over others has resulted in frequent civil and interstate wars.

For peoples more accustomed to resolving disputes with bullets than barristers, civil war has a decidedly different impact than for those less prone to violence. When war is endemic to a state or a regional subset of states, the resolution of a civil conflict takes on a markedly different character than one in which the belligerents view war as an aberration—a breakdown in normal relations (Eckstein, 1964, 1–32). Though war may mean to some states that the system is broken, for other states the occurrence of war implies no such thing.

To countries such as the United States that view war as an aberration, the end of a civil conflict is often seen as that point at which the shooting stops, a point that usually, though not always, coincides with the belligerents' agreeing to resolve the disputed issues without the force of arms.[14] In raging civil wars, or for states more accustomed to the presence of violence, however, the end of a war is less restrictive; wars end when the shooting mostly stops. Thus when third parties and the state in which the war occurs hold dissimilar views of conflict, no clear consensus emerges regarding what it will take to have the war end.

The international system, as a whole, has a certain tolerance for civil conflict; states, correspondingly, have individual levels of tolerance for this type of conflict as well. While states do not have unlimited tolerance for all types of violence, neither are they incapable of withstanding the incidence of any neighboring conflict, despite a general dislike for war. Indeed, compelling evidence for this tolerance is the fact that though the international system has been regarded as generally stable since 1945, war has been an ever-present fixture on the international scene. As Quincy Wright noted, "hostilities of considerable magnitude have occurred continuously in one part of the world or another [since World War II], under the name of aggression, defense, enforcement measures, intervention, reprisals, or civil strife—in several cases resulting in over a million fatalities" (Wright, 1970, 59).

Though the incidence of war is high (indicating a generally high tolerance for certain types of conflict), clearly some threshold exists above which tolerance for conflict precipitously erodes. In any case, it seems clear that while some may hold the strong belief that war is bad, states' behavior over the decades reveals a more differentiated approach to conflict—wars are more or less bad, depending on how and where they are fought and who is doing the principal fighting.

These two factors—the general notion of warfare (both of the belligerents and the international system) and the relative tolerance for a particular conflict—implicitly contribute to the recognition and exploitation of points at which a civil conflict might be brought to an end. The intervention of third parties for the purposes of ending a civil conflict presents perhaps the clearest evidence of the degree to which a civil war has become internationalized.

Exploration of the numerous and various reasons that third parties intervene in civil conflict lies beyond the scope of this chapter. Nevertheless, two general bases for third-party intervention seem evident: first, when the war threatens to widen in unacceptable ways third parties intervene to control the spread; and second, third parties' former involvement with one or another belligerent may suggest a moral imperative that they intervene, particularly as a civil conflict appears to go on without real prospects for resolution. Britain's involvement in terminating the Zimbabwe civil war illustrates the point.

Thus, as a civil war becomes increasingly internationalized, external forces could moderate the effects of a belligerent's dominant battlefield position in order to introduce tactical pause and probe possible settlement initiatives to see whether or not the conditions for achieving an enduring peace obtain. International influences to end the war in this way will prevent the inevitable desires for belligerents' short-term tactical gains from dominating an appreciation of the long-term strategic costs and work to undermine the immediate military contest as the principal means through which belligerents achieve war aims. Moreover, third-party withdrawal from a conflict could have similar effects. Without the support of a powerful patron, belligerents may be forced to cease their military effort and seek a settlement in more peaceful ways. Often, third parties intervene with a principal goal of establishing a basis for regional stability in the hope that this goal might be attained at a point far short of total military victory and unconditional surrender for either side. Differing views of conflict mean that often for external actors, a stable situation does not require the absence of violence, only that the principal belligerents maintain their violence at acceptable levels. While one may not know what levels are precisely acceptable, it often becomes clear over the course of a civil war what levels are not. As an aim of war termination, an 'enduring peace' should be envisioned not as an eternal state of affairs, but rather, and more realistically, as one that can be sustained long enough for indigenous institutions to emerge that can moderate antagonisms and broker future conflict in less violent ways.

Greater internationalization of a civil conflict introduces other factors into the belligerents' war termination decision-making calculus. Such things as reputational concerns, the effects of the warfare on extrinsic economic interests, and absolute power considerations (as contrasted with the relative valuation of power that dominates wartime decision-making) may come to matter more to the belligerents than who has the upper hand on the battlefield as they consider their postwar position in the larger context of the international community (Ikle, 1971, chapter 4).

Even in civil war, a belligerent's reputation both as warrior and negotiator is important for the signal it sends to its adversary. Its importance, however, extends beyond the immediate conflict and influences outside observers. Similarly, the absolute power capability of a belligerent becomes an important consideration as the war drains assets and prevents their application to other uses. Civil wars are particularly debilitating in this regard.

The international system provides a wider context for evaluating the status of one's power; evaluating one's position within the international system in various potential postwar orders can cause a belligerent either to seek peace more rapidly—if it perceives that its position will only erode—or become obstinate—if it perceives that its position can only be strengthened with delay.[15] Belligerents can become concerned with how the costs of the war have diluted their ability to conduct affairs with other states, in other issue areas. A state greatly weakened by civil war, even if the incumbent leadership has the upper hand in that war, may be inclined to seek a premature settlement if it perceives that continued struggle serves to undermine its economic or diplomatic position with other states. Over time, then, the international aspects of a conflict tend to become accentuated and assume a larger role informing the timing and shape of the settlement. The military contest between the belligerents becomes correspondingly less important.

As previously noted, greater internationalization of a civil conflict creates opportunities for outside states to join a war as active participants. A civil war widened in this way accentuates the difficulties associated with managing the interactive relationship between one's own incentives, perceptions, and expectations and those of one's opponent by introducing the complicating factor of coalition management.

Either side to a civil war can exploit the vulnerabilities associated with coalitions such as the political integrity of the coalition or command and control of forces. The ambiguity that surrounds civil conflict can be made to work to the belligerents' advantage. It is neither necessary nor always desirable that the incentives of coalition partners perfectly coincide; civil wars are often characterized by unnatural alliances in which formerly unconnected, even hostile, groups join together to face a common threat.

The primary belligerent that must combine with a disparate group of partners in a civil war will expend efforts trying to force those partners into a specific behavior. The task of winning may be achieved more easily because a range of supporting behaviors is in fact acceptable as long as all share basic preferences and incentives regarding simple victory in the war.[16]

In sum, the longer a civil war lasts, the greater the opportunity for the conflict to become internationalized. The involvement of outside forces, either as active participants or as added sources of pressure on the belligerents, will cause extenuating factors to assume greater importance to the belligerents than the simple military balance between them.

Conclusion

This chapter sought to address broadly how the process of waging a civil war shapes the process of terminating that war. More specifically, it endeavored to develop an understanding of how the battlefield situation in civil war can affect the belligerents' desire for and ability to reach accommodation in a negotiated settlement.

Activity on the battlefield clearly is an important factor that will influence efforts to terminate a civil war. This chapter has argued that for a number of reasons relating to how groups conceive of and use force to resolve differences, a civil war can develop to the point where the military contest between the belligerents becomes only one of a number of factors important for resolving the conflict.

Through the years, countless peoples and groups have tried to redress contentious issues through civil war. They often make this choice believing that conflict is the only decisive step toward the resolution of their grievances. For lasting resolution, however, the war must also work. Recognizing when it does not may be the first step toward ending it.

Notes

1. The rich literature on the causes of wars offers a profusion of arguments that address the general use of force and factors incident to the onset of conflict. The explicit relationship between a war's beginning and its end, however, has received markedly less systematic attention. In a typical treatment Geoffrey Blainey writes: "Wars usually end when the fighting nations *agree* on their relative strength, and wars usually begin when fighting nations *disagree* on their relative strength" (1973, 122, emphasis original). Though Blainey does go on to identify categories of factors important for understanding the onset of a particular war, the way in which the relationships between those factors enhance or impede efforts to terminate the conflict remains unexamined.

2. There are, of course, extensive literatures on both of these conflicts. They share the characteristic that decisive military victory conveyed political victory by forcing the defeated side to capitulate. The difference, of course, is that in the American case the victors were the incumbents and in the Spanish civil war, the insurgents dominated.

3. Systematic analysis of the tortured history of the fifteen-year civil war in Lebanon remains a future challenge for scholars. For a thoroughgoing journalistic account of these years, see Fisk, 1990.

4. The American experience in Vietnam suggests clearly that battlefield supremacy alone is insufficient to deliver victory in war. " 'You know you never defeated us on the battlefield,' said the American colonel. The North Vietnamese colonel pondered this remark a moment. 'That may be so,' he replied, 'but it is also irrelevant' " (Summers, 1982, 1).

5. Pillar (1983, 18–21) codes at least five cases in which a civil war was concluded with a negotiated settlement: Yemen (1962–1970); Jordan (1970); The Sudan (1971–1972); Lebanon (1975–1976) and Zimbabwe (1972–1979), though the durability of the settlement—such as in Lebanon— may suggest that this claim be more circumspect.

6. The argument here is simply that civil conflicts, especially those of long duration, cannot help but take a major toll on the afflicted population. For discussions of two civil wars that include the general impact on the societies in which they occur, see Oquist, 1980 and Fisk, 1990. For an excellent general introduction to the role of domestic political factors in war termination (though in the context of interstate conflict), see Ikle, 1971, chapters four and five. A more recent effort that evaluates the strength of

290 Jane E. Holl

organizational explanations as they inform war termination decisions is Sigal, 1988.

7. Clearly the studies of war termination that have taken interstate conflict as their focus are applicable here. Civil wars, however, are at least as useful for understanding the complex process of war termination, yet they have received little careful examination in this regard.

8. This, as noted, is a limited study. To understand how the battlefield relates to civil war termination, it takes as its focus the often unanticipated tendency for military developments to become, under certain circumstances, less influential both in efforts to terminate a civil conflict as well as the final shape of the settlement.

9. Pillar (1983, 164) makes the argument that the disposition of a conflict to negotiated settlement will have an impact on the level of fighting and presents this position in the context of war termination as a bargaining problem. The present argument extends Pillar's analysis and suggests that the activity on the battlefield has importance beyond the extent to which it informs negotiations. Because civil wars largely appear less amenable to compromise solutions, the general utility of warfare as a means of achieving war aims should be high for the belligerents. Warfare loses its potency as a policy instrument, however, for a number of reasons to be discussed. The simple issue of whether or not possible compromise solutions are present from the outset of a civil conflict (or emerge over the course of the war) can function either as an important source of strength or as an effective constraint on the fullest application of the military instrument.

10. It is not always obvious to belligerents that possible compromise settlements exist in some wars and not in others. Nevertheless, whether or not a conflict might be settled through compromise is an important observation that has profound implications for the motivations of belligerents in war; when belligerents do not share the same view regarding the possibility of compromise, the effects can be startling. The importance of the phenomenon of asymmetry of motivation was articulated and emphasized in the work of George, Hall and Simons, 1971; see also Pillar, 1983, 154–155.

11. 'Successful' escalation is simply based on the relationship between the gains achieved given their costs. In other words, an escalation can be characterized as successful if the belligerent is better off after escalation than before. Though there are a number of problems with the term 'better off,' decision-makers often have clear perceptions regarding whether escalation has conveyed advantage along whatever dimension they determine important.

12. This simplification is used only to make the point that the effects of the military contest will be different in civil wars where possible compromise solutions exist than in conflicts where they do not appear accessible.

13. A comprehensive examination of the vast array of international and domestic factors that contributes to the initiation and conclusion of hostilities

presents a daunting challenge and may be ultimately unmanageable in any single study. For important contributions on how key policymakers generally perceive and interpret these factors, see George, 1969, and Jervis, 1976. Moreover, a considerable amount of scholarly work has been done on the bargaining processes that go on between belligerents. For a general introduction see Snyder and Diesing, 1977 and Young, 1968. Though these studies take interstate conflict as their principal focus, they do offer insights into the problems of bargaining in civil wars.

14. The classic description of the American approach to war is Osgood, 1957. For extended discussions of national style in security decision-making, see Gray, 1986 and 1988, chapters 5–6 and Lord, 1985.

15. Belligerents' expectations regarding their status in the international system following the civil war often influence their termination efforts in important ways. Relevant discussions are contained in Modelski, 1964b and Rosenau, 1964. Falk, 1971 approaches civil conflict and its termination from the perspective of international legality and includes case discussions of the postwar implications of several conflict settlements; see also Luard, 1972.

16. Insight into the impact of incentives on behavior can be found in March and Simon, 1958, 58–65 and 132–133. On the general uses and problems of coalition warfare as they relate to civil conflict see Deutsch and Kaplan, 1964.

The views expressed in this chapter are those of the author and do not reflect the official position of the Department of the Army, the Department of Defense, or any other agency of the U.S. government. The author would like to thank Daniel J. Kaufman for his invaluable assistance in the preparation of this chapter.

Political Order and the "Settlement" of Civil Wars

Harvey Waterman

Whatever else they may be, civil wars are conflicts over political order. They may arise when an existing order is challenged and their termination depends on agreement on a new one. The circumstances of that agreement, therefore, can be understood as *the re-creation of the conditions for a viable, common political order*. These conditions may not, in the end, produce a viable order and levels of conflict may increase, perhaps even rekindling the large-scale violence called "civil war." The common order created may not be a centralized one; indeed, it may, as a result of a separation, be an order maintained by two or more autonomous polities. But the ending of a civil war clearly entails agreement on the part of the combatants that the incentives to overt conflict have declined relative to those for institutional accommodation and that one such institutional arrangement is acceptable for the moment. Understanding how civil wars end must therefore mean understanding the changes in costs, risks and benefits perceived by those who will make the new order.

That, of course, is not much more than a polysyllabic way of saying that civil wars end in a deal and that the deal is about political institutions. Nevertheless, it is worth having said it at the outset, I think, because discussions of civil war become so entangled in the fascinating detail of military dispositions and intergroup negotiations that one can sometimes lose sight of the fact that a constitution is, in effect, being written, re-written, reinstated or promised at the end of almost every such war. Having said this, how do we move on to understanding it better?

Since, in some sense, all of political science is concerned, distantly or proximately, with the nature of political order, there is a wide gamut of approaches from which to choose. Traditional studies of constitutions, anthropological and sociological studies of plural societies, social psychological studies of ethnic relations, politico-economic studies of incentive structures, the political sociology of mobilization and collective action and the politico-historical study of national political development all have something to offer—a palette richer than Hamlet's for the theater.

For present purposes, we might best begin by reviewing what we think we know about the breakdown of political order and, thereby, about its repair. The common theme I shall follow in all this is the *constitutional deal*. I shall suggest that, as in many bargaining situations, the outcome is the acceptance of a deal that might have been had much earlier, and that the conflict has served as a necessary demonstration that certain alternatives were not in fact available. And I shall conclude that, among the many factors that may affect the outcome of a civil war, it is the nature and autonomy of the competing leaderships (the institutions of authority) that are crucial to the making of the deal that ends the fighting.

Collective Action

Armed combat is rarely thought of as "collective action," a term more often reserved for what have been seen as more "spontaneous"—or at least more "domestic"—forms of behavior involving large numbers of people. Yet most examples of collective action have been organized activities based on existing institutions or identities, with some form of leadership making decisions on behalf of the whole. The mobilization of large numbers of people is always "domestic," even if they are then sent abroad for the intended activity. Even governments must provide the incentives and the means for collective action they wish to sponsor. If mobilizing a national army can produce a kind of collective action on the part of its members, surely we can see the mobilization of internal armies contesting the national deal in the light of the collective action literature.

What does it tell us that might interest the student of the ending of civil wars?[1] It tells us that those in power are likely to mobilize when newly threatened and that those not in power are likely to do so when a new opportunity arises that increases their incentives. It tells us that one of the most common of such opportunities is the perception of a weakening of central authority, often accompanied by a division among those in power. It tells us that provocation by a weak government is particularly prone to result in a violent response and that politically open governments are less likely to encounter violence from their challengers. It tells us that violence is instrumentally used and its use is related to the weakness of the target. It tells us that early successes are a crucial prelude to sustained mobilization.

Whence come these eruptions? It now seems clear that they are almost invariably communal, based on primary ties, preponderantly youthful. Collective action occurs when the participants see minimal risk and grounds for optimism about success. While there is much emotion associated with these events, it is not very helpful to emphasize anger or frustration in efforts to explain its occurrence: emotions tend to follow as much as to precede action and sustained large-scale action is the product of fairly rational decisions based on available information.

Who are these people? Anyone can play, but there do seem to be some patterns: Those motivated by threat tend to be those who are already established in the polity, while those motivated by opportunity are likely to be contestants for new status (or for the re-creation of old statuses perceived to have been lost). While material goals are often important in the minds of the participants, constitutional conflicts that may develop into civil wars invariably call primarily upon contested status demands having to do with citizenship and/or ethnicity (Bendix, 1969; Marshall, 1964; Mannheim, 1941; Rustow, 1970; Horowitz, 1971; Horowitz, 1985, chapters 3–4).

Civil wars are occurrences of collective action that have direct constitutional stakes, are highly mobilized and sustained and employ organized violence. They are responses, on the part of the challengers at least, to governmental weakness or provocation or growing collective resources or the discovery of new allies. If that is so, once the war has begun to take its toll and reveal the military prospects of the two sides, the ending of civil war should be a matter of readjusting statuses, rights and material benefits to the *postbellum* balance of threats, opportunities, risks and incentives. It is, of course, rarely so simple and never easy.

Leaders

Each new collective political activity, including those that launch civil wars, entails willingness on the part of many people to take certain risks, to associate themselves with certain ventures. While doing so may certainly involve admissions that previous policies have proven unsuccessful, the fact that mobilization has occurred at all implies the presence of leaders willing to countenance its use for assertive actions. Popular feeling is not always aggressive or warlike, but the part of it that is most loudly heard in unsettled situations often is and provides ready support to those who favor such action. Thus, from the point of view of leaders, a decision in favor of action is often an "easy" one to take.

Making a deal to resolve conflicts is not so easy. Some expectations will have to be disappointed. Leaders will have to climb down from the heights of earlier rhetoric. Coalition members will have to be satisfied. Reasonable concerns for the minimum conditions of the losers will run up against the anger and fear of the winners, aggravated by the conflict now ending. Each of the parties to the deal will have to satisfy a constituency, but each will have to make a deal less favorable than at least part of that constituency will want to accept. The dealers will not only have to make the deal, they will have to be willing and able to insulate themselves from its repercussions.

Case studies of pre- and postwar negotiations are replete with the heroics of clever diplomats and politicians and generals finding ways to turn some of these tricks. Indeed, it is one of the times in politics when individuals can matter a great deal. Still, there are ways in which collectivities are structured and leaders empowered that largely determine the possibilities for solutions. Such questions as why some civil wars are compromised early and others are fought to a bitter end can be approached as questions about the structure of authority in contesting groups and the nature of coalitions.

The relevant literature here is the extensive one that describes plural societies and the "consociational" arrangements that have been used to enable settlements after periods of conflict and to facilitate subsequent decision-making (Rustow, 1970; Lijphart, 1968; Daalder, 1974; Rabushka and Shepsle, 1972; Horowitz, 1971; Horowitz, 1985). The gist of this is that accommodation takes place best when each collectivity has a strong organizational expression that, in turn, allows leaders the autonomy to act on its behalf. If leaders lack that autonomy, they are subject to competitive bidding from individuals with ambitions to replace them and become unable to consent to the necessary compromises. The better established the organization, the more likely it is that the leaders will enjoy the necessary autonomy.

Autonomy, however, is never assured: waves of discontent can upset even the most oligarchic of organizations. Autonomy, therefore, needs not only appropriate organizational protection but also a situation that favors deal-making. The postwar deals in Western Europe were made possible not only by the highly articulated decision-making structures of Catholic, Socialist, Protestant and Liberal subcultures but by the historical circumstances that induced them to suspend their overt conflicts in the interest of banding together against common enemies or common vicissitudes. In at least some of these cases it can be argued that the fear of further conflict brought the leaders to terms and that the immediate problems of postwar recovery gave them the autonomy to do so. The arrangements then lasted for some time because intrinsic to them were provisions that discouraged direct contact or competition between their constituents.

If one were to project this lesson on to the civil wars of recent history, one might expect that *the conditions for resolving civil wars are sufficient military risk to persuade the leaders to deal and sufficient economic and social trouble to persuade the followers to let them,* even at the expense of strongly held status goals. This will be facilitated if the pre-eminent spokespersons of those goals (e.g., Ian Smith, Jefferson Davis, the leader of the Yemeni Royalists) are calculatedly or fortuitously moved aside, reducing the personal stakes of the deal-makers.

Constitutional deals of the kind under discussion are inherently coalitional. Coalitions of multiple actors are usually seen as a source of problems, since they increase the number of players who must be satisfied with the outcome. On the other hand, they increase the possibilities for trade-offs and accommodations (as in Yemen). Minimum coalitions that are sufficient for parliamentary governments may be insufficient for constitutional bargains intended to end civil wars and avert new ones. Universalistic rules may have to give way to special arrangements designed for one or more of the contestants in the civil war. Again, *increasing the number of actors that must be included in a postwar arrangement helps to facilitate agreement when the leaders are autonomous and have not gotten themselves too far out on a rhetorical limb; when they are populist leaders subject to competitive bidding, accommodation will be very difficult and the required threshold of pain will rise accordingly, until the way to bid for power becomes the promise of peace, rather than war* (Eisenhower's "I will go to Korea;" the field commanders behind both Smith and Mugabe in Zimbabwe).

The reference, above, to "status goals" can refer to a number of ways in which groups of people define themselves collectively, but in most civil war cases these will be ethnic in some sense, especially if one understands "nationalism" to be a generalized form of ethnic feeling. As Horowitz (1985) demonstrates, at its core ethnic conflict is status conflict. Status, including ethnic status, is expressed through institutions. Even where these have not previously been codified into formal organizations, civil war will do so in order to form the combat forces that engage in the war. The symbols which give these organizations their meaning may then become the sticking points in efforts to conclude hostilities. This happens because the organizational changes usually demanded as part of a settlement come to be seen as representing painful status concessions that lend themselves poorly to compromise. The high visibility of such symbols undermines leadership autonomy and makes leaders especially vulnerable to being bid up by competitors for their jobs. In these circumstances, a *deus ex machina* from the battlefield or the international arena may be needed to bail out the leadership.

The staying power of the coalition created by a settlement is itself a function of the autonomy of the leaders entering into coalition, both as the deal is made and afterward. Here the role of international intervention looms large. It is not enough that the leaders have freedom from immediate pressures from below; if the deal depends on foreign intervention it will fall apart when the foreign actors lose interest or coercive power. Thus local leaders may well use foreign intervention as their excuse for accepting an unpopular settlement, but they do so at their peril if the settlement is not one that can be lived with after the foreign promoters/guarantors are gone. From this, it may follow that *intervention may hasten or delay the settlement of a civil war, but will usually have less to do with the shape of the settlement itself.*

The Settlement

While in a larger sense the settlement is a constitutional deal, in the short term it is also an exercise in threat reduction. Clearly two or more armed camps have much to fear from each other and need a great deal of reassurance if they are to lay down their arms. The case studies of civil wars make this very clear and describe it well. The search for reassurance, oddly, may be at cross-purposes with the search for a settlement. Here is why I think that may be so:

The normal workings of a reasonably stable polity entail, at the highest political levels, a process of conflict management. Conflict is expected to occur, is legitimate within certain circumscribed bounds, and is channeled through the political institutions or through other institutions accepted by them. This is most clearly seen in such matters as industrial relations, where mechanisms for bargaining and for handling the breakdown of bargaining are based on the expectation of conflict and the understanding that the parties have a mutual interest in managing it within certain parameters. These mechanisms work to the degree that they can stand a certain amount of strain; if conflict becomes too violent they are perceived to be inadequate and new ones must be devised. Indeed, the occurrence of civil war is itself the extreme example of such a breakdown in conflict management: civil war is the least managed of major domestic conflicts.

When violence breaks out and new reassurances are needed to end it, those reassurances are usually seen as going beyond the creation of mechanisms to manage conflict. They are, rather, hoped to be mechanisms that *end* conflict, that "resolve" rather than "manage" it. That is a tall order, all the more so if the civil war has been fought with unconventional means and there is uncertainty about who can speak for whom. The escalation of violence is followed by an escalation of goals from management to resolution. It is no longer enough to find a way to deal with existing conflicts; the conflicts themselves are to be ended, because the thought of one's enemies continuing the conflict by other means is so threatening. Instead of an ongoing process of politics, demands come to be for an obliteration of the original political conflict. This, perhaps, is what is meant by "winning."

The perceptive reader will have recognized the traditional view of the balance of power in Europe. In that view, one pulled one's punches in war and foreign relations because today's opponent might be tomorrow's ally and the ongoing political process was assumed to continue into the future. The popular civil wars of our time, like the total wars of our century, have shortened the perspective of political rhetoric and have raised the stakes, by making it difficult to view the future as no more than an adjustment to the past. *War may, indeed, be the continuation of politics by other means, but we have a hard time saying so and, consequently, a hard time bringing war to an end. Thus, war costs and military stalemates are often not enough to provide the political justification for settlement. That, in turn, is one reason why civil wars based on ethnic conflicts tend to require perceived military victories as a condition of their termination.*

Violence

Occasional, small scale-violence may be accidental, but large-scale, organized violence is a matter of choice. It is a strategic or even tactical option deliberately taken in the context of a specific set of incentives, a product of cost-benefit analysis. Its occurrence is always idiosyncratic, no matter how "structural" the underlying conflict may be seen to be. Whether the issue is one of local autonomy, economic competition, threatened group status or adaptation to social change, violence is typically seen as one option in a defense against change or as a response to the actual or anticipated violence of others.

One reason the ending of large scale violence such as civil wars is interesting is that the beginning and ending of violence are not symmetrical problems. In a decisional sense, violence is easy to start, difficult to stop. This is so well understood that the difficulty of stopping violence becomes one of the disincentives to starting it. Once started, violence brings with it a web of commitments and costs that demand compensations difficult to arrange in a war-terminating settlement. Revenge is not the least of these compensations and it is available only to the "victors," who, in turn, avail themselves of it only by risking the settlement itself.

The way in which this problem is resolved may perhaps be understood as a bargaining process in which what is being bargained is the definition of magnanimity. The militarily more successful party defines its own revenge (and other compensations) and then publicly accedes to a lesser benefit in return for the acceptance of its terms by the less successful combatant(s). Its magnanimity is accepted by most of its own people because they "won"; its terms are accepted by the "losers" because the terms are magnanimous. (The Nigerian civil war is a particularly clear example of this.) The substantive settlement is imposed by the winners with the connivance of the losers and has a chance of durability because the acknowledgment

of military defeat demonstrates the unavailability of alternative settlements more desirable to the losers—ones that might have provided
incentives for reviving the original terms of the conflict. In other
words, a fresh basis for normal politics has been established.

The problem of violence also brings us back to the autonomy of
leaders. In a civil war, there is always a problem keeping violence
under control, keeping it organized. Leaders are likely to find that
they are spending as much time controlling the armed combatants
on their own side as they are defeating those on the other. Disarming
the combatants becomes not only a condition of settlement for the
leaders but a condition of continued leadership and autonomy within
their own domains. In the face of all the impediments to settlement
mentioned above, *the need to control violence eventually makes the
opposing leaders conspirators in the search for a settlement* that may
allow them to retain their positions and influence. And so settlements
occur after all.

Violence, historically, tends to be associated with hard times. Participating in violent acts has substantial costs for the participants; a
great deal has to be at stake personally in order to sustain such
participation, even when it is being coerced. While fear of personal
or group physical harm may be the dominant motivation, the atmosphere of violence in which such fear takes root usually comes
out of economic disasters in the form of food shortages and/or massive unemployment. These disasters may be natural or artifactual; in
either case, they are unlikely to be much alleviated by the civil wars
that ensue. Yet the discussions of these wars and their settlement
barely touch on such economic events. What were the economic
conditions at the outbreak of the civil wars in Greece, in Nigeria, in
Zimbabwe?

We ought to know. And yet, it is not clear that we will be much
helped. The wars do not likely end because economic conditions
have improved. They end in political and institutional settlements
that may say little about economic affairs and the rhetoric surrounding these events is focused on status and politics. Ironically, economic
suffering, having brought people to violence, may in time become
one of the reasons that the termination of violence is accepted.

There is one other aspect of the violence that is brought out in
the cases but is elsewhere insufficiently emphasized. Someone has
to *do* the violence. Armies and their generals do not always want to
persist in doing it. More often than not, they are the first to recognize

a stalemate or an imminent loss and the ones most cognizant of the human and economic cost of the fighting. It is the politicians whose commitments and personal standing move them to want to press on in a losing or futile cause. In a number of cases (most clearly in the U.S., in Yemen and in Zimbabwe, perhaps) the war ends and the settlement is made because the combatants force the political leaders to swallow the bitter pill of a negotiated peace. Climbing down from the rhetoric of war becomes, not something that must be voluntarily agreed to, but a response to a *fait accompli*.

The Stakes

Why do some civil wars get fought "to the death," with a surrender or annihilation in place of a constitutional "deal"? Not surprisingly, the answer would seem to be that this happens when the stakes do not lend themselves to such a deal, when the losers have no legitimacy in the eyes of the winners. The case that most clearly fits that criterion is the Greek civil war.

Most modern civil wars end with an agreement that the losers can continue to exist as a collectivity but under constitutional rules that reduce their autonomy and relative power. In the Greek case, the Cold War context led the Greek government leadership to interpret the persistence of the Communist insurgency as a "Slavic horse" that would ultimately subvert the polity with the help of international Communism. The ideological rhetoric of the time made it almost impossible to contemplate the continuation of politics with a chastened minority playing by any new set of rules. If "normal" politics could not include them, then they had to be annihilated as a political force and the costs of continuing the war had to be paid. Since those costs *could* be paid with the help of foreign powers, they were.

One ought to be skeptical of arguments about human events that are based on the moving force of ideologies. It is always prudent to seek better explanations. The rebels were a rather small minority in the North with relatively little to offer any new coalition and they could be chased out of the country, so that compromise was never necessary for the strongly supported government. Yet the Greek case is a telling one: in comparison to the other civil wars it appears as an *uncivil* war, one in which the rhetoric of one side is not simply heightened by the emotions of violent conflict but is specifically based on an ideology that rejects the "normal" politics on which any postwar settlement would have to be based. In this sense, the Communism of the Stalin period and the Cold War that formed around it were *not* the continuation of politics by other means, and the resumption of politics was not then seen as an option. Now that the period has come to a definitive end, we have a right to hope that the civil wars of our time will be more "settleable" and reach earlier and therefore less costly ends.

Conclusion

I have argued that civil wars end in a constitutional deal and that they are allowed to do so by the fact that the war itself has demonstrated that certain options cannot be imposed. I have emphasized the decisional autonomy of leadership groups as a help to deal-making through consociational arrangements. I have distinguished between conflict management and conflict resolution and accused the latter goal of being overambitious and an impediment to a return to normal politics. In the same spirit, I have found radical ideology to be equally inimical to the remaking of the constitutional settlement.

Paradoxically, all this emphasis on political institutions and political bargains has had the effect of highlighting the importance of military matters in the ending of civil wars. The identification of winners and losers determines the options available to the settlement makers. The prospect of military reversals is one of the most powerful incentives to deal. In situations where leaders are subject to rhetorical outbidding, military or economic exhaustion may open the possibility of bidding on behalf of peace. Termination itself must have the support of the military and, in many cases, is forced on political leaders by military ones. Military victory resolves conflict where it cannot be safely managed. It is little wonder that civil wars tend to be seen as "won" or "stalemated" first, settled afterward.

Ultimately, however, a war cannot be declared "won" or "stalemated" until the new political order can be discerned on the horizon and the outlines of the new deal clear enough to justify the risks of negotiation. Societies pay a high price for having let their problems come to the point of civil war, but victories in such wars need not be Pyrrhic ones. Political order is the highest of social stakes.

Notes

1. The following summary is taken from Waterman, 1981.

THIRTEEN

What Have We Learned and Where Do We Go from Here?

Roy Licklider

The authors in this book have attempted to explain how civil wars end and why they do not resume in terms of five questions or variable clusters: the issues in dispute, the internal politics of the various sides, the activities of third parties, battlefield outcomes, and the nature of the settlement. What, if anything, have we learned from this exercise?

Settlements under Many Different Circumstances

Perhaps the clearest lesson is that *settlements of civil wars can emerge under a remarkable variety of conditions.* We have found settlements of conflicts with separatist and revolutionary goals, united and divided contestants, intense warlike and peaceful activities and no action at all by third parties, battlefield victories and stalemates, and agreements ranging from elimination of one side to status quo ante to new constitutions with devolved powers and new central power-sharing arrangements.

To put this point more dramatically, there seems to be no simple, direct relationship between any of these factors and the termination of civil war. However, the authors also agree that these five factors are important in determining the results in their cases, and there are clearly many similarities across individual cases which are consistent with plausible theory. What are we to make of this apparent conundrum?

In fact this is only a problem if we assume that all civil wars end in the same way. This heroic assumption was useful in the early phase of the project, since it allowed us to bring in a wide variety of materials without making any initial judgments about how they should be divided. However, it now seems more useful to conceive of the termination of civil violence as a set of *different processes* in which there are certain *critical choice points*. Selections at these points form *alternate strategies* of conflict termination. Instead of a single pattern which all cases will follow, there seem to be a number of different patterns.

The cases have also allowed us to explore the relationships between the different individual factors or variable clusters and the outcomes of civil violence. While our initial ideas were often oversimplified, real and intriguing theoretical connections do seem to exist, as discussed below.

Underlying Issues

Interestingly, it was often difficult to isolate the underlying issues in the conflicts; even the distinction between a war of secession and a revolution was sometimes elusive. Sudan is usually regarded as a secessionist conflict, for example, but the current rebellion is being fought to restore the prior Sudanese constitution, so it could be classified as a revolution. On the other hand, presumably the constitution was attractive to the South because it guaranteed regional autonomy. Ethnicity in particular proved to be a difficult concept to work with; most of the case authors argued that their cases did indeed involve some ethnic divisions but also that the conflict was more than ethnic. Antagonists sometimes manipulated and even invented such identification issues in order to increase hatred of the opposition; in Greece, for example, the rebels were described as "Slavo-communists," even though the vast majority were not Slavs. This variable was thus subject to manipulation by political leaders, who seemed unworried about the risk of deepening animosities which might limit their freedom to negotiate successfully at a later stage.

This made it difficult to evaluate the hypothesis that conflicts fueled by identity issues are either harder or easier to resolve by negotiation than those involving other issues (presumably political or economic). Nonetheless, we can confront the issue by making some crude divisions among the cases. Of the seven examples, identification issues seem to have divided the contestants more deeply in Nigeria and Sudan (where separatist wars were fought by sides in which ethnic membership was important) and Yemen and Zimbabwe (where identity groups contended for control of the state) than in Colombia, Greece, and the United States. We can also distinguish between *victories* and *negotiated settlements*, that is settlements in which both sides retain significant military forces in being and have the option of rejecting settlement terms if they so choose.

There is no clear relationship between identification issues and negotiated settlement. Of the cases where these issues were important, there are two negotiated settlements (Sudan and Yemen), one intermediate case (Zimbabwe), and one total victory (Nigeria). When identification issues were less important, there was one negotiated settlement (Colombia), one intermediate case (the United States), and one total victory (Greece). Since these cases are not random samples of a larger universe and all involve the ending of civil conflict, we cannot definitively reject the relationship between the type of issue and the kind of resolution. Nonetheless, at a minimum the relationship needs to be demonstrated in comparative analysis before it is assumed to be true.

The classic image of an identification conflict is two groups, each united by internal links against the other. In fact, all four of the conflicts we have labeled "identification" show a much more complex pattern, with both sides being composed of *coalitions* of identification groups. The Nigerian government won in part because the population of Biafra included many non-Ibos who wound up supporting the government. In the Sudan, only about three-fifths of the Northerners were Arab, and the Southerners were divided along religious and ethnic lines. Both sides in Yemen were coalitions, and groups routinely defected from one to the other for a variety of motives. Zimbabwe was probably the closest to a classic identification conflict, with the division between blacks and whites, but by the Lancaster House conference there were black politicians in the government who were not simply fronts for white interests, and the ethnic divisions among the rebels were quite serious.

The necessity to manage coalitions of different identification groups presumably moderates some of the extreme responses which civil wars tend to produce. This suggests a pattern similar to cross-cutting cleavages in domestic politics, where actors who are opposed on one issue find themselves united on another and are thus encouraged to moderate their hostility toward their adversaries, since they may well be allied with them in the future. Nigeria is particularly interesting since, in order to maintain its coalitions, the government changed the constitution in a way that allowed the rebels to be integrated fairly easily when the violence ended, redrawing the provincial boundaries and giving more autonomy to the provinces. The addition of black politicians to the Rhodesian government must have made it easier for the whites to accept the new Zimbabwean government. The significance of coalition management in civil war termination needs to be investigated using a wider set of cases.

Identification issues are not irrelevant. The fear of ethnic violence prevented the Biafrans from negotiating a surrender, even when it was clear that they had lost the war. The Greek government deliberately tried to paint the conflict as an ethnic one to its own supporters, assuming that the conflict would be more intense if identification issues were dominant. A more striking case is Reconstruction after the American Civil War, where guerrilla resistance was mounted after the Southern military defeat, not to support Southern independence, but to ensure white supremacy; the identity issue was thus stronger than the political issue of independence. Nonetheless, while identification issues may thus increase the intensity of conflict, they can be manipulated by elites and resolved by negotiated settlements under the proper circumstances. The initial issue of the conflict seems less important than other aspects of the situation in its resolution.

Internal Politics of Each Side

The internal politics of each side were often important, but sometimes in ways that seemed contradictory. Decisions to end a war are, by definition, policy changes. Our first hypothesis was that they were more likely to occur in conjunction with *leadership change*, since the new leadership was likely to be less committed to the policies of previous leaders, had an incentive to do something different, and might be more acceptable as a negotiating partner to the opposition. The cases suggest an addendum: leadership change is likely to be more important when policy change is substantial, that is when the side either has lost the war or agrees to a negotiated settlement; if the side wins a military victory and can impose its will, leadership change will be less necessary to end the war.

A separate argument is that decisions to end a conflict by a negotiated settlement may well require *strong, united leadership* on both sides (ironically, more than continuing the war, which may be a sign of a weak leadership). This is likely to be a particular problem in civil wars where both sides are often alliances of disparate factions. These coalitions seem likely to come under particular pressure at several different times. (a) When the side is losing, the leadership's control may be reduced. But it may require a strong internal leadership to carry out a surrender, which is hardly likely to be a popular policy and which often occurs precisely when control over the armed forces is tenuous. (b) Coalitions may also be divided when negotiations are about to begin, since this forces them to specify their priorities, often undercutting the ambiguity which has helped hold the coalition together. Negotiations are thus like budgets for domestic political groups, forcing hard and often divisive choices to be made. (c) Ironically, coalitions may also be undercut when victory is at hand. Victory means that expectations among the victors rise, wartime coalitions end, and the automatic priority of this issue declines (Kaplan 1980, 75). In the Sudan, a negotiated settlement was facilitated by a shift to more concentrated power on both sides. Nimeiry and Lagu were not political newcomers, but each was able to establish control of his own coalition, at roughly the same time, in processes which were quite independent of one another, so that policy change seemed appropriate and possible. Clearly it was also critical that, for different reasons, both decided that a settlement was in their best interests. However, these decisions do not seem particularly idiosyncratic; other individuals in their offices at the time might reasonably have reached similar conclusions. Their personalities may have had more impact on their ability to *implement* this policy change (by creating unity) than on the actual *choice* of policy. This was an unusually clear case where unity on both sides helped bring about a negotiated settlement.

Yemen, on the other hand, involved two coalitions, neither of which ever seems to have really solidified. Despite this, both sides decided to opt for a negotiated settlement, excluded people on both sides who opposed this strategy, and were able to reach an agreement and carry it out, a very impressive achievement. There was significant *leadership change* but not much *leadership concentration*.

Colombia involved leadership change in the state, since the expulsion of General Rojas was critical to the settlement. However, the leadership of the parties did not change significantly, and the prestige and power of these established leaders helped to make the settlement stick. Nonetheless, the rebel leaders controlled only some of the forces opposing the government; as a result large-scale conflict continued for several years after the settlement.

Zimbabwe and the American Civil War differ from the other negotiated settlements because one side was clearly losing militarily. It is unusual to regard the American Civil War as a negotiated settlement, but there were still Confederate armies in the field after Lee's surrender, and Jefferson Davis never surrendered and was captured fleeing into the mountains to lead a guerilla war which never materialized.

In order for the wars to stop, the losing sides had to make important policy changes, while the winners had to change much less. In Zimbabwe, Mugabe took control of the rebels, which was one reason a settlement could be reached. But the other requirement for settlement was that Ian Smith, who had strongly opposed ending the war, be removed from power; this leadership change involved something very like a coup by the military and intelligence leaders of the Rhodesian government. Similarly in the American Civil War Lincoln's reelection (partly because of soldiers' votes) solidified his control of the North and marked the effective defeat of the South. The Confederate government eventually came apart, with the military surrendering on its own authority, isolating Jefferson Davis who wanted to continue the struggle. A settlement was facilitated in these two cases by *power concentration on the winning sides* and *leadership changes on the losing sides*.

The sequence in both cases is the same. A change in the military balance is followed by a leadership change on the losing side which in turn is followed by settlement. This suggests that battlefield outcomes may facilitate settlement by inducing leadership change.

Although key individuals were replaced, there were no major changes of leadership on either side during the Nigerian and Greek civil wars, the two cases where no negotiated settlement proved possible. Power seems to have been fairly concentrated, but there was no change of leadership; policies didn't change either, and the losing sides fought until their armed forces were crushed in the field and the leadership itself was forced to flee into exile. Negotiated settlements would presumably have required some sort of leadership change; whether it would also have required more power concentration is unclear but entirely possible, since changing an accepted policy may well require more political power than preserving it even if it is clearly losing.

On balance, then, the cases suggest that negotiated settlements are linked to leadership change and (perhaps) power concentrations on both sides, while military victories are facilitated by such change on the losing side. Obviously these are necessary rather than sufficient causes; leadership changes and power concentration can certainly take place without facilitating a settlement. But it seems very difficult to bring about a settlement *without* such political change on the side(s) from which policy change is required, on the losing side if there is one and probably on both sides if the military balance is stalemated and the result is a negotiated settlement.

Military Balance

The military balance was clearly a factor in all seven settlements, although it was influential mainly as it shaped *perceptions of the future* rather than for its own sake. Zartman's concept of the "hurting stalemate" is deceptively hard to work with. "Stalemate" can be defined without undue difficulty but will not produce a settlement by itself; both sides must *perceive* the current situation as untenable and unlikely to improve *in the future*. (Thus escalation which fails may actually lead to settlement, since it demonstrates that the major goals of the escalating side cannot be achieved at a tolerable cost.) The concept is difficult to operationalize without being tautological; we want to know if a hurting stalemate exists in order to predict whether or not the parties will alter their policies, but we only know if it exists if the parties do alter their policies. (Druckman and Green [1986; 1993] have attempted to operationalize this concept and use it to predict the initiation of negotiations in the Philippines.)

Such conditions seem to have existed in Sudan, Colombia, and Yemen, opening the way to successful negotiations there. The concept also helps explain why no negotiated settlement occurred in Greece; the battlefield situation shifted so quickly that each side perceived itself as either winning or losing, with no real incentives for negotiations at any time.

In Zimbabwe, on the other hand, no hurting stalemate existed on the battlefield since the rebels were winning. However, Britain was able to *create* such a situation by persuading Mozambique and Zambia, the rebel suppliers, to threaten to cut off rebel supplies if a settlement was not reached.

While the Confederacy could still have resisted (and did so effectively during Reconstruction), all concerned in the surrender shared the common perception that the regular Southern forces had been defeated, and the individual commanders surrendered their separate forces. This suggests that the hurting stalemate is just a special case of a more general argument, that if both sides *share an expectation of future battlefield outcomes*, fighting is unnecessary, and a settlement based on these expectations should be viable; as Harrison Wagner and Jane Holl note, this is a central conclusion of Blainey (1988) on international war.

On the other hand, the fact that regular forces have been defeated need not signal the end of resistance. Clearly it means an end to one stage of the struggle; the next question is whether a settlement based on this military outcome should be accepted or the *form* of the struggle should shift to civilian resistance and guerrilla warfare. We do not know whether this shift is a common response to military defeat; while it is a common fear when ending civil wars, it is difficult to find examples. Any group which has used conventional military force for some time will find it difficult to switch to guerrilla war, since the two tactics require entirely different mindsets and organizations.

Among our cases, the two clearest examples of this shift are the United States and Colombia. Not only was political violence during Reconstruction in the United States above our threshold definition of civil war, but it achieved a real political end, the abandonment of the Reconstruction governments and the reestablishment of white supremacy in the settlement of 1876. On the other hand, it's not clear that there was multiple sovereignty in the South during this time; the population often did not give allegiance to the central government, but no single organization took its place.

Violence continued at a fairly high level in Colombia as well after the settlement, but it seems to have had relatively little political purpose or impact except perhaps to confirm the wisdom of the National Front system whose rigidity would later be partially responsible for the development of another civil conflict. On balance, then, guerrilla war does not seem a likely consequence of military defeat, even in civil wars where this might have been expected given the high stakes involved.

We do not know why the defeated sides in Greece and Nigeria did not resort to guerilla war after their defeat. Perhaps the sheer magnitude of the defeat made guerilla warfare seem too costly. However, the American Civil War suggests another interpretation. Violence did not begin immediately in 1865; instead it began a year or two later, when the first Southern elections with blacks voting were held, and it ended with the new settlement in 1876. This suggests that the violence was a response to a settlement which was seen as unacceptable. When the settlement was changed, the violence ended as well. We may then have to look to the *terms of settlement* to explain why no such pattern of violence developed in the other states, and we will do so shortly.

Third Parties

The role of *third parties* in these conflicts varied enormously. They seem to have had no impact at all in Colombia. In the United States, third parties were important in a negative way, because they decided *not to intervene* (presumably on the side of the South). In Sudan external mediation was very helpful in reaching a negotiated settlement, although not by itself decisive. In Greece and Nigeria third parties largely determined the military balance and therefore the course of the war, but external mediation attempts were entirely unsuccessful. In Zimbabwe third parties created the conditions which brought about a settlement through diplomacy. And in Yemen third party intervention seems to have created a common enmity toward outsiders which caused the two warring sides to carve out a settlement which they otherwise would probably not have reached.

Third-party involvement can be categorized rather crudely as military aid and assistance on the one hand and mediation efforts of various sorts on the other (Modelski 1964a, 24–26).

(1) Military aid was clearly critical in establishing the military balance in Nigeria and Greece, where the side with the most military assistance (in both sides the government) won. Greece is a particularly striking case since both sides received extensive military assistance, and the decision by Yugoslavia to cut off this aid as part of its conflict with the Soviet Union was a major turning point leading to government success. In Nigeria and the United States, third parties

decided *not* to intervene militarily in support of the rebels, thus allowing the government to establish and maintain military superiority and defeat the rebel forces.

Strong external military support to governments seems to militate against a negotiated settlement; Greece and Nigeria are the two cases where such agreements were never reached. A government which expects to win has no incentive to negotiate. Zartman points out in his chapter that internal negotiations are inherently asymmetric; if the rebels cannot establish some sort of military balance, they have no leverage.

It's not clear whether this sort of balance increases the total amount of violence. On the one hand, if the government has no reason to negotiate, it will presumably fight until it wins. But the resulting violence may actually be less than the consequences of dragging out the conflict over a long time by creating a military balance by either cutting aid to the government or aiding the rebels. Modelski (1964b, 145–149) argues that outside powers should try to strengthen the center parties between the two extremes to reduce violence. Clearly we would need to know both when the rebels understand they will lose and how they respond to this knowledge. The latter choice is presumably influenced by the terms of settlement, which we will discuss later.

(2) Two examples show how the notion of mediation includes very different patterns of activity. Over a period of years church groups in the Sudan established credibility with both sides and opened lines of communication. After several failures, the two parties were brought into negotiation. When the negotiations deadlocked, Haile Selassie of Ethiopia was persuaded to recommend a settlement and to back it by threatening sanctions against both sides. The result was a settlement which held for over a decade and which seems to have been undermined primarily by the willfulness of the Sudanese president. This was the embodiment of "quiet mediation"; indeed much of this process is still secret.

On the other hand, British involvement in Zimbabwe exemplifies the concept of "mediation with muscle," that third-party intervention is more likely to succeed if it is backed with the power either to coerce or to give substantial rewards and that, in the global arena, such resources are still controlled by governments. As the primary supporter of the white government, Britain had a great deal of leverage with its client. As noted above, it was also able to persuade the rebels' regional supporters to apply pressure as well. The British used this leverage in a highly charged set of negotiations at Lancaster House in London which they controlled rigorously, producing a negotiated settlement against what they themselves thought were very heavy odds. (Another example of this technique was the Camp David negotiations, which hinged on pressure from the U.S. and its willingness to commit large sums of money to both Egypt and Israel to facilitate a settlement.)

While the distinction between these techniques is important and useful, it can be overstated. In the Sudan case, it was still necessary to involve a government which was able to threaten both sides. Moreover, the British based their strategy on knowledge from years of quiet negotiation, sometimes by themselves and sometimes by others, much of which had failed but which provided an information base on which they could build.

But when are third parties likely to intervene, what strategies will they use, and when may they change their minds (as in the case of Greece)? As usual our ignorance is substantial, although not total. Donald Horowitz (1985, 273) notes that third parties to civil conflicts are likely to change their positions, since they will have multiple objectives which can be used in bargaining with others. Perhaps it makes sense to talk about "hurting stalemates" for third parties as well (the regional powers around Zimbabwe may be an example of this phenomenon), although it is probably hard to create such a situation since military aid by itself is usually fairly inexpensive for a third party. Jane Holl in her chapter argues that third parties are more likely to intervene as the civil war winds down.

Terms of Settlement

Settlements of civil violence often do not hold. This is hardly surprising. At the end of a civil war, the state is often left with inadequate social, political, and economic bases of support, general access to weapons, a sense that civil violence is now expected rather than unusual, and a massive demobilization problem often involving two armies. This sounds like a recipe for beginning rather than ending civil violence (Rosenau 1964, 74; Tilly 1978, 219; Higham 1972, 52–53). To put it differently, few of the conditions which led to the civil violence are likely to have been much improved by the ensuing carnage, other than reducing doubt about the military balance of the major parties and the consequences of not settling the underlying issues. J. Bowyer Bell (1972, 225) argues that "civil war inoculates a nation against a second attack," but the empirical evidence does not entirely support this position since it simply ignores failed settlements.

Moreover, the global system seems to be reducing the alternatives of governments when ending civil violence. One logical solution to these kinds of problems, especially those with some ethnic or regional basis, is secession, bringing state and nation into alignment. But there have been remarkably few successful secessions since World War II (the obvious exceptions are Israel from Palestine, Pakistan from India, Bangladesh from Pakistan, Cyprus, and the recent events in Eastern Europe), despite many separatist conflicts. The most persuasive explanation of this phenomenon is probably that of Donald Horowitz (1985, 229–230 and 272–277), who argues that while secession movements are *created* domestically, their *success* is determined by international factors, since by definition they are weaker than their governments. However, other governments are generally reluctant to encourage secessions, both because so many would themselves be threatened by similar movements in their own country and because the government under attack can make concessions to persuade other governments to stop supporting the rebels. At any rate, secession seems to be unavailable to participants today except under very unusual circumstances. (The most interesting recent case is certainly the Soviet Union; it is particularly striking that this is secession without civil war. In any case, it's not clear this will change the situation in much of the Third World.)

If you can't split off a dissident group within a state, the other extreme solution is to kill all of its members or at least its elites (Bell 1972, 224–225). But while genocide is easier technologically in the contemporary global system, it has become more difficult politically. The rise of human rights as an international issue has put pressure on some very unlikely governments to behave more acceptably toward portions of their own population.

A less draconian strategy is to require or encourage mass expulsion of the losers. For example, perhaps 100,000 Loyalists left the United States after the American Revolution out of a total white population of about two million (Evans 1969, 190), a higher percentage than left France after the French Revolution (Robert Palmer, cited in

Evans 1969, 192). However, this has also become more difficult in modern times, although there are a few examples such as Cuba and Vietnam; significant numbers of rebels also fled the country after the failure of the Greek revolution. This change is a major moral improvement, but it further limits the flexibility of governments in dealing with major civil violence. Increasingly, disputants are forced to coexist in the same state; the question remains under what conditions can this be done so that the likelihood of renewed civil violence is reduced.

The kind of *polity* which emerges after the settlement will presumably influence the likelihood of renewed civil violence. We can examine the new polity along several different dimensions: *power balance*; *participation*, especially of the losers; *policy choices* in areas like disarmament, demobilization (of at least one and perhaps two or more armies), economic reconstruction and development, and national security, which are common to all such regimes; and responses to the *underlying issues* of the original civil war.

Internal Power Balance

Much of this analysis has assumed that negotiated settlements are a good thing, presumably because they end the conflict with fewer casualties than a total victory would require. However, a number of practitioners have suggested that negotiated settlements of civil wars are more likely to break down into large-scale violence than military victories. In his chapter, Harrison Wagner reaches a similar conclusion with a much more sophisticated analysis, arguing that negotiated settlements are likely to create balance of power situations in which it will be difficult to change the political and social structure to create a society in which violence seems unnecessary as a way to resolve problems.

Our cases lend some support to this argument. Of the seven examples, large-scale violence broke out after the settlement in Colombia and the United States, while in Sudan the settlement held for over five years but eventually dissolved. No fewer than two of the three negotiated settlements thus were followed by violence, as opposed to neither of the military victories and one of the two examples of military dominance. A negotiated settlement may not be an unmitigated blessing if the major objective is to reduce future large-scale civil violence.

Participation

The conflict resolution literature argues that conciliation of at least some of the losers is necessary if the new polity is to be stable (Kaplan 1980, 78–84; Gray 1980, 154; Azar 1986, 33–35; Rothchild and Foley 1988). The record of the cases on this issue is mixed. As one might expect, the three compromise settlements in Yemen, Sudan, and Colombia all showed a fairly high level of integration of former rivals in the new system (otherwise why would they agree to the settlement when they still had military options available?). More interestingly, this was also true of the cases of military dominance (Zimbabwe and the United States) and in one case of military victory, Nigeria.

On the other hand, in Greece the defeated leaders were not allowed back into the political system for over twenty years; indeed that process of integration is still taking place. While this may be repugnant to outsiders, it seems to have worked in Greece. The success of this repressive policy gives pause to the assumption that such integration is just and necessary for a lasting settlement. There are certainly specific reasons why the policy worked in Greece; as John Iatrides notes, the rebel leaders who went into exile in the Soviet Union angered Stalin and were dispersed, isolated from one another as well as from their base of support in Greece. Nonetheless, it is striking that, while the Greek political system after 1949 has not been especially stable, no major political contender seems to have found it useful to appeal specifically to the people who supported the Greek revolution, as distinguished from the partisans of the World War II resistance movement. This seems to support Iatrides' argument that the social base of the Greek rebels was always weak and was further undermined by the government's success in painting it as an "anti-Greek" movement. If so, this Punic strategy may be effective only in cases where the rebellion was weak to start with. Of course, as Bikash Roy has noted, this implies that the strategy was irrelevant since *any* strategy would have worked as well. Spain may be another example.

We know less than we should about the mechanisms for such participation, but a recent study (Shugart 1992) tells us a lot about getting rebels involved in elections.

Policy Choices

Integrating the former enemy is also often proposed as part of the solution for the problems of disarmament, demobilization, economic recovery and development, and national security. It is striking to see significant numbers of the opposing armed forces brought together in places like the Sudan (where Southerners composed the personal bodyguard of the president who had been their enemy) and Zimbabwe (where the white heads of the army and intelligence system were kept at their positions for over a year by the rebels after the settlement). Yemen is an even more interesting case—weapons were simply retained by most men on both sides. People with administrative experience from the other side were also used in several cases, including the American South.

Again Greece is the obvious exception, although not the only one. In the United States, for example, Confederate veterans were elected to the Congress in great numbers and many Southerners served in the American army during the last half of the nineteenth century. However, they were excluded from both the military affairs committees in Congress and command positions within the military (Bensel 1990, 411–413).

Postwar Policy toward the Underlying Issues

This was sometimes difficult to determine, since there was often disagreement about what the major issues were. In many cases the issue seems to have been removed from the political agenda by mutual consent. In the United States, for example, the eventual bargain after Reconstruction was that the defeated whites could control the South as long as secession and slavery were excluded. Something similar happened in Nigeria, Yemen, the Sudan, and Colombia. On the other hand, in Greece the government simply imposed its own policies with its own personnel.

Coalition Maintenance and Civil War Termination

It may be useful to sketch out a more dynamic framework for analysis suggested by this discussion. Given our definition, a civil war requires at least two substantial coalitions of individuals and groups to be maintained over time; otherwise the required levels of violence and political control can't occur. Each leadership must preserve its own coalition and attempt to undermine that of the opposition. Moreover, like any sizeable organization, each will develop organizational momentum, a tendency to do today what it did yesterday. We have taken situations in which both sides are engaged in large-scale violence, and we want to know why they might agree to stop such violence and then not resort to it later.

Given this approach, the internal politics of both sides becomes absolutely critical for the analysis, but it also becomes a dependent variable—we want to explain under what circumstances internal politics will change so that both sides are likely to be willing to agree on some sort of settlement. We are thrown back on other variables to explain why this might occur.

Presumably the coalitions will change policy when they perceive the costs of the present policy to be significantly higher than those of an alternative. Obviously this oversimplifies a complex process; there will be disagreement among different members as to the weights assigned to each, and these perceptions in turn will be more or less influential depending on the position of the individual involved. Moreover, tracing such changes in perception in current events or history can be quite difficult. Nonetheless the simplification focuses our attention on two important sets of variables which will probably influence these estimates: battlefield results of current policies and terms of settlement which are perceived to be available.

Battlefield results clearly play an important role, but they are not decisive by themselves. Even if one side is militarily defeated, it retains the option to resort to other forms of resistance, from guerrilla warfare to passive resistance of various sorts. Nor is this an empty threat; the communist government of Poland in the late 1980s found itself in complete military control of the country but unable to get its citizens to work for it. The issue then is not resolved by determining whether one coalition has suffered military defeat but how it will respond to such a defeat.

Our cases suggest that indeed military defeat often is seen as a turning point by many on both sides and serves as an important indicator of the costs of future resistance. Despite rhetoric, no side voluntarily fights until the last man, woman, and child, and while guerilla warfare after military defeat is clearly possible, it does not often occur in our cases. Thus it did not develop in Nigeria or Greece after total military defeats, in Zimbabwe after a settlement avoided an inevitable military defeat, or in Yemen or Sudan (for at least five years after the war) after a military stalemate led to a negotiated settlement.

On the other hand, guerilla warfare did appear after settlements in Colombia and the United States, for quite different reasons. In

Colombia the leaders did not control much of the fighting, which was not tightly organized; thus they could deliver only a portion of the rebels to their agreement. However, they correctly calculated that this would be sufficient to build a new government which could eventually reduce the level of conflict drastically, and this happened over time.

In the American case, on the other hand, the rebel military leaders controlled their armed forces, and the surrender went remarkably smoothly, including some armies still in the field. The problem arose later, with popular revulsion among white Southerners over black enfranchisement, combined with an unwillingness by many white Northerners to pay a high price to enforce such enfranchisement. The result was a renewal of large-scale violence until the settlement was revised, leaving the South securely within the Union but disenfranchising blacks for generations. Clearly the terms of settlement were critical here. If the Union had said initially that all Confederate officers would be shot for treason, the Southern army would not have surrendered in 1865. After the settlement was revised in 1876, the guerrilla violence disappeared.

Obviously battlefield outcomes and terms of settlement are related. If you want to put pressure on the enemy coalition, you can offer harsh terms of settlement if they expect negative battlefield outcomes in the future. The extreme case is Greece, where no negotiations or formal terms were offered at all, and large numbers of rebels and their supporters were punished directly. On the other hand, we can imagine a situation in which all inhabitants of the area expect to be killed or deported from the country. Resistance is likely to be desperate; something like this seems to have occurred in Nigeria for a time. This extreme example points up the fact that there are always some terms of settlement, although they may not be stated explicitly (no genocide, for example). A reputation for keeping one's word may be helpful in making terms of settlement palatable to the opposition as well.

Seen within this perspective, third-party activities can play an important but limited role. A third party can keep a conflict going by persuading one coalition that it cannot be defeated since the third party will supply whatever supplies, support, or asylum is necessary to prevent it. These assertions by themselves may not be sufficient if the coalition divides for other reasons; something like this seems to have happened in Vietnam and Afghanistan. Moreover, third par-

ties have much less potential influence in bringing about a settlement, even assuming good will; the cases show clearly that their
impact is limited by what the locals are prepared to do.

Although it is counter-intuitive, whether the war started as a revolution or a separatist attempt seems less important in its outcome
than these other factors, assuming third parties are involved. The
issues certainly have some impact. Separatist movements find it much
more difficult to widen their coalitions than revolutionary movements; there are few examples of different separatist groups uniting
against a single government (Ethiopia comes to mind). Moreover,
separatist movements tend to get less foreign support because most
governments are reluctant to encourage secession even from their
enemies, again reducing the separatists' ability to build coalitions.
These two factors explain why secessionist revolutions have been so
much less successful than political ones since World War II and something of the different intervention records of the two superpowers
(Sensi 1991). However, our cases suggest that the nature of the issue
acts as a background condition influencing actions rather than a prox-
imate cause of a coalition change.

Future Research

We are left, then, with a number of intriguing patterns and hypotheses. What should be done with them? How can we move forward from this point? There are several different paths for future
research suitable for people with different research agendas.

(1) One possibility is to probe some or all of these seven cases in
more detail. Our deceptively simple framework actually puts great
demands on the case authors. The question of what issues really
caused the initial conflict, for example, is extremely difficult to answer for any of these examples. We often know little about the internal politics of both sides or the perceptions of different actors of
the military balance on the battlefield and their expectations of future
success or failure. Sometimes even the actions of third parties are
obscure, not to mention their motivation. And any discussion of the
settlement terms leads directly into the question of how the successor
state was formulated, why it took the form it did, how it might have
developed in different ways, and how all this influenced the likelihood of future civil violence, the lifestyle of the population, and the
behavior of the new state. The discussion of these issues by our case

authors has been exemplary, but none of them would claim to have the last word on these issues.

(2) Another approach would be to add more cases. I deeply regret not accepting Robert Whealey's generous offer to do a case study of the Spanish Civil War. China and Vietnam would also be excellent additions, not to mention the large number of anti-colonial struggles. The utility of the American Civil War case suggests that the approach might be profitably pushed back into earlier historical cases, not only to civil wars such as the American Revolution (which, given the number of colonists who supported the British and emigrated after the settlement, could reasonably be called a civil war), the Glorious Revolution of England, the French Revolution, the wars of religion in Europe, the Taiping Revolution in China, and the Great Mutiny in India, but also to wars of conquest, potentially a very long list indeed. There is a variety of fascinating possibilities for comparative case studies, which are probably more useful than single examples. An interesting example of this strategy is Goldman 1990.

(3) Rather than analyzing a few cases through a framework with several different variable clusters, a larger number of cases could be included focusing on particular hypotheses. Our theory chapters suggest several intriguing possibilities such as the relationship between terminating international and civil wars, the role of battlefield success in settlement, or what sorts of settlements seem more likely to last. Other possibilities include the impact of outside actors on civil war settlement, the role of shifting coalitions within one or both sides, the significance of varying underlying issues, and the circumstances of changing goals by one or both sides. This technique can also be used to explore the utility of variables excluded from our analysis; a number of people have speculated about the effect of a strong vs. a weak state or a prewar state which was democratic or not, for example, both in initiating and terminating civil violence.

(4) We now have a number of different data bases on civil wars from different perspectives (Small and Singer 1982; Pillar 1983; Stedman 1991; Gantzel and Meyer-Stamer 1986; Sivard 1988; Miall 1992; Gurr and Scarritt 1989). A systematic comparison of these would be helpful in allowing us to move toward hypothesis testing on a broader scale than a relatively few cases, especially since the same examples tend to recur in case analyses.

(5) We need analyses rooted in different intellectual traditions and frameworks. The approach in this volume, borrowing from James

B. Rule's analysis (1988, 178–179) of Charles Tilly's work, sees large-scale violence as purposeful and rational, reflective of perceived collective interests, and one of several different types of collective action which groups may use for their own ends, in a word, *political*. It is probably not coincidental that most of the authors in this volume are political scientists. This is emphatically not the only approach to explaining the outbreak of civil violence, as Rule and others eloquently demonstrate; analyses of the *termination* of such conflict from these different perspectives would be very useful indeed.

Nor need we be restricted to social science and history. The development of myths to explain the outcomes of civil wars, for example, is probably central to the process of reconciliation, but we know little about it. Indeed the whole concept of victory could profitably be reexamined (for an evocative exploration, see Carroll 1980).

(6) This project has been iterative, moving back and forth between theory and cases. It may now be time to move back to theory, to try to build on what we have learned (particularly in Harvey Waterman's chapter) to try to develop some ideas about the *process of state formation* by which civil wars end, the alternative *strategies* which can be used, the likelihood that such strategies can remove or reduce the use of large-scale violence within the repertoire of collective action (Tilly 1978), and the *consequences* of such strategies for the people, the state, and the international system. This is the area I hope to explore myself.

Clearly these are only some of the options available. Other people will have other ideas, and we are far from being able to say which will be the most useful in our search for the explanation of how civil wars end.

Bibliography

Acheson, Dean. 1969. *Present at the Creation: My Years in the State Department.* New York: Norton.

"The Addis Ababa Agreement on the Problem of South Sudan." 1972. *Grass Curtain* 2, 3 (May): 17–26.

Africa Confidential. 1971. 12, 21 (October 15).

———. 1974. 15, 4 (February 22).

———. 1981. 22, 24 (November 25).

Africa News. 1985. 24, 3 (February 11).

Alier, Sayed Abel. 1976. *Peace and Development in the Southern Region.* Khartoum: Ministry of Culture and Information.

All Africa Conference of Churches. 1971. *AAAC Follow-up of Reconciliation and Relief Initiatives in the Sudan.* World Council of Churches Archives, Geneva, May 25.

Amen, Michael Mark. 1978. *American Foreign Policy in Greece, 1944/1949: Economic, Military and Institutional Aspects.* Bern: Lang.

Americas Watch Committee. 1989. *The Killings in Colombia.* Washington, D.C.

Amy, Douglas James. 1983. "Environmental Mediators: An Alternative Approach to Policy Stalemates." *Policy Sciences* 15:345–365.

Anderson, Benedict. 1983. *Imagined Communities: Reflections on the Origin and Spread of Nationalism.* London: Verso Editions and NLB.

Anderson, Terry H. 1981. *The United States, Great Britain, and the Cold War, 1944–1947.* Columbia: Missouri University Press.

Ankrah, Kodwo E. 1971. *Sudan: [Report of the] First Mission by SSLM European Representatives to Africa.* World Council of Churches Archives, Geneva, August 30.

———. 1972. "Sudan: The Church and Peace." *Africa,* no. 9 (May): 58–63.

323

Assefa, Hizkias. 1987. *Mediation of Civil Wars: Approaches and Strategies—The Sudan Conflict.* Boulder: Westview.

Austin, Reginald. 1975. *Racism and Apartheid in Southern Africa, Rhodesia: A Book of Data.* Paris: UNESCO.

Azar, Edward. 1986. "Protracted International Conflicts: Ten Propositions" in Edward D. Azar and John W. Burton, eds., *International Conflict Resolution: Theory and Practice.* Boulder: Lynne Rienner, 28–39.

Ballard, Michael B. 1986. *A Long Shadow: Jefferson Davis and the Final Days of the Confederacy.* Jackson: University of Mississippi Press.

Baumhogger, G. 1984. *The Struggle for Independence: Documents on the Recent Development of Zimbabwe (1975–1980), Volumes 1–7.* Hamburg: Institute of African Studies, Africa Documentation Center.

Bell, J. Bowyer. 1972. "Societal Patterns and Lessons: The Irish Case" in Robin Higham, ed., *Civil Wars in the Twentieth Century.* Lexington: University Press of Kentucky, 217–227.

Bendix, Reinhard. 1969. *Nation-Building and Citizenship: Studies of Our Changing Order.* New York: Anchor Books.

Bensel, Richard Franklin. 1990. *Yankee Leviathan: The Origins of Central State Authority in America, 1839–1877.* New York: Cambridge University Press.

Beringer, Richard E., Herman Hattaway, Archer Jones, and William N. Still, Jr. 1986. *Why the South Lost the Civil War.* Athens, Georgia: University of Georgia Press.

Beshir, Mohamed Omer. 1975. *The Southern Sudan: From Conflict to Peace.* London: C. Hurst.

Betts, Tristram. 1974. *The Southern Sudan: The Ceasefire and After.* London: Africa Publication Trust.

Blainey, Geoffrey. 1973. *The Causes of War.* New York: Free Press.

———. 1988. *The Causes of War.* 3rd ed. New York: Free Press.

Blake, Robert. 1977. *A History of Rhodesia.* London: Eyre Methuen.

Bokhari, Imtiaz. 1993. "Two-Tiered Negotiations: Afghanistan" in I. William Zartman, ed., *Negotiating Internal Conflicts.* Columbia: University of South Carolina Press.

Bowman, Larry. 1973. *Politics in Rhodesia: White Power in an African State.* Cambridge: Harvard University Press.

Brams, Steven. 1985. *Superpower Games.* New Haven: Yale University Press.

British Diplomat A., Participant, Lancaster House. 1987. Interview by Stephen John Stedman, April 24, London. Notes.

British Information Services. 1953. *The Sudan, 1899–1953.* New York: British Information Services. (I.D. 1179).

Bueno de Mesquita, Bruce. 1981. *The War Trap.* New Haven: Yale University Press.

Buijtenhuijs, Robert. 1978. *Le FROLINAT et les révoltes populaires du Tchad.* The Hague: Mouton.

Burton, John W. 1987. *Resolving Deep-Rooted Conflict: A Handbook*. Lanham, Md.: University Press of America.

Campbell, M. A., E. W. Downs, and L. V. Schuetta. 1964. *The Employment of Airpower in the Greek Guerrilla War, 1947–1949*. N.p.: U.S. Aerospace Studies Institute.

Carrington, Lord Peter, British Foreign Secretary, Chairman of Lancaster House Conference. 1987. Interview by Stephen John Stedman, June 3, Brussels. Notes.

Carroll, Bernice A. 1980. "Victory and Defeat: The Mystique of Dominance" in Stuart Albert and Edward C. Luck, eds., *On The Endings of Wars*. Port Washington, N.Y.: National University Publications, Kennikat, 47–71.

Channing, Steven A. 1974. *Crisis of Fear: Secession in South Carolina*. New York: W. W. Norton.

Churchill, Winston S. 1953. *Closing the Ring*. Boston: Houghton Mifflin.

Cilliers, J. K. 1985. *Counter-insurgency in Rhodesia*. Sydney: Croom Helm.

Clark, Robert. 1990. *Negotiations with the ETA: Obstacles to Peace in the Basque Country*. Reno: University of Nevada Press.

Claude, Inis L. 1962. *Power and International Relations*. New York: Random House.

Clausewitz, Carl von. 1976. *On War*. Edited and translated by Michael Howard and Peter Paret. Princeton: Princeton University Press.

Cloete, Stephanus. 1991. *Negotiations in South Africa*. Boulder: Lynne Rienner.

Collins, Robert O. 1985. "African-Arab Relations in the Sudan." Paper presented to the Middle East Studies Association, New Orleans, November.

Colombia, Office of the President. N.d. *The Fight Against Drug Traffic*. Bogotá.

Conflict Research Society. 1973. *Intermediary Activity and the Southern Sudanese Conflict*. Draft report of a symposium held at the Richardson Institute, London, November. Mimeo.

Coser, Lewis. 1964. *The Functions of Group Conflict*. New York: Free Press.

Coufoudakis, Van. 1981. "The United States, the United Nations, and the Greek Question, 1946–1952" in John O. Iatrides, ed., *Greece in the 1940s: A Nation in Crisis*. Hanover, N.H.: University Press of New England, 275–297.

Couloumbis, Theodore A., John A. Petropulos, and Harry J. Psomiades. 1976. *Foreign Interference in Greek Politics*. New York: Pella.

Cronje, Suzanne. 1972. *The World and Nigeria*. London: Sidgwick and Jackson.

Daalder, Hans. 1974. "The Consociational Democracy Theme." *World Politics* 26 (July): 604–621.

Davidow, Jeffrey. 1984. *A Peace in Southern Africa: The Lancaster House Conference on Rhodesia, 1979*. Boulder: Westview.

Day, Arthur. 1986. "Civil Conflict in Lebanon" in Arthur Day and Michael Doyle, eds., *Escalation and Intervention*. Boulder: Westview, 31–53.

Deeb, Mary Jane, and Marius Deeb. 1993. "Negotiation under Intervention: Lebanon" in I. William Zartman, ed., *Negotiating Internal Conflicts*. Columbia: University of South Carolina Press.

de la Espriella, Adriana. 1988. "Panorama de los derechos humanos en Colombia." Bogotá: Centro de Estudios Internacionales, Universidad de los Andes, Documentos Ocasionales No. 4 (July-August).

Deng, Francis. 1993. "Negotiating Identity: Sudan" in I. William Zartman, ed., *Negotiating Internal Conflicts*. Columbia: University of South Carolina Press.

Deng, Francis, and Prosser Gifford. 1987. *The Search for Peace and Unity in the Sudan*. Washington: Woodrow Wilson Center.

Deng, Francis, and I. William Zartman, eds. 1991. *Conflict Resolution in Africa*. Washington, D.C.: Brookings Institution.

Deutsch, Karl W. 1968. *The Analysis of International Relations*. Englewood Cliffs, N.J.: Prentice Hall.

Deutsch, Karl W., and Morton A. Kaplan. 1964. "The Limits of International Coalitions" in James N. Rosenau, ed., *International Aspects of Civil Strife*. Princeton: Princeton University Press, 170–184.

Djilas, Milovan. 1962. *Conversations with Stalin*. New York: Harcourt.

Donald, David. 1978. *Liberty and Union*. Lexington, Mass.: D. C. Heath.

Dresch, Paul. 1989 *Tribes, Government, and History in Yemen*. New York: Oxford University Press.

Druckman, Daniel, and Justin Green. 1986. *Political Stability in the Philippines: Framework and Analysis*. Monograph Series in World Affairs, vol. 22, book 3. Denver: University of Denver.

———. 1993. "Negotiating a Rural Insurgency: Philippines" in I. William Zartman, ed., *Negotiating Internal Conflicts*. Columbia: University of South Carolina Press.

Dupree, Louis. 1986. "Afghanistan 1984: Crisis after Crisis, Internal and External" in Arthur Day and Michael Doyle, eds., *Escalation and Intervention*. Boulder: Westview, 99–122.

Eckstein, Harry. 1964. *Internal War: Problems and Approaches*. New York: Free Press.

Eliou, Philippos. 1979–1980. "The Civil War in Greece." (In Greek.) Serial in Athens daily *Afgi*. December 2-January 23.

Elster, Jon. 1978. *Ulysses and the Sirens: Studies in Rationality and Irrationality*. Cambridge: Cambridge University Press.

Epps, Dwain C. 1971. Letter to Canon Burgess Carr. World Council of Churches Archives, Geneva. August 6.

Eprile, Cecil. 1972. "Sudan: The Long War." *Conflict Studies* 21 (March): 3–6.

Escott, Paul D. 1978. *After Secession: Jefferson Davis and the Failure of Confederate Nationalism*. Baton Rouge: University of Louisiana Press.

Eudes, Dominique. 1972. *The Kapetanios: Partisans and Civil War in Greece*. New York: Monthly Review Press.

Evans, G. N. D. 1969. *Allegiance in America: The Case of the Loyalists.* Reading, Mass.: Addison-Wesley.

Falk, Richard A. 1971. *The International Law of Civil War.* Baltimore: Johns Hopkins University Press.

Fatouros, A. A. 1981. "Building Formal Structures of Penetration: The United States in Greece, 1947–1948" in John O. Iatrides, ed., *Greece in the 1940s: A Nation in Crisis.* Hanover, N.H.: University Press of New England, 239–258.

Fehrenbacher, Don Edward. 1987. *Lincoln in Text and Context.* Stanford: Stanford University Press.

Fellman, Michael. 1989. *Inside War: The Guerrilla Conflict in Missouri during the American Civil War.* New York: Oxford University Press.

Fellner, Jamie. 1988. "A Murderous Democracy: Chapters from a Dirty War." *Commonweal* 115 (January 15): 6–8.

Fisk, Robert. 1990. *Pity in the Nation.* New York: Atheneum.

Flower, Ken. 1987a. *Serving Secretly: An Intelligence Chief on Record, Rhodesia into Zimbabwe 1964 to 1981.* London: John Murray.

———. 1987b. Interview by Stephen John Stedman, May 21, Harare, Zimbabwe. Notes.

Foner, Eric. 1988. *Reconstruction: America's Unfinished Revolution, 1863–1877.* New York: Harper and Row.

Frederica. 1971. *A Measure of Understanding: Queen Frederica of the Hellenes.* New York: St. Martin's.

Fredrickson, George M. 1975. *A Nation Divided.* Minneapolis: University of Minnesota Press.

———. 1981. *White Supremacy: A Comparative Study in American and South African History.* New York: Oxford University Press.

Galtung, Johan. 1969 "Violence, Peace, and Peace Research." *Journal of Peace Research* 6, 3:167–191.

Gamson, William A. 1975. *The Strategy of Social Protest.* Homewood, Ill.: Dorsey.

Gantzel, Hans Jurgen, and Jorg Meyer-Stamer. 1986. *Die Kriege nach dem Zweiten Weltkrieg bis 1984: Daten und erste Analysen.* Munich: Weltforum Verlag.

Garang de Mabior, Col./Dr. John. 1984. *Appeal to the Sudanese People on the Founding of the Sudan People's Liberation Army (SPLA) and Sudan People's Liberation Movement (SPLM).* SPLM/SPLA, March 3. Mimeo.

———. 1987. *John Garang Speaks.* Edited by Khalid Mansour. London: KPI.

Garcia, Daniel. 1993. "Exclusive and Inclusive Negotiations" in I. William Zartman, ed., *Negotiating Internal Conflicts.* Columbia: University of South Carolina Press.

George, Alexander. 1969. "The 'Operational Code': A Neglected Approach to the Study of Political Leaders and Decision-Making." *International Studies Quarterly* 13 (June): 190–222.

George, Alexander, David K. Hall, and William R. Simons. 1971. *The Limits of Coercive Diplomacy*. Boston: Little, Brown.

Gillette, William. 1979. *Retreat from Reconstruction, 1869–1879*. Baton Rouge: University of Louisiana Press.

Goldman, Ralph M. 1990. *From Warfare to Party Politics: The Critical Transition to Civilian Control*. Syracuse, N.Y.: Syracuse University Press.

Gray, Colin S. 1986. *Nuclear Strategy and National Style*. Lanham, Md.: Hamilton.

————. 1988. *The Geopolitics of Super Power*. Lexington: University Press of Kentucky.

Gray, J. Glenn. 1980. "Ending With Honor" in Stuart Albert and Edward C. Luck, eds., *On The Endings of Wars*. Port Washington, N.Y.: National University Publications, Kennikat, 145–156.

Grey, Richard. 1971. "The Southern Sudan." *Journal of Contemporary History* 6 (1): 108–120.

Guardian (London). 1984. August 24.

Gueyras, Jean. 1983. "Oil Holds Promise for Sudan." *Manchester Guardian Weekly* 129, 20 (November 13): 14.

Gurdon, Charles. 1988. "Sadiq Fiddles while Sudan Burns." *New African*, no. 250 (July): 9–11.

Gurr, Ted Robert. 1988. "On the Outcomes of Violent Conflict" in Ted Robert Gurr, ed., *Handbook of Political Conflict: Theory and Research*. New York: Free Press, 238–294.

————. 1990. "Ethnic Warfare and the Changing Priorities of Global Security." *Mediterranean Quarterly* 1 (Winter): 82–98.

Gurr, Ted Robert, and James R. Scarritt. 1989. "Minority Rights at Risk: A Global Survey." *Human Rights Quarterly* 11 (August): 375–405.

Guzmán, Alvaro. 1988. Oral communication to Jonathan Hartlyn, August.

Hancock, Ian. 1984. *White Liberals, Moderates and Radicals, 1953–1980*. London: Croom Helm.

Hartlyn, Jonathan. 1988. *The Politics of Coalition Rule in Colombia*. Cambridge: Cambridge University Press.

————. Forthcoming. "The Impact of Drug Trafficking on Democracy in Colombia" in Bruce M. Bagley and Annette Traversie Bagley, eds., *Drugs, Human Rights, and Democracy in Colombia*.

Heraclides, Alexis. 1987. "Janus or Sisyphus? The Southern Problem of the Sudan." *Journal of Modern African Studies* 25, 2 (June): 213–231.

Herbst, Jeffrey. 1990. *State Politics in Zimbabwe*. Berkeley: University of California Press.

Higham, Robin, ed. 1972. *Civil Wars in the Twentieth Century*. Lexington: University Press of Kentucky.

Hobsbawm, Eric. 1963. "The Anatomy of Violence." *New Society* 1 (April 11): 16–18.

Hondros, John L. 1983. *Occupation and Resistance: The Greek Agony, 1941–44*. New York: Pella.

Horowitz, Donald L. 1971. "Multiracial Politics in the New States: Toward a Theory of Conflict" in Robert J. Jackson and Michael B. Stein, eds., *Issues in Comparative Politics: A Text with Readings.* New York: St. Martin's, 164–180.

———. 1985. *Ethnic Groups in Conflict.* Berkeley: University of California Press.

Howard, Harry N. 1949. *Greece and the United Nations, 1946–1949: A Summary Record.* Department of State publication 3645. Washington, D.C.

———. 1966. "Greece and Its Balkan Neighbors (1948–1949): The United Nations' Attempts at Conciliation." *Balkan Studies* 7 (1): 1–26.

Howard, Michael E. 1979. "The Forgotten Dimensions of Strategy." *Foreign Affairs* 25 (Summer): 975–986.

Howell, John. 1978. "Horn of Africa: Lessons from the Sudan Conflict," *International Affairs* 54: 421–436.

Hugo, Pierre. 1988. "Towards Darkness and Death: Racial Demonology in South Africa." *Journal of Modern African Studies* 26 (4): 567–590.

Iatrides, John O. 1972. *Revolt in Athens: The Greek Communist "Second Round": 1944–1945.* Princeton: Princeton University Press.

———. 1980. "American Attitudes toward the Political System of Postwar Greece" in Theodore A. Couloumbis and John O. Iatrides, eds., *Greek American Relations: A Critical Review.* New York: Pella, 49–73.

———. 1981. "Civil War, 1945–1949: National and International Aspects" in John O. Iatrides, ed., *Greece in the 1940s: A Nation in Crisis.* Hanover, NH: University Press of New England, 195–219.

———. 1987. "Perceptions of Soviet Involvement in the Greek Civil War, 1945–1949" in Lars Baerentzen, John O. Iatrides, and Ole L. Smith, eds., *Studies in the History of the Greek Civil War, 1945–1949.* Copenhagen: Museum Tusculanum, 225–248.

Ikle, Fred C. 1971. *Every War Must End.* New York: Columbia University Press.

International Labour Office. 1976. *Growth, Employment and Equity: A Comprehensive Strategy for the Sudan.* Geneva.

Isaacman, Allen. 1985. "Mozambique: Tugging at the Chains of Dependency" in Gerald J. Bender, James S. Coleman, and Richard Sklar, eds., *African Crisis Areas and U.S. Foreign Policy.* Berkeley: University of California Press, 129–157.

Isaacman, Allen, and Barbara Isaacman. 1983. *Mozambique: From Colonialism to Revolution.* Boulder: Westview.

Jervis, Robert. 1976. *Perception and Misperception in International Politics.* Princeton: Princeton University Press.

Johannsen, Robert Walter. 1985. *To the Halls of the Montezumas: The Mexican War in the American Imagination.* New York: Oxford University Press.

Johnson, Douglas H. 1988. *The Southern Sudan.* Report No. 78. London: Minority Rights Group.

Jones, Howard. 1989. *"A New Kind of War"*: *America's Global Strategy and the Truman Doctrine in Greece*. New York: Oxford University Press.

Jones, Joseph M. 1955. *The Fifteen Weeks*. New York: Viking.

Kahneman, Daniel, and Amos Tversky. 1979. "Prospect Theory: An Analysis of Decision under Risk." *Econometrica* 47 (March): 263–291.

——— . 1984. "Choices, Values, and Frames." *American Psychologist* 39 (April): 341–350.

Kaplan, Jay L. 1980. "Victors and Vanquished: Their Postwar Relations" in Stuart Albert and Edward C. Luck, eds., *On The Endings of Wars*. Port Washington, N.Y.: National University Publications, Kennikat, 72–117.

Kasfir, Nelson. 1976. "Still Keeping the Peace." *Fieldstaff Reports* 21, 4. Northeast Africa Series. Hanover, N.H.: American Universities Field Staff.

——— . 1977. "Southern Sudanese Politics since the Addis Ababa Agreement." *African Affairs* 76, 303 (April): 143–166.

——— . 1987. "One Full Revolution: The Politics of Sudanese Military Government, 1969–1985" in John W. Harbeson, ed., *The Military in African Politics*. New York: Praeger, 141–162.

Kecskemeti, Paul. 1958. *Strategic Surrender: The Politics of Victory and Defeat*. Stanford: Stanford University Press.

——— . 1970. "Political Rationality in Ending War." *The Annals of the American Academy of Political and Social Science* 392 (November): 105–115.

Kennedy, Paul. 1988. *The Rise and Fall of the Great Powers*. New York: Random House.

Keohane, Robert O. 1986. *Neorealism and Its Critics*. New York: Columbia University Press.

Kissinger, Henry A. 1957. *A World Restored*. Boston: Little Brown.

——— . 1969. "The Vietnam Negotiations." *Foreign Affairs* 47, 2 (January): 211–234.

Kitchen, Helen. 1987. *Angola, Mozambique and the West*. New York: Praeger.

KKE (Communist Party of Greece). 1987. *Official Documents* 6 (1945–1949). (In Greek.) Athens: Synchroni Epohi.

——— . 1988. *Short History of the KKE: A Draft, Part A: 1918–1949*. (In Greek.) Athens: Synchroni Epohi.

Kofos, Evangelos. 1964. *Nationalism and Communism in Macedonia*. Salonica, Greece: Institute for Balkan Studies.

Kontis, Basil. 1984. *Anglo-American Policy and the Greek Problem, 1945–1949*. (In Greek.) Salonica, Greece: Paratiritis.

Kriesberg, Louis, Terrell A. Northrup, and Stuart J. Thorson. 1989. *Intractable Conflicts and Their Transformation*. Syracuse, N.Y.: Syracuse University Press.

Kuniholm, Bruce B. 1980. *The Origins of the Cold War in the Near East*. Princeton: Princeton University Press.

Kuper, Leo. 1981. *Genocide: Its Political Use in the Twentieth Century.* New Haven: Yale University Press.

Lagu, Joseph. 1978. Letter to Mading de Garang, Owiny Ki-Bul. World Council of Churches Archives, Geneva. October 30.

———. 1981. *Decentralisation: A Necessity for the Southern Provinces of the Sudan.* Khartoum: Samar P.

Laitin, David. 1983. "The Ogaadeen Question and Changes in Somali Identity" in Donald Rothchild and Victor Olorunsola, eds., *State vs. Ethnic Claims.* Boulder: Westview.

Laqueur, Walter. 1976. *Guerrilla: A Historical and Critical Study.* Boston: Little, Brown.

Leal Buitrago, Francisco. 1988. "Democracia Oligárquica y Rearticulación de la Sociedad Civil: El caso Colombiano." Unpublished manuscript. Bogotá.

Legg, Keith. 1987. "Musical Chairs in Athens: Analyzing Political Instability" in Lars Baerentzen, John O. Iatrides, and Ole L. Smith, eds., *Studies in the History of the Greek Civil War, 1945–1949.* Copenhagen: Museum Tusculanum, 9–24.

Legum, Colin. 1971. *Africa Contemporary Record, 1969–70.* New York: Africana.

———. 1988a. "The Sudan: Warnings of Catastrophe." *Third World Reports* K.P/1 (November 2): 1–4.

———. 1988b. "Sudan: Only the OAU Can Now Avert Disaster." *Third World Reports* K.Q/2 (November 9): 1–6.

Licklider, Roy. 1988. "Civil Violence and Conflict Resolution: A Framework for Analysis." Paper presented at the International Studies Association, St. Louis, Mo., April 1.

———. 1992. "How Civil Wars End: Preliminary Results from a Comparative Project" in Stephen J. Cimbala and Sidney R. Waldman, eds., *Controlling and Ending Conflict: Issues Before and After the Cold War.* New York: Greenwood, 219–237.

Lijphart, Arend. 1968. "Typologies of Democratic Systems." *Comparative Political Studies* 1 (April): 3–44.

Lord, Carnes. 1985. "American Strategic Culture." *Comparative Strategy* 5: 269–293.

Luard, Evan. 1972. *The International Regulation of Civil Wars.* New York: New York University Press.

Lyons, Terrence. 1991. "The Transition in Ethiopia." *CSIS Africa Notes* 127 (August 27): 1–8.

Mack, Andrew J. R. 1975. "Why Big Nations Lose Small Wars." *World Politics* 27 (January): 175–200.

MacVeagh, Lincoln. 1980. *Ambassador MacVeagh Reports: Greece, 1933–1947.* Edited by John O. Iatrides. Princeton: Princeton University Press.

Majok, Aggrey A. 1989. Letter to Donald Rothchild. January 20.

Malwal, Bona. 1985. *The Sudan: A Second Challenge to Nationhood.* New York: Thornton Books.

Manchester Guardian Weekly. 1984. 131, 15 (October 7).

Mannheim, Karl. 1941. *Man and Society in an Age of Reconstruction.* New York: Harcourt, Brace.

March, James G., and Herbert E. Simon. 1958. *Organizations.* New York: John Wiley and Sons.

Marcum, John. 1978. *The Angolan Revolution.* Cambridge: M.I.T. Press.

Marshall, T. H. 1964. "Citizenship and Social Class" in T. H. Marshall, *Class, Citizenship, and Social Development.* Garden City, N.Y.: Doubleday, 65–122.

Martin, David, and Phyllis Johnson. 1981 *The Struggle for Zimbabwe: The Chimurenga War.* London: Faber and Faber.

Maullin, Richard. 1973. *Soldiers, Guerrillas, and Politics in Colombia.* Lexington, Mass.: D. C. Heath, Lexington Books.

Mavrogordatos, George T. 1981. "The 1946 Election and Plebiscite: Prelude to Civil War" in John O. Iatrides, ed., *Greece in the 1940s: A Nation in Crisis.* Hanover, N.H.: University Press of New England, 181–194.

Mayer, Arno. 1971. *The Dynamics of Counterrevolution in Europe, 1870–1956: An Analytic Framework.* New York: Pantheon.

Mazrui, Ali A. 1969. "Pluralism and National Integration" in Leo Kuper and M. G. Smith, eds., *Pluralism in Africa.* Berkeley: University of California Press, 333–349.

McClintock, Cynthia. 1989. "Peru's Sendero Luminoso Rebellion: Origins and Trajectory" in Susan Eckstein, ed., *Power and Popular Protest.* Berkeley: University of California Press, 61–101.

McCormick, Shawn. 1991. "Angola: The Road to Peace," *CSIS Africa Notes* 125 (June 6): 1–12.

McDonald, John and Diana Bendahmane. 1985. *Perspectives on Negotiation.* Washington, D.C.: State Department Foreign Service Institute.

McNeill, William H. 1949. "The Outbreak of Fighting in Athens, December 1944." *American Slavic and East European Review* 8: 239–251.

———. 1957. *Greece: American Aid in Action, 1947–1956.* New York: Twentieth Century Fund.

McPherson, James. 1982. *Ordeal by Fire: The Civil War and Reconstruction.* New York: Harper and Row.

———. 1988. *Battle Cry of Freedom.* New York: Oxford University Press.

Mearsheimer, John J. 1983. *Conventional Deterrence.* Ithaca, N.Y.: Cornell University Press.

Miall, Hugh. 1992. *The Peacemakers: Peaceful Settlement of Disputes since 1945.* New York: St. Martin's.

Minter, W. and E. Schmidt. 1988. "When Sanctions Worked: The Case of Rhodesia Reexamined." *African Affairs* 87 (April): 207–237.

Mitchell, Christopher. 1991. "Classifying Conflicts: Asymmetry and Resolution" in I. William Zartman, ed., *Resolving Regional Conflicts: Inter-*

national Perspectives, The Annals of the American Academy of Political and Social Science 518 (November): 23–38.

——— . 1992. "Protracted Internal Conflicts" in I. William Zartman, ed., *Cooperative Security: Reducing Third World Wars.* Syracuse, N.Y.: Syracuse University Press.

Mitchell, Reid. 1988. *Civil War Soldiers: Their Expectations and Their Experiences.* New York: Viking Press.

Modelski, George. 1964a. "The International Relations of Internal War" in James N. Rosenau, ed., *International Aspects of Civil Strife.* Princeton: Princeton University Press, 14–44.

——— . 1964b. "International Settlement of Internal War" in James N. Rosenau, ed., *International Aspects of Civil Strife.* Princeton: Princeton University Press, 122–153.

Montville, Joseph, ed. 1990. *Conflict and Peacemaking in Multiethnic Societies.* Lexington, Mass.: D. C. Heath, Lexington Books.

Moorcraft, P., and P. McLaughlin. 1982. *Chimurenga! The War in Rhodesia, 1965–1980.* Marshaltown, South Africa: Sygma/Collins.

Moore, Barrington. 1966. *The Social Origins of Dictatorship and Democracy.* Boston: Beacon Press.

Most, Benjamin, and Harvey Starr. 1983. "Conceptualizing 'War': Consequences for Theory and Research." *Journal of Conflict Resolution* 27: 137–59.

Mubako, Simbi, ZANU legal adviser at Geneva, Lancaster House. 1987. Interview by Stephen John Stedman, May 28, Harare, Zimbabwe. Notes.

Mueller, John. 1989. *Retreat from Doomsday: The Obsolescence of Major War.* New York: Basic Books.

Murray, Col. J. C. 1954. "The Anti-Bandit War." *Marine Corps Gazette* 38 (January-May).

New African (London). 1984. No. 198 (March).

Newhouse, John. 1983. "Profiles: Lord Carrington." *New Yorker* 58 (February 14): 47–83.

Niilus, Leopoldo J. 1972. Communication to Dwain Epps, Addis Ababa. World Council of Churches Archives, Geneva. February 17.

——— . 1973. "Peace in the Sudan: Reflections on Questions for a Written Interview from Mrs. Barbara Hampton." World Council of Churches Archives, Geneva. March 12.

Nimeiri, Lewa Gaafar Mohamed. 1971. *Speeches of Chairman of the Revolutionary Command Council and Other Relevant Policies on The South.* World Council of Churches Archives, Geneva, November. Mimeo.

Niou, Emerson M. S., and Peter C. Ordeshook. 1989. "Conflict and Stability in Anarchic International Systems." Working Paper No. 700. Pasadena: California Institute of Technology.

Niou, Emerson M. S., Peter C. Ordeshook, and Gregory F. Rose. 1989. *The Balance of Power.* New York: Cambridge University Press.

O'Ballance, Edgar. 1966. *The Greek Civil War, 1944–1949*. New York: Praeger.

———. 1977. *The Secret War in the Sudan: 1955–1972*. London: Faber and Faber.

O'Connell, James. 1967. "The Anatomy of a Pogrom: An Outline Model with Special Reference to the Ibos in Northern Nigeria." *Race* 9, 1 (July): 95–100.

———. 1969. "The Ibo Massacres and Secession." *Venture*, 21, 7 (July): 22–25.

Olson, Mancur. 1971. *The Logic of Collective Action*. Cambridge: Harvard University Press.

O'Meara, Patrick. 1975. *Rhodesia: Racial Conflict or Coexistence?* Ithaca, N.Y.: Cornell University Press.

Oquist, Paul. 1980. *Violence, Conflict, and Politics in Colombia*. New York: Academic Press.

Osgood, Robert E. 1957. *Limited War*. Chicago: University of Chicago Press.

Ottoway, Marina. 1993. "Eritrea: Negotiating Transitional Conflicts" in I. William Zartman, ed., *Negotiating Internal Conflicts*. Columbia: University of South Carolina Press.

Paludan, Phillip S. 1989. *A People's Contest*. New York: Harper and Row.

Partsalidis, Mitsos. 1978. *Double Rehabilitation of the National Resistance*. (In Greek.) Athens: Themelio.

Petropulos, John A. 1981. "The Traditional Political Parties of Greece during the Axis Occupation" in John O. Iatrides, ed., *Greece in the 1940s: A Nation in Crisis*. Hanover, N.H.: University Press of New England, 27–36.

Pillar, Paul R. 1983. *Negotiating Peace: War Termination as a Bargaining Process*. Princeton: Princeton University Press.

Pizarro, Eduardo. 1990. "Insurgencia crónica, movimiento guerrillero, y proceso de paz en Colombia." Paper presented to a Conference on Violence and Democracy in Colombia and Peru, Columbia University, November.

Pollis, Adamantia. 1981. "U.S. Intervention in Greek Trade Unions, 1947–1950" in John O. Iatrides, ed., *Greece in the 1940s: A Nation in Crisis*. Hanover, N.H.: University Press of New England, 259–274.

Potter, David. 1968. *The South and the Sectional Crisis*. Baton Rouge: University of Louisiana Press.

———. 1976. *The Impending Crisis: 1848–1861*. Completed and edited by D. Dehrenbacker. New York: Harper and Row.

Rabushka, Alvin, and Kenneth A. Shepsle. 1972. *Politics in Plural Societies: A Theory of Democratic Instability*. Columbus, Ohio: Merrill.

Ramage, James. 1988. *Rebel Raider: The Life of General John Hunt Morgan*. Lexington: University Press of Kentucky.

Randle, Robert F. 1970. "The Domestic Origins of Peace." *Annals of the Academy of Political and Social Science* 392 (November): 76–85.

———. 1973. *The Origins of Peace: A Study of Peacemaking and the Structure of Peace Settlements*. New York: Free Press.

Renwick, Robin. 1981. *The Rhodesia Settlement*. Cambridge: Center for International Affairs, Harvard University.

Republic of the Sudan. 1956. *Southern Sudan Disturbances, August 1955*. Khartoum: Ministry of Interior.

Rhodesia, Central Statistical Office. 1971. *1969 Population Census, Interim Report, Volume 1: The European, Asian, and Coloured Populations*. Salisbury.

———. Ministry of Finance. 1975. *Economic Survey of Rhodesia*. Salisbury.

Richter, Heinz. 1980. "The Battle of Athens and the Role of the British" in Marion Sarafis, ed., *Greece: From Resistance to Civil War*. Nottingham: Spokesman, 78–90.

———. 1986. *British Intervention in Greece: From Varkiza to Civil War*. London: Merlin.

———. 1987. "The Second Plenum of the Central Committee of the KKE and the Decision for Civil War: A Reappraisal" in Lars Baerentzen, John O. Iatrides, and Ole L. Smith, eds., *Studies in the History of the Greek Civil War, 1945–1949*. Copenhagen: Museum Tusculanum, 179–187.

Rosenau, James N. 1964. "Internal War as an International Event" in James N. Rosenau, ed., *International Aspects of Civil Strife*. Princeton: Princeton University Press, 45–91.

Rothchild, Donald. 1986. "Hegemonial Exchange: An Alternative Model for Managing Conflict in Middle Africa" in Dennis L. Thompson and Dov Ronen, eds., *Ethnicity, Politics, and Development*. Boulder: Lynne Rienner, 65–104.

———. 1991. "An Interactive Model for State-Ethnic Relations" in Francis Deng and I. William Zartman, eds., *Conflict Resolution in Africa*. Washington, D.C.: Brookings Institution, 190–215.

———. 1993. "The Roads to Gbadolite and Estoril" in I. William Zartman, ed., *Negotiating Internal Conflicts*. Columbia: University of South Carolina Press.

Rothchild, Donald, and Michael W. Foley. 1988. "African States and the Politics of Inclusive Coalitions" in Donald Rothchild and Naomi Chazan, eds., *The Precarious Balance: State and Society in Africa*. Boulder: Westview, 233–264.

Rubin, Jeffrey, and Bert Brown. 1975. *The Social Psychology of Bargaining and Negotiation*. New York: Academic.

Rule, James B. 1988. *Theories of Civil Violence*. Berkeley: University of California Press.

Rustow, Dankwart A. 1970. "Transitions to Democracy: Toward a Dynamic Model." *Comparative Politics* 2 (April): 337–363.

Sánchez, Gonzalo. 1985. "*La Violencia* in Colombia: New Research, New Questions." *HAHR: Hispanic American Historical Review* 65 (November): 789–807.

Sánchez, Gonzalo, and Danny Meertens. 1983. *Bandoleros, gamonales y campesinos: El caso de la Violencia en Colombia.* Bogotá: El Ancora Editores.

Sánchez, Gonzalo, et. al. [Comisión de estudios sobre la violencia]. 1987. *Colombia: Violencia y democracia: Informe presentado al Ministerio de Gobierno.* Bogotá: Universidad Nacional de Colombia.

Sensi, Luigi. 1991. "The Burden of Hegemony: Superpower Intervention in Civil Wars." Unpublished Ph. D. dissertation, Political Science Department, Rutgers University.

Sewell, Richard H. 1988. *A House Divided: Sectionalism and Civil War, 1848–1865.* Baltimore: Johns Hopkins University Press.

Shugart, Matthew Soberg. 1992 "Guerrillas and Elections: An Institutionalist Perspective of the Costs of Conflict and Cooperation." *International Studies Quarterly* 36 (June): 121–151.

Sigal, Leon V. 1988. *Fighting to a Finish: The Politics of War Termination in the United States and Japan, 1945.* Ithaca, N.Y.: Cornell University Press.

Sithole, Masipula. 1977. *Zimbabwe: Struggles within the Struggle.* Harare, Zimbabwe: Rujeko.

Sivard, Ruth. 1988. *World Military and Social Expenditures 1988.* Leesburg, Va.: World Priorities.

Skocpol, Theda. 1985. "Bringing the State Back In: Strategies of Analysis in Current Research" in Peter Evans, Dietrich Rueschemeyer, and Theda Skocpol, eds., *Bringing the State Back In.* Cambridge: Cambridge University Press, 3–37.

Small, Melvin, and J. David Singer. 1982. *Resort to Arms: International and Civil Wars, 1816–1980.* 2d ed. Beverly Hills: Sage.

Smith, Anthony D. 1986. "Conflict and Collective Identity: Class, Ethnie and Nation" in Edward D. Azar and John W. Burton, eds., *International Conflict Resolution: Theory and Practice.* Boulder: Lynne Rienner, 63–84.

Smith, D., and C. Simpson. 1981. *Mugabe.* London: Sphere Books.

Smith, Ian. 1987. Interview with Stephen John Stedman, May 22, Harare, Zimbabwe. Tape recording.

Smith, Ole L. 1987. "Self-defense and Communist Policy, 1945–1947" in Lars Baerentzen, John O. Iatrides, and Ole L. Smith, eds., *Studies in the History of the Greek Civil War, 1945–1949.* Copenhagen: Museum Tusculanum, 159–171.

Snyder, Glenn H., and Paul Diesing. 1977. *Conflict among Nations.* Princeton: Princeton University Press.

Solidarity Committee of the Southern Members 4th People's National Assembly, Omdurman. N.d. *The Redivision of the Southern Region: Why It Must Be Rejected.* Juba, Sudan: Nile Press.

South Sudan Resistance Movement. N.d. *The Anya-Nya Struggle: Background and Objectives.* London: Southern Sudan Association.

Spykman, Nicholas J. 1942. *America's Strategy in World Politics: The United States and the Balance of Power.* New York: Harcourt, Brace.

Stampp, Kenneth. 1980. "The Southern Road to Appomattox" in Kenneth Stampp, ed., *The Imperiled Union*. New York: Oxford University Press, 246–269.

Stavrakis, Peter J. 1989. *Moscow and Greek Communism, 1944–1949*. Ithaca, N.Y.: Cornell University Press.

Stavrianos, L. S. 1950. "The Mutiny in the Greek Armed Forces (April 1944)." *American Slavic and East European Review* 9: 302–11.

———. 1952. "The Greek National Liberation Front (EAM): A Study in Resistance Organization and Administration." *Journal of Modern History* 14: 1 (March): 42–55.

Stedman, Stephen John. 1991. *Peacemaking in Civil War: International Mediation in Zimbabwe, 1974–1980*. Boulder: Lynne Rienner.

Stedman, Stephen John, Thomas Ohlson, Khete Shubane, and Rob Davies. 1992. *Conflict Resolution in Southern Africa*. Washington, D.C.: Brookings Institution.

Strausz-Hupé, Robert, William R. Kintner, James E. Dougherty, and Alvin J. Cottrell. 1959. *Protracted Conflict*. New York: Harper.

Stremlau, John. 1977. *The International Politics of the Nigerian Civil War 1967–70*. Princeton: Princeton University Press.

SUDANOW. 1981. 6, 3 (March).

———. 1983. 8, 11 (November).

Summers, Harry G., Jr. 1982. *On Strategy: The Vietnam War in Context*. Carlisle, Penn.: U.S. Army War College.

Swain, Geoffrey. 1989. "The Comintern and Southern Europe, 1938–43" in Tony Judt, ed., *Resistance and Revolution in Mediterranean Europe*. New York: Routledge, 29–52.

Thomadakis, Stavros B. 1981. "Black Markets, Inflation, and Force in the Economy of Occupied Greece" in John O. Iatrides, ed., *Greece in the 1940s: A Nation in Crisis*. Hanover, N.H.: University Press of New England, 61–80.

Thompson, Virginia, and Richard Adloff. 1981. *Conflict in Chad*. Berkeley: University of California Press.

Tilly, Charles. 1978. *From Mobilization to Revolution*. Reading, Mass.: Addison-Wesley.

Tinker, Jon. 1978. "Sudan: The Ecology and Economics of the Jonglei Canal." *Weekly Review* (Nairobi). April 28: 24.

Touval, Saadia, and I. William Zartman. 1985. "Introduction: Mediation in Theory" in Saadia Touval and I. William Zartman, eds., *International Mediation in Theory and Practice*. Boulder: Westview, 7–17.

Tsoucalas, Constantine. 1981. "The Ideological Impact of the Civil War" in John O. Iatrides, ed., *Greece in the 1940s: A Nation in Crisis*. Hanover, N.H.: University Press of New England, 319–341.

UANC Delegate A., Participant, Victoria Falls, Geneva, Lancaster House. 1987. Interview by Stephen John Stedman, May 19, Harare, Zimbabwe. Notes.

United Kingdom. 1979. *Constitutional Conference, Lancaster House, London: Conference Papers and Summaries of Proceedings*. Unpublished documents. National Archives, Harare, Zimbabwe.

United Nations, Security Council. 1947. *Report by the Commission of Investigation Concerning Greek Frontier Incidents to the Security Council*. May 23, 1947. Vols. 1–3. New York: United Nations.

United States, Department of State. 1969. *Foreign Relations of the United States 1946. Vol. 8, The Near East and Africa*. Washington, D.C.: Government Printing Office.

——, Senate, 80th Congress. 1973. *Hearings before Committee on Foreign Relations March-April 1947*. Washington, D.C.: Government Printing Office.

Van Fleet, James. 1967. "How We Won in Greece." *Balkan Studies* 8 (2): 387–393.

Vlavianos, Haris. 1989. "The Greek Communist Party: In Search of a Revolution" in Tony Judt, ed., *Resistance and Revolution in Mediterranean Europe*. New York: Routledge, 157–212.

Wagner, R. Harrison. 1986. "The Theory of Games and the Balance of Power." *World Politics* 38: 546–76.

———. 1991. "What Was Bipolarity?" Paper presented at the Annual Meeting of the International Studies Association, Vancouver, British Columbia.

Wai, Dunstan M. 1973. *The Southern Sudan: The Problem of National Integration*. London: Frank Cass.

———. 1981. *The African-Arab Conflict in the Sudan*. New York: Africana.

———. 1983. "Geoethnicity and the Margin of Autonomy in the Sudan" in Donald Rothchild and Victor A. Olorunsola, eds., *State vs. Ethnic Claims*. Boulder: Westview, 304–330.

Wallensteen, Peter. 1991. "Is There a Role for Third Parties in the Prevention of Nuclear War?" in Philip E. Tetlock, Jo L. Husbands, Robert Jervis, Paul C. Stern, and Charles Tilly, eds., *Behavior, Society, and Nuclear War, Volume 2*. New York: Oxford University Press, 193–253.

Wallimann, Isidor, and Michael N. Dobkowski. 1987. *Genocide and the Modern Age: Etiology and Case Studies of Mass Death*. New York: Greenwood.

Waltz, Kenneth. 1979. *Theory of International Politics*. Reading, Mass.: Addison-Wesley.

Waterman, Harvey. 1981. "Reasons and Reason: Collective Political Activity in Comparative and Historical Perspective." *World Politics* 23 (July): 554–589.

Wedge, Bryant. 1986. "Psychology of the Self in Social Conflict" in Edward D. Azar and John W. Burton, eds., *International Conflict Resolution: Theory and Practice*. Boulder: Lynne Rienner, 56–62.

Weekly Review (Nairobi). 1984. June 1.

Welton, Gary L., Dean G. Pruitt, and Neil B. McGillicuddy. 1988. "The Role of Caucusing in Community Mediation." *Journal of Conflict Resolution* 32, 1 (March): 181–202.

Wilkinson, A. R. 1980. "The Impact of the War." *Journal of Commonwealth and Comparative Politics* 38: 110–123.

Wittman, Donald. 1979. "How a War Ends: A Rational Model Approach." *Journal of Conflict Resolution* 23 (December): 743–763.

Wittner, Lawrence S. 1982. *American Intervention in Greece, 1943–1949.* New York: Columbia University Press.

Wolfers, Michael, and Jane Bergerol. 1983. *Angola in the Front Line.* London: Zed.

Woodhouse, C. M. 1976. *The Struggle for Greece, 1941–1949.* London: Hart-Davis.

———. 1981. "The National Liberation Front and the British Connection" in John O. Iatrides, ed., *Greece in the 1940s: A Nation in Crisis.* Hanover, N.H.: University Press of New England, 81–101.

———. 1982. "Recent Crisis in Free Greece" in Lars Baerentzen, ed., *British Reports on Greece, 1943–44.* Copenhagen: Museum Tusculanum, 47–103.

Wriggins, Howard. 1993. "The Tamil Insurgency" in I. William Zartman, ed., *Negotiating Internal Conflicts.* Columbia: University of South Carolina Press.

Wright, Quincy. 1965. *A Study of War.* 2d ed. Chicago: University of Chicago Press.

———. 1970. "How Hostilities Have Ended: Peace Treaties and Alternatives." *Annals of the American Academy of Political and Social Science* 392 (November): 51–61.

Young, Oran R. 1968. *The Politics of Force: Bargaining during International Crises.* Princeton: Princeton University Press.

ZAPU Delegate A., Participant, Geneva, Lancaster House Conferences. 1987. Interview by Stephen John Stedman, May 11, Harare, Zimbabwe. Notes.

Zartman, I. William. 1985. *Ripe for Resolution: Conflict and Intervention in Africa.* New York: Oxford University Press.

———. 1986. "Conflict in Chad" in Arthur Day and Michael Doyle, eds., *Escalation and Intervention.* Boulder: Westview, 13–30.

———. 1989. *Ripe for Resolution: Conflict and Intervention in Africa.* 2d ed. New York: Oxford University Press.

———. 1990. "Negotiations and Prenegotiations in Ethnic Conflict: The Beginning, the Middle, and the Ends" in Joseph Montville, ed., *Conflict and Peacemaking in Multiethnic Societies.* Lexington, Mass.: D. C. Heath, Lexington Books, 511–533.

———. 1991. "Regional Conflict Resolution" in Victor Kremenyuk, ed., *International Negotiation: Analysis, Approaches, Issues.* San Francisco: Jossey-Bass, 302–314.

———. 1993a. "Introduction" in I. William Zartman, ed., *Negotiating Internal Conflicts.* Columbia: University of South Carolina Press.

―――― . 1993b. "Negotiating Régime Transformation: South Africa" in I. William Zartman, ed., *Negotiating Internal Conflicts*. Columbia: University of South Carolina Press.

Zartman, I William, and Johannes Aurik. 1991. "Power Strategies in Deescalation" in Louis Kriesberg and Stuart Thorson, eds., *Timing the Deescalation of International Conflicts*. Syracuse: Syracuse University Press, 152–181.

Zartman, I. William, and Maureen Berman. 1982. *The Practical Negotiator*. New Haven: Yale University Press.

Contributors

JONATHAN HARTLYN is associate professor of political science at the University of North Carolina at Chapel Hill.

CAROLINE HARTZELL is a Ph.D. student in the Department of Political Science at the University of California, Davis.

JANE E. HOLL is a major in the United States Army and associate professor of social science at the United States Military Academy, currently on the National Security Council staff.

JOHN O. IATRIDES is professor of political science at Southern Connecticut State University.

ROY LICKLIDER is professor of political science at Rutgers University, New Brunswick.

JAMES O'CONNELL is professor of peace studies at the University of Bradford in the United Kingdom.

DONALD ROTHCHILD is professor of political science at the University of California, Davis.

STEPHEN JOHN STEDMAN is assistant professor of African studies and comparative politics at the Paul Nitze School of Advanced International Studies, Johns Hopkins University.

ROBERT HARRISON WAGNER is professor of political science at the University of Texas, Austin.

HARVEY WATERMAN is associate professor of political science and associate dean of the Graduate School at Rutgers University, New Brunswick.

MANFRED W. WENNER is associate professor of political science at Northern Illinois University.

I. WILLIAM ZARTMAN is the Jacob Blaustein Professor of International Organization and Conflict Resolution at the Paul Nitze School of Advanced International Studies, Johns Hopkins University.

Index

Abboud, Ibrahim, 73, 77
Abdullah, Sayed Abdel Rahman, 79
Abolitionists, 171–175, 178–179
Addis Ababa agreement. *See* Sudan,
  settlement terms
Adefope, Henry, 139
Afghanistan, 4, 23–24, 29, 34, 269,
  319
African National Council. *See*
  Zimbabwe, internal politics
Ahmad, 96, 97
al-Ahmar, Abdullah, 99
Aiken, Arthur, 93
Albania, 210, 214, 221, 222, 224, 228
Algeria, 107, 111, 114
Alier, Abel, 70, 71, 72, 86, 87, 93
All Africa Conference of Churches, 76–
  77, 81–84, 92
Alliance for Progress, 49
American Civil War. *See* United States
  of America, civil war
Amin, Idi, 74
Amnesty, in Colombia, 40, 53, 55, 59;
  in Greece, 215, 232; in Nigeria, 198;
  in United States of America, 166,
  180, 181, 183–184
Anarchy, 235, 248, 254
Andersonville, 183–184
Angola, 3, 21, 33, 125
Ankrah, Kodwo, 82, 93
Appomattox, 166, 167

Arabian Sea, 101
Argentina, 168
al-Arif, Abd al-Karim, 114
Asaba, 203
Asika, Ukpabi, 197
Asir, 120
Australia, 139

Bab al-Mandab, 101
al-Badr, Muhammad, 96, 97, 105, 120
Bakheit, Gaafar Mohamed Ali, 79
Balance of power, 247–251, 261, 266,
  267, 298–299
Bangladesh, 5, 314
Barco, Virgilio, 52–53, 55, 60
Bargaining. *See* Negotiations
Basques. *See* Spain
Beauregard, P. T., 166
Ben Bella, Ahmad, 114
Benidorm, Declaration of, 44
Benjamin, Judah, 166
Bensel, Richard, 15
Bentiu, 88
Betancur, Belisario, 52, 53, 55
Blainey's argument. *See* Convergent
  expectations
Botha, Pik, 146
Boulkes, 221
Brazil, 168
Breckinridge, John, 165, 167
Brewster, Kingman, 150

343

British South African Company, 126
Brown, John, 175
Bulawayo, 129, 132, 162
Bulgaria, 210, 221, 222
Bunche, Ralph, 113
Bunker, Ellsworth, 113

Cambodia. *See* Kampuchea
Canada, 115
Carr, Burgess, 82, 84
Carrington, Lord, 138–157
Carter, Jimmy, 5, 150
Case studies, 10, 11
Casualties, 9, 10, 11, 312; in Colombia,
  37, 38–43, 56, 60; in Greece, 228,
  229; in Nigeria, 192, 193; in United
  States of America, 164, 168, 181,
  182; in Zimbabwe, 135–137, 161,
  162
Causes of war. *See* Issues
Census, Nigeria, 191
Centralization. *See* Federal structure;
  Settlement terms
Chad, 22–23, 27, 30, 34
Chevron, 88
Chicken Dilemma Game, 30, 31
Chitepo, Herbert, 132
Choice points, 304
Churchill, Winston, 207, 212, 223
Civic Front. *See* Colombia, settlement
  terms
Civil war, and conflict, 10; and
  interstate wars, 7–8, 19, 20, 24,
  257–258, 263–264; and negotiation,
  24–27, 257–263, 271–272; in
  Colombia, 8, 11, 12, 19, 23, 36–61;
  definition of, 9–10, 60, 115; in
  Ethiopia, 21, 27, 32, 33, 125, 320; in
  Great Britain, 4, 321; in Greece, 12,
  19, 204–232, 300; importance of, 5–
  6; in Jordan, 100, 101, 111, 112,
  289; in Lebanon, 3, 23, 27, 29, 33,
  268, 269, 271, 289; in Nigeria, 5,
  12, 19, 188–203, 262, 299, 300; in
  Spain, 5, 198, 270, 289; in Sudan, 8,
  11, 12, 19, 21, 62–93, 125, 289; in
  United States of America, 4, 5, 11,
  12, 13, 19, 164–187, 262, 270, 289,

296, 301; in Yemen Arab Republic,
  8, 12, 19, 94–123, 265, 289, 296,
  301; in Zimbabwe, 9, 10, 12, 19,
  124–163, 289, 296, 297, 300, 301
Coalition management, 305–306, 317–
  318. *See also* Internal politics
Cold War, end of, 4
Collective security system, 252
Colombia, amnesty, 40, 53, 55, 59;
  civil war, 8, 11, 12, 19, 23, 36–61;
  casualties, 37, 38–43, 56, 60;
  constitutional convention, 53, 57, 60;
  democracy, 45; drug trafficking, 42,
  43, 50, 51, 53–59; guerrilla war,
  43–44, 50–58, 54, 58, 310, 315,
  318–319; internal politics, 38–39,
  43–48, 59, 308; issues, 29, 38–43,
  45–47, 305, 317; landowners, 43,
  54, 55; land, 50; leadership, 47, 50–
  51, 308; map, 36; military balance,
  45, 53, 309; mutual hurting
  stalemate, 47–48, 309; negotiations,
  43–45, 53; participation, 41, 49–52,
  306, 316; peasants, 39; Protestants,
  48; redistribution, 50; Roman
  Catholic Church, 47, 49, 60;
  settlement terms, 30, 31–33, 49–52,
  59, 60–61, 306, 315, 316, 317, 318–
  319; state capacity, 43, 50, 53–60;
  third party intervention, 45, 48–49,
  54, 56–58, 311; Union of Soviet
  Socialist Republics, 57; United States
  of America, 48–49, 54, 56–58
Commitment, 25, 245
Commonwealth, and Greece, 225; and
  Nigeria, 200; and Zimbabwe, 139,
  140, 146, 147, 150–152
Compromise of 1850, 172
Conflict resolution theory, 6–7, 16–17,
  37
Conquest. *See* Wars of conquest
Consociational democracy, 46, 295–
  296. *See also* Settlement terms
Constitution. *See* Settlement terms
Contest of punishment, 238–239, 244,
  247, 254, 260, 267
Convergent expectations, 242–264,
  289, 310
Correlates of War project, 6

Counterforce duel, 238, 246, 247, 248, 251, 254, 258, 260, 265, 266, 267
Credibility, 245
Critendon-Johnson Resolutions, 179
Cuba, 49, 172, 315
Cyprus, 22, 27, 29, 30, 33–34, 232, 314

Dachau, 209, 219
el-Dahab, Abdel Rahman Siwar, 90, 91
Davis, Jefferson, 165–178, 184, 296, 308
Day, Derek, 144
DeGaulle, Charles, 203
Democracy, 321
Development, 7, 28
Dimitrov, Georgi, 222, 223
al-Din, Hamid, 117
Disarmament, 17, 19, 298, 313, 315–317; in Yemen Arab Republic, 115–116
Douglas Home, Alec, 128
Douglas, Stephen, 173
Dred Scott decision, 173

EAM, 207, 208, 218, 221
East Germany. See German Democratic Republic
Effiong, Philip, 195
Egypt, 101, 104–114, 118–119, 313
Eisenhower, Dwight David, 101, 297
El Salvador, 24
ELAS, 207, 208, 221
Elections, 316; in Angola, 21; in Greece, 208, 209, 212, 227; in Nigeria, 191; in Sudan, 87, 90; in United States of America, 165, 182, 183, 308, 311; in Yemen Arab Republic, 117, 118; in Zimbabwe, 126, 133, 134–135, 137–138, 141, 147–159
Emancipation Proclamation, 178, 179
England. See Great Britain
Enugu, 203
Epps, Dwain, 93
Eritrea. See Ethiopia
Erkwit, 104, 114
Escalation, 31

Escobar, Pablo, 58
Ethiopia, civil war, 21, 27, 32, 33, 125, 320; and Sudan, 69, 74–75, 84–85, 312
Ethnic divisions, 5, 7, 15, 32, 304–306. See also Issues
Evatt, Herbert, 224
Expulsion, 314–315. See also Settlement terms

Faisal. See Faysal ibn Abd al-Aziz
Falklands, 269
FARC (Revolutionary Armed Forces of Colombia), 41, 49, 53, 55
Faysal ibn Abd al-Aziz, 105–107, 114, 120
Fearless, 128
Federal structure, 17, 32; in Nigeria, 189, 192, 197, 200–202; in Sudan, 78, 80, 89–90; in United States of America, 186
Florina, 210
Flower, Ken, 137, 158, 159
Framework, 10–11, 14–17
France, and Nigeria, 195, 203; revolution, 4, 314–315, 321
Fraser, Malcolm, 139
Frederica, 209–210
Fugitive Slave Act, 172
Fulani, 190, 196, 201–202

Gaitán, Jorge Eliécer, 39
Galán, Luis Carlos, 55, 56
Game theory, 266. See also Prisoners' Dilemma Game; Chicken Dilemma Game
Garang, Joseph, 69–70, 71
de Garang, Mading, 77, 93
Garang de Mabior, John, 88, 89–91
Garrison, William Lloyd, 172
Gaviria, Cesar, 53, 56–57
Genocide, 7, 8, 31, 245, 314, 319; in Nigeria, 194, 195, 200
George II, 206–209, 217
German Democratic Republic, 154
German Federal Republic, 197
Germany, 187, 199, 221
Gilmour, Ian, 143, 150, 151

Gómez, Laureano, 39, 43, 44, 45, 47
Gonatas, Stylianos, 216
Gowon, Yakubu, 192–193, 197, 199, 203
Grammos-Vitsi range, 214, 228
Grant, Ulysses S., 164, 179, 186
Great Britain, civil war, 4; and Falklands, 269; Glorious Revolution, 321; and Greece, 207–213, 218, 221–225, 227, 231, 232; and Nigeria, 190, 194–195, 203; and Sudan, 65–68, 69; and United States of America, 177–178; and Yemen Arab Republic, 101, 106, 107, 111, 115, 118; and Zimbabwe, 126–129, 133–135, 136, 138–159, 161–162, 286. *See also* Northern Ireland
Greece, and Albania, 210, 214, 221, 222, 224, 228; amnesty, 215, 232; casualties, 228, 229; civil war, 12, 19, 204–232, 300, 301–302; and Commonwealth, 225; and Cyprus, 29, 232; elections, 208, 209, 212, 227; and Great Britain, 207–213, 218, 221–225, 227, 231, 232; guerilla warfare, 208, 211, 214, 231, 309, 318; internal politics, 209–220, 308–309; issues, 206–210, 301–302, 304, 305, 306; junta, 232; leadership, 215–220, 308–309; Macedonia, 208, 215, 219; map, 204; military balance, 205–206, 209, 210–215, 227–230, 311, 312; mutual hurting stalemate, 230, 309; negotiations, 212–213, 224; participation, 232, 316, 317; Second Round, 207, 208, 212; settlement terms, 205–206, 214, 215, 230–232, 316, 317, 319; state capacity, 226; third party intervention, 207–215, 218, 220–232, 311, 312; and Union of Soviet Socialist Republics, 205, 207–215, 218, 220–232, 311, 316; and United Nations, 210, 223–224, 227; and United States of America, 208–213, 218, 221–232; weapons, 210, 213–214, 222, 227–299; and Yugoslavia, 208, 210, 213–215, 220–223, 228, 311

Grenada, 269
Grevena, 210
Guatamala, 115
Guerrilla warfare, 15, 255, 258, 310–311, 318–319; in Colombia, 43–44, 50–58, 54, 58, 310, 318–319; in Greece, 208, 211, 214, 231, 311, 318; in Nigeria, 194, 311, 318; in Sudan, 73–74, 90, 92, 318; in United States of America, 165–168, 186–187, 306, 310, 318–319; in Yemen Arab Republic, 110, 318; in Zimbabwe, 128, 129–131, 132–133, 135–137, 318
Gwelo, 129
Gweru, 162

Hadjivasiliou, Chrissa, 219
Harad, 105
Harare, 162
Harper's Ferry, 175
Hausa, 190, 196, 201–202
Hegemony, 250–251, 267
Hierarchy, 235–236
High Executive Council, 85, 86, 87
History, 6
Honwanna, Fernand, 157, 158
Horn of Africa, 101
Horn, Carl von, 114
Hoxha, Enver, 222, 224
Hudaydah, 121
Hurting stalemate. *See* Mutual hurting stalemate
ibn Husayn, Muhammad, 108

Ibibio, 194, 196
Identification conflict, 304–306. *See also* Issues
Identity issues. *See* Ethnic divisions; Issues
Idoma, 196
Ijaw, 194, 196
Ikle, Fred, 4, 9
India, 22, 314, 321
Indian Ocean, 101
Integration, 316. *See also* Settlement terms; Participation
Intensity, 3

Internal politics, 15, 17–18, 240–241, 244, 247, 295–297, 306–309, 317–320, 321; in Chad, 27; in Colombia, 38–39, 43–48, 59, 308; in Cyprus, 27; in Ethiopia, 27; in Greece, 209–220, 308–309; in Lebanon, 27; in Nigeria, 191–196, 308–309; in Sudan, 27, 69–72, 89–91, 307; in Sri Lanka, 27; in United States of America, 164–169, 174–186, 308; in Yemen Arab Republic, 100–109, 116–117, 307; in Zimbabwe, 127–128, 130–137, 141–161, 308
Internal power balance, 315. *See also* Settlement terms
Internal Security Negotiations, Conference on, 13
International war. *See* Interstate war
International politics, 235–268
International Monetary Fund, 54
Interstate war, 4, 237–241, 263–264, 285–286
Intervention. *See* Third party intervention
Ioannidis, Yiannis, 219
Iran, 100, 111, 202, 267
Iraq, 5, 9–10, 111, 114, 267–268
Ireland, Republic of, 115, 198
Ironsi, 192
Islam, in Nigeria, 190, 191, 202–203; in Sudan, 65, 67, 68, 69, 78, 89, 91, 92; in Yemen Arab Republic, 95, 96, 120
Israel, 9, 314; and Egypt, 312; and Palestine, 267; and Lebanon, 269; and Sudan, 70, 74, 75, 89; Yom Kippur War, 269
Issues, 5, 12, 13–14, 17–18, 28–29, 235–268, 271–272, 275–278, 294, 301–302, 304–306, 315, 317, 320, 321; in Afghanistan, 23–24, 29; in Angola, 21; in Chad, 22–23; in Colombia, 29, 38–43, 45–47, 305, 317; in Cyprus, 22; in Ethiopia, 29; in Greece, 206–210, 301–302, 304, 305, 306, 317; in Lebanon, 23, 29; in Mozambique, 21–22, 29; in Nigeria, 189–194, 202, 305, 306, 317; in Philippines, 22, 29; postwar

policies, 317; revolutionary or secessionist, 320; in South Africa, 29; in Sri Lanka, 22, 29; between Spain and the Basques, 22, 29; in Sudan, 21, 29, 64–68, 304, 305, 317; in United States of America, 164–165, 168–179, 185–186, 305, 306, 317; in Yemen Arab Republic, 97–100, 305, 317; in Zimbabwe, 125–131, 305, 306
Italy, 221

Jamaica, 139, 150
Japan, 5
Johns Hopkins University, 13
Johnson, Andrew, 167, 181, 182, 184–185
Johnston, Joseph, 166–167
Jonglei Canal, 88
Jordan, 100, 101, 111, 112, 289
Justice, 13–14

Kalabari, 196
Kampuchea, 3, 24
Kanellopoulos, Panaviotis, 216
Kansas, 172–173
Kansas-Nebraska Act, 173, 174
Kanuri, 190
Kaunda, Kenneth, 132, 133, 139, 146, 151–152, 155
Kennedy, John F., 101, 112–113
el-Khalifah, Sir el-Khatim, 73, 78
Khama, 133
Khamir, 105
Khartoum Summit Conference, 107
Kissinger, Henry, 133, 138
KKE, 207, 209–215, 218–232
Konitsa, 210
Korea 4, 48, 260, 297
Kosti, 88
Kurds, 268
Kuwait, 5, 9–10, 114, 268

Lagu, Joseph, 67, 70, 71–72, 85, 86, 89–90, 307
Land, in Colombia, 50; in United States of America, 174, 183; in Zimbabwe, 126, 129, 130, 133, 145, 160, 162

Land Tenure Act, 126–127
Land Apportionment Act, 126
Laos, 268
Leadership, 295–297, 306–309, 317–318; in Colombia, 47, 50–51; in Greece, 215–220; in Nigeria, 190, 202; in Sudan, 70–72, 85–91. *See also* Internal politics
Lebanon, 3, 23, 27, 29, 33, 268, 269, 271, 289
Lee, Robert E., 165–167
Legitimate use of force, 235–236, 256, 261–262
Levy, Jack, 5
Lexicographic preferences, 178, 187
Lincoln, Abraham, 165, 166, 174, 178, 179, 181, 186, 308
Lleras, Alberto, 44, 45
Luce, Richard, 149

M-19 (Movement of the 19th of April), 50, 52, 55, 60
Macedonia, 208, 215, 219
Machel, Samora, 133, 157, 158
MacVeagh, Lincoln, 217, 225–226
Maghoub, Mohammed Abmed, 73
al-Mahdi, Sadiq, 73, 91
Manley, Michael, 139, 150
Maps, of Colombia, 36; of Greece, 204; of Nigeria, 188; of Sudan, 62; of Yemen Arab Republic, 94; of Zimbabwe, 124
Markos (Vafiadis), 210, 214, 215, 220, 227
Massacres, 9
Mavromihalis, Petros, 216
Mediation with muscle, 16, 312–313
Metaxas, John, 206, 207, 217, 219
Middle Belt people, 190, 192, 195, 196
Military balance, 15–16, 17–18, 19, 34, 269–291, 299–301, 303, 308, 309–311, 313–314, 318, 320, 321; in Afghanistan, 34; in Chad, 34; in Colombia, 45, 53, 309; in Greece, 205–206, 209, 210–215, 227–230, 309; in Mozambique, 34; in Nigeria, 193–197; in Philippines, 34; in Spain, 34; in Sri Lanka, 34; in Sudan, 34,

72–74, 91, 309; in United States of America, 165–166, 177, 310; in Yemen Arab Republic, 109–111, 309; in Zimbabwe, 128–129, 130–137, 310
Missouri Compromise, 171–172
Morocco, 101, 111
Moros. *See* Philippines
Mortal combat, 238
Mortimer, Robert, 9
Movement of the 19th of April. *See* M-19
Mozabmique, 21–22, 125
Mozambique, 21–22, 29, 30, 34, 125; and Zimbabwe, 129, 130, 132, 135, 137, 139, 146, 152, 157, 158, 162, 163, 310
Mugabe, Robert, 128, 132, 136–137, 140–162, 297, 308
Multiple sovereignty, 9, 10
Muslim. *See* Islam
Mutare, 162
Mutual hurting stalemate, 16, 24–25, 26, 260, 271, 309; in Colombia, 47–48; in Greece, 230, 309, 316; in Sudan, 72–74, 91, 309; third parties, 313; in Yemen Arab Republic, 107, 110–111; in Zimbabwe, 310
Muzorewa, Abel, 128, 129, 134–159
Myths, 322

Najran, 120
Namibia, 21, 125
Nasir, Gamal Abdel, 105–107, 114
Nasser. *See* Nasir
National Front. *See* Colombia, settlement
National Liberation Army (ELN), 50, 53
Ndebele, 132, 161
Negotiated settlements, 8, 12, 16, 17–18, 30–34, 259–263, 269–291, 305, 311, 315; in Sri Lanka, 31. *See also* Settlement terms
Negotiations, 24, 25, 258–263, 310; in Colombia, 43–45, 53; and equality, 25, 26; in Greece, 212–213, 224; in Nigeria, 200–201; and spokesmen,

26; in Sudan, 68, 71–72, 76–85; in
   United States of America, 166–168;
   in Yemen Arab Republic, 104–109;
   in Zimbabwe, 134–135, 140–157
Nicaragua, 172, 268
Nigeria, amnesty in, 198; casualties,
   192, 193; census, 191; civil war, 5,
   12, 19, 188–203, 262, 299, 300; and
   Commonwealth, 200; elections, 191;
   federal structure, 189, 192, 197,
   200–202; and France, 195, 203;
   genocide, 194, 195, 200; and Great
   Britain, 190, 194–195, 203; guerilla
   warfare, 194, 311, 318; internal
   politics, 191–196, 306; Islam, 190,
   191, 202–203; issues, 189–194, 202,
   305, 306, 318; leadership, 190, 202,
   308–309; map, 188; Middle Belt
   people, 190, 192, 195, 196; military
   balance, 193–197, 311–312;
   negotiations, 200–201; oil, 189, 193,
   196, 200, 202–203; and Organization
   of African Unity, 200; participation,
   197–198, 201–203, 316; settlement
   terms, 197–203, 316, 318, 319;
   starvation, 198–199; third party
   intervention, 194–201, 203, 311–
   312; and Union of Soviet Socialist
   Republics, 194, 195; weapons, 194–
   195; and Zimbabwe, 139, 146
Niilus, Leopoldo, 93
el-Nimery, Gaafar, 69, 71, 72, 73, 78,
   79, 85–90, 92, 307
Nitze School of Advanced International
   Studies, 13
Nkala, Enos, 161
Nkomo, Joshua, 128, 132, 137, 138,
   144, 146, 147, 150–161
Normal politics, 27–30
Norman, Ken, 159
Normative issues, 13–14
North Yemen. See Yemen Arab
   Republic
Northern Ireland, 3, 24, 198, 267
Nsukka University, 197
Nullification Crisis, 172
Nu'man, Ahmad Muhammad, 105, 119
Nyerere, Julius, 132, 133, 139, 157

Obasanjo, 195
Obote, Milton, 75
Ogoja, 196
Oil, in Nigeria, 189, 193, 196, 200,
   202–203; in Sudan, 88–89; in Yemen
   Arab Republic, 123
Ojukwu, Odumegwu, 192–196, 198,
   199, 201
Okigbo, Pius, 198
Oman, 111
Organization of American States, 44, 48
Organization of African Unity, 200
Organizational advantage, 253–257,
   261
Orner, Jan, 93
Ospina, Mariano, 39, 43, 44
Outside intervention. See Third party
   intervention
Owen, David, 133

Pact of March (1957), 44
Pakistan, 5, 314
Palestinians, 9, 10, 23
Panama, 58, 269
Papagos, Alexander, 218, 229, 230
Papandreou, George, 207, 208, 216
Paraguay, 168
Participation, 16–17, 315, 316–317; in
   Colombia, 41, 49–52; in Greece,
   232, 317; in Nigeria, 197–198, 201–
   203; in Sudan, 65, 80, 86, 87, 317;
   United States of America, 180–186,
   317; in Yemen Arab Republic, 115–
   118, 122–123, 317; in Zimbabwe,
   127–128, 148, 158–162, 317
Partisan warfare. See Guerilla warfare
Partition, 8
Partsalidis, Dimitris, 219
Patriotic Front. See Zimbabwe, internal
   politics
Patriotic Unity party. See UP
Paul, 209–210
Peace, 13–14
Peoples Regional Assembly, 85, 86, 87
Peoples Democratic Republic of Yemen
   (South Yemen), 95, 107, 116, 117,
   120; and Great Britain, 111; and
   Union of Soviet Socialist Republics,
   101

Peoples Republic of China, 132, 268, 321
Performance on postwar issues. *See* Settlement terms
Persian Gulf, 100
Persian Gulf War, 267, 268
Peru, 24
Philippines, 22, 29, 34
Pinilla, Luis, 60
Plastiras, Nikolaos, 216
Poland, 318
Policide, 7
Political will, 279–281
Political science, 6
Political parties. *See* Internal politics
Popular sovereignty, 173
Popular Liberation Army (EPL), 50
Port Harcourt, 197
Portugal, 129, 132
Power, 25
Power balance, 315. *See also* Settlement terms
Power-sharing, 46. *See also* Settlement terms
Prisoners' Dilemma Game, 30, 267
Protracted conflicts, 7, 20, 24

Ramphal, Shridath, 139, 146, 150
Realism, 235–236, 248, 252
Reconstruction. *See* Settlement terms, United States of America
Red Sea, 101, 118–119
Regions. *See* Federal structure
Repression, 316. *See also* Settlement terms; Participation
Republic of Yemen. *See* Yemen, Republic of
Reputation, 287
Research strategy, 10–17
Revolution, theory of, 7. *See also* Issues
Revolutionary Armed Forces of Colombia. *See* FARC
Rhodes, Cecil, 126
Rhodesia. *See* Zimbabwe
Rhodesian Front, 127
Risk-acceptant, 243, 265, 278
Rojas, Gustavo, 40, 41, 43, 44, 46, 48, 49, 50, 60, 308

Rousos, Petros, 219
Roy, Bikash, 316
Rutgers University, ix, 12–13
Rwanda, 24

Sa'ud ibn Abd al-Aziz, 120
Salih, Ali Abdullah, 117
Salisbury, 129
al-Sallal, Abdullah, 105, 119
Sana'a, 108, 121
Saudi Arabia, 100–101, 104–108, 111–114, 117, 118–120, 122–123
Scherf, Theresa, 93
Secession, 314. *See also* Settlement terms
Second Arab League Summit Conference, 104
Selassie, Haile, 74, 84–85, 200, 312
Separatism. *See* Issues
Settlement terms, 5, 16–19, 24, 38, 121, 261, 273, 292–302, 303–304, 311, 313–317, 320, 321; in Angola, 30, 32, 33; in Colombia, 30, 31–33, 49–52, 59, 60–61, 316; in Ethiopia, 29, 32, 33; in Chad, 29, 30; in Cyprus, 29, 33–34; in Greece, 205–206, 214, 215, 230–232, 311, 315, 316, 319; in Lebanon, 30, 33; in Mozambique, 30; in Nigeria, 197–203, 311, 316, 319; in Sri Lanka, 29, 30; in South Africa, 32, 33; in Spain, 316; in Sudan, 29, 30, 32, 33, 63–64, 85–93, 316, 317; in United States of America, 165, 166, 180–186, 316, 317; in Yemen Arab Republic, 115–118, 121–123, 316, 317; in Zimbabwe, 125, 141–147, 159–162, 316, 317
Shagari, 146
Sheridan, Philip, 165
Sherman, William T., 164–167, 179, 186
Siantos, George, 219
Sitges, Pact of, 45
Sithole, Ndabaningi, 128, 132, 134, 148, 162
Smith, Ian, 127–149, 162, 296, 297, 308

Smith, David, 143
Smith, Kirby, 166
Soames, Lord, 157, 159
Social science, 13–14
Sociology, 6
Sofoulis, Themistoclis, 213, 216, 217
Somalia, 24
South Carolina, 172, 175
South Africa, 23, 29, 33; and
    Zimbabwe, 126, 128, 130, 133, 139,
    146, 154, 157, 161–162
South Yemen. *See* Peoples Democratic
    Republic of Yemen
Southern Provinces Regional Self-
    Government Act, 71, 85
Southern Rhodesia. *See* Zimbabwe
Southern Policy. *See* Sudan, issues
Spain, Basque conflict 22, 29, 34; civil
    war 5, 198, 270, 289, 321; and
    Colombia, 48; settlement terms, 316
Sri Lanka, 22, 27, 29, 30, 31, 34
Stakes, 9
Stalemate, 26–27, 260, 271, 309; in
    Yemen Arab Republic, 107, 110–
    111. *See also* Mutual hurting
    stalemate
Stalin, Josef, 213, 215, 220, 222–223,
    231, 232, 316
Stanton, Edwin, 167
Starvation, 198–199
State formation after civil war, 18–19,
    32–33, 322
State capacity, 321; in Colombia, 43,
    50, 53–60; in Greece, 226; in Sudan,
    71, 72, 86, 93
Strategies of conflict termination, 304
Structural violence, 13
Sudan, All Africa Conference of
    Churches, 76–77, 81–84, 92;
    amnesty, 78; civil war, 8, 11, 12, 19,
    21, 62–93, 125, 289; elections, 87,
    90; and Ethiopia, 69, 74–75, 84–85;
    federal system, 78, 80, 89–90; and
    Great Britain, 65–68, 69; guerrilla
    war, 73–74, 90, 92, 318; internal
    politics, 27, 69–72, 89–91, 307; and
    Islam, 65, 67, 68, 69, 78, 89, 91, 92;
    and Israel, 70, 74, 75, 89; issues, 21,
    29, 64–68, 304, 305, 317; Kampala

Group, 77, 82; leadership, 70–72,
    85–91, 307; map, 62; Makere Group,
    77, 82; military balance, 34, 72–74,
    91, 309; mutual hurting stalemate,
    72–74, 91, 309; negotiations, 68,
    71–72, 76–85; oil, 88–89;
    participation, 65, 80, 86, 87, 316,
    317; refugees, 86; Round Table
    Conference, 78, 79; settlement terms,
    29, 30, 32, 33, 63–64, 85–93, 316,
    317; state capacity, 71, 72, 86, 93;
    third party intervention, 70, 74–77,
    81–85, 91–92, 93, 311, 312, 313;
    and Uganda, 69, 74, 75, 82; water,
    88; World Council of Churches, 76–
    77, 81–84, 92
Sufyan, 123
Sweden, 114
Syria, 23, 33, 107, 111, 112

Ta'if, 105
Ta'izz, 121
Tamils. *See* Sri Lanka
Tanzania, 132, 155, 163
Thant, U, 113, 114
Thatcher, Margaret, 137–138, 150–
    152, 155
Theories, 10; and case studies 11, 12
Theotokis, John, 216
Third party intervention, 4, 5, 12, 16,
    17–18, 27, 265, 271, 274–275, 283–
    288, 303, 311–313, 319–320, 321;
    in Colombia, 45, 48–49, 54, 56–58,
    311; governments vs. private parties
    16; in Greece, 207–215, 218, 220–
    232; in Nigeria, 194–201, 203, 311,
    312; in Sudan, 70, 74–77, 81–85,
    91–92, 93, 311, 312, 313; in United
    States of America, 177–178, 311–
    312; in Yemen Arab Republic, 100–
    115, 117, 118–123, 311–312; in
    Zimbabwe, 126–159, 161–162, 286,
    310, 311, 312–313
Tiger, 128
Tito, Josip Broz, 208, 213, 215, 222–
    223, 231
Tiv, 196
Tongogara, Josiah, 146, 155, 156, 157

Torit, 73
Tribal Trust lands, 126
Truman Doctrine, 212
Tsaldaris, Constantine, 209, 213, 216
Tsaldaris, Panatges, 217
Turbay, Julio César, 52
Turkey, 212, 225, 232

Uganda, 125; and Sudan, 69, 74, 75, 82
Ulster. See Northern Ireland
Umtali, 129
Uncertainty, 244, 248, 266, 267, 278–279
Union of Soviet Socialist Republics, 267, 314; and Afghanistan, 269; and Colombia, 57; and Greece, 205, 207–215, 218, 220–232, 311, 316; and Nigeria, 194, 195; revolution, 262; and Yemen Arab Republic, 101, 106, 107, 108, 111, 118; and Zimbabwe, 132, 154
United Nations, and Greece, 210, 223–224, 227; and Yemen Arab Republic, 104, 112–115; and Zimbabwe, 147, 150
United States of America, amnesty, 166, 180, 181, 183–184; Camp David accords, 313; casualties, 164, 168, 181, 182; civil war 4, 5, 11, 12, 13, 19, 164–187, 262, 270, 289, 296, 301, 321; and Colombia, 48–49, 54, 56–58; elections, 165, 182, 183; federal structure, 186; and Great Britain, 177–178; and Greece, 208–213, 218, 221–232; and Grenada, 269; guerilla warfare, 165–168, 186–187, 306, 310, 311, 315, 318–319; internal politics, 164–169, 174–186, 308; issues, 164–165, 168–179, 185–186, 305, 306, 317; land, 174, 183; Mexican War, 171–172, 187; military balance, 165–166, 177, 310, 311–312; negotiations, 166–168; and Panama, 269; participation, 180–186, 316, 317; revolution 4–5, 176–177, 314–315, 321; settlement terms, 165, 166, 180–186, 316, 317, 318–

319; slavery, 166, 170–175, 178–182, 184, 186; third party intervention, 177–178, 311–312; Vietnam War, 269, 289; and Yemen Arab Republic, 101, 104, 106, 111–115; and Zimbabwe, 133–134, 136, 146–147, 150
United Nations High Commissioner for Refugees, 86
United Kingdom of Great Britain. See Great Britain
United States Institute of Peace, ix, 12–13
United Nations Yemen Observation Mission, 113–115
United Arab Republic. See Egypt
University of Lagos, 191
UP (Patriotic Unity party), 53–54, 55, 59
Uruguay, 168

Vafiadis, Markos. See Markos
Valencia, Guillermo León, 44
Van Fleet, James, 213, 226
Vance, Cyrus, 133
Varkiza accord, 207, 208
Venizelos, Eleutherios, 216, 217
Venizelos, Sofoclis, 216
Verwoerd, Hendrik, 131
Victory, 5
Vietnam, 4, 247, 260, 267, 269, 289, 315, 319, 321
La violencia. See Colombia, civil war
Vorster, John, 131, 133

Walls, Peter, 137, 144, 149, 157, 158–159, 160
War, causes of. See Issues
War. See Interstate war; Civil war
Wars of conquest, 4, 9–10
al-Wazir family, 117
Weapons, in Greece, 210, 213–214, 222, 227–299; in Nigeria, 194–195; in Yemen Arab Republic, 106, 109–110, 115–116
Western Sahara, 27
Whealey, Robert, 321
Wirz, Henry, 183–184

World Council of Churches, 76–77,
81–84, 92
World Bank, 48–49

Yahya ibn Muhammad, 95–96, 97
Yemen, North. *See* Yemen Arab
Republic
Yemen Arab Republic (North Yemen),
assassination, 116; civil war, 8, 12,
19, 94–123, 265, 289, 296, 301;
creation, 95–97; disarmament, 115–
116, 317; and Egypt, 101, 104–114,
118–119; elections, 117, 118; and
Great Britain, 101, 106, 107, 111,
115, 118; guerrilla war, 110, 318;
internal politics, 100–109, 116–117,
307; and Islam, 95, 96, 120; Isma'ili
sect, 96, 99; issues, 97–100, 305,
317; Jidda Agreement, 105–106,
114; Jews, 96; leadership, 307; map,
94; military balance, 109–111, 309;
mutual hurting stalemate, 107, 110–
111; National Peace Conference,
105; negotiations, 104–109; oil, 123;
Ottoman Empire, 95, 98;
participation, 115–118, 122–123,
316; poison gas, 110; qadis, 98, 117;
republicans, 99, 103–104; royalists,
99, 103–104; and Saudi Arabia, 100–
101, 104–108, 111–114, 117, 118–
120, 122–123; sayyids, 98, 117;
settlement terms, 115–118, 121–
123, 316–317; Shafi'i sect, 96, 98,
99, 100, 103; stalemate, 107, 110–
111; Third Force, 105; third party
intervention, 100–115, 117, 118–
123, 311; tribes, 96–97; and Union
of Soviet Socialist Republics, 101,
106, 107, 108, 111, 118; and United
Nations, 104, 112–115; and United
States of America, 101, 104, 106,
111–115; weapons, 106, 109–110,
115–116; Zaydi sect, 95, 96, 97, 99,
100, 103, 108. *See also* Yemen,
Republic of
Yemen, Republic of, 95
Yemen, South. *See* Peoples Democratic
Republic of Yemen

Yom Kippur War, 269
Yoruba, 191, 196
Yugoslavia, 208, 210, 213–215, 220–
223, 228, 311

Zahariadis, Nikos, 209, 214, 219–231
Zambia, 132, 133, 135, 137, 139, 146,
152, 154–155, 162, 163, 310
Zimbabwe, casualties, 135–137, 161,
162; civil war, 9, 10, 12, 19, 124–
163, 289, 296, 297, 300, 301; and
Commonwealth, 139, 140, 146, 147,
150–152; cease-fire, 153–157;
declaration of independence (UDI),
128; economic sanctions, 130;
elections, 126, 133, 134–135, 137–
138, 141, 147–159; emigration, 135–
136; and Front Line States, 133, 138,
146–147, 155, 163; and Great
Britain, 126–129, 133–135, 136,
138–159, 161–162, 286, 310, 312–
313; guerrilla war, 128, 129–131,
132–133, 135–137, 318; internal
politics, 127–128, 130–137, 141–
161, 306, 307; Internal Settlement,
134–135; issues, 125–131, 305, 306;
land, 126, 129, 130, 133, 145, 160,
162; leadership, 307, 308; map, 124;
military balance, 128–129, 130–137,
310; and Mozambique, 129, 130,
132, 135, 137, 139, 146, 152, 157,
158, 162, 163, 310; mutual hurting
stalemate, 310; negotiations, 134–
135, 140–157; and Nigeria, 139,
146; participation, 127–128, 148,
158–162, 316, 317; Pearce
Commission, 128–129, 130; and
People's Republic of China, 132;
settlement terms, 125, 141–147,
159–162, 316, 317; Smith-Home
pact, 128–129, 130; and South
Africa, 126, 128, 130, 133, 139,
146, 154, 157, 161–162; and
Tanzania, 132, 155, 163; third party
intervention, 126–159, 161–162,
310; and Union of Soviet Socialist
Republics, 132, 154; and United
Nations, 147, 150; and United

Zimbabwe, *(Continued)*
  States of America, 133–134, 136,
    146–147, 150; and Zambia, 132,
    133, 135, 137, 139, 146, 152, 154–
    155, 162, 163, 310, 311, 312–313
Zimbabwe African National Union
  (ZANU). *See* Zimbabwe, internal
  politics

Zimbabwe African Peoples Union
  (ZAPU). *See* Zimbabwe, internal
  politics
al-Zubayri, Muhammad Mahmud, 105,
  119
Zvobgo, Edison, 143, 150, 157